Illona Ward.

Limit States Design in Structural Steel

by

G.L. Kulak, P.Eng.
Professor Emeritus

and

G.Y. Grondin, P.Eng.
Professor

Department of Civil and
Environmental Engineering
University of Alberta
Edmonton, Alberta

Canadian Institute of Steel Construction
2001 Consumers Road, Suite 300
Willowdale, Ontario M2J 4G8

ISBN 978-088811-119-7

Printed in Canada by
Quadratone Graphics Ltd.
Toronto, Ontario

PREFACE

Preface to Eighth Edition

The Seventh Edition of this text introduced the changes to the 2001 edition of CSA–S16 standard and saw the addition of sections on torsion, welding processes and procedures and a new presentation of the chapter on stability analysis of frames and the design of beam-columns. The Eighth Edition reflects significant changes that have been made in the National Building Code of Canada. Additional design examples have been added to Chapter 8 to illustrate various analysis procedures for multi-storey frames. The design examples in that chapter have been adapted to the 2005 edition of the National Building Code. Additional design examples were added to Chapter 9 to illustrate the use of weld symbols and to emphasize some design aspects of rigid beam-to-column moment connections.

The first two chapters of the book deal with the interrelationship of design and analysis, various aspects of steel construction, the structural steels and sections available, the International System of Units, and the philosophy of the limit states design approach. With the 2005 edition of the National Building Code, the factored loads in the limit states design approach have been redefined, with the implementation of a companion load approach. The design of tension members, presented in Chapter 3, reflects changes to S16–01 with respect to failure by tension plus shear block in gusset plates and in coped beams. (This mode of failure was called block shear failure in the earlier editions of the Standard.) The changes are meant to provide a more rational and, in some cases, a safer approach.

The S16–01 Standard has brought flexural-torsional buckling of columns into the main body of the standard. The design of columns presented in Chapter 4 addresses this failure mode. Chapter 5, Beams, saw the introduction in the Seventh edition of a section on beams subjected to the combined action of bending and torsion, a specialty topic. Chapters 6 and 7 go on to describe the design processes needed for particular kinds of beams—composite beams and plate girders. The stability of members and frames has always been a difficult area for instructors to teach and for students to understand. Chapter 8 in the Seventh edition integrated analysis and design topics in this area. A design example was added in the eighth edition to illustrate the analysis procedure for multi-storey frames. Additional design examples have been added to Chapter 9 to illustrate the use of weld symbols and the design of rigid beam-to-column connections. The example design of framed building presented in Chapter 10 has been updated to the new edition of the National Building Code. Finally, Chapter 11 deals with fatigue. Although it is likely that most instructors will not be able to include it in the undergraduate teaching program, it should be useful as students begin their professional career and to practicing engineers who need to know more about this topic.

The intent of the authors still remains to provide a reference document for the training of those who will be responsible in the future for the design of steel structures. The book is intended primarily for a one or two term course in the subject at the third or fourth year university level.

The authors acknowledge the contributions of the co-authors of previous editions of this book. These are Peter Adams, the principal co-author of technical material in editions through the Fifth, and Michael Gilmor and Hugh Krentz, responsible for industry-related material and who acted as Publishers through the Sixth Edition. Their contributions and influence continue in this edition.

August, 2006   *G.L. Kulak*
                                                            G.Y. Grondin

TABLE OF CONTENTS

Chapter 7   *PLATE GIRDERS*

Chapter 8   *BEAM-COLUMNS*

Chapter 9   *CONNECTIONS*

Chapter 10   *BUILDING DESIGN*

Chapter 11   *FATIGUE*

FOREWORD

For many years the CISC has supported the educational efforts of Canadian universities and other educational institutions by providing research grants, scholarships, films, slides, video tapes, computer programs, Handbooks, and other literature. As part of this continuing interest in education, the CISC is pleased to publish this textbook.

The Canadian Institute of Steel Construction does not assume responsibility for the contents of this book, nor for errors or oversights resulting from use of the information contained herein. All suggestions for improvement of this book will be forwarded to the authors for their consideration for future printings.

CISC is located at 201 Consumers Road, Suite 300, Willowdale, Ontario, M2J 4G8. Contact may also be made as follows; telephone 416–491–4552, facsimile 416–491–6461, electronic mail _info@cisc-icca.ca_. A web site is also available: _www.cisc-icca.ca_.

CHAPTER 1

INTRODUCTION

1.1 The Design Process

Structural design is a creative art and, at the same time, a reasonably exact science. A structural designer must endeavour to:

1. Provide a safe, reliable structure that satisfactorily performs the function for which it was intended;

2. Provide a structure that is economical to build and to maintain;

3. Whenever possible, provide a structure that is aesthetically pleasing.

The design process for any structure contains many steps, not all of which involve the structural designer, although he should be involved in most of them. These steps are:

1. A prospective owner must have a need for the structure and must arrange the financing necessary to build the structure.

2. For a building, an architect and an engineer must familiarize themselves with the applicable building by-laws and building codes in order to ensure that fire protection, health and safety requirements will be met.

3. Geological and geotechnical investigations must be carried out in order to determine the type of foundation most suitable for the site and for the structure.

4. For a bridge, an engineer must ensure that navigation clearances, highway or railway geometric requirements are met, and any interference with the body of water that may exist below the bridge during and after construction meets the approval of environmental protection agencies.

5. The structural designer must investigate the site to determine how site conditions will affect the structure (e.g., buried water mains on a building site. potential ice jams at a bridge site).

6. The form, shape, and size of the structure must be determined.

7. The probable loads (wind, earthquake, occupancy loads, ice pressures on a bridge, differential settlements, etc...) must be estimated by the designer.

8. The most suitable structural material, or materials, must be selected, with due consideration of required performance, life cycle cost, supply, transportation to the site, and construction on the site.

9. The structural designer must compare various structural systems and arrangements of structural members.

10. A structural analysis must be carried out in order to determine the forces that the anticipated loads will impose on the structural members.

11. The structural designer must arrange and proportion the elements of the structure so that the expected loads are carried safely and that the elements and the structure as a whole perform satisfactorily.

12. The structural designer must convey to the fabricator, erector, and the general contractor his concept of the structure, principally by means of drawings and specifications.

13. The structural designer must inspect the work of the fabricator, the erector, and the general contractor in order to ensure that the structure is built in accordance with the plans and specifications.

These 13 steps summarize the major portions of the design process for a structure. This book will deal with several of these steps, but will cover in detail only Step 11—the arranging and proportioning of the structural elements in order to safely carry the expected loads and to ensure that the elements and the structure perform satisfactorily.

For simplicity, most explanations and examples will deal specifically with the design of elements of buildings. For bridges and other structures, design procedures are similar to those followed in the design of buildings, although the governing design standards may differ in some requirements. The major difference between buildings and such structures as bridges, crane girders, or any application where there is the possibility of a large number of repeated loads is that failure by fatigue must be considered in the latter. Of course, all structures must meet the static strength requirements. The aspect of design for fatigue life is presented in Chapter 11.

1.2   Codes, Specifications, and Standards

Building codes are written to protect the public, and they contain information such as wind loads, snow loads, and earthquake loads for a given locality. Recommended design floor loads for buildings of various types and sizes are provided. Fire protection requirements for buildings fulfilling various functions are stipulated.

Building codes also contain rules governing the ways in which the loads are to be considered to be applied to buildings. Design requirements for steel, concrete, and other materials are included in building codes, either in the form of detailed rules or by reference to other standards.

A building code represents the consensus of opinion of experienced engineers, architects, and others. It does not cover in detail every situation that a structural designer may encounter, and the designer often must exercise judgment in interpreting and applying the requirements of a building code.

The National Building Code of Canada [1.1], first written in 1941, serves as a model code and single source for technical requirements for all Canadian jurisdictions. The individual provinces have the responsibility for their own building codes and these provide uniform requirements for all cities and municipalities located within that province. All provinces have mechanisms to adopt the National Building Code of Canada without technical change soon after its publication. The National Building Code usually is reviewed, revised, and updated on a five-year cycle.

Project specifications, along with design drawings, comprise the designer's instructions to the builder. Specifications and drawings vary from company to company, but they include items such as the materials that are to be used in the structure, sizes of structural members, methods of joining the members, and general instructions on how the construction work is to be conducted. Unambiguous specifications expedite the successful completion of a structure. In many companies, specifications are written by professional specification writers, but the structural designer should always be involved in preparing or approving the technical contents of a specification.

Standards make it possible for the construction industry to function efficiently. Without standards governing such things as quality of steel, dimensions of screw threads on bolts, and dimensions of steel beams, each structure would be "custom-made" and would be prohibitively expensive.

In Canada, the preparation of standards for all commodities is co-ordinated under the auspices of the Standards Council of Canada. Various standards-writing organizations, accredited by the Standards Council of Canada, are responsible for writing standards in specific subject areas. Standards for steel structures are written under the auspices of the Canadian Standards Association (CSA). Standards of the Canadian General Standards Board (CGSB) and the Steel Structures Painting Council (SSPC) are used for paint. The American Society for Testing and Materials (ASTM) and the American National Standards Institute (ANSI) standards are used for certain steel products. Design and construction standards of the American Welding Society (AWS), the American Association of State Highway and Transportation Officials (AASHTO), the American Railway Engineering and Maintenance-of-Way Association (AREMA), and similar organizations are also used to some extent.

Loading on long span roof trusses can be critical during construction

Canadian Standards Association standards govern the design and construction of most Canadian steel structures. Several of the more important are:

1. For buildings: CSA–S16–01, "Limit States Design of Steel Structures."

2. For bridges: CAN/CSA–S6–00, "Canadian Highway Bridge Design Code."

3. For welded structures: CSA–W59 "Welded Steel Construction (Metal-Arc Welding)."

4. For steel: CSA–G40.20/G40.21–04, "General Requirements for Rolled or Welded Structural Quality Steel / Structural Quality Steel."

5. For cold-formed steel members: CSA–S136, "Cold Formed Steel Structural Members."

In this book, since most of the design explanations deal with buildings, most references will be to the current (2001) edition of CSA S16 [1.2]. References to steel material Standards will usually be to CSA G40.20/G40.21 [1.3], although some ASTM Standards also will be used.

CSA Standards are written by committees representing producers, designers, educators, fabricators, government bodies, and other interested parties. Most steel standards are under continual review and new editions are issued every few years. National Standards of Canada, written by the CSA, are identified by the designation CAN/CSA before the standard number.

1.3 Loads on Structures

One of the most important steps in the total design process is determination of the design loads for the structure. Typical loads that a designer considers for a building are dead load, live load, wind load, earthquake load, and temperature effects [1.1]. Consideration sometimes needs to be given to impact and vibrations that may occur in structures involving cranes, elevators, or machinery. In bridge design, loads resulting from the centrifugal force and the longitudinal force of moving vehicles, ice pressures, earth pressure, buoyancy, and stream flow pressure must be considered. The nature of the loads can also be different during construction. Special attention should be given to the ability of the structure to resist the loads applied during the construction stage, a period during which the structure is particularly vulnerable since all the load-resisting elements are not yet in place.

Dead load consists of the weight of the structure itself plus the weight of permanently installed equipment. It includes the weight of the structural members, floors, ceilings, ductwork, exterior walls, permanent partitions, and unusual items such as water in swimming pools. Dead load can usually be estimated with reasonable accuracy, but these estimates should be checked after the structure has been designed. Published information [1.4] is available to assist the designer in estimating dead loads.

Live load includes the loads specified by building codes for various uses and occupancies of the building. These specified loads encompass the occupants, furniture, movable equipment, fixtures, books, etc., and are the minimum gravity live loads for which the building can be designed, within the jurisdiction of that building code. In some circumstances, the designer may be justified in using higher design live loads. Live load also includes loads due to snow, ice or rain, earth or hydrostatic pressure, and the weight of loads being lifted by cranes.

The loads and the ability to resist loads of a cable-stayed bridge are significantly different during construction compared to its in-service condition.

Design wind loads are stipulated in building codes. The National Building Code of Canada [1.1] is one of the most progressive in the world in its treatment of wind load. For most structures, wind load can be treated as a static load and is computed with the aid of reference velocity pressures, gust factors, exposure factors, and shape factors. Particularly tall or slender buildings and bridges must be designed using a dynamic approach [1.5] or with the aid of experimental methods such as wind tunnel tests. Some of the most significant structures in the world have been designed with the aid of testing done at the Boundary Layer Wind Tunnel at the University of Western Ontario—the Tsing Lung suspension bridge in Hong Kong; Sears Building, Chicago; World Trade Center, New York; Commerce Court, Toronto; Petronas Towers, Kuala Lumpur, Malaysia, and many others.

Building codes also stipulate earthquake loads. Conventional earthquake (seismic) design procedures replace the dynamic earthquake loads with equivalent static loads. Alternatively, the National Building Code of Canada specifies that a dynamic analysis may be used. The earthquake loads that are stipulated in most codes are recognized to be much less than the maximum loads possible from a very severe earthquake. However, most codes attempt to prescribe earthquake loads large enough to:

1. Prevent structural damage and minimize other damage in moderate earthquakes that might occur occasionally;

2. Avoid collapse or serious damage in severe earthquakes, which seldom occur.

Wind loads must receive special attention in the design of suspension bridges

Temperature effects is a category intended to include contraction or expansion due to temperature changes, shrinkage, or moisture changes; creep in component materials; and movement due to differential settlement.

The designer must consider combinations of the various loads that can be imposed on the structure. The loads are divided into two groups: the principal loads and the companion loads. Only a fraction (50% or less) of the companion load is assumed to act with the principal loads in order to account for the improbability of the maximum value of each load occurring simultaneously.

For bridges, the design standards [1.6, 1.7] provide detailed information that covers most design situations. For railway bridges, live load classes ("E" loading) are established that are intended to simulate the wheel loads of railway locomotives and the cars they pull. In Canada the standard for highway bridges is CAN/CSA–S6–00, Canadian Highway Bridge Design Code. This standard use a load set called the "design truck" whose wheel loads and axle spacing have been derived from extensive field studies of actual vehicle loads and axle spacing of trucks using Canada's highway system. Since bridges carry different types and volumes of traffic depending on their location, the actual magnitudes of the loads for which bridges are to be designed customarily are established by the owner of the bridge.

1.4   Structural Systems

The art of structural design is manifested in the selection of the most suitable structural system for a given structure. The arrangement of beams, girders, joists, trusses, and columns to support the vertical (gravity) loads and the selection of a method to resist the horizontal (lateral) loads determines the economy and functional suitability of a building. Much of the cost of a multi-storey building is in the floor system, and numerous trial designs might be necessary to ensure that the most suitable system has been selected. Judicious use of design aids, such as handbooks [1.4], graphs, tables, spreadsheets, and computer programs [1.8, 1.9] make such studies practical in a design office. For relatively high buildings, the "premium for height" necessitates a thorough study of lateral load resisting systems. Again, computer programs and other design aids can be very useful.

In bridge design, the choice of continuous or simple-span structures, plate girders, box girders or trusses, steel orthotropic deck (bridge floor), or concrete deck will determine not only economy but aesthetic appeal.

Open web joists, beams and columns are used extensively
(Photo courtesy of Cohos Evamy)

Some broad classifications of structural systems for buildings can be listed. The applicability of any system to any particular type or size of structure varies from place to place and from time to time.

1. Bearing-wall construction – The ends of rolled beams or open-web steel joists (light trusses) are supported on bearing walls, usually of masonry construction. This is generally suitable for one or two storey industrial buildings, commercial buildings, schools, or residential-type buildings. However, this type of construction has also been used for apartment buildings exceeding ten storeys in height.

2. Rigid-frame, single storey construction – Structural frames consisting of two vertical columns and two sloped beams rigidly connected into one unit, usually by welding, form a pitched-roof type of structure. Roof beams (purlins) and wall supports (girts) span between rigid frames. They are generally used for industrial structures, stores, arenas, and auditoriums, but are also used for churches because of their aesthetic appeal.

3. Beam and column construction – This comprises the majority of steel framed structures. It is suitable for low structures of multiple spans, such as large industrial buildings, shopping plazas and schools, or for multi-storey buildings,

such as office buildings, hospitals, or student residences. It consists essentially of regularly spaced columns joined by beams or girders. Open-web joists or secondary beams span between the girders or main beams and provide direct support to the floors or roof.

Beam and column construction is treated in design standards as either rigid, simple, or semi-rigid [1.2]. The distribution of forces within the structure will be a reflection of the method of construction chosen. Simple construction assumes that the ends of beams and girders are connected to transmit transverse shear only and are free to rotate under load in the plane of bending. Connections are usually made by welding plates or angles to a beam or column in the fabrication shop and then bolting to the connecting column or beam on the building site. Lateral forces are generally resisted by direct-acting bracing in one storey buildings, often using angles or flat bars to form vertical or horizontal trusses. The unbraced portion of the building frame in effect leans on the braced portion in order to maintain the required stability of the structure. In multi-storey buildings, vertical steel bracing trusses can be used, but "cores" of reinforced concrete or infill steel plates are often used instead.

Continuous construction assumes that beams and girders are continuous over, or rigidly framed to, supports and that beam-to-column connections hold the original angles virtually unchanged at least up to the specified load level. Connections are usually made, in both shop and field, by welding. Lateral forces are resisted by the flexural action of the rigid-frames of the structure, or sometimes by a combination of rigid-frame action and bracing.

In semi-rigid construction, also known as partially restrained construction, the assumption is that angle changes can take place between the members as the loads are applied. The consequence of this is that redistribution of moments between members must occur. The redistribution response must have been established by tests, whether job specific or as presented in the technical literature.

4. Long-span construction – Long spans between columns, such as are necessary for large arenas, auditoriums, ballrooms, theatres, airport hangars, etc. require special consideration. Deep welded plate girders or box girders, long span open web joists or trusses may suffice. For very long spans, deep trusses or arches may be necessary. Space frame structures, using two-way trusses, lattice-work domes, or cable suspended roofs, may be used to cover very large open spaces. Long-span construction is also frequently used in office buildings. Here, closely spaced open-web joists or trusses span from exterior wall to exterior wall without interior columns, or span from exterior walls to an internal core. In addition to providing large open areas for office flexibility, this system, with its open trusswork, facilitates the installation of electrical and mechanical building services.

5. High-rise construction – Tall buildings become an economic necessity in large cities, where land costs are very high. To build tall buildings economically, the designer must pay particular attention to the resistance required to accommodate lateral forces. The framed tube system simulates the action of a perforated

hollow tube by utilizing closely spaced exterior columns joined to, and interacting with, deep spandrel (exterior wall) beams. The 110-storey World Trade Center towers in New York used this system, as does the 72-storey First Bank Tower in Toronto. The 100-storey John Hancock Center in Chicago uses a trussed tube system. In this case, large exterior columns are connected with diagonal members, making all exterior columns act together as a rigid tube. Carrying the tube concept still further, one of the world's tallest buildings (442 metres), the Sears Building in Chicago, uses a bundled tube arrangement. In this concept, a number of relatively small framed tubes or diagonally trussed tubes are bundled together for great efficiency in resisting lateral forces.

Tubular steel sections were used for the arches of the Humber River Bridge
(Photo courtesy of Terri Meyer Boake)

1.5   Analysis and Design

In the structural design process, *analysis* usually means the determination of the force effects (shear forces, axial forces and bending and torsional moments) that the individual structural members must resist. *Design* can mean the development of the structural layout or arrangement of members, but in the context used in this text it is taken to mean the selection of shape and sizes of members to resist the imposed forces and bending moments.

For statically determinate structures, the analysis is relatively simple, and the requirements of static equilibrium can be used to determine the forces and moments on each member. These depend only on the geometry of the structure and methods used to connect the members. The relative stiffnesses of intersecting members do not affect the analysis. When the analysis has been completed and the forces and moments on each member are known, the member size can be selected using an appropriate design method and there is normally no need for a re-analysis and re-design of the structure. Of course, assumptions made regarding member dead loads and the like must be checked.

For statically indeterminate structures, the procedure is more complex. The equations of statics alone are no longer sufficient to determine internal forces and moments. Numerous analytical methods have been developed over the years, but the most common method of analysis today is use of the force or displacement methods. These lend themselves well to computer-based computations. Whatever technique is used, assumptions must be made regarding the relative stiffnesses of connecting members. After the analysis has been completed and the members have been designed, it is necessary to re-analyze the structure in order to check the validity of the original assumptions. Re-design of the members may then be necessary. For complex structures, several cycles of analysis and design may be required. Section 8.1 deals in more detail with the implications of the assumptions made in the analysis upon the design.

When designing statically indeterminate structures, it is often advantageous to arrive at preliminary member sizes using approximate methods. Handbooks [1.4] provide formulae and coefficients to simplify the preliminary design of continuous or rigidly-framed members.

Although the standard CSA S16–01 covers both structures analysed elastically and those analysed plastically, most steel buildings in Canada are analysed elastically.

1.6   Limit States Design

Limit states design is a design method in which the performance of a structure is checked against various limiting conditions at appropriate load levels. The limiting conditions to be checked in structural steel design are ultimate limit states and serviceability limit states. Ultimate limit states are those states concerning safety, for example, load-carrying capacity, overturning, sliding, and fracture due to fatigue or other causes. Serviceability limit states are those states in which the behaviour of the structure under normal operating conditions is unsatisfactory, and these include excessive deflection, excessive vibration, and excessive permanent deformation.

In essence, the designer attempts to ensure that the maximum strength of a structure (or elements of a structure) is greater than the loads that will be imposed upon it, with a reasonable margin against failure. This is the ultimate limit state criterion. In addition, the designer attempts to ensure that the structure will fulfill its function satisfactorily when subjected to its service loads. This is the serviceability limit state criterion.

The ultimate limit state criterion is illustrated by Figure 1.1. Neither the loads nor the resistance are deterministic quantities. Figure 1.1 shows hypothetical frequency distribution curves for the effect of loads (S_i) on a structural element and the strength, or resistance, of the structural element (R). Where the two curves overlap, shown by the shaded area, the effect of the loads is greater than the resistance of the element, and the element will fail. The structure must be proportioned so that the overlap of the two curves is small, and hence the probability of failure is small enough to be acceptable. (It has to be recognized that no structure can be designed with zero probability of failure.)

The basic equation for checking the ultimate limit state condition is the following:

$$\phi R \geq \alpha_i\, S_i \tag{1.1}$$

In this equation,

ϕ = resistance factor

R = nominal resistance of a structural element

α_i = load factor

S_i = load effect under specified loads

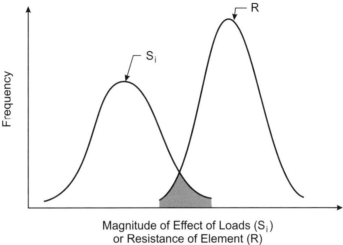

Figure 1.1 – Frequency Distribution Curves

Considering first the left hand side of Equation 1.1, the resistance factor, ϕ, is a factor applied to the nominal member strength, or resistance, to take into account the fact that the actual strength of a member may be less than anticipated because of variability of material properties, dimensions, and workmanship. In some limit states design methods, the resistance factor also takes into account the type of failure anticipated for the member and uncertainty in prediction of member resistance. In CSA–S16–01, these are not in the resistance factor, ϕ, but have been included as a constant in the formulas that establish the theoretical member strengths (or member resistances). In general, ϕ is 0.90 for steel components and is 0.60 for concrete components. There are a number of exceptions, however, and these will be explained in the text as they arise.

The *nominal* resistance, R, of a structural element is the strength calculated using the specified material properties, nominal dimensions, and equations describing the theoretical behaviour of the member, connection, or structure. Thus, in limit states terminology the *factored* resistance of a structural element, ϕR, is the product of the nominal resistance and the resistance factor. As expressed in Equation 1.1, the factored resistance must equal or exceed the effect of the factored loads (the right hand side of Equation 1.1).

The right hand side of Equation 1.1 deals with loads applied on the structure. The factor α_i is a load factor used to account for the variability of loading and the probability of having loads from various sources acting simultaneously on the structure. The load effects, S_i, consist of axial force, bending moment, or other load effect, resulting from the application of the specified loads on the structure. The specified loads consist of:

1. Dead load (D), which is a permanent load that includes the weight of the structure and stationary equipment;

2. Earthquake load (E), which results from ground motion during an earthquake.

3. Live load (L) due to use of occupancy of the building, including loads due to cranes;

4. Snow load (S), representing loads due to snow and ice and associated rain or rain alone;

5. Wind load (W) resulting from the action of wind on the structure.

In order to account for the importance of the structure, which is based on the building use and occupancy, the specified snow, wind, and earthquake loads are multiplied by the importance factors presented in Table 1.1 for the different categories of buildings described in Table 1.2. Because ultimate limit states pertain to safety of the occupants, the importance factors for ultimate limit states are generally higher than the importance factors used for the serviceability limit states. Snow loads on buildings that represent low hazard to human life represent the only exception to this rule.

Table 1.1 - Importance factors

Importance category	Ultimate limit states			Serviceability limit states		
	Snow, I_s	Wind, I_w	Earthquake, I_E	Snow, I_s	Wind, I_w	Earthquake, I_E
Low	0.8	0.8	0.8	0.9	0.75	See NBCC 2005, Section 4.1.8.13 and Commentary J
Normal	1.0	1.0	1.0	0.9	0.75	
High	1.15	1.15	1.3	0.9	0.75	
Post-disaster	1.25	1.25	1.5	0.9	0.75	

The importance factors used for serviceability limit states, such as those associated with deflection under snow or wind load, reflect the return period, i.e., the severity of the snow load or wind load a structure is designed for. Since the snow load used for the ultimate limit states calculations represents the 1 in 50 year values, which are approximately 10% larger than the 1 in 30 year values used for serviceability calculations, the load factor for serviceability applied to the specified snow load is 0.9.

Deflections due to wind are checked for a 1 in 10 year wind pressure. However, the wind pressure for the ultimate limit states corresponds to the 1 in 50 year value. The ratio of the 1 in 10 year reference pressure to the 1 in 50 year reference pressure varies from 0.82 to 0.71. A value of 0.75 was selected.

Since live load deflections are usually checked under specified live load due to use and occupancy, the serviceability limit state load factor applied to the specified live load is 1.0.

The load factor α_i in Equation 1.1 accounts for the variability in loading as well as the probability of having loads of different sources acting simultaneously on the structure. In this respect, loads are separated into two groups: the principal loads and the companion loads. Five load cases are considered, as outlined in Table 1.3. Since dead loads are always part of the loads applied on a structure, they are always considered to be a principal load. With the exception of dead loads, the principal loads are factored by a factor greater than or equal to 1.0. When dead loads counteract the effect of the other applied loads, such as for overturning, uplift, sliding, or stress reversal, the load factor is taken as 0.9. The load factor applied to the companion load is always less than 1.0 in order to account for the reduced probability of having the companion load at its maximum value when the principal load is at its maximum value. When the live load is used as a companion load (load cases 3, 4 and 5), the live load factor shall be increased to 1.0 for structures or parts of structures used for storage, housing of equipment, or consist of service rooms. The load factor on dead load and earthquake load is 1.0 when earthquake loading is considered. This reflects the level of conservatism used in the definition of the earthquake load in the National Building Code [1.1].

Table 1.2 – Building importance categories

Use and occupancy	Importance category
Buildings that represent a low direct or indirect hazard to human life in the event of failure, including • low human-occupancy buildings, where it can be shown that collapse is not likely to cause injury or other serious consequences • minor storage buildings	Low
All buildings except those listed in low, high, and post-disaster categories	Normal
Buildings that are likely to be used as post-disaster shelters, including buildings whose primary function is as • an elementary, middle, or secondary school • a community centre Manufacturing and storage facilities containing toxic, explosive, or other hazardous substances in sufficient quantities to be dangerous to the public, if released	High

Post-disaster buildings that include
 	
• hospitals, emergency treatment facilities, and blood banks
 	
• telephone exchanges
 	
• power generating stations and electrical substations
 	
• control centres for air, land, and marine transportation
 	
• sewage treatment facilities
 	
• buildings of the following types, unless exempted from this designation by the authority having jurisdiction:
 	
  • emergency response facilities
 	
  • fire, rescue, and police stations and housing for the vehicles, aircraft, or boats used for these emergency services
 	
  • communication facilities, including radio and television stations
	Post-disaster

In addition to the load combinations in Table 1.3, the effect of factored loads 1.5H, 1.0P, and 1.25T shall be included in the load combinations presented in Table 3 when any of these loads affects structural safety. The load H is the permanent load due to lateral earth pressure, P is the prestress load, and T represents the load effects due to contraction, expansion, or deflection.

Table 1.3 – Load combinations for ultimate limit states

Case	Load combination	
	Principal loads	Companion loads
1	1.4D	—
2	(1.25D or 0.9D) + 1.5L	0.5S or 0.4W
3	(1.25D or 0.9D) + 1.5S	0.5L or 0.4W
4	(1.25D or 0.9D) + 1.4W	0.5L or 0.5S
5	1.0D + 1.0E	0.5L + 0.25S

As an example of the use of specified loads and factored loads, Figure 1.2 illustrates the basic design checks required for a beam. The deflection, Δ_s, when the beam is subjected to bending moment, M_s, computed using specified loads, must be within the limits specified in CSA–S16–01. When the bending moment reaches M_f, computed using factored loads, the beam would fail or be on the verge of failure. The value of the deflections at this load level is not usually of interest.

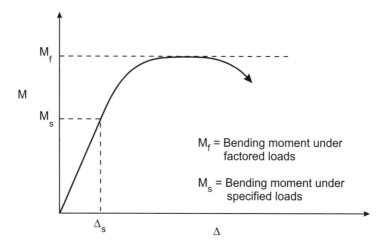

Figure 1.2 – Moment vs. Deflection Curve

More information on limit states design is widely available and reference [1.10] can be used as a convenient starting point. Chapters 3 to 11 inclusive contain more detailed information on the design of members using limit states design procedures. The design function is facilitated in practice by the use of design aids such as handbooks, manuals [1.4] and computer programs [1.8, 1.9].

Example 1.1

Given

The loading conditions for a roof beam in a school building are to be determined using limit states design. The specified loads are:

Snow on roof $= S = 1.50 \text{ kN/m}^2 = 1.50 \text{ kPa}$ (see Section 1.7)

Dead load on roof $= D = 2.00 \text{ kN/m}^2 = 2.00 \text{ kPa}$

Solution

For ultimate limit states, such as yielding or buckling of the beam due to applied bending moment, factored loads must be used. Using Tables 1 and 2, it is established that the building belongs to the high importance category and the importance factor for snow load, I_s, is 1.15. Referring to Table 3, it is seen that all five load cases involve either the dead load, the snow load, or both. It can readily be observed, however, that load case 3 is a more critical case than any of load cases 2, 4, and 5 when dead loads and snow loads are the only two loads acting on the structure. Therefore we only need to check load cases 1 and 3.

Load case 1

$$\alpha_i S_i = \alpha_D D = 1.4 \times 2.00 \text{ kPa} = 2.80 \text{ kPa}$$

Load case 3

$$\alpha_i S_i = \alpha_D D + \alpha_S S I_s = 1.25 \times 2.00 \text{ kPa} + 1.5 \times 1.50 \text{ kPa} \times 1.15 = 5.09 \text{ kPa}$$

In order to design the beam for the ultimate limit states, factored load case 3 would be used to determine M_f, the bending moment under factored loads (see Figure 1.2).

For serviceability limit states, such as deflection, the specified loads are used. Normally, live load or snow load deflection is of most concern, in which case the specified snow load, 1.50 kPa, multiplied by the importance factor of 0.9, namely, 1.35 kPa, would be used in the design check. The bending moment determined using this reduced snow load would correspond to M_s in Figure 1.2.

If a dead load deflection check was required, the specified dead load, 2.00 kPa, would be used to determine M_s; if the total deflection needs to be obtained, the sum of the specified loads, 3.35 kPa, should be used.

1.7   The International System of Units

The International System of Units is a coherent system that includes the metre as the base unit of length and the kilogram as the base unit of mass. The international abbreviation of the name of this system, in all languages, is SI. The policy of the Canadian government since 1970 has been that all measurements eventually be converted to the metric system. In the construction and related industries, material and design standards, building codes, and technical literature the transition to the SI system is largely complete.

Designers using SI units must transform loads given in mass (kilograms) to forces, using the relationship force = mass × acceleration. In the design of structures on earth, acceleration is the acceleration due to gravity, designated by "g" and established as 9.80665 metres per second per second at the third General Conference on Weights and Measures in 1901. (Because the designer usually uses loads given in handbooks and similar sources as the starting point, the conversion from mass to loads is already established.)

The unit of force to be used in design is the newton (N) (or multiples thereof), where a newton is defined as the force that, when applied to a body having a mass of one kilogram (kg), gives the body an acceleration of one metre (m) per second squared (s^2). Thus, $N = kg \cdot m/s^2$. The unit of stress is the pascal (Pa), which is one newton per square metre (N/m^2). Because this is a very small quantity, designers of steel structures will generally use megapascals (MPa), where one megapascal is one million pascals and equals one newton per square millimetre (N/mm^2).

The kilopascal (kPa), one thousand pascals, usually will be a convenient unit to use for uniformly distributed loads (or forces). For example, the National Building Code of Canada, 1995 edition, lists design floor loads in kilopascals. Designers can write either kN/m^2 or kPa, but kPa seems to be the more convenient notation and it will be used in this book.

Properties and dimensions of steel sections will be given in millimetre (mm) units and millimetres should be used for dimensioning steel structures. In this book, mm dimensions are used on drawings and, in general, the mm units are not shown. If other units are used, they will be shown. Some relationships and values of interest to steel designers are as follows:

1. Density of steel = 7850 kg/m^3

2. Modulus of elasticity = 200 000 MPa

3. Shear modulus of steel = 77 000 MPa

4. Coefficient of thermal expansion of steel = $11.7 \times 10^{-6}/C°$

5. Acceleration due to gravity = 9.80665 $m/s^2 \approx 9.81\, m/s^2$

6. One kN/m^2 = one kPa

7. One kN/m = one N/mm

8. $10^6\ N \cdot mm$ = one $kN \cdot m$

Reference [1.11] recommends that multiples of base units that represent 10 raised to a power that is a multiple of 3 should be used. Thus, common structural steel design units are:

Force — kilonewton (kN), or meganewton (MN)

Distributed Load — Newtons per square metre (N/m^2) or pascals (Pa), kilonewtons per square metre (kN/m^2), or kilopascals (kPa)

Stress — pascal (Pa), kilopascal (kPa), or megapascal (MPa)

Length — millimetre (mm) or metre (m)

Mass — kilogram (kg), megagram (Mg)

The tonne is a special unit, equal to 1 000 kg (or 1 Mg) that is used in the basic steel industry, but it should not be used in structural design calculations.

For a more complete description of SI, Reference [1.11] can be consulted.

1.8   Construction Contracts

The procedure used to select the steel fabricating company (fabricator) who will actually build the steel structure conceived by the designer can have a significant effect upon the speed with which the structure is erected and, in some cases, the quality of the completed structure.

For a large or complex project, it is common for the future owner (usually as represented by the architect, engineer, or project manager) to negotiate a contract with one of a few selected firms that is considered capable of completing the project to the satisfaction of the owner. In this case, the cost of the structure and construction time schedule are negotiated, and the contract is awarded to the company that offers the best combination of price, technical capability, experience, and schedule for completing the structure. For commercial projects, such as office buildings, a saving in construction time can mean earlier renting of the premises and increased revenue for the owner. Thus, speed of construction is an important aspect of the construction process.

For publicly-owned structures, such as bridges, and for many privately owned structures, contracts are awarded after the calling of public tenders. In this case, the fabricator submitting the lowest bid is usually awarded the contract, provided that the fabricator meets any prequalification requirements stipulated in the tender call. For steel buildings and bridges, it is good practice to stipulate that the fabricator be certified by the Canadian Welding Bureau in accordance with the requirements of CSA Standard W47.1 "Certification of Companies for Fusion Welding of Steel Structures." This Standard provides three Divisions of certification, based primarily upon the qualifications of the personnel employed by the fabricator who are responsible for welding. It is usually advantageous for the owner (or his representative) to stipulate that the fabricator be certified in the Division that seems most appropriate for the structure under consideration. CSA–S16 for buildings and CAN/CSA–S6 for bridges each stipulate that fabricators assuming responsibility for welded construction must be certified for Division 1 or Division 2.1 of CSA Standard W47.1.

For many structures, it is desirable to consider other methods of prequalifying bidders, in addition to certification by the Welding Bureau, to ensure that only competent fabricating firms submit bids.

For construction contracts, good practice is to use a Canadian Standard Form of Construction Contract developed by a joint committee of the Canadian Construction Association, The Royal Architectural Institute of Canada, The Association of Consulting Engineers of Canada, Construction Specifications Canada, and the Engineering Institute of Canada. Six different types of contract are provided, three of which depend upon the method of payment. These are:

1. Stipulated Price Contract

2. Unit Price Contract

3. Cost Plus-a-Fee Contract

4. Construction Management Contract

5. Design–Build Stipulated Price Contract

6. Partnering.

The Cost Plus-a-Fee Contract is relatively rare and is usually used for emergency repairs or renovations or for a structure that must be completed with maximum speed and minimum notice of intention to build. It will often cover design, fabrication, and erection. As the name implies, is based on the actual cost of the work performed plus a fixed fee.

The Stipulated Price (or Lump Sum) is probably the most common contract and provides for a fixed sum of money to cover the cost of fabricating and erecting the structure as described in the job specification and drawings. This type of contract is advantageous when the structure can be designed completely before tenders are called. Since it is not unusual for modifications to be made to the structure after the contract is signed, it is desirable to include provisions in the tender call and the contract for additions or deletions to the lump sum contract.

The Unit Price Contract is used when it is not possible to call for Stipulated Price tenders because the design drawings are not complete. In this type of contract, the fabricator provides unit prices for various structural steel members and the final contract price is determined when the design has been completed and total weights can be computed. In this type of contract, it is necessary to have a standard method of computing contract weights, and the method normally used is described in the CISC Code of Standard Practice for Structural Steel. This Code covers usual industry practice with respect to the furnishing of structural steel for buildings. It should normally be specified in tender calls to ensure uniformity of bidding practice.

In those cases where the owner relies on a construction manager to provide administrative and technical services for a fee, the Construction Management Contract allows work to start before the design is complete.

The Design–Build Stipulated Price Contract is similar to a Stipulated Price Contract, but in this case the contract is between an owner and the contractor, who then hires the structural engineer and other consultants. The owner usually selects the contractor whose proposal best suits his needs.

Partnering is a team building process in which working relationships are established among all the parties involved in a construction process. The objectives are mutually agreed upon and then formalized. The process improves communications and expedites resolution of problems. This process is used on large projects to achieve savings in time and costs.

1.9   The Construction Process

The construction process is the end result of the design process. For a steel structure, the construction process involves the fabrication, erection, and inspection of the structural steel. Inspection is a part of the construction process and also the final step of the design process.

In its broadest sense, the term *fabrication* includes interpreting design drawings and specifications, preparing shop fabrication and field erection drawings, procuring the required material, cutting, forming, assembling and fastening the material into units, and shipping the material to the construction site. It is the responsibility of the designer to convey to the fabricator sufficient information to permit him to properly interpret the design drawings and specifications. Guidance for the designer is provided in S16–01 and other publications. Fabricators may stock some of the most popular sizes of beam and column sections and some steel plate. However, this stock material will normally be adequate to supply the material for only relatively small structures. For larger structures, some or all of the steel must be ordered from a steel mill.

Steel mills usually roll structural sections and plate in accordance with a published rolling schedule, based on demand for the various rolled steel products. Thus, several weeks may elapse between the time a fabricator orders steel from a mill and the arrival of that steel at his plant. This lead time is used by the fabricator for preparation of shop (fabrication) drawings. Nevertheless, to speed up the construction process, the designer should endeavour to supply the fabricator the design information required for ordering steel as early as possible. For rush jobs and small orders, if the required steel is not in the fabricator's own stock, he may order it from a steel warehouse. However, warehousing requires more handling and hence higher overhead costs, necessitating a higher retail price for the steel. Thus, if large quantities of steel must be ordered from warehouses, the cost of the structure will be increased.

Shop drawings, sometimes called detail drawings, are prepared by the fabricator in order to show in detail the information required to make the component parts of the structure and assemble them into shipping pieces. Erection drawings are also prepared. They comprise a set of plans with elevations and cross-sections that locate all pieces and provide information required by the erection crews.

Fabrication operations usually include cutting main members to the correct length, cutting connection pieces from larger pieces, and possibly cutting pieces from steel plate. Cutting is usually carried out by flame-cutting with oxygen-acetylene, or other gas mixture, torches. These are usually controlled automatically. Thin material may be cut with heavy shears and, for very smooth cuts or extreme precision, cold sawing with specially hardened blades can be performed. If bolts are to be used to connect pieces, the holes are punched or drilled. Heavy punches can punch various size holes, singly or several at a time, in all but very thick or very hard material. In general, the diameter of the hole punched should equal or exceed the thickness of the plate.

Drilling can be performed on material of any thickness with single or multiple drills, but the process is slower and more expensive than punching. For this reason, fabricators usually try to place holes for connections in thin material so it can be punched and weld connection material in the shop to thick main members. The location of holes produced by either punching or drilling can be accurately controlled with modern methods.

Dimensional tolerances permitted by standards for straightness of structural sections and plate supplied by steel mills may sometimes permit deviations from straightness that are unacceptable in the finished structure. Such material is straightened by using rolls or presses, or sometimes by the local application of heat.

After the holes have been punched or drilled and the pieces cut to the required size or shape, the components necessary to form an assembly are fitted together and connected by bolts or, more often in the shop, by welding. The use of rivets for structural steelwork in Canada has disappeared. Fabricators try to plan their fabrication operations to make maximum use of automatic or semi-automatic welding equipment. This provides improved weld quality and permits maximum efficiency. Machine finishing (usually called "milling" or "facing") may be required for the ends of certain compression members required to have a truly flat or a very smooth bearing surface. Bridge bearing plates and thick base plates for large building columns may also require milling.

After assembly in the shop, identification numbers are painted on the shipping piece or bar codes are provided and the piece is stored until it can be shipped to the construction site. When required for aesthetics or architectural appearance, or when subject to corrosive atmospheres, the shipping pieces will be given a coat of paint in the shop before the identification numbers are applied.

The erection of structural steel is the phase of the construction process where the ingenuity and experience of the fabricator/erector can save considerable time and money. Few structural designers have extensive experience in on-site construction, and therefore for large or unusual structures the designer should consult with an experienced fabricator/erector to ensure that the designer's proposed structure can be built economically. The erection of structural steel often requires further calculations by the fabricator/erector in order to ensure that adequate margins of safety are maintained when erecting the structure. It is customary to use lower margins of safety for erection loads than for the design loads on the completed structure. Thus, often a structure will be subject to its most severe stress condition while it is being constructed.

Several types of erection cranes are used for lifting the component parts of the structure. A truck crane is a crane mounted on a heavy truck-type chassis. It can travel over highways under its own power and is widely used to erect low buildings involving relatively light individual pieces. Some of the larger truck cranes are used, often in pairs or triplets, to lift heavy bridge girders for overpasses. Crawler cranes are similar to truck cranes, except that they have caterpillar tracks instead of wheels. Unlike truck cranes, they must be transported to the job site.

Guy derricks are used principally for the erection of tall, multi-storey buildings. A guy derrick consists essentially of a long vertical column (called a "mast") supported at intervals by guy wire cables. An inclined member, called a "boom" is attached to the base of the mast. Its tip can be raised or lowered and can swing in a complete circle, thus enabling the derrick to cover a large hoisting or erection area. Guy derricks are unique inasmuch as they lift themselves up a building as the building rises. This self-lifting capability, combined with the maximum height of column that can be handled when the boom is extended to its maximum reach, makes it possible to erect columns for multi-storey buildings in pieces two or three storeys high. This provides important economies in steel erection. Closely related to the guy derrick is the stiffleg derrick, in which the guy wires are replaced by two inclined structural members capable of resisting either tension or compression.

Tower cranes, characterized by tall vertical towers and horizontal or inclined booms are widely used. Various types of climbing or creeping cranes have been used recently in the erection of tall buildings. Derrick barges, locomotive cranes, and traveller cranes are specialized types of cranes developed principally for the erection of large bridges. New ideas in erection equipment are continually being tried by ingenious erection engineers.

Pre-assembly of modules can save considerable erection time
(Photo courtesy of Waiward Steel Fabricators Ltd.)

Inspection of the structure and its component members is the final step of the design process. The quality control programs of fabricators involve inspection of members before they are shipped to the construction site, and the quality assurance philosophy is being increasingly emphasized by fabricators, designers, and owners.

However, it is the responsibility of the structural designer to ensure that the structure has been fabricated and erected in accordance with the drawings and specifications. Non-destructive testing techniques have been developed for testing the components of high-strength bolted joints and welded joints. It is completely impractical to test every connection joint in a structure. A comprehensive inspection programme will test the more critical joints of a structure (such as a welded splice in a highly stressed bridge girder tension flange) and representative joints elsewhere. The purpose is primarily to ensure that the welding or bolting technique being used provides the required quality in the connection. Knowledge of the significance of weld defects is particularly important for the designer. Many times, a weld "defect" detected by a sensitive inspection method will not be particularly detrimental to the behaviour of the structure, whereas a repair of the defect may introduce a condition that is more serious. Thus, an acceptance level for defects must be established by the designer for the guidance of the inspectors.

1.10 The Role of the Structural Designer

The suitability and economy of any steel structure is determined by the structural designer. He or she is the key person in most of the steps in the design process listed earlier. In a building, heating and air conditioning requirements or other factors may dictate the use of a structural system that is not necessarily the most suitable from a purely structural viewpoint, but which is best in the overall consideration of the total building. It is the role of the structural designer to ensure that the best structural system is selected within the scope of the imposed constraints. Furthermore, a structural designer may fill one of several roles in the design and construction process. The structural designer may be employed by an architectural or consulting engineering firm and be responsible for the actual design of the structure, may work for a fabricator and do "detail design" or prepare erection schemes, or may work for an owner and be responsible for supervision and inspection. All roles are important and require a good knowledge of structural design.

Today's structural designer can use handbooks, computer programs, and other design aids that minimize the need to personally perform extensive computations. Ideally, this means that more time can be spent thinking of design concepts. Should the building have a lateral bracing system to provide stability under gravity loads and resistance to wind and earthquake loads, or should the flexural capacity of a rigid-frame type of building be used? If bracing is used, should it be in the form of a concrete core, steel truss or steel infill plate core, or a bracing system in the exterior walls of the structure? Can the floors act as diaphragms to transmit lateral loads from points of application to points of resistance (bracing system)? Can steel cladding on the walls be utilized to stiffen the structure and reduce the amount of other bracing required? Are expansion joints needed in long industrial buildings to minimize temperature effects? Is the building shape such that severe torsional effects may be encountered under wind and earthquake loads? Is the layout of floor beams and girders the most efficient and economical that can be used?

Selection of the most suitable grade of steel is an important design decision. In the past it has been customary for structural designers to assume that least weight means least cost for a steel building. This is a good general principle, but it should not be carried to extremes. Using a very high strength steel to reduce weight often will not reduce cost because the increased unit price of the higher strength steel will make the lighter design more costly than a design using a less expensive, lower strength steel. The most economical design, for buildings in particular, is usually achieved by using a steel with a reasonably high strength and relatively low base cost. In most parts of Canada, CSA G40.21 grades 300W or 350W steels will prove to be economical for buildings. However, for many buildings comparative designs using various structural layouts and different grades of steel are justified and can be prepared quickly and economically with the help of design aids.

For bridges, a higher-strength steel, such as CSA G40.21 grade 350A will often be the most suitable steel to use. In addition to economy, the bridge designer is interested in using a steel that is "tough" (to resist the propagation of cracks) and that has good resistance to atmospheric corrosion.

In bridges and buildings, the type of corrosion protection selected by the designer will greatly affect the economy of the structure. Certain steels, such as CSA G40.21 grade 350A and 350R provide their own protection against atmospheric corrosion by forming a dense, tightly adhering coat of rust that inhibits further corrosion. These steels require no paint or other coating for most environments. Other steels exposed to the weather can usually be protected satisfactorily with several coats of paint, such as those listed in CSA–S16–01. For severe corrosive environments, special treatment such as galvanizing with zinc may be justified. However, in most buildings, where the steel will be protected from the weather and the ambient environment is basically non-corrosive, no corrosion protection at all need be applied to the steel.

The protection of buildings and building occupants against the hazards of fire is an important consideration for designers and owners. Building codes stipulate fire protection requirements based on the proposed use of the structure (type of occupancy) and the size of the structure. Life-safety is a primary consideration, and restrictions on the composition of finishing materials (carpets, wall coverings, etc.) in a building, use of smoke detectors, and automatic sprinkler systems are being given increased attention in building codes. Building codes also stipulate that beams and columns must have certain "fire ratings." The required ratings differ for different types of buildings. For some buildings or parts of buildings, unprotected steel is adequate; for others, some type of insulating material or fire protective system is added to the steel. Fire protection can be an important consideration in the overall cost of a building and must be given a complete examination. Guidance on fire protection of steel construction is available in published literature [1.12].

Suitability for the intended function, safety, economy, and aesthetics must all be considered by the structural designer. Structural steel is a versatile material that can be used for virtually any type of structure. For most structures, the designer should attempt to use a grade of structural steel that is readily available, keep the structural layout and structural details as simple as possible, and use the maximum possible repetition of sizes and lengths and connection details.

References

1.1   National Research Council of Canada, "National Building Code of Canada 2005," Ottawa, Ontario.

1.2   Canadian Standards Association, CAN/CSA–S16–01, "Limit States Design of Steel Structures," Toronto, Ontario, 2001.

1.3   Canadian Standards Association, CSA-G40.20–04/G40.21–04, "General Requirements for Rolled or Welded Structural Quality Steel / Structural Quality Steel," Toronto, Ontario, 2004.

1.4   Canadian Institute of Steel Construction, "Handbook of Steel Construction," Ninth Edition, Toronto, Ontario, 2006.

1.5   National Research Council of Canada, "The National Building Code of Canada 2005," Structural Commentaries (Part 4 of Division B), Ottawa, Ontario.

1.6   Canadian Standards Association, CAN/CSA–S6–00 (R2005), "Canadian Highway Bridge Design Code," Toronto, Ontario, 2005.

1.7   American Railway Engineering and Maintenance-of-Way Association, "2002 Manual for Railway Engineering, Volume 2 – Structures," Landover, MD, 2002.

1.8   Canadian Institute of Steel Construction, "Column Selection Program (CSP)," Toronto, Ontario, 1987.

1.9   Canadian Institute of Steel Construction, "Gravity Frame Design V4.0 (GFD4)," Toronto, Ontario, 1994.

1.10   Theodore V. Galambos, F.J. Lin, and Bruce G. Johnston, "Basic Steel Design with LRFD," Prentice–Hall, 1996.

1.11   Canadian Standards Association, CAN3–Z234.1–00, "Metric Practice Guide," Toronto, Ontario, 2000.

1.12   Canadian Steel Construction Council, "Fire Protection Bulletin," Series, Toronto, Ontario.

CHAPTER 2

STRUCTURAL STEEL

2.1   Composition and Manufacture

The Industrial Revolution that changed Western society starting in the mid-1800s was driven by technological advances in three major areas—iron and steel, textiles, and power. From that central position in determining how we live, steel is still one of the most useful metals known to mankind. It is seen in items ranging from paper clips to space vehicles, and its appeal has increased in recent years because it is highly recyclable. As a structural material, steel is widely used for buildings, bridges, towers, and other structures.

Although composed almost entirely of iron, steel also contains minute quantities of other elements and these greatly affect the physical properties. Carbon is the most important of these elements. Increasing the carbon content of steel causes an increase in strength and hardness, but causes a decrease in ductility and toughness. Accordingly, standard specifications [2.1, 2.2] for structural steel limit the carbon content so that it comprises no more than about 0.15 percent to 0.30 percent of the total chemical composition.

Manganese affects steel properties in a manner similar to carbon, except that increasing the manganese content increases the toughness of steel. In structural steel, the ratio of carbon to manganese is carefully controlled so as to obtain the desired combination of strength, ductility, and toughness. Structural steel normally contains from 0.50 percent to 1.75 percent manganese.

Phosphorus, sulphur, silicon, copper, vanadium, nickel, chromium, columbium, molybdenum, and aluminum are some of the other elements that may be added to, or restricted in, structural steel. Most of these are added to impart some beneficial properties to the steel, but phosphorus and sulphur are considered to be impurities. Although the elimination of these two elements is impractical, their content is strictly limited and their detrimental effect on toughness is minimized by the addition of manganese. A good overview of the metallurgical characteristics of steel is available in [2.3]. Table 1 of Appendix A summarizes the chemical composition of structural steels used in Canada.

The manufacture of steel at an integrated steel mill begins at the blast furnace. Iron ore, limestone, and coke (made from coal) are charged into the top of this huge vessel and molten pig iron issues forth at the bottom. At this stage the pig iron contains from 3 to 4.5 percent carbon. Since most steel used today contains less than 1 percent carbon, the pig iron is converted into steel in special steelmaking furnaces. These are the basic oxygen furnace and the electric arc furnace.

Oxygen is essential to steelmaking processes. It is used to oxidize the excess of elements such as carbon, but must be carefully controlled to avoid creating gas pockets in the steel, especially at the stage when the molten steel is cast into ingots. Gas pockets can lead to defects in the final rolled steel product.

Because excess oxygen can combine with elements in the steel such as manganese, with a resultant negative effect on the steel properties, deoxidizers, such as silicon or aluminum, are used. Steel with the highest degree of deoxidation is termed killed steel; semi-killed steel has an intermediate degree of deoxidation, while rimmed steel has the lowest degree of deoxidation. Structural steel is customarily produced either as a killed or semi-killed product, depending on thickness and intended use.

Basic oxygen furnaces require a large capital investment. In North America, the majority of structural steel is now produced in electric arc furnaces (EAF). In this process, scrap steel is the main ingredient, and it is used together with smaller amounts of limestone and fluxes. Direct reduced pellets of iron ore that are rich enough in iron content may also be added. After the furnace is charged with the scrap steel, large graphite electrodes are lowered into the furnace until electric arcs are formed between the electrodes and the scrap steel. The heat so produced is sufficient in itself to reduce the scrap steel to a molten state. Electric arc furnaces take advantage of the fact that steel is highly recyclable.

The chemical composition of the steel dictates its potential mechanical properties, but its final mechanical properties are also influenced by rolling practice, including the finishing temperature, cooling rate, and subsequent heat treatment (if any). In the rolling process, the material is passed through two rollers revolving at the same speed in opposite directions. Rolling shapes the steel, reduces it in cross-section, elongates it, and increases its strength.

From the steelmaking furnaces, the molten steel normally is poured directly in the continuous casting process, but in some mills it may be poured into ingots which are then first rolled into slabs, billets, or blooms and later rolled into final form (plates, bars, or shapes) in a finishing mill. In the continuous casting process, steel is cast directly as slabs or blooms (bypassing the ingot stage) and subsequently rolled into the final product form (plates, bars, or shapes).

A chemical analysis, known as the heat analysis, is performed on samples taken from the molten metal. This analysis is reported on the mill test certificate covering the related "heat" of steel. A heat of steel is one production lot of steel from a steelmaking unit. Most heats of steel produced in North America are from fifty tons to three hundred tons of metal, depending on the size of the furnace. The time required to produce a heat of steel ranges from one hour to eight hours, depending on the type of furnace used.

Some of the steps in the steelmaking process are illustrated schematically in Figure 2.1. This figure shows two paths. In one, the raw materials enter the blast furnace are then processed in a basic oxygen steelmaking furnace. In the other, the process starts as scrap steel enters the electric arc furnace. In either case, the molten steel is poured from the furnace into ingot form or into the continuous caster. Conventional continuous casting generally produces slabs for rolling as structural plates in what is termed a reversing mill. Ingots are subsequently re-heated in a "soaking pit," and then passed through the bloom mill, the breakdown mill, and finally the finishing mill, where the product achieves its final shape. In the continuous casting process, the slabs from the continuous caster are passed directly to the rolling mills. Of course, some steps in the steelmaking process at any particular steel mill could differ from those illustrated in Figure 2.1.

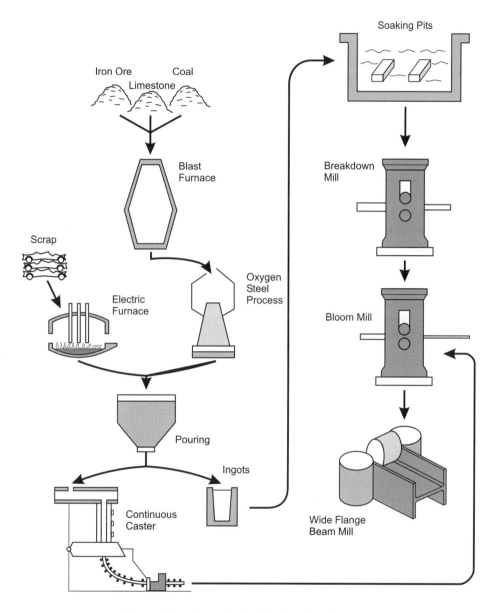

Figure 2.1 – Steps in the Steelmaking Process

Tests to determine mechanical properties of the steel are conducted on material taken from the final rolled product. One or more tensile tests to determine yield strength, tensile strength, and elongation (a measure of ductility) are set out in standard specifications [2.1], and are recorded on the mill test certificate. These reported mechanical properties, which normally exceed the specified properties by a significant amount, simply certify (along with the other information reported) that the heat of steel covered by the test certificate meets the requirements of a specific steel material specification. It should not be assumed that each piece of steel from the heat of steel covered by the mill test certificate has precisely the properties listed thereon. For this reason, designers should always use the properties set out in the standard steel specification for design purposes and not the test values reported on the mill test certificate. This is set out as a requirement in Clause 5.1.2 of the S16–01 Standard [2.4].

2.2   Strength and Ductility

Structural steel is important to designers because of its favourable strength and ductility properties, ease of fabrication and erection, and relatively low cost. Although the majority of steel structures are relatively small buildings or bridges, the great strength of steel also makes it possible to build unusual structures or structures of long clear span. Any steel structure also has the attribute of low dead weight, thereby reducing foundation costs. The high inherent ductility of steel means that local overstress in portions of a structure is not especially deleterious because yielding permits a redistribution of stresses in the structure.

Strength and ductility of steel are customarily measured by means of a standard tension test. This test consists of pulling a standard-size prepared specimen [2.1] until fracture occurs. From the load vs. elongation relationships, the yield point (or similar property), tensile strength, and percentage of elongation occurring within a prescribed gauge length can be computed. A stress vs. strain curve can also be drawn, using the load vs. elongation data.

A typical stress vs. strain curve for a structural steel is shown in Figure 2.2, and an enlargement of the initial portion of the curve is shown in Figure 2.3. Referring to these curves, it can be seen that steel obeys Hooke's law under initial load because the elongation (strain) is directly proportional to the applied load (stress). This straight line relationship holds true until the proportional limit is reached. The steel continues to behave elastically (no permanent deformation) until the elastic limit is reached. In most tension tests it is difficult to distinguish between the proportional limit and the elastic limit, and they are often considered to occur at the same point on the response curve.

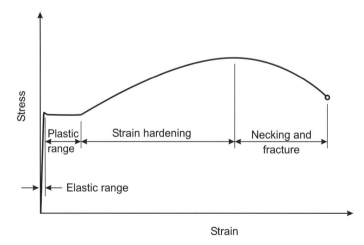

Figure 2.2 – Typical Stress vs. Strain Curve

When passing from the elastic range to the plastic range, gradual yielding of the cross-section begins. Low and medium strength structural steel test specimens exhibit a definite yield point. The yield point is defined [2.5] as the first stress in a material, less than the maximum attainable stress, at which an increase in strain occurs without an increase in stress. The yield point is manifested in the stress vs. strain curve by a long, flat plateau. The strain that the specimen undergoes between the attainment of the yield point and the beginning of strain-hardening[1] is typically ten to fifteen times as great as the strain incurred in the elastic range.

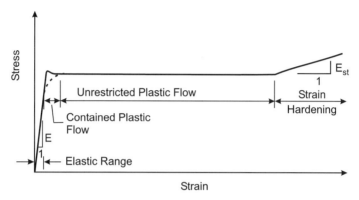

Figure 2.3 – Initial Portion of Stress vs. Strain Curve

When the specimen begins to strain-harden, the load-carrying capacity of the specimen increases until the maximum load is attained. At this point the cross- section of the specimen begins to reduce rapidly, the load that can be carried decreases, and the specimen fractures.

A typical stress vs. strain curve (Figure 2.2) indicates that the stress in the specimen is reduced between the time the maximum stress is attained and the point at which the specimen fractures. However, this is only a mathematical phenomenon. It occurs because, conventionally, the stress is computed by dividing the applied load by the original cross-sectional area of the specimen. The response curve depicted in this way is termed the "engineering" stress vs. strain curve. In fact, the cross-sectional area is continually reducing, particularly after the maximum load is attained. If the reduced area were to be used in the computations, it would be seen that the actual stress in the specimen continually increases, as would logically be expected. The result is the "true" stress vs. strain curve. The difficulty in measuring the cross-sectional area as it decreases with increasing force means that the engineering stress vs. strain curve is almost always the one used (or, implied) in structural engineering applications.

Some steels (notably high-strength quenched and tempered steels) do not exhibit a well-defined yield point, but yield gradually. Since the yield point is considered by designers to mark the limit of structural usefulness of many structural steel members, an arbitrary value, called the yield strength, is selected for these steels that do not exhibit a

---

[1] Yielding of steel occurs as dislocations move unimpeded through the crystal structure. When obstacles such as grain boundaries and other dislocations are encountered, more work is required to move the dislocation and the material is said to have strain-hardened.

yield point. Yield strength is defined [2.5] as the stress at which a material exhibits a specified limiting deviation from the proportionality of stress to strain. The deviation is expressed in terms of strain. The term yield stress [2.5] is often used to denote either the yield point or the yield strength, as applicable.

The other strength characteristic measured in a standard tension test is the tensile strength. This is defined [2.5] as the maximum tensile stress that a material is capable of sustaining, and it corresponds to the highest point on the stress vs. strain curve.

The ability of a material to undergo large plastic deformation without fracture is termed "ductility." In a standard tension test, ductility is measured by the amount of elongation the specimen undergoes over a standard gauge length (200 mm or 50 mm). Elongation is usually expressed as a percentage, and standard steel material specifications [2.1] normally require from fifteen to twenty percent elongation in a 200 mm gauge length. A ductile steel is characterized by large total strain before fracture.

The favourable ductility characteristics of steel enable many structural parts to be designed using simplified, but not necessarily precisely correct, assumptions and still perform satisfactorily. When ductility is reduced, through poor design details or fabrication practices, brittle fracture or low fatigue strength can result.

2.3   Cross-Section Properties

A characteristic of importance to designers is the local buckling strength of steel. Relatively thin steel elements subjected to compressive loads can buckle before reaching the yield point, an undesirable situation. The local buckling strength of these elements depends primarily upon the ratio of the width of the element to its thickness and upon the types of support provided at the edges of the element. The compression flange of a beam, for instance, supported at only one point (the beam web) will buckle (for the same applied load) at a lower width-to-thickness ratio than will the web of a beam, which is supported at two edges by the beam flanges. Design standards [2.4] limit the width-to-thickness ratios of elements subject to compression. Thus, the designer need not be concerned with the local buckling problem if steel members are selected that conform to the width-to thickness limits specified. Provisions allow designers to deviate from the specified limits, when necessary, by performing a buckling analysis.

Another characteristic of interest to designers is residual stress. Residual stresses are the stresses that remain in an unloaded member after it has been formed into a finished product. Examples of such stresses include, but are not limited to, those induced by cold-bending, cooling after rolling, or by welding.

Residual stresses are of particular importance in column design (Chapter 4). When a hot-rolled steel product cools, certain portions cool more quickly than others. In an I–shape for instance, the flange tips and the middle of the web cool more quickly than the junction between the flanges and the web, where there is more material. As steel cools, it shrinks. When the flange tips and the middle of the web cool down, their shrinkage is unhindered by the hot web–flange junctions (hot steel has negligible yield strength). When the flange–web junctions cool down, the flange tips and web mid-section have already gained strength and shrinkage of the web–flange junction exerts a compressive force on the cooler flange tips and middle of the web. This compressive force is resisted by the cooler portions, which have now gained some strength. At the time that the whole cross-section has cooled, therefore, the flange tips and middle of the web will contain residual compressive stress and the remainder of the cross-section will contain residual tensile stress. The presence of these locked-in stresses will affect the load-carrying capacity of all structural steel columns to some degree. This effect will be treated in subsequent chapters.

Residual stresses resulting from the steel rolling procedure usually range from about 70 to 100 MPa. Not all residual stresses reduce the load-carrying capacity of columns. For instance, box sections formed of four welded plates will generally have residual tensile stress at the corners—a desirable residual stress pattern for columns subject to axial load plus bending.

2.4   Other Properties

Toughness, the capacity to absorb large amounts of energy, can be an important design criterion, particularly for structures subject to impact loads (e.g., bridges) and for structures subject to earthquake loads. Tough materials usually fracture after large plastic deformations have taken place, i.e., they fail in a ductile manner. At room temperature, common structural steels are very tough and fail in a ductile manner. As the temperature drops, a point is reached at which the steel loses its toughness and fails in a brittle, rather than a ductile, manner. This characteristic usually is measured by means of a Charpy V-Notch impact test [2.1]. In this test, a standard notched specimen is subjected to an impact load imparted by a swinging pendulum. The temperature of the specimens is varied, the energy absorbed by each specimen is recorded, and an energy vs. temperature curve (Figure 2.4) is plotted. From this curve, a transition temperature corresponding to some level of energy absorption (usually 20 or 27 joules) can be selected. The transition temperature is the temperature below which fractures are mostly brittle and above which fractures are mostly ductile.

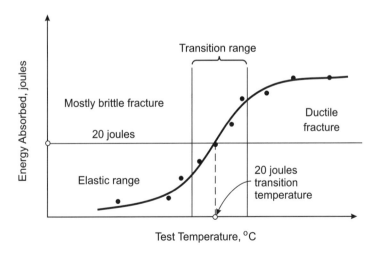

Figure 2.4 – Energy vs. Temperature Transition Curve

Structural steels differ greatly in toughness. A fully killed, fine-grain steel with a suitable chemical composition or a specially heat-treated steel will exhibit considerable toughness. Several tough steels have been developed for use in Canada, where low ambient temperatures are an inescapable design condition for exposed structures. Under low temperature conditions, a structural member with a severe notch or other stress raiser, subject to a significant tensile stress, may be susceptible to brittle fracture. Selection of a tough steel for this design condition will help to minimize the possibility of brittle fracture. Guidance in the selection of a suitable steel is provided elsewhere [2.3, 2.6].

Most steel structures are fabricated and erected with the aid of welding. Many structures are assembled with welds and bolts—but seldom with bolts only. Thus, the weldability of the structural steel to be used is almost always a design consideration. All structural steels are weldable in the sense that two pieces can be connected with a weld. However, the ease with which the welding can be accomplished, the cost, and the quality of the welds differ from steel to steel. Standard specifications [2.1, 2.7] provide information on those structural steels considered readily weldable, while other sources [2.3, 2.8] provide more details on the weldability of steel.

Atmospheric corrosion resistance may be an important design consideration when structures are exposed to the weather. Special steels have been developed that eliminate the need for paint or other protective coatings under most atmospheric conditions [2.1, 2.3].

Toughness, weldability and corrosion resistance are important for highway bridges.
(Photo Courtesy of Buckland & Taylor Ltd.)

The modulus of elasticity (Young's modulus) for structural steel is practically constant, and the value usually used is 200 000 MPa. Poisson's ratio (ratio of transverse to longitudinal strain) is taken as 0.30 in the elastic range. The density of steel is 7 850 kg/m^3 and the coefficient of thermal expansion, at atmospheric temperatures, is approximately $11.7 \times 10^{-6} / C°$. The coefficient of thermal expansion is the change in length per unit of length for a change of one degree of temperature.

2.5 Types of Structural Steel

In 1924, the first standard of the Canadian Standards Association (CSA) dealing with the design of steel buildings was published. Designated A16, this building standard contained a material specification for the type of steel to be used—mild steel with a specified minimum yield point of 190 MPa. Over the years, steel grades with greater strength properties were introduced, and at present a wide range is available. Yield strengths range from 245 MPa to 700 MPa. Today the designer can select structural steels from five general categories.

Carbon steel—Carbon and manganese are the principal strengthening elements. The specified minimum yield point ranges from about 245 to 300 MPa, and the specified minimum tensile strength from about 380 to 450 MPa.

High strength carbon steel—Adding carbon increases the steel strength but reduces ductility, toughness, and weldability. For transmission towers and other structures where relatively light members are joined together by bolts, this steel has proven to be satisfactory. The specified minimum yield point ranges from 350 MPa to about 400 MPa, and the specified minimum tensile strength from about 480 to 550 MPa.

High strength low-alloy steel—The carbon content is kept low and strength is increased by adding alloys such as vanadium or columbium. The specified minimum yield point ranges from about 300 to 480 MPa, and the tensile strength from 450 to 550 MPa.

Atmospheric corrosion resistant steel—This is a low-alloy type steel in which the alloying elements are chosen so that the long-term atmospheric corrosion resistance is at least four times that of plain carbon structural steel. Also known as "weathering steels," these steels are often left unpainted. The yield point is generally 350 MPa and the tensile strength about 480 MPa.

High strength quenched and tempered steel—These are steels heat-treated to develop high strength. They are generally weldable and tough, but special welding techniques are usually required. The specified minimum yield strength ranges between 550 and 700 MPa, with specified minimum tensile strengths between 700 and 950 MPa.

The large variety of structural steels available gives the designer freedom to select the type of steel most suitable for the particular structure. At the same time, however, the task is complicated by this very variety. In 1973, the Canadian Standards Association published a comprehensive steel standard that considerably simplifies the designer's task of selection. This is described in Section 2.6.

2.6 Structural Steel Material Standards

CSA Standards G40.20 and G40.21 [2.1][2] are companion standards that permit the user to completely define the structural steel material needed for purchase and description of structural steel products in Canada. The first standard (G40.20) lists requirements common to all structural quality steel plates, shapes, and so on, and the

---

[2] These are separate standards, but they are published as a single document.

second provides specific information in these product areas. More particularly, CSA G40.20 covers the testing, inspection, marking, and delivery requirements for the G40.21 structural steels, as well as the dimensional tolerances permitted for the various rolled and welded products. CSA G40.21 specifies chemical compositions, strength levels, methods of manufacture, methods of identification, etc. for the grades of steel covered by the standard. It is only necessary for the designer to specify that the structural steel to be used shall be CSA Standard G40.21, grade 350W (or other suitable grade).

Table 2 of Appendix A shows a matrix of the grades of steel available under the G40.20/G40.21 standards. Each is identified by a number and a letter. The number is the specified minimum yield of the thinnest plate and lightest section available in that grade of steel. (The yield strength in some grades decreases for the larger plate or shape thicknesses.) The letter refers to the characteristics of the six types of steel available, as follows:

Type W – Weldable Steel

Type WT – Weldable Notch Tough Steel

Type R – Atmospheric Corrosion-Resistant Steel

Type A – Atmospheric Corrosion-Resistant Weldable Steel

Type AT – Atmospheric Corrosion-Resistant Weldable Notch Tough Steel

Type Q – Quenched and Tempered Low Alloy Steel Plate

Type QT – Quenched and Tempered Low Alloy Notch Tough Steel Plate

Tables 3 and 4 of Appendix A enable the user to identify the specific strength properties available for a given shape or plate size as a function of the grade of steel. For example, a steel plate designated as grade 300W will have a yield strength of 300 MPa if the thickness is ≤ 65 mm but will have a yield strength of 280 MPa if the thickness is >65 mm. This information is obtained from Table 4. A rolled shape described as a W310×86 section[3] and of Grade 350WT steel is a Group 3 shape (Table 3), for which the yield strength is 350 MPa (Table 4).

2.7   Structural Steel Products

Structural steel products are the basic elements from which structural members such as beams and columns are fabricated. A complete list of items used in buildings that the Canadian structural steel fabricating industry considers to be covered by the term "structural steel" is contained elsewhere [2.9]. The most widely used items can be described according to following categories:

Flat rolled products — plate, flat bars, sheet and strip

Sections — rolled shapes, rolled bar-size shapes and hollow structural sections

Bolts

Welding electrodes.

---

[3] The ways to describe structural steel products are covered in Section 2.7.

Complex structures may use more than one type of steel.
(Photo Courtesy of Michael I. Gilmor)

In broad terms, plate is flat-rolled steel over 200 mm wide and over 6 mm in thickness, sheet is flat-rolled steel over 300 mm wide and less than 6 mm thick; strip is flat rolled steel less than 300 mm wide and 6 mm or less in thickness. For most applications, the structural engineer will specify the use of plate.

Structural-size rolled shapes are sections with flanges that have at least one dimension of the cross section 75 mm or greater; bar-size shapes have all dimensions less than 75 mm. Welded shapes are sections with flanges and which are produced by welding together two or more components. Hollow structural sections are hollow square, rectangular, or round sections and which are produced by either hot-forming or cold-forming. Properties, dimensions and illustrations of all sections generally available in Canada are contained in the CISC Handbook of Steel Construction [2.10].

When designating structural steel products on drawings, it is desirable that a standard method of abbreviation be employed that will identify the product without reference to the manufacturer. The following nomenclature is used.

Welded Wide Flange Shapes	WWF 900×169
W Shapes	W 610×113
M Shapes	M 100×19
Standard Beams (S Shapes)	S 380×64
Standard Channels (C Shapes)	C 230×30
Structural Tees	
– cut from WWF Shapes	WWT 250×138
– cut from W Shapes	WT 305×56.5
Equal Leg Angles:	
(leg dimensions× thickness, all in mm)	L 64×64×7.9
Unequal Leg Angles	
(leg dimensions× thickness, all in mm)	L 127×89×13
Plates (thickness× width, both in mm)	PL 8×500
Square Hollow Structural Sections:	
(outside dimensions× thickness, both in mm; G40.20 class)	
	HSS 102×102×4.8 Class H
Round Hollow Structural Sections	
(outside diameter× thickness, both in mm; G40.20 class)	
	HSS 60×3.2 Class H
Rectangular Hollow Structural Sections	
(outside dimensions× thickness, both in mm; G40.20 class).	
	HSS 203×102×6.4 Class H

Rolled shapes, plates and high strength bolts are commonly used in buildings.
(Photo Courtesy of The Canam Group)

The bolts most widely used in steel construction are those conforming to ASTM Standard A325 [2.11]. These high-strength bolts are used extensively for connecting structural members at the job site, and, to a lesser extent, in the steel fabrication shop. Under certain conditions it may be desirable to use a higher strength bolt, such as ASTM

A490 [2.12] Metric standards for high strength bolts, designated A325M and A490M, are also available. In many structures, lower strength bolts, conforming to ASTM Standard A307 [2.13] are suitable. Design standards [2.4] stipulate conditions under which these bolts can be used.

Welding electrodes are the rods or wire that are used to produce welds. They must conform to standards such as the CSA W48 series of standards on electrodes. Each electrode is suitable for use with a certain type of steel, using a particular type of welding equipment and specific welding procedures. Each electrode is designated by a code number that identifies the minimum tensile strength of the deposited weld metal, the welding positions for which the electrode is suitable, and the deposition characteristics of the electrode. The selection of the most suitable electrode to use in a given situation requires specialized knowledge of welding. Normally, this decision should be left to the fabricator, after consultation with the designer as to the required performance and service conditions.

Hollow Structural Sections of CSA G40.21 350W steel were used for the Toronto SkyDome roof trusses.
(Photo Courtesy of Canada Wide / Fred Thornhill)

References

2.1 Canadian Standards Association, CSA–G40.20/G40.21–04, "General Requirements for Rolled or Welded Structural Quality Steel / Structural Quality Steels," Toronto, Ontario, 2004.

2.2 American Society for Testing and Materials, "ASTM Book of Standards, Part 4," Philadelphia, Pennsylvania.

2.3 Lay, M.G., "Structural Steel Fundamentals, Australian Road Research Board, Victoria, Australia, 1982.

2.4 Canadian Standards Association, CAN/CSA–S16–01, "Limit States Design of Steel Structures," Toronto, Ontario, 2001.

2.5 Ad Hoc Committee on Nomenclature, Administrative Committee on Metals of the Structural Division, "Glossary of Terms," Journal of the Structural Division, ASCE, Vol. 97, No. ST8, August, 1971.

2.6 Barsom, J.M. and Rolfe, S.T., "Fracture and Fatigue Control in Structures; Applications of Fracture Mechanics," Third Edition, West Conshohocken, PA : ASTM, 1999.

2.7 Canadian Standards Association, CSA–W59–03, "Welded Steel Construction (Metal-Arc Welding)," Toronto, Ontario, 2004.

2.8 Patchett, B. M. and Bringas, J. E., "Metals Blue Book, Welding Filler Metals," Third Edition, CASTI Publishing, Edmonton, Canada and American Welding society, Miami, FL., 2000.

2.9 Canadian Institute of Steel Construction, "CISC Code of Standard Practice for Structural Steel," CISC Handbook of Steel Construction, Part 7, Toronto, Ontario, 2002.

2.10 Canadian Institute of Steel Construction, "Handbook of Steel Construction," Ninth Edition, Toronto, Ontario, 2006.

2.11 Specification for Structural Bolts, Steel, Heat-Treated, 120/105 ksi Minimum Tensile Strength, ASTM A325-00.

2.12 Specification for Heat-Treated Steel Structural Bolts, 150 ksi Minimum Tensile Strength, ASTM A490-00.

2.13 Specification for Carbon Steel Bolts and Studs, 60 000 PSI Tensile Strength, ASTM A307-00.

CHAPTER 3

TENSION MEMBERS

3.1 Introduction

Tension members are those structural elements that are subjected to direct axial loads that tend to elongate the members. They occur as components of trusses, hangers, and cables for floors or roofs, in bracing systems, as tie rods, and similar members. The design of tension members is one of the simplest problems with which the structural engineer is faced. In limit states design, the basic requirement is simply that enough cross-sectional area be provided in order that the factored resistance of the member is equal to or greater than the factored load in the member.

Tension members are used as major load-carrying elements in this building

In discussing the resistance of a tension member, it is pertinent to examine the qualitative behaviour of a typical member as the load on it is increased to failure. Figure 3.1(a) shows such a member and plots its behaviour in terms of the elongation response to load. Figure 3.1(b) shows an enlarged plot of the initial portion of this curve. Like a coupon of the same material, the initial portion of the curve shows an elastic response, that is, unloading of the member anywhere in this region will cause it to return to its original undeformed shape. However, local yielding starts at a value less than the yield point of the material as obtained from a tension coupon. This is due to the inevitable eccentricity of load, dimensional variations in the cross-section, and the presence of residual stresses. Eventually, all the material in the cross-section reaches the yield point, terminating this region of "contained plastic flow." Deflections now will increase rapidly under no increase in load until the fibres start to strain-harden and the load again increases. Although this region of "unrestricted plastic flow" defines one limit of usefulness, the member still has considerable additional load-carrying capacity. The other limit of usefulness is that given by the ultimate resistance of the member. Both of these limits are used by S16–01 in establishing the criteria for tension members. As is the case for all members proportioned according to Limit States Design, the deformation of the tension member under the specified load must also be examined.

3.2   Tension Member Resistance

For the usual case, wherein the connections are made either by means of bolts or by welding, S16–01 requires (Clause 13.2(a)) that the resistance of a tension member be taken as the least of the following three conditions:

$$T_r = \phi A_g F_y \tag{3.1}$$

$$T_r = 0.85 \phi A_n F_u \tag{3.2}$$

$$T_r = 0.85 \phi A_{ne} F_u \tag{3.3}$$

In all three of these cases, the resistance factor, ϕ, is to be taken as 0.90.

The requirement given by Equation 3.1 follows directly from the examination of the behaviour of a typical tension member that was made using Figure 3.1, namely, that one limiting load condition is attained when excessive elongation occurs. This is calculated as the product of the yield strength of the material, F_y, and the cross-sectional area of the member. In this case, the gross cross-sectional area, A_g, is used, rather than the net cross-sectional area, A_n. When yielding occurs on the net cross section, that is, in the region immediately around the holes, it does not result in very much elongation. The regions of yielding are confined and the length of the connection is relatively small. Thus, it is considered that not until the entire cross-section, A_g, has yielded is there any undesirable behaviour, in this case excessive deformations.

The requirements given in Equations 3.2 and 3.3 are similar to one another in appearance, and they also follow from the examination of Figure 3.1. They both represent the limiting load as established by fracture of the tension member—its ultimate load. Because there is no reserve of any kind beyond the ultimate resistance, an additional multiplier, 0.85, is introduced. This has the effect of increasing the safety index from its usual value of about 3.0 up to 4.5.

The terms in Equations 3.2 and 3.3 describing the cross-sectional area require more explanation. In general, the least cross-sectional area (A_n) must be used, but this quantity can take different forms. The possibilities for net area are described in Clause

12.3 of the Standard. If the potential fracture plane is normal to the force, Figure 3.2(a), then the net area is simply the product of the net width (w_n) and the thickness (t). However, if a segment of the potential fracture surface is inclined to the force, Figure 3.2(b), its net area is calculated as the net area across the inclined element (w_n t) plus a correction term, $s^2/4g$. The quantities s (stagger, or, pitch) and g (gauge) are shown in the figure. The correction term is largely empirical.

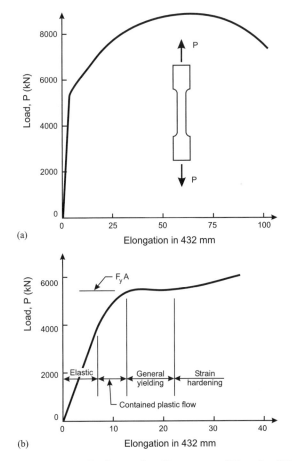

Figure 3.1 – Load vs. Deformation Response of Tension Member

The net width, w_n, is calculated by subtracting the diameters of all holes contained within the scope of the segment being examined from the gross width, taken at right angles to the direction of the load. The specified diameter of a hole is normally 2 mm greater than the bolt diameter itself. If it is known that the holes are to be drilled, then the actual diameter of the hole can be used in the calculations. However, if punched holes are used, a common fabrication procedure, then an allowance for distortion around the hole is made. In this case, the calculations for net area should be made using a notional hole diameter 2 mm larger than the one specified.

The net area, A_n, calculated in accordance with the above requirements is the quantity to be used in Equation 3.2. The term A_{ne}, used in Equation 3.3, is calculated initially in the same way, but a further adjustment is required. It is introduced to account for a phenomenon known as "shear lag." This is discussed in Section 3.3.

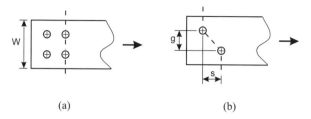

(a)   (b)

Figure 3.2 – Tension Member – Net Section

To summarize, Clause 12.3.1 of the Standard requires that the effective net area be calculated as the sum of the net areas, A_n, of each segment along the path of a potential failure plane computed as follows:

For a segment normal to the force—

$$A_n = w_n \, t \tag{3.4}$$

and for a segment inclined to the force—

$$A_n = \left(w_n + s^2/4g \right) t \tag{3.5}$$

Examples of net area calculations are given in the following sections and in Section 9.9.

The capacity for distortion before failure is considered to be of importance in any structural assemblage because it allows for the re-distribution of forces as the structure proceeds towards its ultimate capacity [3.1]. For commonly used steels the spread between yield point and ultimate tensile strength is relatively large. For example, the yield and ultimate values are 350 MPa and 450 MPa, respectively, for G40.21 350W steel. Usual member proportions will permit yielding to occur before the ultimate strength is attained, and failure of the member by actual physical separation of parts would be preceded by considerable distortion, a desirable feature. In cases like this, Equation 3.1 is likely to govern and the associated safety index is 3.0. On the other hand, a steel such as G40.21 700Q has a much lower spread between yield and ultimate strength; the figures are 700 MPa and 800 MPa, respectively. If material is removed in the form of holes when making the end connections, the situation can easily arise wherein the ultimate strength of a 700Q steel tension member is reached by fracture of the material at the net section of the connection before yielding takes place in the main portion of the member, where no holes are present. If failure did occur, this means that it would happen suddenly and with little warning. In recognition of this, S16–01 introduces the modification to the resistance factor (0.85) that has the effect of increasing the safety index to 4.5 from the usual value of 3.0.

Pin-connected members are used infrequently. If they are required, the factored resistance is established as 0.75 times the product of $\phi \, A_n \, F_y$ (Clause 13.2(b)). The basic expression here is similar to Equation 3.1 except that the net area is to be used in recognition that holes used to accommodate pins will be relatively large as compared with bolt holes. The 0.75 reduction factor recognizes the greater non-uniformity of stress that will occur around a hole that is large relative to the material in which it is formed.

3.3   Shear Lag

Physical tests of tension members have demonstrated that the actual fracture load can sometimes be less than that predicted on the basis of the product of the net area and coupon strength of the material [3.2]. If a reduction in capacity occurs, it can be attributed to such factors as the method of making holes (punched or drilled), the ratio of the gauge of the holes to the fastener diameter, the ductility of the steel, and the amount of the cross-section that has actually been connected. Of all the possible factors, it is the latter that is most significant and its effect will be discussed in this section.

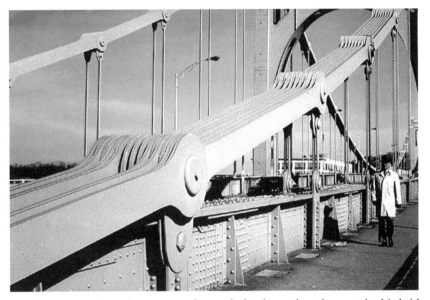

Large pin-connected members are used as main load carrying elements in this bridge.

Figure 3.3(a) shows a W-shape in which the connection is made using gusset plates attached to the flanges. This would be a common configuration: it is seldom practical to connect both the web and the flanges. It is obvious that the web cannot be expected to be fully effective in the region of the connection. As shown pictorially in Figure 3.3(b), it is only some distance away from the region of the connection that the assumption of uniform stress (actually, uniform strain) throughout the connection will be fulfilled. Because the internal transfer of forces from the flange region into the web region will be by shear and because one part lags behind the other, the phenomenon is referred to as "shear lag."

The researchers who investigated the shear lag problem suggested that the net area calculated according to Equations 3.4 and 3.5 be modified when situations like that depicted in Figure 3.3 are encountered. The empirical relationship suggested was [3.2]

$$A_{ne} = \left(1 - \frac{e}{L}\right) A_n \tag{3.6}$$

43

The term L is the length of the connection and e is the distance from the face of the gusset plate to the centroid of the area tributary to that gusset plate (see Figure 3.3(b)).

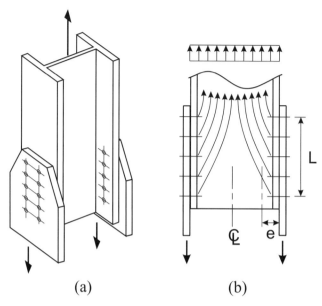

(a)   (b)

Figure 3.3 – Shear Lag in Tension Member

Equation 3.6 can be usefully employed to deal with unusual situations, but in routine design it means that the connection must be fully detailed in order that the shear lag effect can be determined. An examination of a large number of hypothetical cases involving the most commonly used structural shapes has led to simplified rules, which are provided in Clause 12.3.3.2 of the Standard. Those rules directly provide the adjusted effective net area (A_{ne}) required for use in Equation 3.3. The specific requirements when a bolted connection is used are as follows:

For WWF, W, M, or S shapes with flange widths not less than 2/3 the depth and for structural tees cut from these shapes, when only the flanges are connected and there are three or more transverse lines of bolts—

$$A_{ne} = 0.90 \, A_n \tag{3.7a}$$

For angles connected by only one leg and with four or more transverse lines of bolts—

$$A_{ne} = 0.80 \, A_n \tag{3.7b}$$

For angles connected by only one leg and with less than four transverse lines of bolts—

$$A_{ne} = 0.60 \, A_n \tag{3.7c}$$

For all other structural shapes connected by three or more transverse lines of bolts—

$$A_{ne} = 0.85 \, A_n \tag{3.7d}$$

For all other structural shapes connected by two or one transverse lines of bolts—

$$A_{ne} = 0.75\,A_n \tag{3.7e}$$

A similar requirement should apply when welds are used to connect tension members and this is treated in the Standard in Clause 12.3.3.3. In this case, the elements comprising the cross-section of the tension member are examined separately to determine the reduction for shear lag for that element. The amount of the reduction is dependent upon the manner in which the load is transmitted to each individual element of the cross-section.

For elements of the cross-section connected by welds transverse to the tension field, no reduction for shear lag is necessary. Thus, for such elements, the contribution to the total net area is—

$$A_{n1} = w\,t \tag{3.8a}$$

The connection of an element using longitudinal welds also raises the possibility of shear lag across its width. For the case of weld length, L, not less than the element width, w, and considering the welds to be placed at the longitudinal edges of the plate, then—

when $L \geq 2\,w$, $A_{n2} = 1.00\,w\,t$ (3.8b)

when $2w > L \leq w$, $A_{n2} = 0.50\,w\,t + 0.25\,L\,t$ (3.8c)

when $w > L$, $A_{n2} = 0.75\,L\,t$ (3.8d)

Where the element is connected by a single line of weld located a distance $\bar{x}$ with respect to the centroid of the element, a reduction based on Equation 3.6 is used—

when $L \geq w$ $A_{n3} = \left(1 - \dfrac{\bar{x}}{L}\right) w\,t$ (3.8e)

when $w > L$ $A_{n3} = 0.50\,L\,t$ (3.8f)

The reduced effective net area of the entire cross-section is then determined by summing the individual reduced net areas of each of the elements comprising the total cross-section. Hence—

$$A_{ne} = A_{n1} + A_{n2} + A_{n3} \tag{3.9}$$

3.4   Tension and Shear Block Failure[1]

Tensile fracture, which has been discussed in Sections 3.2 and 3.3, can also take place in combination with shear. In cases like that shown in Figure 3.4, it is observed in tests that it is possible to have tensile fracture across A–B accompanied by shear yielding along A–D and B–C [3.3]. The usual representation of the shear component is to describe the shear resistance of steel in terms of the tensile strength and to use the von Mises

---

[1] In the previous edition of the Standard, tension and shear block failure was called block shear failure.

criterion, i.e., $\tau_y \approx \sigma_y / \sqrt{3}$. Rounding off the value and using the symbols employed by the S16 Standard, the shear strength is taken as $0.60\, F_y$. Thus, the expression given in the S16 Standard for this case (Clause 13.11(a)(i)) is

$$T_r + V_r = \phi\, A_{nt}\, F_u\ +\ 0.60\, \phi\, A_{gv}\, F_y \tag{3.10a}$$

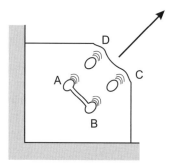

Figure 3.4 – Tension and Shear Block Failure of Gusset Plate

It is possible that the product $A_{gv}\,(0.60\, F_y)$, which describes shear yielding, is greater than shear fracture, i.e., $A_{nv}\,(0.60\, F_u)$. To cover this possibility, an upper limit to Equation 3.10(a) is prescribed

$$T_r + V_r \ \leq\ \phi\, A_{nt}\, F_u\ +\ 0.60\, \phi\, A_{nv}\, F_u \tag{3.10b}$$

The term, A_{gv}, is the gross area (i.e., no deduction for holes) taken along the potential shear planes and A_{nv} is the net shear area. The term A_{nt} is the net area in tension, where the area under examination is that consistent with the block of material under examination. This area should not be confused with the net area A_n associated with the design of the tension member itself.

3.5   Design Requirements

In equation form, the basic design requirement for a tension member can be expressed as

$$T_r \geq T_f \tag{3.11}$$

or, if shear is also a possibility

$$T_r + V_r \geq T_f \tag{3.12}$$

In these equations, T_f is the tensile force in the member resulting from the factored loads. T_r is the factored tensile resistance of the member calculated by Equation 3.1, 3.2, or 3.3 and V_r is the factored shear resistance, given by the second term in the right-hand side of Equation 3.10. When these expressions are substituted for T_r and V_r, the left-hand side of Equation 3.11 or 3.12 will contain the term A, the required cross-sectional area.

The design equation implies that all fibres of a cross-section are uniformly stressed, or, more precisely, that all fibres undergo the same elongation. Excluding for the moment the disturbing effects introduced if holes are used in making the end connections, this assumption will generally be valid if the load axis is coincident with a longitudinal axis through the centre of gravity of the member. Unavoidable eccentricities do arise, however. In those cases where only part of the member is connected at its ends, such as an angle fastened only by one leg, the rules given for shear lag (Equations 3.7 and 3.8) can be used. (In the case of angles, it probably is not wise to apply those rules to unequal leg angles that are connected only by the short leg [3.4]. The designer should be alert to cases where the load is definitely not coincident with the centroidal axis of the member. The additional effect of the bending should then be considered.

The introduction of holes for purposes of making end connections will result in local stresses higher than a nominal stress calculated on the basis of the least area available to carry the load. At the level of the working loads, this increase theoretically can be quite large for the case of a plate with a hole [3.5]. However, the situation is ameliorated by the fact that such a hole is normally filled by a bolt—the fastener introduces a localized compressive stress into the plate adjacent to the region of theoretically high tensile stress. In any event, the stress rise is highly localized and does not produce any undesirable behaviour in the member. At factored load levels, the assumption of uniform stress across the section becomes even more valid because of material yielding and the resulting redistribution of stresses [3.5].

Taking all of these factors into consideration, the effect of stress concentrations around holes is neglected when dealing with holes used for bolts in fabricated steel members. In these cases, the stress is assumed to be uniformly distributed over the area of a cross-section through one or more holes.

As has already been indicated, one notable exception to this rule is made when dealing with the substantially larger holes that are needed for pins in eyebars or in pin-connected plates.

The choice of section or shape to be used as a tension member is governed to a considerable extent by the type of end connection that will be used. Some of the sections available, exclusive of cables, are shown in Figure 3.5.

Round and flat bars are used infrequently. In the sizes generally required, the flexural stiffness of these members will be very low and they may sag under their own weight or that of workers and maintenance personnel. Their small cross-sectional dimensions also mean high slenderness values and, as a consequence, they may tend to flutter under wind loads or vibrate under moving loads. Design standards commonly place an upper limit on slenderness (ratio of unsupported length to least radius of gyration, L/r) to guard against these undesirable features. The S16 requirement limits the slenderness ratio of tension members to 300 (Clause 10.4.2.2). This may be waived if the designer takes other steps to control possible sag, flutter, or vibration.

Angles, used singly or in multiples, are often selected for use when tension member loads are light to medium. It is considered good practice to provide angles in pairs rather than singly. At least one axis of symmetry is then present and eccentricity in the end connection is minimized [3.6]. When angles or other shapes are used in this fashion, they should be interconnected at intervals to prevent rattling, especially when moving loads are present.

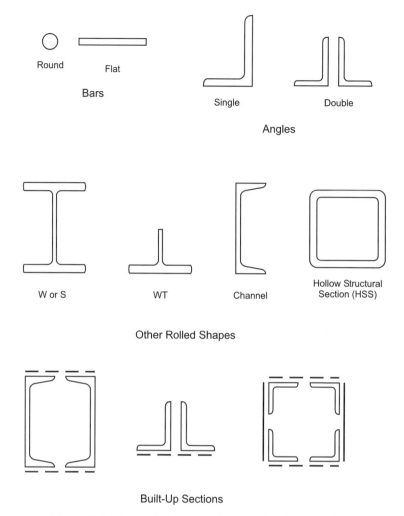

Round   Flat

Bars

Single   Double

Angles

W or S   WT   Channel   Hollow Structural
                                        Section (HSS)

Other Rolled Shapes

Built-Up Sections

Figure 3.5 – Typical Sections Used as Tension Members

Larger tension loads may be carried by W or S-shapes, channels, or built-up sections. The built-up sections are also tied together either at intervals (batten plates) or continuously (lacing or perforated cover plates). Except when perforated cover plates are used, these ties are not considered to add load- carrying capacity in themselves, but they do serve to provide rigidity and to distribute the load among the main elements.

3.6   Calculation of Effective Area of Tension Members

If the connection of a tension member is made using welds, such as shown in Figure 3.6, then potentially all of the chosen cross section is available for carrying load and the design can proceed in accordance with the requirements of Equation 3.11. (Depending on the arrangement of welds, shear lag may have to be considered, however, as discussed in Section 3.3) On the other hand, a connection made using bolts means that material has been removed from the cross-section in the form of holes. Only a portion of the cross-section is now available to carry load and this is termed the net section. It has already been described, in Section 3.2.

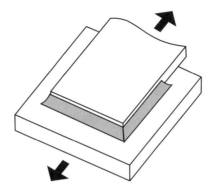

Figure 3.6 – Tension Member with Welded End Connections

Consider fasteners laid out in a simple fashion, such as shown in the "lap" splice of Figure 3.7(a). Starting from plate A, it can be seen that the load is transferred in some manner into the six fasteners, then from the fasteners the load is transferred back into plate B. (Connection design is fully discussed in Chapter 9.) Plates A or B here represent a simple form of tension member. Failure of member A might occur by fracture through a pair of fastener holes such as shown as Section 1–1 in Figure 3.7(a) and illustrated pictorially in Figure 3.7(b). If, for example, $w = 200$ mm and $t=25$ mm , then the gross cross-sectional area A_g is 5000 mm^2. Assuming bolts of 22 mm diameter and punched holes, the net area can be calculated using Equation 3.4 as—

$$A_n = w_n \; t = [\,200 - 2 \times (\,22 + 4\,)\,]\ \text{mm} \times 25\ \text{mm} = 3700\ \text{mm}^2$$

In this example, fracture through Section 1–1, or an equivalent section in member B, is the only possible net section fracture location. An example in which the area of a staggered section must be calculated will follow.

Carrying this illustration to its conclusion, the tensile capacity of member A now can be determined. For G40.21 300W steel, $F_y = 300$ MPa and $F_u = 450$ MPa. Calculation of the tensile resistance, T_r, using Equations 3.1 and 3.2 gives

$$T_r = \phi \; A_g \; F_y = 0.90 \times 5000\ \text{mm}^2 \times 300\ \text{N}/\text{mm}^2 = 1350 \times 10^3\ \text{N}$$
$$= 1350\ \text{kN}$$

or $\quad T_r = 0.85 \; \phi \; A_n \; F_u = 0.85 \times 0.90 \times 3700\ \text{mm}^2 \times 450\ \text{N}/\text{mm}^2$

$$= 1\,274 \times 10^3\ \text{N} = 1274\ \text{kN} \qquad\qquad \text{(Governs)}$$

The value of the factored resistance, $T_r = 1274$ kN, can now be compared with the effect of the factored loads in the member under consideration. It should also be noted that the yield point of this steel was taken to be 300 MPa. In fact, the yield strength of plates is a function of thickness. Table 4 of Appendix A shows that the yield strength for Grade 300W steel is 300 MPa for plate thicknesses up to 65 mm. Since the plate thickness used in this example is 25 mm, the assumption used here is valid.

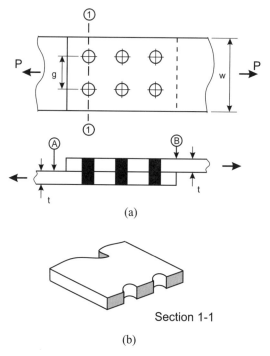

(a)

Section 1-1

(b)

Figure 3.7 – Tension Member – Lap Splice

This example will not be used to investigate the possible tension and shear block failure. That will be illustrated later.

Referring to the preceding example, a cross-section of 3700 mm^2 will be loaded to its maximum permissible capacity under a factored load of 1274 kN. However, a cross section of 5000 mm^2 was provided for most of the length of the member. This means that 35% more cross-sectional area than is necessary is being used for a greater part of the member. While the ideal of 100% efficiency is not attainable when mechanical fasteners are used, the designer might look for a more favourable fastener pattern. One alternative is shown in Figure 3.8. Two cases will be examined, a tearing of the plate directly across Section 1–1 or through in a zig-zag fashion as in Section 2–2.

Referring again to Figure 3.8 and assuming values of w = 200 mm, s = 80 mm, and g = 115 mm, and the use of 22 mm diameter bolts in punched holes, the net areas are:

Section 1–1 $A_{ne} = [200 - (22 + 4)]$ mm $\times$ 25 mm=4 350 mm^2

Section 2–2 $A_{ne} = \left[200 - 2 \times (22 + 4) + \dfrac{80^2}{4 \times 115}\right]$ mm $\times$ 25 mm=4 048 mm^2

Section 2–2 governs, and the net area (A_n) to be used in Equation 3.2 is 4048 mm^2.

The efficiency of this connection is now $4048/5000 = 81\%$, a considerable improvement over that obtained with the previous fastener arrangement. The improvement does come at the expense of having to make a longer joint, however.

50

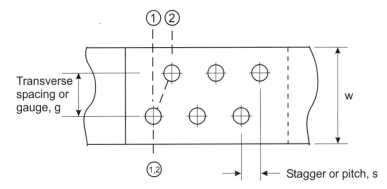

Figure 3.8 – Tension Member – Staggered Fasteners

The capacity of this member can now be established. Since the plate thickness involved is less than 65 mm, the yield strength of the Grade 300W material is 300 MPa. Checking Equations 3.1 and 3.2 gives, respectively,

$$T_r = 0.90 \times 5000 \text{ mm}^2 \times 300 \text{ N/mm}^2 = 1350 \times 10^3 \text{ N}, \quad \text{or}$$

$$T_r = 0.85 \times 0.90 \times 4048 \text{ mm}^2 \times 450 \text{ N/mm}^2 = 1394 \times 10^3 \text{ N}$$

The capacity based on the yield criterion (Equation 3.1) governs, and the factored resistance of this member (1350 kN) can now be compared with the effect of the factored loads.

In some instances, a member may be connected by using fasteners in more than one plane. If the fasteners are staggered, such as those shown in Figure 3.9, the usual procedure is to develop the cross-section into an equivalent flat plate by revolving about the centrelines of the component parts. The critical net section can then be established by the procedure described for plates. An illustration of the calculations involved is given in Example 3.3.

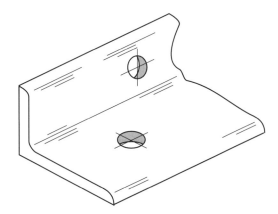

Figure 3.9 – Net Section – Fasteners in More Than One Plane

Examples of net section calculations will also be found in Chapter 9.

3.7 Design Examples

The preceding sections have set out the basis of design of tension members. As has been noted, one of the main criteria affecting the design will be the connection details. If the end connection is to be made using welds, there generally is no resulting reduction in cross-section and, if there is no shear lag reduction to be made, the design of the member can proceed directly. When bolts are to be used, however, the design of the member is influenced by the amount of material removed in making the connection. In turn, the design of the connection itself cannot proceed without a knowledge of the shape to be used. As with most design problems, the engineer must work in a trial and error fashion until all relevant aspects have been satisfied.

Example 3.1

Given

Design the tension diagonal of an all-welded Pratt roof truss in which the chords are made from WT 265×61.5 sections. The factored load (T_f) in the member under consideration is 630 kN and its length is 4 m. Use G40.21 300W steel ($F_y = 300$ MPa, $F_u = 450$ MPa).

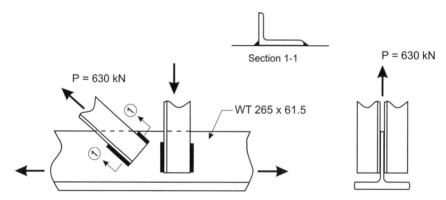

Figure 3.10 – Tension Member – Welded End Connections – Example 3.1

Solution

Since welded end connections will be used, the net and gross areas of the cross-section will be equal (A). Examination of Equations 3.1 and 3.2 gives

$$T_r = \phi \, A \, F_y = 0.90 \times 300 \text{ MPa} \times A = 270 \, A \qquad \text{or,}$$

$$T_r = \phi \, 0.85 \, A \, F_u = 0.85 \times 0.90 \times 450 \text{ MPa} \times A = 344 \, A$$

(These resistances will be in newtons when the area is given in mm^2.)

Now, we must satisfy the requirement that $T_r \geq T_f$. Because the requirement based on yield provides the lower resistance, it governs and this means that

$$270A \geq 630 \times 10^3$$

and the required area is obtained as

$$A = \frac{630 \times 10^3 \text{ N}}{270 \text{ MPa}} = 2333 \text{ mm}^2$$

As shown in Figure 3.10, it will be convenient to use a pair of angles, one welded on each side of the WT. Since there is no reduction in member area due to a physical hole, the only reduction that may be required is for shear lag, depending on the configuration of the welds. From the CISC Handbook, try $2 - 76 \times 64 \times 9.5$ angles, long legs back to back. The area provided by two angles is 2480 mm^2 and $r_{min} = 13.3$ mm for one angle (see Handbook, Part 6).

In order to determine if shear lag reductions apply, it is necessary to know the configuration of the weld. It will be assumed here that the 76 mm leg will be welded to the stem of the WT by a 120 mm long weld on the toe of the angle and by a 250 mm long weld along the heel of the 76 mm leg, as illustrated in Figure 3.10. (Proportioning of the welds is covered in Chapter 9).

Considering the long leg first, the average weld length, L is $(120 + 250)/2 = 185$ mm. Since 185 is more than twice the leg width of 76 mm, it is not necessary to make a reduction for shear lag (Equation 3.8b). Thus, for the connected leg we have

$$A_{n2} = 1.00 \times (76 - 9.5) \text{ mm} \times 9.5 \text{ mm} = 632 \text{ mm}^2$$

For the outstanding leg, the eccentricity of this element, e, is $64/2 = 32$ mm and $L = 250$ mm. Using Equation 3.8(e), the effective area of this leg is

$$A_{n3} = (1 - \frac{32}{250}) \times 64 \text{ mm} \times 9.5 \text{ mm} = 530 \text{ mm}^2$$

Finally, using Equation 3.9, the effective net area (for one angle) is

$$A_{ne} = 632 \text{ mm}^2 + 530 \text{ mm}^2 = 1162 \text{ mm}^2$$

Checking Equations 3.1 and 3.2 gives

$$T_r = 0.90 \times 2480 \text{ mm}^2 \times 300 \text{ MPa} = 670 \times 10^3 \text{ N} = 670 \text{ kN}$$

$$T_r = 0.85 \times 0.90 \times (2 \times 1162) \text{ mm}^2 \times 450 \text{ MPa} = 800 \times 10^3 \text{ N} = 800 \text{ kN}$$

The governing value is 670 kN and we note that this is still > 630 kN.

Although there was a reduction for shear lag in this case, it was not large enough to influence the selection of the member. In other cases, either a new member size must be tried or a different weld arrangement used.

The radius of gyration, 13.3 mm, is the radius of gyration about the z–axis. Since it has not been identified that the angles are interconnected along their length, the least radius of gyration of one angle must be used in the slenderness ratio calculation. Thus—

$$\text{max} \quad \frac{L}{r} = \frac{4000 \text{ mm}}{13.3 \text{ mm}} = 301$$

Although this is greater than the permissible value of 300 given in Clause 10.4.2.2 of S16–01, the amount of underdesign is quite small. Also, the length given for the member, 4 m, is the length between the intersection of the members at each end, i.e., between working points. The unsupported length between the limits of the connected material is unknown at this stage but it would be significantly less than 4 m.

The nominal yield strength of angles 9.5 mm thick must be checked. Using Tables 3 and 4 of Appendix A, this is found to be 300 MPa, as assumed in the calculations.

Use $2 - 76 \times 64 \times 9.5$ angles, long legs back to back, as shown.

Example 3.2

Given

Redesign the member of Example 3.1 assuming that fabrication will be made using 20 mm diameter high-strength bolts. Angles of Grade 300W steel will be used for all members, including the chords, as shown in Figure 3.11, and connections will be made using 10 mm thick gusset plates.

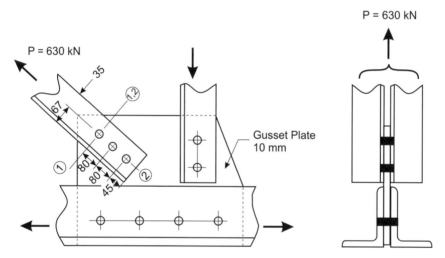

Figure 3.11 – Tension Member – Bolted End Connection – Example 3.2

Solution

Assume that the factored resistance of the member will again be governed by Equation 3.1, that is

$$T_r = 270\,A_g$$

where A_g is now the gross cross-sectional area required. After the member has been selected, the possible application of Equation 3.2 or 3.3 will have to be checked.

From $T_r \geq T_f$, the required gross area is

$$A_g = \frac{630 \times 10^3 \text{ N}}{270 \text{ MPa}} = 2333 \text{ mm}^2$$

Try 2 – 102×76×11 angles, long legs back to back. From the CISC Handbook, $A_g = 3710$ mm^2 for the pair and $r_{min} = r_z = 16.3$ mm. Since the area provided is greater than that required, it is obvious that the member selected will be satisfactory if Equation 3.1 governs the design.

In order to check Equation 3.2 or 3.3, the effective net area must be calculated. Since angles with leg sizes less than 125 mm can accommodate fasteners along only one gauge line (Table 5 of Appendix A), the arrangement of fasteners must be like that shown in the figure. (The bolt spacing shown meets the requirements of S16.) Assume that at least three bolts will be required.

The two possible ways in which the angles can tear from the gusset plate are indicated in Figure 3.11. Section 1–1 shows that one possibility is a tear that extends across the connected leg (passing through the hole) and then moves up through the unconnected leg. In this case, it is easier to simply deduct the area of one hole from the gross area of the angle than to apply Equation 3.4. Thus, for Section 1–1

$$A_n = 3710 \text{ mm}^2 - [(20+4) \text{ mm} \times 11 \text{ mm}] \times 2 \text{ holes (one each angle)}$$
$$= 3182 \text{ mm}^2$$

Since this calculation includes both area that is directly connected and unconnected area (the outstanding leg of the angle), Equation 3.7 must be used to calculate the effective net area reduced for shear lag, A_{ne}. An angle connected by one leg and containing three transverse lines of fasteners will fall under the provisions of Equation 3.7(c). Therefore, the effective net area of Section 1–1 reduced for shear lag is

$$A_{ne} = 0.60 \times 3182 \text{ mm}^2 = 1909 \text{ mm}^2$$

and the corresponding capacity of the pair of angles is

$$T_r = 0.85 \times 0.90 \times 1909 \text{ mm}^2 \times 450 \text{ MPa} = 657 \times 10^3 \text{ N} = 657 \text{ kN}$$

Section 2–2 indicates tearing of the connected leg of the angle across to the first hole in combination with shear yielding or rupture down the length of the angle. This condition was described by Equation 3.10(a). For one angle, the net tensile area is

$$A_n = [35 - 0.5 \ (20+4))] \text{ mm} \times 11 \text{ mm} = 253 \text{ mm}^2,$$

the gross shear area, A_{gv}, is $(80 + 80 + 45)$ mm $\times 11$ mm $= 2255$ mm^2,

and the net shear area, A_{nv}, is 2255 mm$^2 - 2.5 \ (20 + 4)$ mm $\times 11$ mm $= \ 1595$ mm^2

Finally, the tension and shear block capacity (of one angle) calculated according to Equation 3.10(a) is—

$$T_r + V_r = \phi \ A_{nt} \ F_u + 0.60 \ \phi \ A_{gv} \ F_y$$
$$= (0.90 \times 253 \times 450) + (0.60 \times 0.90 \times 2255 \times 300) = 467 \ 775 \text{ N} = 468 \text{ kN}$$

Equation 3.10(b), which is the upper limit of tension and shear block failure, is—

$$T_r + V_r = \phi \ A_{nt} \ F_u + 0.60 \ \phi \ A_{nv} \ F_u$$

$$= (0.90 \times 253 \times 450) + (0.60 \times 0.90 \times 1595 \times 450) = 490\,050 \text{ N} = 490 \text{ kN}$$

Note that no adjustment for shear lag is necessary for the tension and shear block cases since only connected area is included in the calculations.

The governing tension and shear block resistance is that corresponding to tensile fracture plus shear yielding, i.e., 468 kN. Thus, the calculated capacity for the tension and shear block failure for the pair of angles is 2×468 kN $= 936$ kN. Since the capacity calculated for tensile fracture along (Section 1–1) was only 657 kN, the governing factored resistance is the latter, i.e., 657 kN.

Recall that the member was selected on the basis of Equation 3.1, using the factored load of 630 kN. Obviously, Equation 3.1 is satisfied. Since the calculated factored resistance of 657 kN is larger than the factored load of 630 kN, the selected member is satisfactory.

Finally, checking the slenderness ratio

$$\max \quad \frac{L}{r} = \frac{4000 \text{ mm}}{16.3 \text{ mm}} = 245 \; < \; 300 \qquad \text{(Satisfactory)}$$

Use $2 - 102 \times 76 \times 11$ angles, long legs back-to-back, as shown. (If the number of bolts finally selected is different than the three assumed, then the calculations must be reviewed.)

Example 3.3

Given

The lower chord of a large truss consists of two C310$\times$45 sections tied across the flanges with lacing bars. The critical section of the chord occurs just outside a panel point, where it is necessary to splice the member. As shown in Figure 3.12, both web and flange splice plates are provided to transfer the forces from one side of the member to the other. Determine the factored tensile resistance of the channels if the fasteners are 22 mm diameter and G40.21 350A steel is used throughout. (Use Tables 3 and 4 of Appendix A to establish that $F_y = 350$ MPa, $F_u = 480$ MPa.)

Solution

Using the CISC Handbook, the area of 2–C310$\times$45 is

$$A_g = 2 \times 5690 = 11\,380 \text{ mm}^2$$

and the corresponding capacity is (Equation 3.1)

$$T_r = 0.90 \times 11\,380 \text{ mm}^2 \times 350 \text{ MPa} = 3585 \times 10^3 \text{ N} = 3585 \text{ kN}$$

For those net section calculations involving both the web of the channel and its flanges, the cross-section will have to be "developed" as shown. In effect, the section is flattened about the centerline of the material. Thus, the gross width (along the centreline of the cross-section thickness) is

$$w_g = (305 + 80 + 80 - 13 - 13)\ \text{mm} = 439\ \text{mm}$$

The possible net section paths shown in Figure 3.12 as Sections 1–1 and 2–2 will be investigated first.[2] Using Equations 3.4 and 3.5, as appropriate, the calculations (for one channel) are as follows:

Section 1–1 : $A_n = [439 - 3 \times (22 + 4)]\ \text{mm} \times 13\ \text{mm} = 4693\ \text{mm}^2$

Section 2–2 :

$$A_n = \left[439\ \text{mm} - 5 \times (22 + 4)\ \text{mm} + \left(\frac{35^2}{4 \times 108} \right) \text{mm} \times 2 \right] \times 13\ \text{mm} = 4091\ \text{mm}^2$$

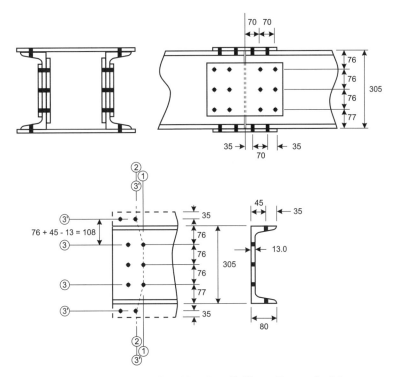

Figure 3.12 – Tension Member Splice – Example 3.3

Note that no adjustment needs to be made for shear lag since each element of the channel cross-section has been fastened.

For this part of the examination, Section 2–2 governs and the capacity of both channels is (Equation 3.2)—

$$T_r = 0.85 \times 0.90 \times (2 \times 4091)\ \text{mm}^2 \times 480\ \text{MPa} = 3004 \times 10^3\ \text{N} = 3004\ \text{kN}$$

---

[2] In the net section calculations, it has been assumed that the thickness of the channel is 13 mm throughout: a small error is introduced since the actual thickness of the flanges is 12.7 mm.

The possibility of tension and shear block failure (Section 3–3) must also be considered. If this were to happen in the web, for example, then an accompanying block of material (Section 3'–3') must also act similarly in each flange. Figure 3.13 shows this pictorially. (In the interest of simplicity, only the section line corresponding to A_{nv} is shown. This is for use when Equation 3.10(b) is used—tensile fracture plus shear fracture. When tensile fracture plus shear yielding is checked, Equation 3.10(a), then the 3 or 3' section line does not pass through the holes.)

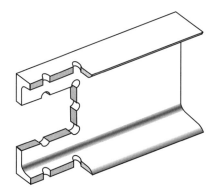

Figure 3.13 – Tension and Shear Block Failure of Channel – Example 3.3

Using Equation 3.10(a) for the case of tensile fracture plus shear yielding—

Section 3–3

$$T_r + V_r = 2 \times \{ 0.90[\, 76 + 76 - 2 \times (22 + 4)] \text{ mm} \times 13 \text{ mm} \times 480 \text{ MPa}$$

$$+ [\, 0.60 \times 0.90 (\, 70 + 70) \text{ mm} \times 13 \text{ mm}] \times 2 \text{ sides} \times 350 \text{ MPa} \}$$

$$= 2 \times (\, 562 \times 10^3 \text{ N} + 688 \times 10^3 \text{ N}) = 2500 \text{ kN}$$

Section 3'–3'

$$T_r + V_r = 2 \times \{ 0.90[\, 35 - 0.5 \times (22 + 4))] \text{ mm} \times 13 \text{ mm} \times 480 \text{ MPa} \times 2 \text{ flanges}$$

$$+ [\, 0.60 \times 0.90 (\, 70 + 35) \text{ mm} \times 13 \text{ mm}] \times 350 \text{ MPa} \times 2 \text{ flanges} \}$$

$$= 2 \times (\, 247 \times 10^3 \text{ N} + 516 \times 10^3 \text{ N}) = 1526 \text{ kN}$$

and the total for both Sections 3–3 and 3'–3' is

$$2 \times (\, 1250 \text{ kN} + 763 \text{ kN}) = 4026 \text{ kN}$$

Using Equation 3.10(b), for the case of tensile fracture plus shear fracture—

Section 3–3

$$T_r + V_r = 2 \times \{ 0.90[\, 76 + 76 - 2.0 \times (22 + 4))] \text{ mm} \times 13 \text{ mm} \times 480 \text{ MPa}$$

$$+ [\, 0.60 \times 0.90 (\, 70 + 70 - 1.5 \times (22 + 4)) \text{ mm} \times 13 \text{ mm}] \times 2 \text{ sides} \times 480 \text{ MPa} \}$$

$$= 2 \times (\, 562 \times 10^3 \text{ N} + 681 \times 10^3 \text{ N}) = 2486 \text{ kN}$$

Section 3'–3'

$$T_r + V_r = 2 \times \{ 0.90[35 - 0.5 \times (22 + 4))] \ mm \times 13 \ mm \times 480 \ MPa \times 2 \ flanges$$

$$+ [0.60 \times 0.90 (70 + 35 - (1.5 \times (22 + 4)) \ mm \times 13 \, mm] \times 2 \ flanges \times 480 \ MPa \}$$

$$= 2 \times (247 \times 10^3 \ N \ + \ 445 \times 10^3 \ N) = 1384 \ kN$$

and the total for both Sections 3–3 and 3'–3' is

$$2486 \ kN + 1384 \ kN = 3870 \ kN$$

In summary, the calculated capacities for the pair of channels are

Gross cross-section yielding (Eq. 3.1):	3585 kN
Net cross-section fracture (Eq. 3.2):	3004 kN
Tensile fracture + shear yielding (Equation 3.10(a)):	4026 kN
Tensile fracture + shear fracture (Equation 3.10(b))	3870 kN

and the governing quantity is 3004 kN.

3.8   Eyebars and Cables

Eyebars were used extensively in the past, particularly as tension members in bridges. The sections are usually made from plate with a hole drilled at each end in an enlarged section. Pins are then used to make the connection. As noted in Section 3.2, the factored resistance of pin-connected members is appreciably lower than that permitted in members where mechanical fasteners or welds are used. Standard S16–01 permits $T_r = 0.75 \, \phi \, A_n \, F_y$ and stipulates a number of other requirements as to dimensions and details (see S16 Clause 12.4). These requirements also apply to pin-connected plates or to pins in built-up members. Pin-connected members are seldom used today.

In contrast to the use of eyebars, cables are being used more in recent years than formerly. They are used in modern suspension and cable-stayed bridges and are also used in longspan structures such as aircraft hangers and cable-suspended and cable-supported roofs for auditoriums.

Cables are generally classified as either strand or rope. Strand consists of an arrangement of individual wires laid in either parallel or helical fashion around a centre wire. It is used for tension members where flexibility or bending is not a major requirement. Wire rope is made by laying a number of strands helically around a central core. The core may be another steel strand or a small wire rope. In both cases, strand and rope, it is standard procedure to use galvanized steel wires. The appropriate ASTM specification can be used to obtain the necessary information on mechanical properties and other details [3.8, 3.9].

Because both rope and strand are made of a multiplicity of individual wires, the first applications of load will cause an appreciable amount of non-recoverable deformation as these individual wires seat themselves. In almost all structural applications, prestretching of the cable will be called for so that this non-elastic deformation is removed before installation of the cables. The ASTM specifications provide information about the modulus of elasticity of the cable along with the metallic core area and the minimum ultimate tensile load. The modulus can be expected to be appreciably less than that associated with a solid steel section of the same area.

Terminal fittings for cables are made using either poured sockets (using zinc or epoxy) or by a pressed-on assembly (swaging). The fittings are usually supplied such that the tensile strength of the cable can be developed before any yielding occurs in the end fitting. The end connection of the socket is then made using pins or heavy hex bolts. More information on design is available in other published literature [3.10, 3.11].

Canopy supported by cables

Example 3.4

Given

A cable-supported roof of 30 m span consists of a series of parallel cables with a sag of 3 m. The uniformly applied load (per metre of horizontal projection of the cable) is 1.60 kN. This is made up of 0.60 kN/m dead load and 1.00 kN/m live load. Choose a suitable cable.

Solution

Using the criteria for factored loads given in Clause 7.2 of the Standard, and assuming that the importance factor for the structure should be 1.0, the factored load is $(1.25 \times 0.60 \text{ kN/m}) + (1.5 \times 1.00 \text{ kN/m}) = 2.25 \text{ kN/m}$. Consideration of the equilibrium conditions for half the cable will establish that the maximum tension in the cable corresponding to this factored load is 90.9 kN.

Since the cable will pass over saddles and then down to anchorages at the edge of the roof or to the ground, rope will be preferred to strand because of its flexibility. From ASTM A603-98, the breaking (ultimate) strength of a 12.70 mm diameter rope with a so-called Class A galvanized coating is 102 kN. Its factored resistance can be taken as 0.9×102 kN = 91.8 kN. The metallic area of the rope is 76.8 mm^2 and it has a mass of 0.62 kg/m. If prestretched, it will have a minimum modulus of elasticity of 140×10^3 MPa.

References

3.1 Lay, M.G., "Structural Steel Fundamentals – an engineering and metallurgical primer," Australian Road Research Board, 1982.

3.2 Chesson, E., Jr., and Munse, W.H., "Behavior of Riveted Truss Type Connections," Transactions, ASCE, Vol. 123, 1958.

3.3 Kulak, G.L., and Grondin, G.Y., "AISC LRFD Rules for Block Shear in Bolted Connections—A Review," Engineering Journal, AISC, Vol. 38, No.4, 2001.

3.4 Madugula, M.K.S. and Mohan, S., "Angles in Eccentric Tension," Journal of Structural Engineering, ASCE, Vol. 114, No. 10, October, 1988.

3.5 Popov, E., "Engineering Mechanics of Solids," Prentice-Hall, 1990.

3.6 Gibson, G.J. and Wake, B.T., "An Investigation of Welded Connections for Angle Tension Members," Welding Journal, Vol. 21, 1942.

3.7 Canadian Institute of Steel Construction, "Handbook of Steel Construction," Ninth Edition, Toronto, Ontario, 2006.

3.8 Standard Specification for Zinc-Coated Parallel and Helical Steel Wire Structural Strand and Zinc-Coated Wire for Spun-In-Place Structural Strand, ASTM A586-98.

3.9 Standard Specification for Zinc-Coated Steel Structural Wire Rope, ASTM A603-98.

3.10 Scalzi, J.B. and McGrath, W.K., "Mechanical Properties of Structural Cables," Journal of the Structural Division, ASCE, Vol. 97, No. ST12, December, 1971.

3.11 Gaylord, E.H., Gaylord, C.N., and Stallmeyer, J.E., Editors, "Structural Engineering Handbook," Fourth Edition, McGraw-Hill, New York, N.Y., 1997.

CHAPTER 4

COMPRESSION MEMBERS

4.1   Introduction

Compression members are those members in a structure that are subjected to loads tending to decrease their lengths. Compression members are used as the vertical load-resisting elements of a building structure, called columns; as the posts that resist the compressive components of a load in a truss; as bridge piers; and as the load-resisting elements in many other situations.

Heavy welded columns are often used in tall buildings.

In a building structure, forces and moments are transmitted to the columns through beams at each floor or roof level in the structure. In some cases, the arrangement of members will be such that the net bending moment acting at the ends of the column is zero. In this situation, the column is required to resist a load acting concentric to the original longitudinal axis of the member and is termed an axially loaded column or, simply, a column. This will be the case treated in this chapter. If the net end moments are not zero, the member will be subjected to an axial load and to bending moments along its length. This type of member is termed a beam-column, and it will be treated in Chapter 8.

An example of an axially loaded column is shown schematically in Figure 4.1. The centroidal axis of the member is shown by a broken line in the figure. The axial load, C, to be resisted by the member is equal to the sum of the beam shears, $V_1 + V_2$. The net moment, M, to be resisted by the column is a result of the difference between the end moments M_1 and M_2 developed by the beams and any additional moment caused by the beam shears acting about the column centroidal axis. There are many practical cases in which the net end moment can be taken as zero. For example, the net end moment for the member shown in Figure 4.1 will be zero if both the end moments and the shears developed in the beams are equal. Where the beams are not connected rigidly to the column, the beams would not develop significant end moments and any moment to be resisted by the column would be due only to the difference in end shears. In many such cases, the net moment is small and the member is designed as an axially loaded column.

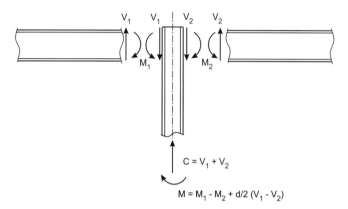

Figure 4.1 – Force Transfer – Axially Loaded Column

Unlike the member subjected to tension, the column is designed on the assumption that its gross cross-sectional area will be effective in resisting the applied load. Bolts are often used to connect the column to adjacent members. As the load is applied the member will contract. It is assumed that the action of the bolts is such that they will replace the material removed for the holes.

When a steel member is subjected to an increasing axial load, its stiffness decreases gradually as the maximum load-carrying capacity is approached. Eventually, the member cannot resist any further increase in the applied force; at this stage the member is said to have failed. The attainment of the maximum load-carrying capacity can be the result of local failure in the plates making up the cross-section (for example the flange or web plates in a wide-flange section) or it can be the result of overall failure of the column. The design relationships developed later in this chapter are based on the assumption that failure will be an overall column type of failure. To ensure that this will always be the case, the width-to-thickness ratios of the plate elements of the cross-section must be limited so that the plates will not buckle locally before the column fails as a unit. For example, the projecting width-to-thickness ratio of the flange of a wide-flange type section is limited in S16–01 to $200/\sqrt{F_y}$ and the clear web depth-to-thickness ratio to $670/\sqrt{F_y}$. If the plate width-to-thickness ratios must exceed these values, the column cannot be designed on the assumption of overall failure [4.1]. These provisions are summarized in Figure 4.2 and are discussed in more detail in Chapter 5. In the example problems used in this chapter it will be assumed in most cases that the plate elements meet the limitations. This will generally be easily attainable for rolled sections of steel having yield stress levels up to and including 400 MPa.

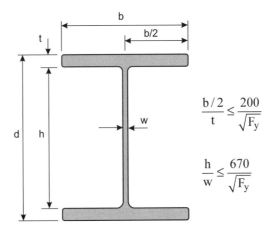

$$\frac{b/2}{t} \le \frac{200}{\sqrt{F_y}}$$

$$\frac{h}{w} \le \frac{670}{\sqrt{F_y}}$$

Figure 4.2 – Cross-Section Nomenclature

4.2   Strength of Steel Columns

The maximum strength of a steel column depends to a large degree on the member length. For discussion, steel columns can be conveniently classified as short, intermediate, or long members. Each range has associated with it a characteristic type of behaviour, and therefore different techniques must be used to assess the maximum strength.

A short column is loosely defined as a member that can resist a load equal to the yield load, C_y. The yield load is defined as the product of the cross-sectional area of the column, A, and the yield stress level, σ_y (i.e., $C_y = A \sigma_y$). In this case, the maximum strength of the member is independent of its length and governed only by the yield strength of the steel and the cross-sectional area.

For longer columns on the other hand, failure is accompanied by a rapid increase in the lateral deflection. If the member is extremely slender, the load at which this increased deflection takes place is not sufficient to significantly yield the member. Thus, the maximum load is not a function of the material strength, but depends on the bending stiffness of the member (EI) and its length.

Columns falling into the intermediate range are more complex to analyze, but they also are the most common category in steel structures. For intermediate length columns, failure is also characterized by a rapid increase in the lateral deflection, but only after some portions of the column cross-section have yielded. Yielding is initiated first in those portions of the cross-section that have large compressive residual stresses. The failure in this case is termed inelastic instability and the maximum strength of the column depends not only on the bending stiffness and length, but also on the yield stress level of the steel, the distribution of residual stresses over the cross-section, and the magnitude of the initial imperfections in the columns.

Figure 4.3 shows schematically the relationship between the maximum strength of a column and its length. The three ranges of column behaviour are shown in the figure, together with the characteristic associated with the attainment of maximum strength. In the Sections following, the determination of the maximum strength will be discussed in detail.

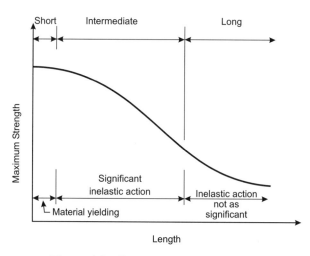

Figure 4.3 – Strength of Steel Columns

4.3   Behaviour of Cross-Section

The stress versus strain curve obtained from a tension test performed on a steel specimen is shown in Figure 2.2. A very similar curve would be obtained from a compression test performed on a suitable specimen. Theoretically, because the applied load on a column is distributed uniformly over the cross-sectional area, the average stress versus average strain curve for a short column should also be similar to that shown in Figure 2.2.

If a short length of wide-flange column is subjected to an axial compressive load, the stress versus strain curve differs from that obtained from a small coupon, however. The average stress versus strain curve for a short column is shown in Figure 4.4, where the applied load has been divided by the product of the cross-sectional area and the yield stress and the resulting strain by the yield strain [4.2]. The term σ/σ_y, plotted on the vertical axis, is equivalent to the ratio C/C_y. The first significant difference between the curves of Figures 2.2 and 4.4 becomes apparent at about load number 15 (Figure 4.4) when the $\sigma - \varepsilon$ curve for the short column deviates from the elastic, straight-line relationship.

The reason for this early yielding lies in the presence of residual strains in the short column. These strains are parallel to the longitudinal axis of the member and a typical distribution over the cross-section is as shown in Figure 4.5(a). Residual strains are the result of the cooling of rolled or welded shapes or the cold-straightening of any shape that is beyond straightness tolerance. For example, as a structural member comes off the rolls, it is allowed to cool in air. The flange tips cool more quickly than the areas adjacent to the flange-to-web junctions and gain strength and stiffness in the process. Then, when the central portions of the flanges and the web cool, that material is restrained by the stiffer areas near the flange tips. The result is a set of residual strains as shown in Figure 4.5(a); the flange tips are subjected to compressive strains, the remainder of the section to tensile strains [4.2].

66

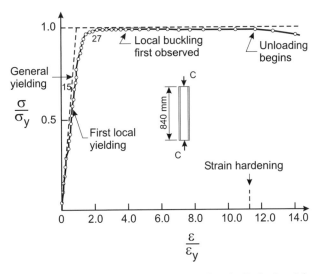

Figure 4.4 – Stub Column Stress vs. Strain Relationship

An applied load produces a uniform strain distribution over the cross-section, as shown in Figure 4.5(b). As the load is increased, the magnitude of the total strain, $\varepsilon_t = \varepsilon_a + \varepsilon_r$, eventually exceeds the yield strain, ε_y, as shown in Figure 4.5(c). On additional loading, the yielded areas are ineffective, since an increase in the magnitude of the applied strain does not produce a corresponding increase in stress. In addition, the width of the yielded area, $\bar{x}$, increases, causing the section to be even more ineffective. This process corresponds approximately to the portion of the $\sigma - \varepsilon$ curve between load numbers 15 and 27 (Figure 4.4). Once the applied strain exceeds the maximum tensile residual strain by an amount ε_y, the entire cross-section will have yielded and the applied load will be equal to the so-called yield load, $C_y = A\,\sigma_y$. This stage corresponds approximately to load number 27 on the curve of Figure 4.4.

In accordance with the stress versus strain curve of Figure 2.2, the load should increase above C_y because of the presence of strain-hardening. However, in compression, as the applied strain is increased the plates composing the cross-section begin to exhibit large local deflections and the load-carrying capacity of the cross-section begins to decrease. Thus, for a column the maximum load-carrying capacity is, in fact, governed by the strength of the cross-section.

4.4 Behaviour of Columns

4.4.1 Flexural Buckling Strength

While the strength of the cross-section is dependent on the yield stress level of the material, the strength of an actual column is, to some extent, independent of the material strength. A column of length L is shown in Figure 4.6. The column is subjected to a load C and is pinned at either end. The pinned connections are assumed to be incapable of resisting bending moments. The column cross-section is shown in Section A–A. In the following development it will be assumed that the cross-section is free to translate in the x direction only so that its motion will tend to bend the member about its weak axis (the y–axis). The moment of inertia about the y–axis will be denoted by I and the material has a modulus of elasticity, E.

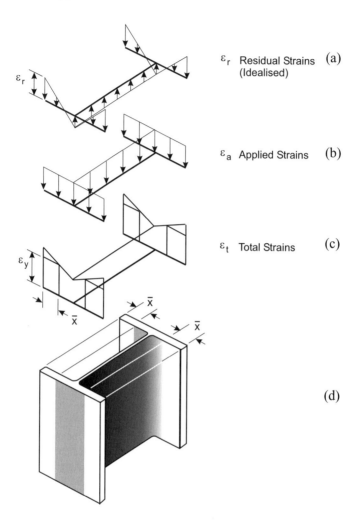

ε_r Residual Strains (a)
   (Idealised)

ε_a Applied Strains (b)

ε_t Total Strains (c)

(d)

Figure 4.5 – Residual and Applied Strains

As the member is loaded, it will remain in a straight position provided that it is free from imperfections of load or geometry. If it is forced into the position shown by the full line in Figure 4.6(a) and then the forcing agency is removed, it will return to the straight position. However, as the load is increased a stage will eventually will be reached at which the member will no longer return to the straight position. At this value of the load, Q_r, the member remains in equilibrium in the deflected position and a free body diagram corresponding to this condition is shown in Figure 4.6(b).

Summing moments at the cut section produces an expression for the moment, M

$$M = C\,x \tag{4.1}$$

The internal resisting moment is also related to the curvature by [4.3]

$$M = -E\,I\,\frac{d^2x}{dz^2} \tag{4.2}$$

Combining Equations 4.1 and 4.2 results in the basic differential equation—

$$E\,I\,\frac{d^2x}{dz^2} + C\,x = 0 \tag{4.3}$$

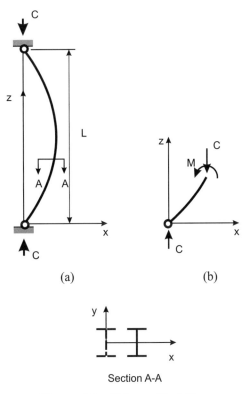

(a)   (b)

Section A-A

Figure 4.6 – Column Buckling

The solution to Equation 4.3 produces an expression for the deflected shape:

$$x = A\,\sin\sqrt{\frac{C}{E\,I}}\,z \ + \ B\,\cos\sqrt{\frac{C}{E\,I}}\,z \tag{4.4}$$

where constants A and B are evaluated by considering the boundary conditions at the member ends. For instance, the deflection x must be zero at $z = 0$ and at $z = L$.

Application of the boundary conditions to the differential equations gives $B = 0$ and

$$\sqrt{\frac{C}{EI}}\,L = n\,\pi \tag{4.5}$$

Solving Equation 4.5, the load $C \equiv C_{cr}$ required to hold the member in a deflected shape is given by:

$$C_{cr} = n^2 \, \pi^2 \, \frac{E\,I}{L^2} \qquad\qquad (4.6)$$

where $n = 0, 1, 2, 3\ldots$ A value of $n = 0$ implies that there is no load on the member and values of $n = 2, 3,\ldots$ imply that an external agency must be present to hold the column in a straight position for the load associated with $n = 1$. Thus, the higher values are not relevant to the physical problem. The critical load is given by:

$$C_{cr} = \frac{\pi^2 \, E\,I}{L^2} \qquad\qquad (4.7)$$

At the instant before buckling (or, bifurcation, the change from the straight to the deflected equilibrium position), the average stress on the cross-section is:

$$\sigma_{cr} = \frac{C_{cr}}{A} = \frac{\pi^2 \, EI}{A\,L^2} = \frac{\pi^2 \, E}{(L/r)^2} \qquad\qquad (4.8)$$

where r is the radius of gyration of the cross-section for bending about the y–axis ($r = \sqrt{I/A}$) and L/r is termed the slenderness ratio of the member.

The development of Equation 4.8 assumes that the resisting moment of the cross-section is given by Equation 4.2, that is, the expression is valid only as long as the load does not induce yielding in the cross-section prior to buckling. This means that the applied stress, σ_{cr}, must be less than $E\,(\varepsilon_y - \varepsilon_r)$, since, at this value of stress, yielding will be initiated in the cross-section as a result of the strains produced by the applied load adding to the residual strains in the cross-section (see Figure 4.5).

Figure 4.7 shows a plot of the average stress, σ, versus the deflection at midspan, $x_{(L/2)}$ for a column failing after elastic buckling. The column remains straight (or returns to the straight position after disturbance) as long as the stress is below that given by Equation 4.8; however, at the critical stress the deflection is that given by Equation 4.4 with $z = L/2$:

$$x_{(L/2)} = A \sin \sqrt{\frac{C}{EI}} \, \frac{L}{2} \qquad\qquad (4.9)$$

where the coefficient A cannot be determined but is not zero. Thus, at the critical stress the deflection increases as shown by the full horizontal line in Figure 4.7.

As the slenderness ratio of a column is reduced, the critical value of the average stress is increased until the member will yield under the applied stress before buckling. Yielding will start in those portions of the cross-section that have high compressive residual stresses.

The residual strain distribution is shown in Figure 4.5(a). The distribution is idealized, but the high compressive strains shown at the flange tips and the tensile strains at the flange-to-web junctions and in the web are a good representation of the actual case. The uniform compressive strain distribution, produced as a result of the applied load, is shown in Figure 4.5(b) and the total strain picture (the algebraic sum at each point in the cross-section) is plotted in Figure 4.5(c). The peak strain values occur at the flange tips, as shown, and now exceed the yield strain. The extent of yielding in the cross-section is shown in Figure 4.5(d). The flanges are yielded over a length $\bar{x}$ extending in from the flange tips; the extent will depend on the magnitude of the applied load.

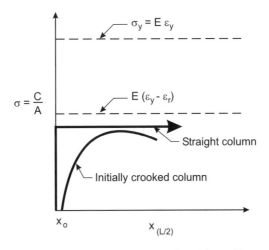

Figure 4.7 – Load vs. Deflection Relationship — Long Column

The strain history for a yielded element of the cross-section is shown in Figure 4.8. The total compressive strain (ε_t) is made up of the residual strain plus the strain due to the applied load, and is sufficient to bring the material to a point A in Figure 4.8. If the column is now subjected to an additional compressive strain, the material will continue to deform at the yield stress level, as shown by the horizontal arrow in this figure. However, if the incremental strain is tensile, the material will unload elastically along the line shown by the inclined arrow.

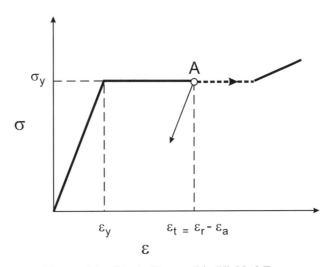

Figure 4.8 – Strain Reversal in Yielded Zone

The deformation upon buckling results in a bending-type motion, so that the incremental strains would appear to be those shown in Figure 4.9(a) for the elastic buckling case. However, Shanley showed by a series of careful experiments that when a column buckles in the inelastic range, the initial motion is accompanied by an increase in load [4.4]. Thus, the strain distribution is actually that shown in Figure 4.9(b), with all elements of the cross-section subjected to an increase in compressive strain.

The load vs. deformation curve for the initially straight column is shown in Figure 4.10, where the applied stress is plotted against the midspan deformation. As the member continues to deform in its buckled shape, the load increases to its maximum value and then drops off. During this process the cross-section continues to yield. The maximum stress is not much greater than the stress at the instant of buckling.

Returning to an examination of the cross-section, if all elements are subjected to an increase in compressive strain at the instant of buckling, then those areas that were yielded at the instant before buckling will not accept an increased stress during buckling and will not contribute to the internal bending moment. In fact, the internal resisting moment will depend on the portion of the cross-section that remains elastic, the portion shown shaded in Figure 4.5(d). The resisting moment would then be given by Equation 4.2, but with the moment of inertia, I, replaced by the moment of inertia of the elastic portion of the cross-section only, I_e. Following through the same derivation as before, the buckling stress is now given by:

$$\sigma_{cr} = \frac{\pi^2 E}{(L/r_e)^2} \tag{4.10}$$

where the radius of gyration, r, in Equation 4.8 has been replaced by an effective radius of gyration

$$r_e = \sqrt{I_e/A} \tag{4.11}$$

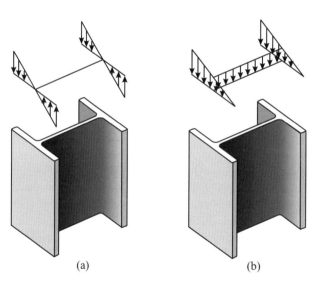

(a)   (b)

Figure 4.9 – Strains Induced by Buckling

The value of r_e will depend on the buckling stress, as well as the magnitude and distribution of the residual strains and on the proportions of the cross-section.

4.4.2   *Torsional and Torsional-Flexural Buckling*

Columns of wide flange section (doubly symmetric cross-section) normally reach their ultimate capacity either by yielding of the cross-section or by flexural buckling, as explained above. Although this covers most practical cases, columns with a cross-section other than the doubly symmetric wide flange (e.g., general asymmetric sections, singly symmetric, cruciform or other bisymmetric sections) can fail either by twisting about the longitudinal axis (torsional buckling) or by a combination of torsion and flexural action (torsional-flexural buckling). The development of the theory of torsional and torsional-flexural buckling is beyond the scope of this text and the reader is referred to other sources [4.5].

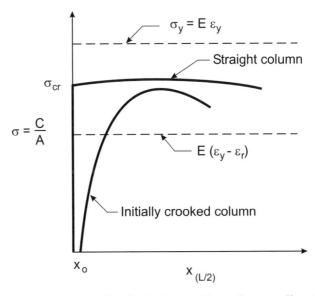

Figure 4.10 – Load vs. Deflection Relationship — Intermediate Column

For doubly symmetric cross-sections (e.g., cruciform sections) and axisymmetric cross-section (e.g., Z sections), buckling can take place independently, either as flexural buckling about one of the two principal axes of the cross-section or as torsional buckling. The elastic buckling strength of the column is taken as the least of:

1) the stress corresponding to flexural buckling of the column about its strong principal axis, given as

$$F_{ex} = \frac{\pi^2 E}{\left(\dfrac{K_x L_x}{r_x}\right)^2} \tag{4.12}$$

2) the stress corresponding to flexural buckling of the column about its weak principal axis, given as

$$F_{ey} = \frac{\pi^2 E}{\left(\dfrac{K_y L_y}{r_y}\right)^2} \tag{4.13}$$

73

or, 3) the stress at which the column will buckle in torsion, given as

$$F_{ez} = \left(\frac{\pi^2 E C_w}{(K_z L_z)^2} + G J \right) \frac{1}{A \bar{r}_o^2}$$ (4.14)

where

K_x, K_y : effective length factors for flexural buckling about the strong and weak principal axes, respectively.

L_x, L_y : unsupported lengths of the column for buckling about the strong and weak principal axes.

K_z : effective length factor for torsional buckling, conservatively taken as 1.0.

r_x, r_y : radius of gyration about the x and y axes, respectively.

C_w : the warping constant of the cross-section.

J : the torsional constant of the cross-section.

A : area of the cross-section

E, G : Young's modulus and shear modulus of the material.

$\bar{r}_o^2 = x_o^2 + y_o^2 + r_x^2 + r_y^2$

where x_o and y_o are the x and y distances from the centroid to the shear center of the cross-section. The location of the shear center and expressions for calculation of the warping constant, C_w, are presented in Figure 4.11. An examination of Equation 4.14 indicates that the resistance of the member to torsional buckling depends upon two distinct components, namely, pure torsion (also referred to as St. Venant torsion and warping torsion. The St. Venant torsion resistance is a function of the stiffness term GJ. The torsional constant for an open cross-section such as a wide flange shape (made up of rectangular plate components) is $J = \frac{1}{3}\Sigma l t^3$, where l and t are the length and thickness of each component. The warping torsion resistance is a function of the stiffness term, $E C_w$. This component of torsion resistance is discussed further in Section 5.10.

For sections that do not have two axes of symmetry, there is coupling between flexural and torsional buckling. Buckling can therefore take place in the form of a coupled flexural and torsional mode. For cross-sections with only one axis of symmetry (singly symmetric), with the y–axis taken as the axis of symmetry, the elastic buckling strength of the column is taken as the lesser of Equation 4.12 or

$$F_{eyz} = \frac{F_{ey} + F_{ez}}{2 \Omega} \left[1 - \sqrt{1 - \frac{4 F_{ey} F_{ez} \Omega}{(F_{ey} + F_{ez})^2}} \right]$$ (4.15)

where

$$\Omega = 1 - \left[\frac{x_o^2 + y_o^2}{\bar{r}_o^2} \right]$$

and F_{ey} and F_{ez} are defined in Equations 4.13 and 4.14, respectively.

For asymmetric sections, the elastic buckling capacity is obtained by solving the following cubic equation for the smallest value of F_e :

$$(F_e - F_{ex})(F_e - F_{ey})(F_e - F_{ez}) - F_e^2 (F_e - F_{ey})\left(\frac{x_o}{r_o}\right)^2 - F_e^2 (F_e - F_{ex})\left(\frac{y_o}{r_o}\right)^2 = 0 \quad (4.16)$$

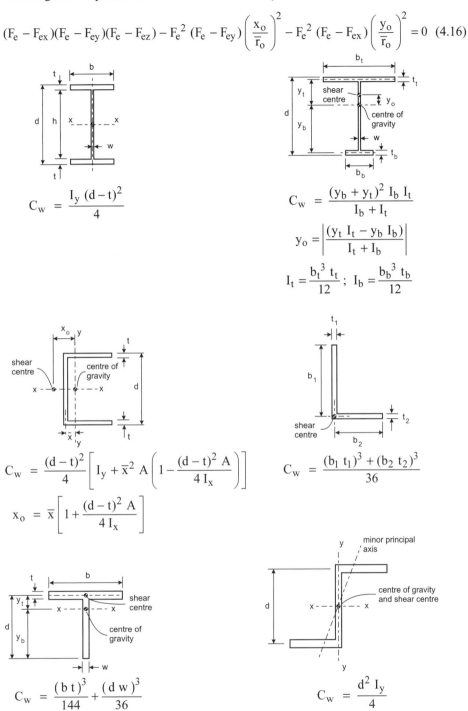

$$C_w = \frac{I_y (d-t)^2}{4}$$

$$C_w = \frac{(y_b + y_t)^2 I_b I_t}{I_b + I_t}$$

$$y_o = \left|\frac{(y_t I_t - y_b I_b)}{I_t + I_b}\right|$$

$$I_t = \frac{b_t^3 t_t}{12} \; ; \; I_b = \frac{b_b^3 t_b}{12}$$

$$C_w = \frac{(d-t)^2}{4}\left[I_y + \bar{x}^2 A\left(1 - \frac{(d-t)^2 A}{4 I_x}\right)\right]$$

$$x_o = \bar{x}\left[1 + \frac{(d-t)^2 A}{4 I_x}\right]$$

$$C_w = \frac{(b_1 t_1)^3 + (b_2 t_2)^3}{36}$$

$$C_w = \frac{(b t)^3}{144} + \frac{(d w)^3}{36}$$

$$C_w = \frac{d^2 I_y}{4}$$

Figure 4.11 – Warping Section Properties for Common Cross-Sections

Equation 4.16 represents a mode of failure where the two flexural buckling modes and the torsional buckling mode interact, resulting in a lower buckling capacity than any one of the buckling modes defined by Equations 4.12 to 4.14.

4.5   Behaviour of Actual Columns

A real column does not behave exactly as described in the previous section. Because of unavoidable disturbances during the rolling and cooling process, the real column will not be perfectly straight. If, for example, the out-of-straightness at mid-height of the column (in the x direction) is x_o, then as soon as the column is loaded the external bending moment at mid-span will be $C x_o$. In this situation, "classical" buckling does not occur. The additional bending moment will cause additional deflections, and, as the average stress is increased, the load vs. deflection curve will take the shape shown by the lower curves in Figure 4.7 or 4.10. As the average stress approaches the critical value, the deflection will increase rapidly and produce large bending moments. These, in turn, will lead to inelastic action and eventual unloading of the member.

For the member shown in Figure 4.6(a), the internal bending moment in the presence of an initial imperfection is given by:

$$M = -EI \left(\frac{d^2x}{dz^2} - \frac{d^2x_o}{dz^2} \right)$$

(4.17)

since the internal moment develops only as a result of the curvatures induced after the load is applied. The resulting equilibrium equation (replacing Equation 4.3) is:

$$EI \left(\frac{d^2x}{dz^2} - \frac{d^2x_o}{dz^2} \right) + Cx = 0$$

(4.18)

Assuming that the initial imperfection is in the form of a sine wave and upon application of the boundary conditions, the deflection at mid-height of the column can be expressed as:

$$x_{(L/2)} = \frac{x_o}{1 - C/C_{cr}}$$

(4.19)

Equation 4.19 is plotted as the initial portion of the lower curve in Figure 4.7 and it is valid until yielding is initiated in the member. The magnitude of the initial imperfection, x_o, is restricted by S16–01. For slender members, the maximum load-carrying capacity is not greatly reduced by the presence of initial imperfections.

For columns of intermediate length the situation is more serious, however. As the axial load is increased, the internal moment is given by Equation 4.17 until yielding occurs in the member. The strain distribution over the cross-section can be obtained by superimposing the distributions of Figure 4.5(a) and (b) and Figure 4.9(a), reflecting the influence of residual strains, axial force, and bending moment, respectively. At any specific loading stage, yielding will have occurred at various locations in the cross-section, wherever the total strain exceeds the yield strain. The yielded zone will extend from the mid-height of the member over a length that depends on the shape of the column cross-section. Corresponding to the yield patterns, there must be a stress distribution on each cross-section that is sufficient to equilibrate C, the axial force, and C x, the bending moment. As the load is increased, the yielded zones grow and the corresponding stress distributions change to maintain these equilibrium relationships.

At some stage of loading it is no longer possible to maintain equilibrium under an increasing axial load. This point marks the maximum load-carrying capacity for an initially imperfect column and corresponds to the peak of the lower curve of Figure 4.10. As the member is deformed beyond this stage, equilibrium cannot be maintained unless the load is reduced. Since the yielded condition changes continually during the loading history, the stiffness values required to determine the deflected shape of the member, and thus the maximum load-carrying capacity, also change. The actual calculation of the maximum strength is accomplished by a numerical integration procedure that is similar to that described in more detail in Section 8.3 for beam-columns.

For columns of intermediate length, the extent of yielding before the maximum strength is attained is significant. Thus, the interaction of the residual strains with those additional strains caused by axial load and bending can influence the maximum strength. Since the additional strains corresponding to bending are triggered by initial imperfections, the interaction of these two variables (residual strain pattern and magnitude of initial imperfection) results in a wide scatter in actual column strengths for intermediate length columns.

4.6   Design of Columns

In order to reflect the influences described above and to provide a convenient tool for design, S16–01 describes the maximum strength of a column using a single equation that depends on non-dimensional slenderness parameter

$$\lambda = \frac{KL}{r} \sqrt{\frac{F_y}{\pi^2 E}} = \sqrt{\frac{F_y}{F_e}} \tag{4.20}$$

and a non-dimensional term n.

Using these parameters, the factored compressive resistance, C_r, is given by:

$$C_r = \phi A F_y \left(1 + \lambda^{2n}\right)^{-1/n} \tag{4.21}$$

In the first part of Equation 4.20, applicable to the most common flexural buckling mode, r is the radius of gyration of the cross-section and L is the member length. The radius of gyration is calculated for the axis about which bending takes place and the quantity L/r is termed the slenderness ratio. The factor K is called the effective length factor, the determination of which will be discussed in detail in Section 4.9. The specified minimum yield strength is denoted by F_y. The second part of Equation 4.20 is more general since F_e accounts also for possible torsional or torsional-flexural buckling for certain cross-section shapes. To account for the expected variations in material properties and cross-sectional dimensions, the expression for compressive resistance contains the resistance factor ϕ. The basis of the resistance factor for axially loaded columns will be discussed in Section 4.7.

Column slenderness affects column strength

The parameter n is used to fit the general curve, Equation 4.21, to two different groups of members. The groupings reflect differences in residual stress patterns and levels and differences in the initial out-of-straightness associated with these groups. For W shapes of Groups 1, 2, and 3 (see Table 3 of Appendix A), fabricated I-shapes, fabricated box shapes, and hollow structural sections of Class C (cold-formed non-stress-relieved), use n = 1.34. The value n = 2.24 is to be used for welded three-plate members with flange edges oxy-flame-cut and for Class H hollow structural sections (i.e., hot-formed or cold-formed and stress-relieved hollow structural sections.) All of these details are in Clause 13.3.1 of the Standard.

Referring to the previous sections, a short column, for example, would be contained in the lower end of the range covered by Equation 4.21. For values of λ less than approximately 0.25 (corresponding to KL/r = 19 for a steel with F_y = 350 MPa) the predicted compressive resistance, excluding the performance factor, will be within 2% of the load given by C_y. For the commonly used steels, slender members can be thought of as those having slenderness parameters greater than about 2.0 (corresponding to KL/r = 150 for F_y = 350 MPa), although there is no definite dividing line between slender and intermediate members.

For extremely slender members the maximum strength is highly sensitive to changes in end conditions and to initial imperfections, and such members cannot safely be designed using Equation 4.21. For this reason, Clause 10.4.2.1 of   S16–01 limits the maximum slenderness ratio for compressive members to KL/r = 200 (which corresponds to λ = 2.7 for F_y = 350 MPa).

4.7   Resistance Factor for Columns

In general, the resistance factor, ϕ, is used to reduce the nominal value of the compressive resistance in order to account for the possibility of under-strength material, under-run in the cross-sectional dimensions, and variations in workmanship. As applied to axially loaded columns, the variations in material strength and cross-sectional dimensions can be expected to have similar effects on columns of different slenderness ratios. As discussed earlier, the influences of variations in column out-of-straightness and residual strain distribution are most severe for intermediate length columns [4.6].

The equation used to predict the compressive resistance (Equation 4.21) in S16–01 has been adjusted to reflect the increased uncertainty in the prediction of the ultimate strength of intermediate columns [4.7]. For this reason the resistance factor ϕ, can be held constant at 0.90 over the entire range of slenderness ratios. This procedure results in a relatively uniform probability of failure for columns of differing slenderness.

4.8   Design Examples

The design provisions of the Canadian Standards Association are shown in Figure 4.12 for steel having F_y = 350 MPa. These curves plot the compressive resistance divided by the cross-sectional area ($C_r/\phi A$) versus the non-dimensional slenderness parameter of the member, λ, for the two different column curves, n = 1.34 and n = 2.24. The column strength relationship given by Equation 4.21 when n = 1.34 and illustrated in Figure 4.12 is applicable to most of the sections in common use in Canada, including H-shape and hollow structural sections manufactured according to G40.20–98 Class C [4.8]. For G40.20–98 Class H hollow structural sections, however, the Standard permits higher capacities and a value of n = 2.24 is applicable.

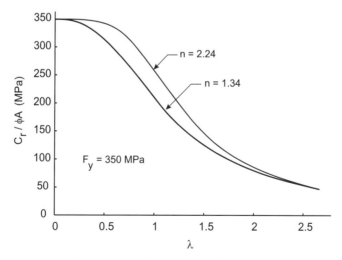

Figure 4.12 – Compressive Resistance

In Canada, many H-shape columns are made by welding together three plate components. The flange-to-web welds induce large residual stresses in the cross-section, which are tensile in the vicinity of the weld and compressive near the flange tips. In some cases the compressive stresses are much higher than normally occur in rolled shapes, and this can result in a section with reduced strength. Studies have indicated that welded H-shapes that have flange edges flame-cut are preferable to those having flange edges rolled, as is the case if unsheared universal mill plate is used. The flame-cutting process induces tensile rather than compressive residual stresses at the edges of the plate. For this reason, the Standard provides higher resistances (n = 2.24) for welded wide flange shapes that have flame-cut flanges and are produced according to the requirements of CSA–G40.20/G40.21–98 [4.8].

The examples that follow treat both the analysis (a checking process) and design of axially loaded pin-ended columns. The examples will be solved using basic principles: however, in many cases tabulated values can be used to reduce the number of computations involved. The values of C_r/A, for example, are given for various values of KL/r in Reference [4.9]. Following the working of each example problem, the alternative solutions using tabulated values will be outlined briefly. Users of the Handbook values should ensure that they understand the principles involved, however.

Example 4.1

Given

A W250×73 section of G40.21 350W steel is used as a pedestal with a height of 1100 mm. Determine the factored compressive resistance.

Solution

The cross-sectional properties of the W250×73 shape are listed in the CISC Handbook as:

A = 9280 mm^2 r_x = 110 mm r_y = 64.6 mm

h (tabulated as d – 2t) = 225 mm   w = 8.6 mm

b (total width of flange) = 254 mm   t = 14.2 mm

First, establish whether the nominal yield strength of 350 MPa is the actual yield strength for this particular section. From Table 3 of Appendix A (or the equivalent table in the CISC Handbook), this is a Group 2 section. Use Table 4 of Appendix A to confirm that the actual yield strength for this Group 2 section is indeed 350 MPa.

Next, establish whether the local buckling requirements are met.

Web: actual $\dfrac{h}{w} = \dfrac{225}{8.6} = 26.2$ limit h/w $= \dfrac{670}{\sqrt{350}} = 35.8$

Flange: actual $\dfrac{b}{2t} = \dfrac{254}{2\times14.2} = 8.9$ limit b/2t $= \dfrac{200}{\sqrt{350}} = 10.7$

In both cases, the actual slenderness of the element is less than the permissible value. This means that the cross-section will not fail by local buckling and its capacity as a column can be predicted using Equation 4.21. Note also that in the case of the flange, it is the projection of the flange relative to its width that is being checked. Although it is conventional to write the limit as b/2t, it would be more precise to write it as (b/2)/t. As shown in Figure 4.2, the CISC Handbook tabulates the total width of the flange, b, not the projecting dimension.

The slenderness ratios are computed assuming that the effective length factor K is 1.0. Thus:

$$\frac{L}{r_x} = \frac{1100}{110} = 10$$

$$\frac{L}{r_y} = \frac{1100}{64.6} = 17 \qquad \text{(Governs)}$$

Now, from Equation 4.20:

$$\lambda = \frac{KL}{r}\sqrt{\frac{F_y}{\pi^2 E}} = 17\sqrt{\frac{350\,\text{MPa}}{\pi^2 \times 200\,000\,\text{MPa}}} = 0.23$$

Thus, for the value of n = 1.34 (the appropriate value for a Group 2 W shape), the factored compressive resistance is (Equation 4.21):

$$C_r = \phi\, A\, F_y \left(1 + \lambda^{2n}\right)^{-1/n}$$

$$= 0.90 \times 9280\,\text{mm}^2 \times 350\,\text{MPa} \left(1 + 0.23^{2 \times 1.34}\right)^{-1/1.34}$$

$$= 2880 \times 10^3\,\text{N} = 2880\,\text{kN}$$

Alternatively, the CISC Handbook can be used to obtain the value of the unit factored compressive resistance (C_r / A) corresponding to the slenderness ratio L/r = 17 and a yield stress of 350 MPa. The permissible load can then be calculated from that information. In addition, the factored compressive resistance for the W250×73 section is tabulated directly in the CISC Handbook for many cases.

Example 4.2

Given

A W250×73 section of G40.21 350W steel ($F_y = 350\,\text{MPa}$) with a length of 11 000 mm is used as a temporary support. Determine the factored compressive resistance of the member. It was verified in Example 4.1 that the actual yield strength for this section is 350 MPa, that the local buckling requirements are met, and that n = 1.34 should be used.

Solution

The cross-sectional properties of the W250×73 shape are listed in the CISC Handbook as:

$$A = 9280\,\text{mm}^2 \qquad r_x = 110\,\text{mm} \qquad r_y = 64.6\,\text{mm}$$

Assuming an effective length factor K = 1.0, the slenderness ratios are computed as:

$$\frac{L}{r_x} = \frac{11\,000}{110} = 100$$

$$\frac{L}{r_y} = \frac{11\,000}{64.6} = 170 \qquad\qquad\qquad \text{(Governs)}$$

The compressive resistance is dependent on the larger slenderness ratio $L/r_y = 170$. According to Equation 4.20, the slenderness parameter is:

$$\lambda = \frac{KL}{r}\sqrt{\frac{F_y}{\pi^2\,E}} = 170\sqrt{\frac{350\text{ MPa}}{\pi^2 \times 200\,000\text{ MPa}}} = 2.26$$

Thus, for the value of n = 1.34, the factored compressive resistance is:

$$C_r = \phi\,A\,F_y\left(1 + \lambda^{2n}\right)^{-\frac{1}{n}}$$

$$= 0.90 \times 9280\text{ mm}^2 \times 350\text{ MPa}\left(1 + 2.26^{2 \times 1.34}\right)^{-\frac{1}{1.34}}$$

$$= 529 \times 10^3\text{ N} = 529\text{ kN}$$

The factored compressive resistance for the W250×73 section is tabulated directly in the CISC Handbook. For extremely slender members (those having $\lambda > 3.6$ but KL/r < 200), the compressive resistance, given by Equation 4.21, is less dependent on the yield strength of the steel. For most of the commonly used steels, columns normally encountered in building construction will not fall in this range, however.

Example 4.3

Given

A W250×73 section of G40.21 350W steel ($F_y = 350$ MPa) is used as a column with a length of 6100 mm. Determine the compressive resistance. As established in Example 4.1, local buckling will not govern and n = 1.34 is to be used in Equation 4.21.

Solution

The cross-sectional properties of the W250×73 shape are listed in the CISC Handbook as:

$$A = 9280\text{ mm}^2 \qquad\qquad r_x = 110\text{ mm} \qquad\qquad r_y = 64.6\text{ mm}$$

Assuming an effective length factor K = 1.0, the slenderness ratios are computed as:

$$\frac{L}{r_x} = \frac{6100}{110} = 56$$

$$\frac{L}{r_y} = \frac{6100}{64.6} = 94 \qquad\qquad\qquad \text{(Governs)}$$

The compressive resistance is dependent on the larger slenderness ratio, $L/r_y = 94$. The corresponding slenderness parameter is given by Equation 4.20:

$$\lambda = \frac{KL}{r}\sqrt{\frac{F_y}{\pi^2 E}} = 94\sqrt{\frac{350 \text{ MPa}}{\pi^2 \times 200\,000 \text{ MPa}}} = 1.25$$

Thus, for the value of $n = 1.34$, the factored compressive resistance is:

$$C_r = \phi A F_y \left(1 + \lambda^{2n}\right)^{-\frac{1}{n}}$$

$$= 0.90 \times 9280 \text{ mm}^2 \times 350 \text{ MPa} \left(1 + 1.25^{2 \times 1.34}\right)^{-\frac{1}{1.34}}$$

$$= 1350 \times 10^3 \text{ N} = 1350 \text{ kN}$$

Again, the CISC Handbook tabulates the factored compressive resistance for the member directly.

Example 4.4

Given

A W310×283 section of G40.21 350A steel ($F_y = 350\,\text{MPa}$) is used as a main member. The column has a length of 4600 mm and is assumed to be pin connected at each end. The cross-section is built up by welding two plates 280 mm× 20 mm, also of G40.21 350A steel, to the outside faces of the flanges. The column is braced at mid-height to prevent movement in the x direction only. Determine the compressive resistance. The column is shown in Figure 4.13.

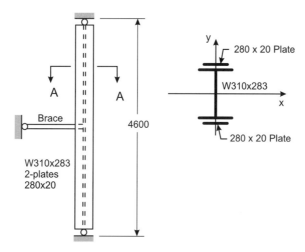

Figure 4.13 – Structural Arrangement — Example 4.4

Solution

The cross-section properties of the W310×283 shape are listed in the CISC Handbook as:

$A = 36\,000 \text{ mm}^2$ $I_x = 787 \times 10^6 \text{ mm}^4$ $I_y = 246 \times 10^6 \text{ mm}^4$

$d = 365 \text{ mm}$ $r_x = 148 \text{ mm}$ $r_y = 82.6 \text{ mm}$

$$h = 277 \text{ mm} \qquad\qquad w = 26.9 \text{ mm}$$

The W310×283 of 350A steel is a Group 3 section, for which F_y is 350 MPa. Likewise, the 20 mm thick flange plates have a yield stress of 350 MPa. Thus, the entire composite section has a yield strength of 350 MPa. (This is not always necessarily the case.) Since the flanges of the W shape have been substantially stiffened by the attachment of the plates, it will be assumed that only web local buckling needs to be examined.

$$\text{Web: actual } \frac{h}{w} = \frac{277}{26.9} = 10.3 \qquad\qquad \text{limit } \frac{h}{w} = \frac{670}{\sqrt{350}} = 35.8$$

Satisfactory re local buckling.

Before the compressive resistance can be determined, the properties of the built-up section must be computed. The calculation of I_x, for example, involves the I_x value for the W shape plus the contribution of the two plates. For each plate this second contribution is composed of the moment of inertia of the plate about its own centroidal axis and the transfer term required to shift the plate moment of inertia to the centroidal axis of the complete section. The moment of inertia of the plate about its own centroidal axis is relatively small and normally is ignored.

$$I_x = I_{x(W310)} + 2\left[I_{x(plate)} + A_{(plate)} \left(\frac{d+t}{2} \right)^2 \right]$$

$$= 787 \times 10^6 + 2\left[\frac{280 \times 20^3}{12} + 280 \times 20 \left(\frac{365 + 20}{2} \right)^2 \right] = 1200 \times 10^6 \text{ mm}^4$$

$$I_y = I_{y(W310)} + 2\, I_{y(plate)}$$

$$= 246 \times 10^6 + 2 \times 20 \times \frac{280^3}{12} = 319 \times 10^6 \text{ mm}^4$$

$$A = A_{(W310)} + 2\, A_{(plate)}$$

$$= 36\,000 + 2 \times 20 \times 280 = 47\,200 \text{ mm}^2$$

$$r_x = \sqrt{\frac{I_x}{A}} = \sqrt{\frac{1200 \times 10^6}{47\,200}} = 159 \text{ mm}$$

$$r_y = \sqrt{\frac{I_y}{A}} = \sqrt{\frac{319 \times 10^6}{47\,200}} = 82 \text{ mm}$$

The slenderness ratios are computed as in the previous examples with the important exception that the brace at mid-height serves to reduce the length for buckling about the y–axis of the section.

$$\frac{KL}{r_x} = \frac{1.0 \times 4600}{159} = 29 \qquad\qquad \text{(Governs)}$$

$$\frac{K L}{r_y} = \frac{0.5 \times 4600}{82} = 28$$

The use of bracing to prevent movement in the x direction has reduced the L/r_y value substantially. Now, the compressive resistance is to be computed on the basis of $K L/r_x = 29$. The corresponding slenderness parameter is (Equation 4.20):

$$\lambda = \frac{K L}{r} \sqrt{\frac{F_y}{\pi^2 E}} = 29 \sqrt{\frac{350 \text{ MPa}}{\pi^2 \times 200\,000 \text{ MPa}}} = 0.39$$

Thus, for the value of $n = 1.34$, appropriate for a Group 3 W-shape, the factored compressive resistance is:

$$C_r = \phi A F_y \left(1 + \lambda^{2n}\right)^{-\frac{1}{n}}$$

$$= 0.90 \times 47\,200 \text{ mm}^2 \times 350 \text{ MPa} \left(1 + 0.39^{2 \times 1.34}\right)^{-\frac{1}{1.34}}$$

$$= 14\,000 \times 10^3 \text{ N} = 14\,000 \text{ kN}$$

In this example, the unit factored compressive resistances tabulated in the CISC Handbook again could be used to compute the factored compressive resistance once the governing slenderness ratio has been calculated. The compressive resistances of built-up shapes are not tabulated directly.

Example 4.5

Given

A 3700 mm long brace consists of two angles $89 \times 64 \times 9.5$ placed with long legs back to back, as shown in Figure 4.14. The two angles are separated by 8 mm thick gusset plates at both ends and are interconnected at intervals close enough that they can be considered to act as a unit. The ends are assumed to be pin-connected. Determine the factored compressive resistance. The angles are of G40.21 300W steel.

Solution

The cross-sectional properties for the double angle member are listed in the CISC Handbook as:

$$A = 2720 \text{ mm}^2 \qquad r_x = 28.0 \text{ mm} \qquad r_y = 27.6 \text{ mm (two angles)}$$

For members built up of angles, the limiting width-to-thickness ratios are the same as for the flange of a wide flange shape. Thus, the governing plate width-to-thickness ratio to prevent premature local buckling of an angle is given in S16–01, Table 1 as:

$$\frac{b}{t} \leq \frac{200}{\sqrt{F_y}}$$

The critical leg is the 89 mm length, and

Flange: actual $\dfrac{b}{t} = \dfrac{89}{10} = 8.9$ limit $\dfrac{b}{t} = \dfrac{200}{\sqrt{300}} = 11.5$

Since the width-to-thickness ratio of the critical leg is less than the limiting value, the compressive resistance will be based on the overall member strength. The slenderness ratios now are computed as:

$$\frac{L}{r_x} = \frac{3700}{28.0} = 132$$

$$\frac{L}{r_y} = \frac{3700}{27.6} = 134 \qquad\qquad\qquad \text{(Governs)}$$

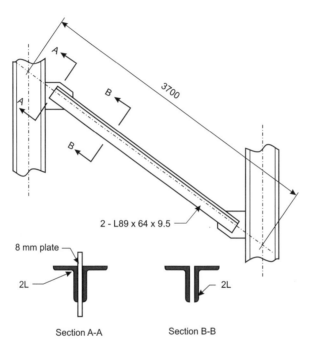

2 - L89 x 64 x 9.5

8 mm plate

2L   2L

Section A-A   Section B-B

Figure 4.14 – Structural Arrangement — Example 4.5

The compressive resistance will be governed by the L/r_y value of 134. It should be noted that the thickness of the gusset plate separates the long legs of two angles. Thus, the thicker the plate, the larger will be r_y. The section properties of two angles separated by the thickness of the gusset plate can be calculated from first principles or can be obtained from the CISC Handbook for several gusset plate thicknesses. The slenderness parameter corresponding to $L/r_y = 134$ is given by Equation 4.20:

$$\lambda = \frac{KL}{r}\sqrt{\frac{F_y}{\pi^2\,E}} = 134\sqrt{\frac{300\ \text{MPa}}{\pi^2 \times 200\,000\ \text{MPa}}} = 1.65$$

Clause 13.3.1 of the Standard does not specifically mention angles when identifying appropriate values of n for use in Equation 4.21. However, the appropriate value for angles (and for channels or for other miscellaneous shapes) is n = 1.34.

Thus, the factored compressive resistance is calculated as:

$$C_r = \phi A F_y \left(1 + \lambda^{2n}\right)^{-1/n}$$

$$= 0.90 \times 2720 \text{ mm}^2 \times 300 \text{ MPa} \left(1 + 1.65^{2 \times 1.34}\right)^{-1/1.34}$$

$$= 226 \times 10^3 \text{ N} = 226 \text{ kN}$$

In the design of double angle struts, advantage can be taken of the tabulated values in the CISC Handbook. For columns composed of double angles of G40.21 300W steel and for certain specific arrangements, the compressive resistance can be determined directly from tables.

Research performed on compression members composed of double angles has shown that the design of such members can be based on the provisions developed for the W shapes [4.10]. For double angle columns, the lateral torsional strength is not significantly below the flexural strength.

Double angles interconnected at discrete locations (rather than connected "continuously," as in this example) must be checked by computing an effective slenderness ratio based on the spacing and type of interconnection [4.11]. See Clause 19.1.4 of S16–01.

Example 4.6

Given

A column is to be designed to resist a load of 13 500 kN. The length of the member is 3600 mm and the ends are assumed to be pin-connected. The column is to be of G40.21 300WT steel.

Solution

The determination of the compressive resistance cannot proceed without a knowledge of the cross-section to be used. Thus, the design procedure becomes a trial and checking process: a particular cross-section is assumed, the factored compressive resistance is determined and then checked against local buckling and the factored load on the member.

A trial section can be selected based on the assumption that the column will be able to reach its maximum strength, namely its yield capacity ($C_r = \phi A F_y$). From this assumption we can compute the minimum cross-sectional area required to carry the factored load as:

$$A = \frac{C_f}{\phi F_y} = \frac{13\,500 \text{ kN} \times 1000 \text{ N/kN}}{0.9 \times 300 \text{ MPa}} = 50\,000 \text{ mm}^2$$

A WWF500×456 (A = 58 200 mm²) is therefore selected as a trial section. As discussed in Chapter 2, the specified minimum yield strength of a plate or section (of a given grade of steel) depends on the plate thickness or the Group classification of the section. For shapes built up by welding plates together, the yield strength depends on the thickness of the source plates. For the WWF500×456, since the component flange plate thickness does not exceed 65 mm, the specified minimum yield stress for 300WT material remains as 300 MPa (see Table 4, Appendix A).

The cross-sectional properties for the WWF500×456 are listed in the CISC Handbook as:

$A = 58\,200\ \text{mm}^2$ $\qquad r_x = 214\ \text{mm}$ $\qquad r_y = 134\ \text{mm}$

$h\,(=d-2t) = 400\ \text{mm}$ $\qquad w = 20.0\ \text{mm}$ $\qquad b = 500\ \text{mm}$ $\qquad t = 50\ \text{mm}$

Check local buckling:

Web: actual $\dfrac{h}{w} = \dfrac{400}{20} = 20$ $\qquad\qquad$ limit $\dfrac{h}{w} = \dfrac{670}{\sqrt{300}} = 38.7$

Flange: actual $\dfrac{b}{2t} = \dfrac{500}{2\times50} = 5.0$ $\qquad\qquad$ limit $\dfrac{b}{2t} = \dfrac{200}{\sqrt{300}} = 11.5$

Since both local buckling limits are satisfied, the capacity of the trial section can now be established on the basis of Equation 4.21.

The slenderness ratios are computed as:

$$\frac{L}{r_x} = \frac{3600}{214} = 17$$

$$\frac{L}{r_y} = \frac{3600}{134} = 27 \qquad\qquad\qquad\qquad \text{(Governs)}$$

The compressive resistance will be governed by the L/r_y value of 27. The corresponding slenderness parameter is given by Equation 4.20:

$$\lambda = \frac{KL}{r}\sqrt{\frac{F_y}{\pi^2\,E}} = 27\sqrt{\frac{300\ \text{MPa}}{\pi^2\times200\,000\ \text{MPa}}} = 0.33$$

Since the trial section selected is a welded wide flange, and assuming that the flanges will be made of flame-cut plates, the appropriate value for n is 2.24. Thus, for the value of $n = 2.24$, the factored compressive resistance is:

$$C_r = \phi\,A\,F_y\left(1+\lambda^{2n}\right)^{-1/n}$$

$$= 0.90\times58\,200\ \text{mm}^2\times300\ \text{MPa}\left(1+0.33^{2\times2.24}\right)^{-1/2.24}$$

$$= 15\,700\times10^3\ \text{N} = 15\,700\ \text{kN}$$

Since the factored compressive resistance of the member is greater than the factored load (15 700 > 13 500), the WWF500×456 is adequate to resist the load. The next lighter section, a WWF500×381, could also be checked. As in the previous examples, use of tabulated values in the Handbook can reduce the computational effort involved.

Example 4.7

Given

A column is built up by welding grade G40.21 300W steel plates together to form the cross-section shown in Figure 4.15. The effective length of the column is 5000 mm. Determine the factored compressive resistance.

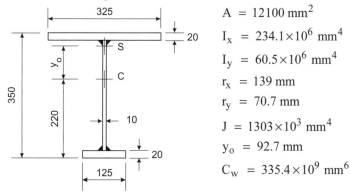

$A = 12100 \text{ mm}^2$

$I_x = 234.1 \times 10^6 \text{ mm}^4$

$I_y = 60.5 \times 10^6 \text{ mm}^4$

$r_x = 139 \text{ mm}$

$r_y = 70.7 \text{ mm}$

$J = 1303 \times 10^3 \text{ mm}^4$

$y_o = 92.7 \text{ mm}$

$C_w = 335.4 \times 10^9 \text{ mm}^6$

Figure 4.15 – Column Cross-Section — Example 4.7

Solution

The column cross-section is singly symmetric (symmetrical about the y–axis only) and it is therefore susceptible to failure by flexural buckling about the strong axis or by torsional-flexural buckling. The cross-sectional properties are shown in Figure 4.15. The location of the shear center, y_o, and the warping constant, C_w, were calculated using the equations shown in Figure 4.11.

We first establish whether the local buckling requirements are met. Since both flanges have the same thickness, only the wider of the two flanges needs to be checked.

Web: actual $\dfrac{h}{w} = \dfrac{350 - 40}{10} = 31$ limit $\dfrac{h}{w} = \dfrac{670}{\sqrt{300}} = 38.7$

Flange: actual $\dfrac{b}{2t} = \dfrac{325}{2 \times 20} = 8.1$ limit $\dfrac{b}{2t} = \dfrac{200}{\sqrt{300}} = 11.5$

The cross-section is satisfactory with respect to local buckling. The elastic flexural buckling strength about the strong axis is given as

$$F_{ex} = \frac{\pi^2 E}{\left(\dfrac{K_x L_x}{r_x} \right)^2} = \frac{\pi^2 \times 200\,000 \text{ MPa}}{\left(\dfrac{5000 \text{ mm}}{139 \text{ mm}} \right)^2} = 1530 \text{ MPa}$$

For singly symmetric cross-sections the flexural buckling mode about the weak axis and the torsional buckling mode are coupled, thus resulting in a reduced capacity. The following calculations apply.

$$\bar{r}_o{}^2 = x_o{}^2 + y_o{}^2 + r_x{}^2 + r_y{}^2 = 0 + (92.7)^2 + (139.1)^2 + (70.7)^2 = 32\,940 \text{ mm}^2$$

$$\Omega = 1 - \left[\frac{x_o{}^2 + y_o{}^2}{\bar{r}_o{}^2} \right] = 1 - \left[\frac{0 + (92.7)^2}{32\,940} \right] = 0.739$$

$$F_{ey} = \frac{\pi^2\,E}{\left(\dfrac{K_y\,L_y}{r_y} \right)^2} = \frac{\pi^2 \times 200\,000 \text{ MPa}}{\left(\dfrac{5000 \text{ mm}}{70.7 \text{ mm}} \right)^2} = 395 \text{ MPa}$$

$$F_{ez} = \left(\frac{\pi^2\,E\,C_w}{(K_z\,L_z)^2} + GJ \right) \frac{1}{A\,\bar{r}_o{}^2}$$

$$F_{ez} = \left(\frac{\pi^2 \times 200\,000 \times 335.4 \times 10^9}{(5000)^2} + (77\,000)(1303 \times 10^3) \right) \frac{1}{12\,100 \times 32\,940}$$

$$= 318 \text{ MPa}$$

$$F_{eyz} = \frac{F_{ey} + F_{ez}}{2\,\Omega} \left[1 - \sqrt{1 - \frac{4\,F_{ey}\,F_{ez}\,\Omega}{\left(F_{ey} + F_{ez} \right)^2}} \right]$$

$$= \frac{395 + 318}{2 \times 0.739} \left[1 - \sqrt{1 - \frac{4 \times 395 \times 318 \times 0.739}{(395 + 318)^2}} \right] = 232 \text{ MPa}$$

It can be observed that, because of the interaction between the flexural buckling mode about the weak axis and the torsional buckling mode, the torsional-flexural buckling stress, F_{eyz}, is lower than either the flexural buckling stress about the weak axis, F_{ey}, or the torsional buckling stress, F_{ez}. The elastic torsional-flexural buckling stress, F_{eyz}, is lower than the strong axis flexural buckling stress, F_{ex}, thereby identifying that torsional-flexural buckling is the critical mode of failure. In order to account for inelastic action, the elastic critical stress F_{eyz} is used to calculate the dimensionless slenderness parameter,

$$\lambda = \sqrt{\frac{F_y}{F_e}} = \sqrt{\frac{300}{232}} = 1.14$$

From which the inelastic torsional-flexural buckling capacity is obtained as:

$$C_r = \phi\,A\,F_y \left(1 + \lambda^{2n} \right)^{-\frac{1}{n}} = 0.9 \times 12\,100 \times 300 \left(1 + 1.14^{2 \times 1.34} \right)^{-\frac{1}{1.34}}$$

$$= 1689 \times 10^3 \text{ N} = 1690 \text{ kN}$$

4.9   Effective Length Concept

In the previous sections of this chapter, design provisions were developed on the assumption that both ends of the column were completely free to rotate as the column reached its ultimate buckling strength. This situation would arise, for example, if the girders were attached to the columns through flexible web connections, as illustrated in Figure 4.16(a). As the compression member is deformed, the rotation of the column end will not induce a corresponding rotation of the girder. Thus the column will act as if it were pin-ended.

Where continuous construction is used, however, the girder-to-column connections are rigid, as illustrated in Figure 4.16(b). In this situation, the column end rotations that take place during the bending motion of the column will induce corresponding rotations in the girder ends. Bending moments will be developed at the connections, and these will restrain the motion of the column and thereby increase its strength.

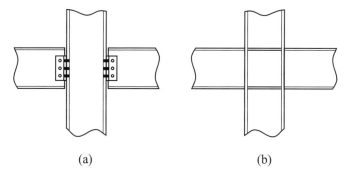

(a)   (b)

Figure 4.16 – Beam-to-Column Connections

In order to use the design rules developed for buckling of a pin-ended column in situations where a column is restrained at its ends, the actual length of the column L, is replaced (in Equation 4.20) by an effective length KL. This corresponds to the length between points of inflection (points of zero bending moment) on the buckled shape [4.4]. Thus, the buckling strength of an ideal column with the actual length and restraining conditions is equal to that for a similar pin-ended column having the appropriate effective length. For simplicity, the ideal column is used in the development of the model for the effective length and the concept will then be applied to real columns with end restraints.

4.10   Effect of Rotational Restraint on Column Buckling Strength

If the column end connections are able to resist bending moments, the buckling strength of the column can be increased significantly above that of the equivalent pin-ended member. Three simple cases are shown in Figure 4.17.

The first is a pin-ended member, where the buckling load given by Equation 4.7:

$$C_{cr} = \frac{\pi^2 \, EI}{L^2}$$

The second column has its lower end clamped so that rotation cannot occur. The buckling load in this situation, obtained from a solution of differential equation using the appropriate boundary conditions, is [4.3]:

$$C_{cr} = 2.05 \frac{\pi^2 \, EI}{L^2}$$

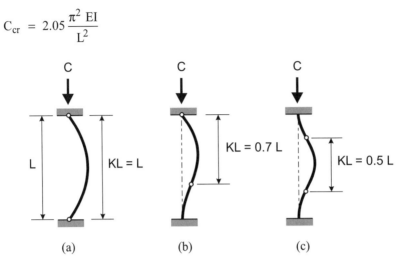

Figure 4.17 – Buckled Shapes — Sway Prevented

Any buckling load can also be expressed in terms of an effective length, KL, defined as the length of a pin-ended column that will give the equivalent buckling load. Thus, for the case shown in Figure 4.17(b)

$$\frac{\pi^2 \, EI}{(KL)^2} \equiv \frac{2.05 \, \pi^2 \, EI}{L^2}$$

Solving, K = 0.7. In other words, a pin-ended column of effective length KL = 0.7 L gives the same buckling capacity as the case shown in Figure 4.17(b) developed from first principles.

If both column ends are clamped, it can be shown that the effective length is 0.5L, as shown in Figure 4.17(c). The buckling load is now:

$$C_{cr} = \frac{\pi^2 \, EI}{(KL)^2} = \frac{\pi^2 \, EI}{(0.5 \, L)^2} = \frac{4.0 \, \pi^2 \, EI}{L^2}$$

In an actual building frame, the ends of the columns will not be clamped, but will be restrained by the bending action of the members rigidly connected to them. A typical frame is shown schematically in Figure 4.18. (The cross-bracing system shown is present to resist the lateral loads acting on the frame.)

In many structures of this type containing direct-acting bracing systems, the girders are connected to the columns through flexible web connections. In the material that follows, however, it will be assumed that all connections are rigid, thus illustrating the effect of end restraint on column strength.

In order to consider the buckling strength of column UL, this portion of the frame has been isolated in Figure 4.19. The dashed lines show the position of this portion of the frame before loads are applied. If the loads are applied symmetrically, the beams will deform as shown and the columns deflect laterally relative to their original vertical position.

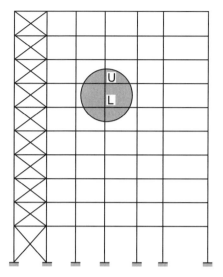

Figure 4.18 – Braced Frame

At the instant of buckling, the additional deformations of the column and adjacent members are shown by the full lines in Figure 4.19. It is assumed in this discussion that buckling will occur in the plane of the frame. (In an actual structure, the possibility of buckling in the perpendicular direction must also be considered, and this is described in Chapter 8.) Assuming that all columns in the frame are designed with approximately the same safety index, it is reasonable to assume that the column sections above and below UL buckle along with UL. During the buckling motion, the ends of the columns rotate through an angle θ_U (or θ_L). The beam ends are also forced through this same rotation.

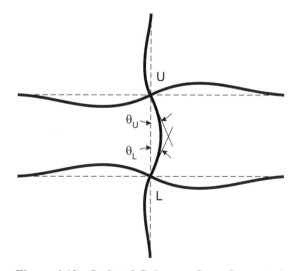

Figure 4.19 – Isolated Column – Sway Prevented

Assuming that both ends of the girder are forced through equal and opposite rotations, θ_U, a resisting moment, M_{UG}, will be developed at the beam-to-column connection equal to [4.12]

$$M_{UG} = \frac{2\,E\,I_g}{L_g}\,\theta_U \qquad (4.22)$$

where E is the modulus of elasticity and I_g and L_g are the moment of inertia of the beam about its axis of bending and the beam length, respectively.

The other beams at the joint will develop similar moments and resist the rotation of the column ends during buckling. The beams at a particular joint will provide resistance to both the column above and to the column below that joint. Assuming that the resistance to buckling is in proportion to the stiffness of the column considered, I_c/L_c, then the net resisting moment, M_U, acting on the column will be:

$$M_U = \frac{(I_c/L_c)}{\Sigma(I_c/L_c)}\times 2\,E\,\theta_U\,\Sigma(I_g/L_g) = \frac{2\,E\,I_c}{G\,L_c}\,\theta_U \qquad (4.23)$$

where G is defined as:

$$G = \frac{\Sigma(I_c/L_c)}{\Sigma(I_g/L_g)} \qquad (4.24)$$

The symbol Σ indicates a summation for all elements rigidly connected to the joint and lying in the plane in which buckling is being considered. I_c is the column moment of inertia and L_c is its length.

The forces acting on column UL are shown in Figure 4.20(a) and a corresponding free body diagram of a portion of the column is given in Figure 4.20(b). The differential equation of equilibrium is no longer that for the pin-ended column, but now must account for the presence of the end moments and shears. The solution to the differential equation can be expressed as [4.4]

$$\frac{G_U\,G_L}{4}\left(\frac{\pi}{K}\right)^2 + \left(\frac{G_U + G_L}{2}\right)\left(1 - \frac{\pi/K}{\tan\,\pi/K}\right) + 2\,\frac{\tan\,\pi/2K}{\pi/K} = 1 \qquad (4.25)$$

where G_U and G_L are defined in Equation 4.24 for joints U and L, respectively, and K is the effective length factor of the column considered, defined as the ratio of the effective length to the actual length.

Equation 4.25 was derived based on a number of simplifying assumptions, namely,

(a) Beams and columns have the same elastic modulus, E.

(b) The behaviour is elastic.

  Although we know that, for intermediate columns, significant inelastic action can be expected, Equation 4.25 has traditionally been used for all columns. Yielding of the cross-section before buckling causes a reduction of the flexural stiffness, EI/L, of the column.

(c) Beam rotation

The solution is based on the assumption that the beams are rigidly connected to the columns.

(d) At buckling of the column, the beams deform in single curvature.

(e) The far end of the beam is rigidly connected to a column.

For other conditions of support at the far end of a beam, the following correction can be made:

$$G = \frac{\Sigma I_c / L_c}{\Sigma f_g \, I_g / L_g}$$

where,

$f_g = $ 1.0 for a beam with both ends rigidly connected to a column

$f_g = $ 0 for a beam pin connected at the column for which K is to be calculated

$f_g = $ 1.5 for a beam pin-connected at the far end

$f_g = $ 2.0 for a beam rigidly connected to a very stiff member at the far end.

(d) Equation 4.25 is based on the assumption that all the columns in the frame buckle simultaneously. Failure to satisfy this assumption actually leads to a conservative estimate of the buckling capacity of the column.

(e) Load and structure symmetry was assumed in deriving Equation 4.25.

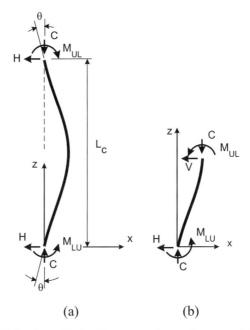

(a)   (b)

Figure 4.20 – Free Body Diagram – Sway Prevented Column

Equation 4.25 is not in a form directly suitable for design use but has been plotted as a nomograph, as shown in Figure 4.21 [4.12]. The nomograph is entered with the calculated values of G_U and G_L and a straight line joining these two values identifies the value of K. For the example shown in the figure, $G_U = 2.0$, $G_L = 0.4$, and K = 0.75. If both G_U and G_L are zero, the implication is that the beams are infinitely stiff as compared to the columns, i.e., $\sum I_g / L_g$ is much greater than $\sum I_c / L_c$ (Equation 4.24), so that no rotation of the column end will occur during buckling. In this case, the buckled shape would correspond to that shown in Figure 4.17(c), and the effective length factor, K, is 0.5.

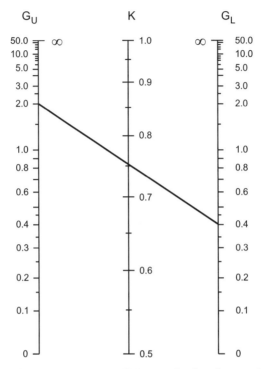

Figure 4.21 – Nomograph – Columns in Continuous Frames

If both G_U and G_L are infinite, the implication is that the beams have no rotational stiffness, and thus the column end can rotate freely during the buckling motion. For this case, $\sum I_g / L_g$ is much less than $\sum I_c / L_c$ in Equation 4.24 and the effective length factor is 1.0. The buckled shape corresponds to that of the pin-ended column shown in Figure 4.17(a). If one value of G is zero and the other infinite, the column corresponds to the one shown in Figure 4.17(b), for which the effective length factor is 0.7.

The value of G given by Equation 4.24 is a measure of the effective rotational restraint delivered by the beams to the column during the buckling motion. However, a special situation exists at the connection of the column end to the foundation. If the connection has been designed to resist a bending moment and the foundation is fairly rigid, then rotation of the column end is restrained during buckling and the effective value of I_g is infinite (G equal to zero). In fact, some rotation will always occur, and to compensate for this G is normally taken as 1.0 for this type of foundation condition.

Where the connection at the foundation is not designed to resist a bending moment, the foundation will offer little rotational restraint to the column and the effective value of I_g is zero. (This corresponds to an infinite value of G.) To compensate for the fact that some small rotational restraint will be offered even in this case, it is recommended that $G = 10$ be used.

4.11   Design Examples

The following design examples were chosen primarily to illustrate the calculation of effective length. Once the effective length (and the corresponding effective slenderness ratio) has been determined, the check for local buckling and the calculation of the load-carrying capacity proceeds in a manner similar to that illustrated in the previous examples of this chapter.

Although the effective length has been developed in terms of the elastic buckling strength of the member, the design of an axially loaded column is based on the maximum strength of an initially imperfect column. Any restraint to the rotation of the ends of the member does, however, provide an increase in the ultimate strength as well as an increase in the buckling capacity. For this reason the effective length is used for the design relationship for axially loaded columns in Equations 4.20 and 4.21.

Example 4.8

Given

A W250×73 section of G40.21 350W steel ($F_y = 350$ MPa) is used as a column with a 3650 mm storey height. The column is shown in Figure 4.22 together with the rigidly connected framing members. The connection at the foundation is not designed to resist moment. Assuming that local buckling will not control the design (see Example 4.1), determine the factored compressive resistance of the member.

Solution

The effective lengths for buckling about the two principal axes must be determined. As a first step, consider buckling in the x–z plane, and compute the relative stiffnesses at the lower and upper ends of the column according to Equation 4.24.

The base plate connection at the lower end of the column is not designed to resist moment and therefore the foundation offers little resistance to the end rotation of the column. Theoretically $G_L = \infty$, but it is common practice [4.9] to use $G_L = 10$ as a reasonable substitution for a large number.

Now, at the upper end:

$$G_U = \frac{\Sigma(I_c / L_c)}{\Sigma(I_g / L_g)}$$

The W250×73 column extends both above and below the floor girders. At the instant of buckling the two column sections bend about their weak (y–y) axes. The moment of inertia about the y–y axis for a W250×73 is given in the CISC Handbook as 38.8×10^6 mm^4. Thus,

$$\Sigma(I_c / L_c) = \frac{38.8\times10^6}{3650} + \frac{38.8\times10^6}{3050} = 23\,400 \text{ mm}^3$$

The beams bend about their strong (x–x) axes as the column buckles. For a W460×74, from the CISC Handbook $I_x = 333\times10^6$ mm^4 and for a W410×54, $I_x = 186\times10^6$ mm^4. Thus,

$$\Sigma\left(I_g/L_g\right) = \frac{333\times10^6}{9200} + \frac{186\times10^6}{7300} = 61\,700 \text{ mm}^3$$

$$G_U = \frac{\Sigma\left(I_c/L_c\right)}{\Sigma\left(I_g/L_g\right)} = \frac{23\,400}{61\,700} = 0.38$$

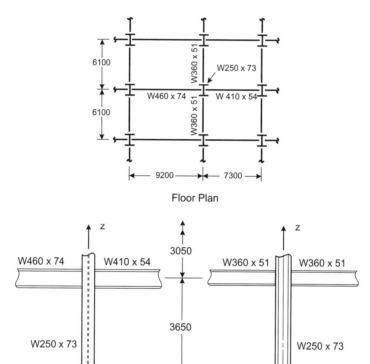

Figure 4.22 – Structural Arrangement — Example 4.8

From the nomograph, Figure 4.21, the effective length factor is read as $K_y = 0.79$ and from the CISC Handbook, $r_y = 64.6$ mm for the W250$\times$73 section. The effective slenderness ratio, $(KL/r)_y$, for buckling in the x–z plane is therefore:

$$\left(\frac{KL}{r}\right)_y = \frac{0.79\times3650}{64.6} = 45$$

Next, the possibility of buckling in the y–z plane should be considered. The relative stiffnesses at the lower and upper ends of the column are computed as before.

$$G_L = 10$$

$$G_U = \frac{\Sigma(I_c/L_c)}{\Sigma(I_g/L_g)}$$

For buckling in the y–z plane, the columns sections above and below the joint bend about their strong (x–x) axes. The moment of inertia about this axis for a W250×73 section is given in the CISC Handbook as 113×10^6 mm^4.

$$\Sigma(I_c/L_c) = \frac{113\times10^6}{3650} + \frac{113\times10^6}{3050} = 68\,000 \text{ mm}^3$$

At the instant of buckling, the W360×51 beams also bend about their strong axes. For a W360×51, $I_x = 141\times10^6$ mm^4.

$$\Sigma(I_g/L_g) = \frac{141\times10^6}{6100} + \frac{141\times10^6}{6100} = 46\,200 \text{ mm}^3$$

$$G_U = \frac{\Sigma(I_c/L_c)}{\Sigma(I_g/L_g)} = \frac{68\,000}{46\,200} = 1.5$$

From the nomograph, Figure 4.21, read $K_x = 0.89$ and from the CISC Handbook, $r_x = 110$ mm for the W250×73 section. The effective slenderness ratio, $(KL/r)_x$, for buckling in the y–z plane is therefore:

$$\left(\frac{KL}{r}\right)_x = \frac{0.89\times3650}{110} = 29.5$$

Since $(KL/r)_y > (KL/r)_x$, failure of the column will be accompanied by bending about the y–y axis and the compressive resistance will be computed using an effective slenderness ratio of 45. From this point on, the determination of the factored compressive resistance follows the steps outlined in the previous sections and only the results of the calculation will be shown. Note that in the equations for column strength developed previously, the actual length or slenderness ratio is replaced by the effective length or slenderness ratio. For a steel having $F_y = 350$ MPa and for a governing slenderness ratio $K_y L/r_y = 45$, the slenderness parameter calculated from Equation 4.20 is $\lambda = 0.60$.

For this section, $n = 1.34$ is to be used (see Example 4.1) and, with a cross-sectional area of 9280 mm^2, the factored compressive resistance for the member is:

$$C_r = 2470 \text{ kN}$$

As in the previous examples, tabulated values in the CISC Handbook could be used to reduce the computational effort once the effective slenderness ratio has been determined.

Example 4.9

Given

Compute the effective slenderness ratio, $(KL/r)_y$, for a WWF500×456 column if the structural arrangement is that shown in Figure 4.23. It is assumed in this example that buckling about the strong axis of the column is prevented by continuous bracing in the y–z plane.

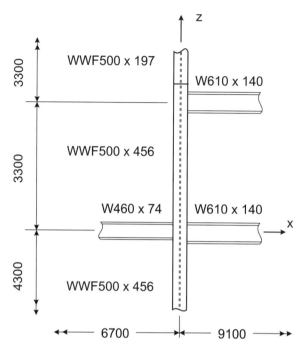

Figure 4.23 – Structural Arrangement – Example 4.9

Solution

As the column buckles, the column sections are bent about their weak (y–y) axes. For the WWF500×456, $I_y = 1040 \times 10^6$ mm^4 and for the WWF500×197, $I_y = 417 \times 10^6$ mm^4, as given in the CISC Handbook. The beams are rigidly connected to the columns and will be bent about their strong (x–x) axes. For the W460×74, $I_x = 333 \times 10^6$ mm^4 and for the W610×140, $I_x = 1120 \times 10^6$ mm^4.

The relative stiffnesses as calculated by Equation 4.24 are:

$$G_L = \frac{\Sigma(I_c/L_c)}{\Sigma(I_g/L_g)} = \frac{\dfrac{1040 \times 10^6}{3300} + \dfrac{1040 \times 10^6}{4300}}{\dfrac{333 \times 10^6}{6700} + \dfrac{1120 \times 10^6}{9100}} = 3.2$$

$$G_U = \frac{\Sigma(I_c/L_c)}{\Sigma(I_g/L_g)} = \frac{\dfrac{417 \times 10^6}{3300} + \dfrac{1040 \times 10^6}{3300}}{\dfrac{1120 \times 10^6}{9100}} = 3.6$$

From the nomograph, Figure 4.21, read $K_x = 0.90$ and from the CISC Handbook, $r_y = 134$ mm for the WWF500×456 section. The effective slenderness ratio for buckling in the x–z plane is therefore

$$\left(\frac{K_y\,L}{r_y} \right)_x = \frac{0.90 \times 3300}{134} = 22$$

4.12 Summary: Effective Length Concept

The calculation of effective column length, which has been treated in Sections 4.9 and 4.10, is applicable to axially loaded columns that fail by buckling only when there is no relative translational displacement between the two ends of the compression member under consideration. If such translational displacement is present, the effect must be included in the analysis. This situation is covered in Chapter 8.

The concept of effective length may also be used in the calculation of the buckling capacity of compression members of trusses provided that the joints at the ends of a member are rigid. However, in this application, it is considered that all members meeting at a joint could reach their capacity simultaneously (yielding of tension members or buckling of compression members), then the effective length factor should simply be taken as unity.

References

4.1 Canadian Standards Association, CAN/CSA–S16–01, "Limit States Design of Steel Structures," Toronto, Ontario, 2001.

4.2 WRC-ASCE Joint Committee, "Plastic Design in Steel, A Guide and Commentary," 2nd Edition, American Society of Civil Engineers, New York, 1971.

4.3 Salmon, C.G. and Johnson, J.E., "Steel Structures," 4th Edition, Harper Collins College Publishers, New York, 1996.

4.4 Structural Stability Research Council, "Guide to Stability Design Criteria for Metal Structures," Fifth Edition, T. V. Galambos Editor, John Wiley and Sons, New York, 1998.

4.5 Galambos, T.V., "Structural Members and Frames," Prentice-Hall, Inc., Englewood Cliffs, New Jersey, 1968.

4.6 Kennedy, D.J.L., Adams, P.F., Allen, D.E., Kulak, G.L., Tarlton, D.L., and Turner, D.K., "Limit States Design," Proceedings of the Canadian Structural Engineering Conference, Canadian Institute of Steel Construction, February, 1976.

4.7 Galambos, T.V. and Ravindra, M.K., "Properties of Steel for Use in Load and Resistance Factor Design," Journal of the Structural Division, American Society of Civil Engineers, Vol. 104, ST9, September, 1978.

4.8 Canadian Standards Association, CSA–G40.20–04/G40.21–04, "General Requirements for Rolled or Welded Structural Quality Steel/Structural Quality Steel," Toronto, Ontario, 2004.

4.9 Canadian Institute of Steel Construction, "Handbook of Steel Construction," Ninth Edition, Toronto, Ontario, 2006.

4.10 Nuttall, N.J. and Adams, P.F., "Buckling Strength of Double Angle Struts," Structural Engineering Report No. 30, University of Alberta, Edmonton, 1970.

4.11 Zahn, C.J. and Haaijer, G., "Effect of Connector Spacing and Flexural-Torsional Buckling on Double-Angle Compressive Strength," Engineering Journal, American Institute of Steel Construction, 3rd. Quarter, Vol. 25, No. 3., 1988.

4.12 Chen, W.F. and Lui, E.M., "Structural Stability—Theory and Implementation," Elsevier, New York, N.Y. 1987.

CHAPTER 5

BEAMS

5.1   Introduction

Beams are the members in a structure that resist loads primarily through flexure. In a building structure, generally the beams (or girders) are horizontal members, spanning between adjacent columns and supporting the loads delivered by the floor or roof system. Beams may also appear in an inclined position as stringers for stairways, ramps, etc., or may be used to support heavy machinery, pipelines, or ductwork. Beams may be required to resist torsional moments in some situations. Although the framing scheme is usually such that torsion is minimized and the primary loading results in bending of the member, in some situations such as crane runway girders torsion is unavoidable.

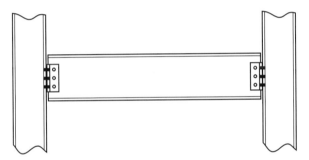

Figure 5.1 – Simply Supported Beam

Beams may be joined to their supporting columns by simple or rigid connections. A simple connection is designed to resist shear only: in this case the connection is assumed to act like a roller or hinged support. Figure 5.1 illustrates schematically a simply supported beam attached to the adjacent columns. The web connections are designed to transmit the beam reactions to the column and are capable of sustaining relatively large rotations without developing significant moments. Such connections usually resist twisting of the beam, but allow distortion, i.e., warping of the cross-section. This makes the connection a simple connection in torsion. In other situations, the designer may wish to connect the beam using a moment-resisting connection, thus achieving a continuous design. In this case the moment developed at the end of the beam is resisted by the connected members. Figure 5.2 illustrates a rigid framing scheme in which the girder is attached to the adjacent columns by connections that have been designed to transmit both moment and shear. In this type of connection, the flanges of the beam are connected to the flanges of the column, whereas in a simple connection only the web of the beam is connected to the columns. Rigid connections in bending may also prevent warping of the cross-section of the beam, making the connection also rigid in torsion.

In a light building structure, the elements supporting floor or roof slabs may be open web joists—a light type of truss. The open web steel joist is an extremely common element in building construction and one that requires careful attention in both the design and production stages. These elements are normally selected from information provided by the manufacturer, and the responsibilities of both designer and manufacturer are delineated in S16–01 [5.1]. In other cases, the beams may be rolled or welded sections, usually wide flange shapes. For longer spans or unusual loads, built-up plate girders may be designed. This chapter will concentrate mainly on rolled and standard welded sections. Chapter 7 contains a discussion of the problems associated with plate girders.

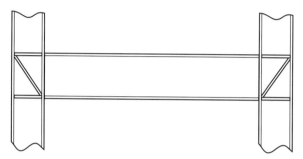

Figure 5.2 – Continuous Beam

A beam or girder is designed primarily on the basis of its flexural strength. Holes in the cross-section tend to reduce this strength. However, tests on beams have shown little reduction, even in sections having as much as 15% of the flange area removed. S16–01 therefore provides that the presence of fastener holes constituting 15% or less of the gross area of a flange may be ignored (Clause 14.1). Larger openings, such as those required for duct work, etc., must be considered in design. The associated problems are beyond the scope of this text [5.2].

5.2   Moment vs. Curvature Relationships for Beams

A small element of beam subjected to a bending moment, M, is shown in Figure 5.3(a). Under the action of the applied moment, strains will develop in the cross-section that are assumed to vary linearly from zero at the neutral axis to a maximum at the extreme fibre, as shown in Figure 5.3(b). For the positive bending moment shown, the top fibres will be in compression, the bottom fibres in tension. The curvature, κ, is the angle change between the original and deformed positions of the cross-section. From elementary strength of materials, if the member behaves elastically [5.3],

$$\kappa = M/EI = \varepsilon/y \tag{5.1}$$

From the stress vs. strain curve of Figure 2.3, if the maximum strain in the cross-section is less than the yield strain, ε_y, the stress distribution is also linear ($\sigma = E\varepsilon$) and is that shown by Part 1 of Figure 5.3(c). However, when the maximum strain exceeds ε_y, the stress cannot increase above the yield stress, σ_y. Thus, yielding must begin to penetrate from the extreme fibres towards the interior of the cross-section. This is shown by Part 2 of Figure 5.3(c).

As strains continue to increase, a limit is reached when the cross-section is fully plastified. (Theoretically, this requires an infinite curvature). At this stage, shown by Part 3 in Figure 5.3(c), the maximum moment capacity has been developed.

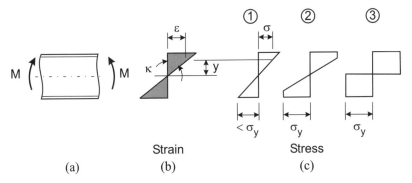

Strain   Stress

(a)   (b)   (c)

Figure 5.3 – Strain and Stress Distributions

The moment that can be carried by the cross-section can be calculated from first principles. If it is desired that the stress nowhere exceed the yield stress, then the corresponding moment is termed the yield moment, M_y. Figure 5.4 represents the M–κ relationship for a beam element, and the moment M_y is shown on the vertical axis. For moment values below M_y, the relationship is linear elastic and the slope of the M–κ curve is equal to E I.

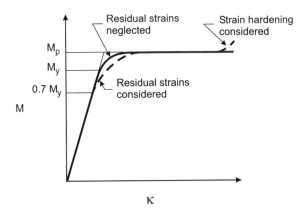

Figure 5.4 – Moment vs. Curvature Relationship

The yield moment is expressed as [5.3]

$$M_y = \sigma_y S \tag{5.2}$$

where the symbol S (elastic section modulus) is used to represent the term I / y. The moment of inertia, I, is that corresponding to the axis about which bending takes place.

The plastic moment capacity is expressed as [5.3]

$$M_p = \sigma_y Z \tag{5.3}$$

where the symbol Z is the plastic section modulus. (The plastic section modulus, Z, is equal to the first moment of area of the tension and compression zones taken about the plastic neutral axis.) The location of M_p on the moment–curvature relationship is shown in Figure 5.4.

Although theoretically an infinite strain is required for the section to reach M_p, in most wide flange shapes approximately 98% of M_p is attained at strains of two times σ_y [5.4].

The moment vs. curvature relationship for a beam element is affected by the residual strains that are present in the rolled or welded cross-section. The residual strains are shown (idealised) in Figure 4.5(a). When the applied bending moment reaches a value of 0.7 M_y, the total strains in the tips of the compression flange will reach ε_y (assuming that the maximum residual strain is $0.3\,\varepsilon_y$ [5.4]). If additional bending moment is applied, the flange tips will be ineffective in accepting the increased stresses, and therefore larger strains than those anticipated will be necessary to develop the required resisting moment. This gradual yielding will modify the behaviour described above and the resulting M–κ relationship will be that shown by the dashed line in Figure 5.4. Since the residual stresses are themselves in equilibrium, the section will still attain its full value of M_p.

The second factor that will modify the behaviour of the cross-section is strain-hardening of the material. As shown in the stress vs. strain curve of Figure 2.2, strain-hardening will occur in the cross-section when the strains are approximately 10 to 12 times the yield strain. The corresponding stresses will then be above σ_y and the resisting moment developed by the cross-section will increase above M_p, as again shown by the dashed portion of Figure 5.4.

5.3 Load vs. Deflection Relationships for Beams

The moment vs. curvature relationship $(M - \kappa)$ reflects only the behaviour of a short element of beam length. To predict the behaviour of a complete member the curvatures corresponding to a given bending moment distribution must be integrated along the length of the member in order to determine the slopes and deflections.

For example, the beam shown in Figure 5.5(a) is assumed to be subjected to a concentrated load, P. The mid-span moment is denoted as M_0 and, at the stage of loading shown, is greater than M_y. The bending moment distribution is shown in Figure 5.5(b) and the corresponding curvature distribution in Figure 5.5(c). The curvatures shown are determined by the M–κ relationship of Figure 5.4.

The mid-span deflections, Δ, are computed using the second moment-area theorem and are plotted in Figure 5.6 as a function of the corresponding mid-span moments. The response of the beam is initially elastic until the mid-span moment is equal to 0.7 M_y. At this point, yielding is initiated in the beam and the central portion "softens." As the load is increased, yielding penetrates through the flanges and spreads along the member length in accordance with the curvature distribution of Figure 5.5(c). On further deformation, the maximum moment increases above M_p due to strain-hardening of the material.

The upper solid curve in Figure 5.6 represents the ideal response and the moment capacity would continue to increase as shown were it not for two phenomena that have not so far been included in the predictions. The first of these is the possibility of local buckling of the component elements that make up the member. In a beam, local buckling of the compression flange is the primary concern, although web buckling can also be of importance, particularly in built-up beams (plate girders). The second factor that can change the behaviour of the beam in a significant way is the possibility of lateral-torsional buckling of the member. This is characterized by the onset of large out-of-plane (or lateral) deflections of the compression flange and an associated portion of the web between points of lateral support [5.4]. Local buckling is discussed in Sections 5.4 and 5.5 and lateral-torsional buckling is treated in Section 5.10.

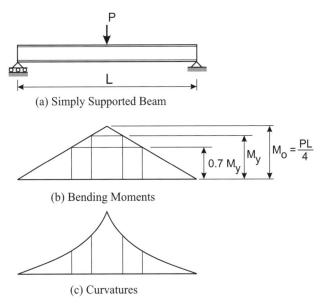

(a) Simply Supported Beam

(b) Bending Moments

(c) Curvatures

Figure 5.5 – Bending Moment and Curvature Distributions

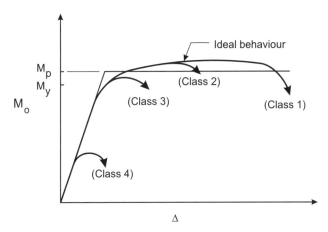

Figure 5.6 – Load vs. Deflection Relationships

5.4 Flange Local Buckling and its Consequences

As the compression region of the beam is subjected to increasing stresses as the external load increases, it is possible that at some level of stress less than the yield strength the plate elements that make up the cross-section (i.e., flange and web elements) will buckle. If this happens, no more load can be applied: attempts at increasing the load simply result in amplification of the buckle. The approach that is used in steel design is to establish limits on slenderness for any of the elements that are in compression such that the desired overall behaviour of the beam can be attained.

A segment of a beam with the compression flange of a beam already buckled is shown schematically in Figure 5.7(a), where the stresses indicated are those computed by the flexure theory. The compression flange is assumed to be braced so that lateral deflections of the flange plate are prevented (this will be discussed below). The web plate is assumed to be stocky enough to prevent vertical buckling of the flange [5.5]. Thus, the buckling mode consists of a twisting motion of the flange, together with a rotation of the web plate. The original cross-section and the buckled shape are shown in Figure 5.7(b).

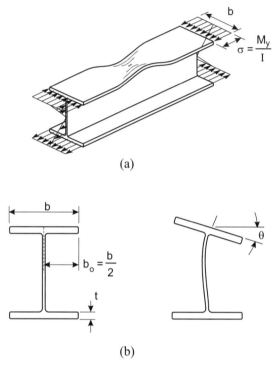

Figure 5.7 – Flange Buckling Considerations

At the critical moment, the flange simply twists about the flange-to-web junction. At this stage, the cross-section is unsymmetrical and further deformation produces a rapid reduction in moment capacity. The driving force behind the buckling motion consists of the component of stress on the plate that produces a twisting moment, T, once the plate assumes the buckled position [5.6]. This force is

$$T = \sigma (b\,t) \frac{b^2}{12} \frac{d\theta}{dx}$$ (5.4)

where $d\theta/dx$ represents the rate of change of the angle of twist along the length of the beam. The torque resisting the motion is produced primarily by the St. Venant (or, uniform) torsional moment developed in the plate and is given by:

$$T_R = JG\frac{d\theta}{dx} = \frac{1}{3}b\,t^3\,G\,\frac{d\theta}{dx} \tag{5.5}$$

where G is the shear modulus of the material and J is the St. Venant torsional constant. Since the plate must be in equilibrium in the deflected shape, the external (Equation 5.4) and resisting (Equation 5.5) torques are equal. Thus:

$$\frac{b}{2t} = \sqrt{G/\sigma} \tag{5.6}$$

Equation 5.6 can be used to restrict the plate width-to-thickness ratio, b /2t, so that the cross-section can develop the desired moment resistance before local buckling takes place. The curve labelled as Ideal Behaviour in Figure 5.6 represents the most favourable response that can be achieved. The moment resistance reaches M_p (the critical cross-section is fully yielded) and then increases slightly with further deformation as strain-hardening takes place. If the plastic moment capacity, M_p, is maintained through relatively large inelastic deformations, the section is called a Class 1 section. Class 1 sections, which have the capacity to both attain their plastic moment capacity and undergo inelastic rotations, enable the complete structure to redistribute bending moments and reach the load-carrying capacity anticipated on the basis of a plastic analysis. The implications of this requirement are discussed in Section 5.15.

For Class 1 sections, the factored moment resistance is specified in Clause 13.5(a) of S16–01, as:

$$M_r = \phi M_p = \phi Z F_y \tag{5.7}$$

Equation 5.6 can now be used to derive the plate proportions necessary to permit the capacity described in Equation 5.7 to be attained. (Sufficient rotation capacity to permit plastic design will also be present, although this does not show up in Equation 5.7). Taking the value of the shear modulus, G, in the yielded condition as 21×10^3 MPa [5.4] and setting the stress level in Equation 5.6 at the yield value, σ_y, the corresponding value of b / 2t is $145/\sqrt{F_y}$. In S16–01, the limitation is expressed in terms of a restriction on the half flange width (i.e., the overhanging width) $b_o = b/2$, and the specified minimum yield stress F_y . Thus, the rule is presented in the Standard as:

$$\frac{b_o}{t} \leq \frac{145}{\sqrt{F_y}} \tag{5.8}$$

The limiting width-to-thickness ratio specified for Class 2 sections is less restrictive than that for Class 1 since the requirements for large inelastic deformations do not exist. The moment resistance developed by the Class 2 section is equal to that of the stockier Class 1 section, however, and S16–01 specifies the moment resistance for both types of sections as that given in Equation 5.7. Tests on steel beams have shown that if

$$\frac{b_o}{t} \leq \frac{170}{\sqrt{F_y}} \tag{5.9}$$

then the member will be capable of developing the full plastic moment capacity [5.7]. This restriction is included in S16–01 Clause 11.2. The moment vs. deflection curve for the member would be similar to that shown for Class 2 sections in Figure 5.6, with the section buckling locally once M_p has been attained.

The width-to-thickness limits for Class 3 sections are still less restrictive than those for Class 2. Referring to Figure 5.6, the plates composing the cross-section should be capable of allowing the member to develop a moment resistance just equal to the yield moment, M_y, and in this condition the stress in the extreme fibre will be equal to the yield stress, σ_y. In general, the plate will behave elastically at this stage, although some deterioration due to the large compressive residual stresses in the flange tips may be expected. Using $G = 77\ 000$ MPa for steel in the elastic range, Equation 5.6 becomes:

$$\frac{b}{2\,t} \le \frac{277}{\sqrt{\sigma_y}} \tag{5.10}$$

If the value of b/2t exceeds that given by Equation 5.10, local buckling will occur before the moment resistance reaches M_y. After a reduction to account for the residual stress effect, the limitation contained in Equation 5.10 is expressed in S16–01 Clause 11.2 as:

$$\frac{b_o}{t} \le \frac{200}{\sqrt{F_y}} \tag{5.11}$$

If the compression flange of the member meets this limit, the behaviour will be that depicted by the curve for Class 3 sections in Figure 5.6.

The factored moment resistance specified for a Class 3 section in S16–01 Clause 13.5(b) is:

$$M_r = \phi\,M_y = \phi\,S\,F_y \tag{5.12}$$

Sections having plate components that are too slender to meet the requirements for Class 3 sections are classified as Class 4 sections. As shown in Figure 5.6, this type of section buckles locally at a moment less than M_y and the moment resistance is a function of the width-to-thickness ratios of the plates composing the section [5.5].

Clause 13.5(c) of S16–01 divides Class 4 sections into three categories. The first category contains those sections having both flange and web plates falling within Class 4. This type of section is designed to the requirements of CSA Standard S136–94, using the material properties appropriate to the structural steel specified [5.8].

The second category contains those sections having flanges meeting the requirements of Class 3 but having webs so slender as to place the section in Class 4. This type of section is designed according to the requirements of Clause 14 of S16–01, which bases the moment resistance on a consideration of the redistribution of load-carrying capacity between the portion of the web in compression and the compression flange. This type of member is discussed in detail in Chapter 7.

For those Class 4 sections having web plates meeting the Class 3 requirements but with compression flanges exceeding Class 3 limits, the moment resistance is governed by local buckling of the compression elements and is to be determined according to the requirements of CSA Standard S136–94. Alternatively, S16–01 permits the factored moment resistance to be computed using an effective elastic section modulus, S_e, determined by limiting the flange width, and calculated as follows:

$$M_r = \phi\, S_e\, F_y \qquad\qquad (5.13)$$

The effective flange width is limited to $670\, t \big/ \sqrt{F_y}$ for flanges supported along two edges parallel to the direction of stress and to $200\, t \big/ \sqrt{F_y}$ for flanges supported along one edge parallel to the direction of stress. A further limitation of $b/t \le 60$ is also imposed on flanges supported along one edge parallel to the direction of stress.

Workmen connect a beam to its supporting columns.

5.5   Web Buckling and Slenderness Limits

Depth-to-thickness limits for webs serve the same purpose as the width-to-thickness ratios prescribed for beam flanges. The individual elements comprising a cross-section must be able to carry the strains imposed upon them without buckling until the strength of the overall cross-section has been attained. This is conveniently, and with reasonable accuracy, done by limiting the width-to-thickness values of the individual elements of the cross-section. As described above, S16–01 does this by referring to Class 1 through Class 4 sections.

111

Web buckling under the action of a bending moment is not generally a problem in beams of usual proportions [5.9]. This is primarily because the stress condition on the web plate is much less severe than that on the compression flange. In addition, most of the resistance to moment is developed by the flange plates; thus, even if the web does buckle, the reduction in moment capacity is not severe.

For Class 1 sections, the web plate must accept strains that are sufficient to allow the cross section to become fully yielded. In order to achieve this condition, the h/w ratio for beams is limited in S16–01 Clause 11.2 to:

$$\frac{h}{w} \leq \frac{1100}{\sqrt{F_y}} \tag{5.14}$$

where h denotes the clear depth of web between flanges and w denotes the web thickness.

The requirements of Equation 5.14 were developed for plastically designed structures. The web slenderness requirements are not as stringent for Class 2 and Class 3 sections, where the strength and stability requirements are less severe. S16–01 thus adopts more liberal requirements for Class 2 and Class 3 sections, in Clause 11.2, respectively [5.10, 5.11].

$$\frac{h}{w} \leq \frac{1700}{\sqrt{F_y}} \quad \text{and,} \tag{5.15}$$

$$\frac{h}{w} \leq \frac{1900}{\sqrt{F_y}} \tag{5.16}$$

For Class 4 sections, the slenderness of the web must be limited so that the flange cannot deflect locally by buckling into the web. This is discussed in Chapter 7.

The limiting width-to-thickness ratios for each class of section are summarised in Table 5.1. In S16–01, these rules are presented in a more general form. In Table 2 of the Standard, the local buckling rules given for webs reduce to the values shown in Table 5.1 when the term C_f in those expressions is set equal to zero.

Table 5.1 – Width-to-Thickness Limits

Class	Flange	Web
Class 1	$b_o/t \leq 145/\sqrt{F_y}$	$h/w \leq 1100/\sqrt{F_y}$
Class 2	$b_o/t \leq 170/\sqrt{F_y}$	$h/w \leq 1700/\sqrt{F_y}$
Class 3	$b_o/t \leq 200/\sqrt{F_y}$	$h/w \leq 1900/\sqrt{F_y}$

5.6   Resistance Factor – Laterally Supported Members

In the S16–01 requirements, the moment resistance of a section is multiplied by a resistance factor, ϕ, to obtain the factored moment resistance. This factored moment resistance is then matched against the bending moments produced by the factored loads. The resistance factor, ϕ, is taken as 0.90 for members subjected to flexure. The purpose of the resistance factor is to take into account the variability of material properties, dimensions, and workmanship. Validity of the use of $\phi = 0.90$ for laterally supported members has been provided in references [5.12] and [5.13].

5.7   Design Examples

In the examples that follow, it is assumed that the members are braced laterally so that their capacities are limited by local buckling. Only the flexural capacities will be considered in these examples. Other factors, such as deflection, bracing spacing, shear, etc., can play a major part in beam design and will be illustrated later in this chapter.

Example 5.1

Given

A W310×52 beam of G40.21 350W steel (F_y = 350 MPa) spans 7300 mm and is connected to columns at either end by means of standard web angle connections. Compute the uniformly distributed factored load that the member can resist.

Solution

The cross-section dimensions and properties are tabulated in the CISC Handbook [5.14] as:

$$Z_x = 841 \times 10^3 \text{ mm}^3$$
$$b = 167 \text{ mm} \qquad d = 318 \text{ mm}$$
$$t = 13.2 \text{ mm} \qquad w = 7.6 \text{ mm}$$

As a first step, the plate proportions of a W310×52 section will be checked against the limiting values for a Class 2 section.

Flange $\quad \dfrac{b}{2t} = \dfrac{167}{2 \times 13.2} = 6.3$

Web $\quad \dfrac{h}{w} = \dfrac{d - 2t}{w} = \dfrac{318 - (2 \times 13.2)}{7.6} = 38.4$

The allowable flange width-to-thickness ratio is calculated according to Equation 5.9 as

$$\frac{170}{\sqrt{F_y}} = \frac{170}{\sqrt{350}} = 9.1$$

and the allowable web depth-to-thickness ratio is given by Equation 5.15 as:

$$\frac{1700}{\sqrt{F_y}} = \frac{1700}{\sqrt{350}} = 90.9$$

Since both the flange and web meet the prescribed limitations, the member is at least a Class 2 section and is capable of developing the plastic moment capacity. It will be assumed throughout that the example members are not intended for use in a plastically designed structure and thus it will not be necessary to meet the requirements for Class 1 sections.

For a Class 2 section, the factored moment resistance is given by Equation 5.7 as:

$$M_r = \phi Z_x F_y = 0.90 \times 841 \times 10^3 \text{ mm}^3 \times 350 \text{ MPa}$$

$$= 265 \times 10^6 \text{ N·mm} = 265 \text{ kN·m}$$

The maximum moment produced by the factored loading is $w_f L^2 / 8$, where w_f denotes the uniformly distributed factored load and L represents the span of the beam. For a satisfactory design:

$$M_r \geq \frac{w_f L^2}{8}$$

$$265 \text{ kN} \cdot \text{m} \geq w_f \times \frac{7.3 \text{ m} \times 7.3 \text{ m}}{8}$$

$$\therefore w_f \leq \frac{265 \text{ kN} \cdot \text{m} \times 8}{7.3 \text{ m} \times 7.3 \text{ m}} = 39.8 \text{ kN/m}$$

Tables contained in the CISC Handbook [5.14] can be used to greatly simplify the calculations. For example, the factored moment resistance is tabulated directly for the W310×52 section, as is the factored load capacity.

Example 5.2

Given

A beam is to be selected to span 11 000 mm. The bending moment diagram has been obtained from an analysis of the structure and is shown in Figure 5.8. The member is to be of G40.21 350W steel (F_y = 350 MPa).

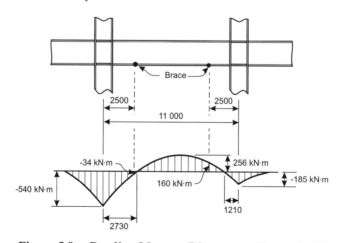

Figure 5.8 – Bending Moment Diagram — Example 5.2

Solution

Before the moment resistance can be determined, the plate width-to-thickness ratios for the section must be known. Most rolled sections at least meet the requirements for Class 2 (for the carbon or low alloy steels), however, and this knowledge can be used to initiate the design.

The factored moment resistance is computed from Equation 5.7, assuming that the member to be selected will be a Class 2 section[1]:

$$M_r = \phi M_p = \phi Z_x F_y$$

The required plastic section modulus for the member is determined on the basis of the maximum bending moment that occurs within the length of the member as a result of the factored loads (Figure 5.8):

$$\text{required } Z_x = \frac{M_{f\,max}}{\phi F_y}$$

$$= \frac{540 \text{ kN} \cdot \text{m}}{0.9 \times 350 \text{ MPa}} = \frac{540 \times 10^6 \text{ N} \cdot \text{mm}}{0.9 \times 350 \text{ N}/\text{mm}^2} = 1714 \times 10^3 \text{ mm}^3$$

Many factors enter into the selection of the member: these will be discussed as they arise. One possible member that has a plastic modulus meeting that required is used in the following calculations.

Try W530× 82, for which $Z_x = 2060 \times 10^3 \text{ mm}^3$

The plate proportions must now be checked to ensure that the member does meet the requirements for a Class 2 section and that the factored moment resistance assumed above is therefore correct. The cross-section dimensions are given in the CISC Handbook and the actual flange and web plate slenderness values are calculated as shown.

$$d = 528 \text{ mm} \qquad\qquad t = 13.3 \text{ mm}$$

$$b = 209 \text{ mm} \qquad\qquad w = 9.5 \text{ mm}$$

$$\text{Flange} \quad \frac{b}{2t} = \frac{209}{2 \times 13.3} = 7.9$$

$$\text{Web} \quad \frac{h}{w} = \frac{d - 2t}{w} = \frac{528 - (2 \times 13.3)}{9.5} = 52.8$$

The limiting width-to-thickness ratios for a Class 2 section flange and web are given by Equations 5.9 and 5.15, respectively:

$$\text{Flange} \quad \frac{170}{\sqrt{F_y}} = \frac{170}{\sqrt{350}} = 9.1$$

---

[1] It should be remembered that the moment capacity for Class 1 and Class 2 sections is identical, and given by Equation 5.7.

Web $\qquad \dfrac{1700}{\sqrt{F_y}} = \dfrac{1700}{\sqrt{350}} = 90.9$

Since both plate slenderness ratios are within the allowable limits, the section is of Class 2, and thus the moment resistance assumed is correct. The W530×82 section may be used. A W460×82 section will also be satisfactory for this situation. In this case, both beams are of equal weight. The W460×82 would be advantageous for use in a multi-storey building because it minimizes the depth of floor construction and would thereby reduce storey height. However, if deflection control is required, then the additional depth of the 528 mm deep section may be necessary. (See Section 5.9 on deflections.)

In the calculations made above it was assumed that the beam is braced laterally to prevent failure of the beam by lateral instability before the capacity of the beam predicted by Equation 5.7 is reached. Lateral stability of beams is treated in Section 5.10.

The Beam Selection Tables contained in the CISC Handbook [5.14] can be used to great advantage in the member selection process. For example, the most economical sections that will provide a factored moment resistance greater than 540 kN·m are listed in this reference.

5.8 The Effect of Shear on Beam Strength

In the selection procedure described above the influence of the shear force was ignored. Theoretically, the presence of a shear force will reduce the flexural strength of the cross-section. However, it is impossible to separate this weakening influence from the increase in strength produced through strain-hardening. In fact, experiments have shown that beams tested under relatively high shear forces will develop moment capacities that are approximately 15% greater than beams tested under pure moment (zero shear) conditions [5.4]. However, the web may fail either by shear buckling or shear yielding before the full flexural capacity of the section has been attained. Thus, the strength of the beam is reduced below its capacity under pure bending. The slenderness of the web of most standard rolled section is often sufficiently small such that buckling will not take place before yielding. The primary problem then is to prevent premature shear yielding of the member [5.4].

According to the von Mises yield criterion, yielding in shear occurs when the shear stress reaches the following value [5.4]:

$$\tau_y = \sigma_y / \sqrt{3} \qquad (5.17)$$

or, in terms of the specified minimum yield stress:

$$\tau_y = 0.58 \, F_y \qquad (5.18)$$

Noting that the major portion of the shear in a wide flange member is carried by the web [5.3], the factored shear resistance is expressed in S16–01 Clause 13.4.1 as:

$$V_r = \phi \, A_w \, F_s \qquad (5.19)$$

where A_w represents the shear area, the gross cross-sectional area of the web. It is taken as equal to $d \times w$ for rolled sections and F_s is taken as 0.66 F_y. Note that the effective value of the shear yield stress, F_s, has been increased above the value given in Equation 5.18 to account for the beneficial effects of strain-hardening.

If the web is relatively slender, it can buckle under the action of the shear stresses before it is completely yielded. In this case, the shear stress, F_s, is reduced from $0.66F_y$. This situation, which arises most often with plate girders, will be covered in Chapter 7. For rolled and standard welded shapes, the shear strength, F_s, can be set equal to $0.66F_y$ provided that, as specified in S16–01 Clause 13.4.1.1,

$$\frac{h}{w} \leq 439 \sqrt{\frac{k_v}{F_y}} \tag{5.20}$$

In Equation 5.20, k_v is a shear buckling coefficient and it has a value of 5.34 for an unstiffened web [5.9]. The restriction imposed by Equation 5.20 ensures that shear buckling will not take place before the web is completely yielded.

Example 5.3

Given

Check the W530× 82 beam of Example 5.2 for shear. The maximum shear force caused by the factored loads is 540 kN.

Solution

The dimensions of the W530× 82 section are given in the CISC Handbook as

d = 528 mm;   t = 13.3 mm;   w = 9.5 mm

As a first step, the clear web depth-to-thickness ratio is computed:

$$\frac{h}{w} = \frac{d - 2t}{w} = \frac{528 - (2 \times 13.3)}{9.5} = 52.8$$

The allowable web slenderness ratio, according to Equation 5.20, is:

$$439 \sqrt{\frac{k_v}{F_y}} = 439 \sqrt{\frac{5.34}{350}} = 54.2$$

Since the actual h/w is less than the limit specified, premature shear buckling is precluded. Yielding will limit the shear strength of the member and Equation 5.19 can be used to compute the factored resistance.

$$V_r = \phi A_w F_s = 0.90 \times 528 \text{ mm} \times 9.5 \text{ mm} \times 0.66 \times 350 \text{ MPa}$$

$$= 1043 \times 10^3 \text{ N} = 1043 \text{ kN}$$

Since the actual shear force produced by the factored loads is less than the factored shear resistance, the W530× 82 is adequate in shear. As a general note, shear will only govern the design of rolled or standard welded sections when the member is used over an extremely short span or is subjected to a large concentrated load. Other potentially dangerous situations may occur when a part of the cross-section is removed.

5.9   Limitations on Deflection

The deflections of a structure are a measure of this general serviceability. If the deflections of the beams and girders are relatively large, cracking may be expected in the floor or roof slabs. Similarly, excessive lateral deflections under wind loading are a sign that cracking of partitions and annoying vibrations may be expected.

The deflections of floor beams or girders may be limited for several reasons. If the deflections are unusually large, the occupants may be affected directly. For example, windows and doors may not operate properly. In extreme cases, the sag of a beam may be visible to the observer, creating an undesirable impression. If the beam or girder supports a plastered ceiling, the deflections of the member may cause cracking of the plaster. Similar distress may occur in brick walls, rigid partitions, piping, etc. In these cases, the non-structural elements are incorporated in the structure during construction. It is usual, therefore, to limit the deflections under live load only (or under the portion of the loads applied after the non-structural element of concern is incorporated to the structure) so that non-structural damage does not occur. For roof beams, similar restrictions have been formulated.

The permissible deflection of a member depends on the nature of the non-structural materials supported by the structure. In many cases, information, based either on test results or on the manufacturer's recommendations will be available for guidance. In the absence of such information, Appendix D of S16–01 recommends limits for both vertical and lateral deflections caused by the specified live loads. For example, the recommended maximum vertical deflections are:

INDUSTRIAL TYPE BUILDINGS

Due to:

Live Load	Members supporting inelastic roof coverings	1/240 of span
Live Load	Members supporting elastic roof coverings	1/180 of span
Live Load	Members supporting floors	1/300 of span
Maximum Wheel Loads (no impact)	Crane runway girders for crane capacity of 225 kN and over	1/800 of span
Maximum Wheel Loads (no impact)	Crane runway girders for crane capacity under 225 kN	1/600 of span

ALL OTHER BUILDINGS

Live Load	Members of floors and roofs supporting construction and finishes susceptible to cracking	1/360 of span
Live Load	Members of floors and roofs supporting construction and finishes not susceptible to cracking	1/300 of span

It is important to note that the deflections considered are those corresponding to the specified load levels, not the factored loads. Deflections must be checked at the specified load levels to ensure that the building will be serviceable but, except for the sway effects discussed in Chapters 8 and 10, deflections do not generally influence the strength of the structure.

The deflections caused by dead loads can also be computed and, if significant, they can be counteracted by cambering the member. In this process, a preset deflection (opposite in sense to that caused by the applied loads) is built into the member. Cambering can be achieved by cold bending, although this is usually practical only for smaller members. For larger members, cambering is done by heating one flange of the member either locally or uniformly along the length [5.15]. Cambering is not usually necessary in building structures having small or moderate spans.

In the past, the restrictions on deflections due to static load have been sufficient in most cases to guard against such problems as walking vibrations associated with the activity of people. However, with the trend to longer spans and lighter construction, more attention must be paid to these effects. The National Building Code of Canada states that a dynamic analysis shall be used to determine the effects of vibrations due to machinery or rhythmic group activities, such as aerobic exercises, if the natural frequency of the floor is less than 6 Hz. Considerable design guidance has been published [5.16, 5.17].

Example 5.4

Given

The W310×52 beam considered in Example 5.1 spans 7300 mm and is subjected to a specified dead load of 7.2 kN/m and a specified live load of 16.6 kN/m. Calculate the dead and live load deflections and check to see that the live load deflection of the member meets the S16 requirements. It is assumed that the member supports an asphaltic roof membrane in an industrial building.

Solution

As shown in Example 5.1, the W310×52 member can safely support a factored uniformly distributed load of 33.9 kN/m.

The moment of inertia about the axis of bending for the W310×52 section is listed in the CISC Handbook as $I_x = 119 \times 10^6$ mm^4 and the maximum deflection due to dead load is calculated as

$$\Delta_D = \frac{5 \, w \, L^4}{384 \, EI} = \frac{5 \times 7.2 \, kN/m \times (7300 \, mm)^4}{384 \times 200\,000 \, MPa \times 119 \times 10^6 \, mm^4} = 11.2 \, mm$$

and the deflection due to live load is:

$$\Delta_L = \frac{5 \, w \, L^4}{384 \, EI} = \frac{5 \times 16.6 \, kN/m \times (7300 \, mm)^4}{384 \times 200\,000 \, MPa \times 119 \times 10^6 \, mm^4} = 25.8 \, mm$$

The allowable live load deflection for a beam supporting an asphaltic roof is given by S16–01 in Appendix D as:

$$\Delta \le \frac{L}{240} = \frac{7300}{240} = 30 \, mm$$

Since the actual live load deflection is approximately 26 mm, less than the limit, the member is satisfactory. The dead load deflection (11 mm) is small and, under normal circumstances, a member of this length would not be cambered to accommodate it.

In the calculation of deflections, the CISC Handbook may also be utilised. The deflections of the member under various loading conditions can be computed by using the tables provided.

5.10   Laterally Unbraced Beams

It has been assumed thus far that the strength of the beam is determined by the capacity of its cross-section and this, in turn, is dependent on the local buckling capacity of its plate elements. In most cases, this assumption is valid. However, if the beam is laterally unsupported the strength may be governed instead by lateral-torsional buckling of the complete member.

A plot of the relationship between the applied moment, M, and the resulting mid-span deflection, Δ, for a member length, L, is shown in Figure 5.9. The member, shown in the insert to the figure, is subjected to end moments producing a uniform bending moment distribution over the length of the span. Lateral supports are assumed to be present at the ends of the member so that the laterally unbraced length is equal to the span length.

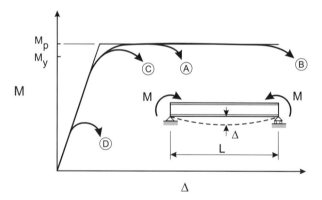

Figure 5.9 – Moment vs. Deflection Relationships

At low values of M, the member will respond elastically. However, as the moment is increased, yielding will occur as a result of the strains produced by the applied moment and the residual strains in the cross-section. Further increases in the applied moment will result in general yielding over the cross-section as the moment approaches M_p.

Figure 5.10 depicts the movement of the cross-section during this loading process. As the member is loaded, the cross-section moves vertically from its initial position. At some stage of loading, however, the cross-section may twist and bend about its weak axis: lateral-torsional buckling has occurred. Lateral-torsional buckling can occur at any stage during the loading history—after the member reached M_p, as shown by curves A and B in Figure 5.9; between M_y and M_p, as shown by curve C; and even at moments below M_y, as shown by curve D. The lateral-torsional buckling capacity of the member

120

depends on its unbraced length, the bending moment distribution along the length of the member, the location of the applied load on the cross section, the restraint conditions at the supports, and on a variety of cross-sectional properties.

The following treatment of lateral-torsional buckling is based on the assumption that the load is applied at the shear centre of the member. Loads applied at the bottom flange tend to stabilize the member, whereas loads applied on the top flange (above the shear centre) would destabilize the member. This is discussed later in the section.

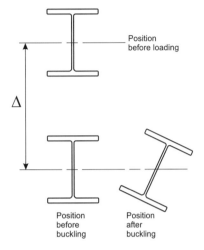

Figure 5.10 – Lateral-Torsional Buckling Motion

Lateral-torsional buckling of a beam is analogous to flexural buckling in a column in that both represent ideal situations. The actual beam will contain imperfections, so that lateral deflections will be present even before loading. These deflections will be amplified as the moment is increased, and, as the critical value is approached, the deflections will grow rapidly. The moment capacity may increase slightly beyond this stage, then drop off rapidly as inelastic action produced by the out-of-plane motion of the beam decreases its resistance.

Just as in the case of axially loaded columns, for purposes of discussion laterally unbraced beams can be classified into stocky, intermediate, and slender members. Figure 5.11 shows schematically the relationship between the moment causing lateral-torsional buckling, M_{cr}, and the length, L, which represents the distance between points of positive lateral support.

A stocky beam is defined as a beam that is able to reach its local buckling capacity before lateral-torsional buckling occurs. (The local buckling capacity has been determined in the previous sections as M_p for a Class 1 or 2 section and M_y for a Class 3 section.) On the other hand, a slender beam buckles laterally before the member yields. The important section properties that are used to determine the lateral-torsional buckling strength can be computed on the basis of full elastic action. For the intermediate member, the bending moment at the instant before lateral-torsional buckling is sufficient to cause portions of the member to yield (the yielding is a result of the strains due to the applied moment adding to the residual strains); thus, the resistance of the member to both lateral and twisting motions is reduced.

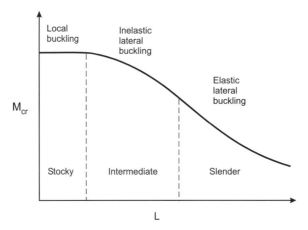

Figure 5.11 – Beam Failure Modes

The resistance of the member to lateral bending depends upon the weak axis bending stiffness of the cross-section, $E\,I_y$. The resistance to a twisting motion can be broken into two portions. One portion is termed the St. Venant resistance and is a function of the stiffness term, $G\,J$, where G is the shear modulus (or, modulus of rigidity) and J is the St. Venant torsional constant for the section. For a section such as the wide flange shape, $J = \sum(l\,t^3)/3$ where l and t represent the length and thickness, respectively, for each plate and the summation extends over all plates in the cross-section. The St. Venant torsional resistance is generated by shear stresses developed by the rotation of adjacent cross-sections and is discussed in detail in texts on mechanics of materials [5.3].

The second component of resistance to twisting, the warping resistance, is developed by cross-bending of the flanges. As the beam twists, the cross-section rotates about its centroidal axis and this motion induces lateral bending strains in the flanges. These strains result in the development of flange bending moments and accompanying shear forces acting in the plane of each flange. The couple produced by the shear forces at a particular section makes up the warping torsional resistance and it is a function of the warping constant for the section, C_w, where $C_w = I_y\,(d-t)^2/4$ for I-shaped sections.

For a beam subjected to end moments producing a constant bending moment distribution and having simply supported boundary conditions[2], the moment at which lateral-torsional buckling will occur is given by [5.18]

$$M_u = \frac{\pi}{L}\sqrt{E\,I_y\,G\,J+\left(\frac{\pi\,E}{L}\right)^2 I_y\,C_w} \qquad (5.21)$$

Equation 5.21 is conservative for most actual situations since the bending moment distribution is not likely to be uniform, as has been assumed, and since the connections between the beams and the supporting columns will provide some restraint.

Equation 5.21 provides a reasonable estimate of the moment at which lateral-torsional buckling will occur, provided that the strains in the member at buckling are less

---

[2] A simple support in torsion implies that twisting is prevented but warping of the cross-section is free to take place.

than the yield strain. Thus, Equation 5.21 is accepted as the basis for the design of slender members.

Because of the presence of relatively large residual stresses in the flange tips, yielding will occur when the applied moment reaches approximately two-thirds of the local buckling capacity of the member, i.e., M_p or M_y, as appropriate. This implies that the maximum residual stress is approximately one-third of the yield stress. Equation 5.21 is thus valid until M_u reaches two-thirds (0.67) M_p for Class 1 or 2 sections, or two-thirds (0.67) M_y for Class 3 or 4 sections. For these cases, S16–01 specifies in Clause 13.6 that the factored moment resistance is to be taken as:

$$M_r = \phi M_u \tag{5.22}$$

For more stocky members, that is, when M_u is above $0.67 M_p$ (for Class 1 or 2 sections) or $0.67 M_y$ (for Class 3 or 4 sections), the assumptions made in deriving the elastic buckling equation are no longer valid because the compression flange has been considerably weakened by yielding at the flange tips. The factored moment resistance is therefore reduced empirically (Clauses 13.6(a) and 13.6(b) of S16–01):

$$M_r = 1.15 \phi M_p \left(1 - \frac{0.28 M_p}{M_u} \right) \tag{5.23}$$

for Class 1 or 2 sections, or

$$M_r = 1.15 \phi M_y \left(1 - \frac{0.28 M_y}{M_u} \right) \tag{5.24}$$

for Class 3 or 4 sections.

Regardless of the results of the lateral-torsional buckling calculations (Equations 5.23 and 5.24), in no case may the moment resistance exceed that based on local buckling. Thus, $M_r < \phi M_p$ for Class 1 and 2 sections (Equation 5.7) and $M_r < \phi M_y$ or $\phi S_e F_y$ for Class 3 and 4 sections, respectively (Equations 5.12 and 5.13).

These provisions are depicted in Figure 5.12, where the moment resistance is plotted against the unbraced length for a W530×92 section of G40.21 350W steel. If the beam has an unbraced length greater than 5200 mm, the factored moment resistance is given by Equation 5.22. If the unbraced length is between 2700 mm and 5200 mm, the factored moment resistance is given by Equation 5.23, and for shorter members, those having lengths less than 2700 mm, lateral-torsional buckling is not a problem and the factored moment resistance is given by Equation 5.7, which is based on local buckling.

The S16 Standard presents calculations of the elastic lateral-torsional buckling strength (given herein by Equation 5.21) in a more general form, namely:

$$M_u = \frac{\omega_2 \pi}{L} \sqrt{E I_y G J + \left(\frac{\pi E}{L} \right)^2 I_y C_w} \tag{5.25}$$

Equation 5.25 is identical to Equation 5.21 except that a modifier ω_2 has been introduced. This accounts for the fact that not all members will be subjected to uniform moment throughout the length of the beam between brace points, as was assumed in the development of Equation 5.21. Any other condition means that the moment resistance will be larger than that given by Equation 5.21. An adequate way of handling this is by the introduction of the moment modifier, ω_2. It depends upon the loading condition, conditions of lateral support, and the moment gradient that exists between the points of lateral support The expression used in S16–01 Clause 18.6 is:

$$\omega_2 = 1.75 + 1.05\,\kappa + 0.3\,\kappa^2 \le 2.5 \tag{5.26}$$

where κ is the ratio of the smaller factored bending moment to the larger factored bending moments at opposite ends of the unbraced length. The ratio κ is positive for members bent in double curvature and negative for members bent in single curvature.

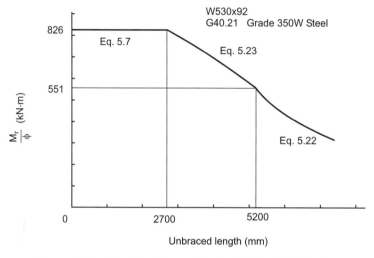

Figure 5.12 – Bending Strength of a W530 × 92 Member

When the bending moment at any point within the unbraced length is larger than the larger end moment or when there is no effective lateral support for the compression flange at one of the ends of the unsupported length, the value of the modifier is to be taken as $\omega_2 = 1.0$.

As indicated in Figure 5.10, the movement of a cross-section during the buckling motion is characterized by lateral deflection of the top (compression) flange and a rotation of the cross-section. During the motion, the tension flange remains relatively straight. A laterally braced point, therefore, is a location at which this buckling motion is prevented. The compression flange might be held laterally by the floor slab or roof deck attached to the beam flange. Alternatively, framing members at right angles to the beam will provide lateral support, provided they are properly anchored. Figure 5.13 illustrates two cases of members framing at right angle. Transverse beams *a* are properly anchored by horizontal bracing and therefore provide lateral bracing to the main beams. Transverse beams *b*, however, are not anchored and do not act as points of bracing for the main beams.

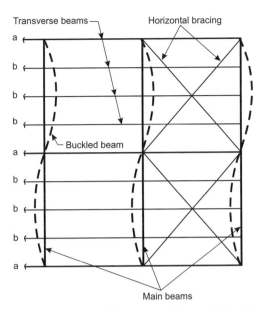

Figure 5.13 – Lateral Bracing of Beams (Plan View)

In cases where it is impossible to brace the compression flange directly, the brace can be attached to the tension flange. A stiffener is then required to prevent distortion of the cross-section and, in addition, the bracing member and the connection must possess sufficient flexural stiffness to prevent rotation of the member cross-section.

In the cases discussed above, it was assumed that the beams were loaded through their shear centre. The application of loads to the top flange tends to make the beam less stable and Equation 5.25 would need to be adjusted for such conditions [5.19]. Although beams that support floor slabs are loaded on their top flange, it is common practice to neglect the beneficial restraint offered by the floor slab. For this reason, the use of Equation 5.25 for beams loaded at their top flange through a floor slab is considered adequate. On the other hand, flexural members such as crane runway girders are often loaded at their top flange and the use of Equation 5.25 for this situation is not conservative. Reference [5.19] can be consulted for guidance in this respect. This reference also addresses the effect of end boundary conditions on the lateral torsional buckling capacity of flexural members.

5.11   Resistance Factor – Laterally Unsupported Beams

In S16–01, the resistance factor, ϕ, is taken as 0.90 for members whose strength is governed by lateral-torsional buckling [5.13]. Earlier studies indicate that, theoretically, ϕ should vary with the cross-section shape and the unbraced length for members buckling laterally after portions of the cross-section have yielded. [5.18] The values for a W610×113 section, for example, having a specified minimum yield stress of 350 MPa range from 0.88 for a slenderness ratio, $L/r_y = 34$ to 0.83 for $L/r_y = 113$ [5.12].

At first glance, S16–01 appears to be slightly non-conservative as compared with the above recommendations, especially for the intermediate range of slenderness ratios. More recent work, however, which has focused on shapes commonly used in Canada, does confirm the validity of the recommended resistance factor [5.13].

125

Example 5.5

Given

The W310×52 beam of Example 5.1 spans 7300 mm and is subject to a uniformly distributed load. What factored load can the member resist if it is braced laterally only at the supports?

Solution

The dimensions and section properties for the W310×52 are listed in the CISC Handbook.

d = 318 mm	t = 13.2 mm	b = 167 mm
w = 7.6 mm	Z_x = 841×10³ mm³	J = 308×10³ mm⁴
I_y = 10.3×10⁶ mm⁴	S_x = 750×10³ mm³	C_w = 238×10⁹ mm⁶

The plate slenderness ratios for the W310×52 were checked in Example 5.1. The member is a Class 2 section and the factored moment resistance for a Class 2 member of G40.21 350W steel (F_y = 350 MPa) based on local buckling is computed according to Equation 5.7 as:

$$M_r = \phi Z_x F_y = 0.90 \times 841 \times 10^3 \text{ mm}^3 \times 350 \text{ MPa}$$

$$= 265 \times 10^6 \text{ N} \cdot \text{mm} = 265 \text{ kN} \cdot \text{m}$$

The critical moment, based on the assumption that failure will be accompanied by elastic lateral-torsional buckling, is computed using Equation 5.25. Using E = 200 000 MPa and G = 77×10³ MPa , the critical moment is:

$$M_u = \frac{\omega_2 \, \pi}{L} \sqrt{E \, I_y \, G \, J + \left(\frac{\pi \, E}{L}\right)^2 I_y \, C_w}$$

$$= \frac{1.0 \, \pi}{7300} \sqrt{A + B}$$

$$= \frac{1.0 \, \pi}{7300 \text{ mm}} \sqrt{488 \times 10^{20} \text{ MPa}^2 \text{ mm}^8 + 182 \times 10^{20} \text{ MPa}^2 \text{ mm}^8}$$

$$= 111 \times 10^6 \text{ N} \cdot \text{mm} = 111 \text{ kN} \cdot \text{m}$$

where

$$A = 200\,000 \text{ MPa} \times 10.3 \times 10^6 \text{ mm}^4 \times 77\,000 \text{ MPa} \times 308 \times 10^3 \text{ mm}^4$$

$$= 488 \times 10^{20} \text{ MPa}^2 \text{mm}^8$$

$$B = \left(\frac{\pi \times 200\,000 \text{ MPa}}{7300 \text{ mm}}\right)^2 \times 10.3 \times 10^6 \text{ mm}^4 \times 238 \times 10^9 \text{ mm}^6$$

$$= 182 \times 10^{20} \text{ MPa}^2 \text{mm}^8$$

and ω_2 has been taken as 1.0 because the bending moment within the unbraced length is larger than the moments at the ends.

If the critical moment given by Equation 5.25 is greater than $0.67\,M_p$ for a Class 2 section, the moment resistance must be reduced to account for inelastic action.

$$0.67\,M_p = 0.67 \times Z_x\,F_y = 0.67 \times 841 \times 10^3 \text{ mm}^3 \times 350 \text{ MPa}$$
$$= 197 \times 10^6 \text{ N} \cdot \text{mm} = 197 \text{ kN} \cdot \text{m}$$

Since $M_u < 0.67\,M_p$, no reduction is required and the factored moment resistance can now be computed according to Equation 5.22 as:

$$M_r = \phi\,M_u = 0.90 \times 111 \text{ kN} \cdot \text{m} = 100 \text{ kN} \cdot \text{m}$$

The actual bending moment (maximum) is $w\,L^2/8$. For a satisfactory design:

$$M_r \geq \frac{w\,L^2}{8}$$

$$100 \text{ kN} \cdot \text{m} \geq \frac{w \times (7300 \text{ mm})^2}{8}$$

$$\therefore w \leq \frac{100 \text{ kN} \cdot \text{m} \times 8}{(7.3 \text{ m})^2} \leq 15 \text{ kN}/\text{m}$$

The factored load-carrying capacity for the unbraced member is 15 kN/m whereas, if the member had been braced laterally, the factored load-carrying capacity would have been 39.6 kN/m (Example 5.1). Thus, the absence of lateral support has reduced the carrying capacity of the member significantly.

The tabulated values in the CISC Handbook [5.14] can be used to reduce the computational effort involved in the design of laterally unsupported beams. For example, the Beam Selection Tables tabulate the factored moment resistance for selected values of laterally unsupported length.

Example 5.6

Given

Select a member of G40.21 350W steel ($F_y = 350 \text{ MPa}$) to span 7300 mm as a simply supported beam. The member is laterally supported only at the ends and must carry a factored uniformly distributed load of 43 kN/m.

Solution

This problem is simply an inverted form of Example 5.5. In order to arrive at a solution, a member first must be selected and then checked. Since the moment resistance depends on the proportions of the cross-section, general rules for selecting members are difficult to formulate. In the absence of design tables such as those given in the CISC Handbook [5.14], a trial and error procedure is necessary. Since these CISC tables cover only members of Grades 300W and 350W steel, the more general procedure will be illustrated.

From the computations of Example 5.5, it is evident that the W310×52 will not be adequate. A heavier section will be selected and checked.

Try a W310×79.

The dimensions and section properties for the W310×79 are listed in the CISC Handbook:

$d = 306$ mm $\qquad\qquad$ $t = 14.6$ mm $\qquad\qquad$ $b = 254$ mm

$w = 8.8$ mm $\qquad\qquad$ $Z_x = 1280 \times 10^3$ mm^3 $\qquad$ $J = 657 \times 10^3$ mm^4

$I_y = 39.9 \times 10^6$ mm^4 $\qquad$ $C_w = 847 \times 10^9$ mm^6

The plate slenderness ratios are first computed to determine whether the member meets the restrictions for a Class 2 section.

$$\text{Flange} \qquad \frac{b}{2t} = \frac{254}{2 \times 14.6} = 8.7$$

$$\text{Web} \qquad \frac{h}{w} = \frac{d - 2t}{w} = \frac{306 - (2 \times 14.6)}{8.8} = 31.5$$

The allowable flange width-to-thickness ratios are given by Equations 5.9 and 5.15 for the flange and web, respectively, as

$$\frac{170}{\sqrt{F_y}} = \frac{170}{\sqrt{350}} = 9.1$$

$$\frac{1700}{\sqrt{F_y}} = \frac{1700}{\sqrt{350}} = 90.9$$

Since the flange and web slenderness ratios are within the specified limits, the cross-section is classified as Class 2, and the factored moment resistance based on the local buckling strength is given by Equation 5.7:

$$M_r = \phi Z_x F_y = 0.90 \times 1280 \times 10^3 \text{ mm}^3 \times 350 \text{ MPa}$$

$$= 403 \times 10^6 \text{ N} \cdot \text{mm} = 403 \text{ kN} \cdot \text{m}$$

The critical moment based on the assumption that failure will be accompanied by elastic lateral-torsional buckling is calculated according to Equation 5.25:

$$M_u = \frac{\omega_2 \pi}{L} \sqrt{E I_y \, G J + \left(\frac{\pi E}{L}\right)^2 I_y \, C_w}$$

$$= \frac{1.0 \times \pi}{7300 \text{ mm}} \sqrt{A + B}$$

$$= \frac{1.0 \times \pi}{7300 \text{ mm}} \sqrt{4037 \times 10^{20} \text{ MPa}^2 \text{ mm}^8 + 2504 \times 10^{20} \text{ MPa}^2 \text{ mm}^8}$$

$$= 348 \times 10^6 \text{ N} \cdot \text{mm} = 348 \text{ kN} \cdot \text{m}$$

where

$$A = 200\,000 \text{ MPa} \times 39.9 \times 10^6 \text{ mm}^4 \times 77\,000 \text{ MPa} \times 657 \times 10^3 \text{ mm}^4$$

$$= 4037 \times 10^{20} \text{ MPa}^2 \text{ mm}^8$$

$$B = \left(\frac{\pi \times 200\,000 \text{ MPa}}{7300 \text{ mm}} \right)^2 \times 39.9 \times 10^6 \text{ mm}^4 \times 847 \times 10^9 \text{ mm}^6$$

$$= 2504 \times 10^{20} \text{ MPa}^2 \text{ mm}^8$$

and ω_2 has been taken as 1.0 because the bending moment within the unbraced length is larger than the moments at the ends.

For a Class 2 section, if $M_u > 0.67 \, M_p$ then the moment capacity must be based on a reduced moment in order to account for the effects of inelastic action.

$$M_p = Z_x \, F_y = 1280 \times 10^3 \text{ mm}^3 \times 350 \text{ MPa}$$

$$= 448 \times 10^6 \text{ N} \cdot \text{mm} = 448 \text{ kN} \cdot \text{m}$$

$$0.67 \, M_p = 0.67 \times 448 = 300 \text{ kN} \cdot \text{m}$$

Since $348 > 300$, the factored moment resistance must be calculated from Equation 5.23:

$$M_r = 1.15 \, \phi \, M_p \left(1 - \frac{0.28 \, M_p}{M_u} \right)$$

$$= 1.15 \times 0.90 \times 448 \left(1 - \frac{0.28 \times 448}{348} \right) = 297 \text{ kN} \cdot \text{m}$$

Finally, this moment capacity of 297 $\text{kN} \cdot \text{m}$, which is based on the lateral-torsional buckling capacity, must be compared with the capacity based on the strength of the cross-section. The latter has been calculated by Equation 5.7 to be 403 $\text{kN} \cdot \text{m}$. Thus, the governing capacity is $M_r = 297 \text{ kN} \cdot \text{m}$.

The actual bending moment on the member is $w \, L^2 / 8 = 1/8 \times 43 \text{ kN/m} \times (7.3 \text{ m})^2 = 286 \text{ kN} \cdot \text{m}$. Since the factored moment resistance for the $W310 \times 79$ has been calculated to be 297 $\text{kN} \cdot \text{m}$, the choice is therefore satisfactory.

Using the tables in the CISC Handbook [5.14] the member can be selected with ease, although interpolation will be required in most cases. The tables are scrutinized for the lightest section that will provide the factored moment resistance according to the unbraced length in question. In this example, the factored bending moment of 297 $\text{kN} \cdot \text{m}$ and the unbraced length of 7300 mm are the governing conditions. Perusal of the tables in the Handbook indicates that a $W310 \times 79$ section of Grade 350W steel is a suitable choice, as expected.

Example 5.7

Given

If the W530×82 section used in Example 5.2 is supported laterally along the top flange by the attachment of the floor deck and the bottom flange is braced at 2500 mm from the columns centreline as indicated in Figure 5.8, is additional bracing required in the negative moment region?

Solution

The W530×82 is a Class 2 section in G40.21 350W steel (See Example 5.2). The factored moment resistance, based only on local buckling considerations, is calculated from Equation 5.7:

$$M_r = \phi Z_x F_y = 0.90 \times 2060 \times 10^3 \text{ mm}^3 \times 350 \text{ MPa}$$

$$= 649 \times 10^6 \text{ N} \cdot \text{mm} = 649 \text{ kN} \cdot \text{m}$$

Since the maximum bending moment produced by the factored loads is 540 kN·m, as shown in Figure 5.8, the W530×82 section will be satisfactory in those regions where the member can develop (approximately) its fully braced capacity. The bending moment values at the columns and at the bottom flange braced points are shown on the diagram of Figure 5.8. One potentially critical area is that adjacent to the left support. In order for the W530×82 section to be satisfactory without additional bracing of the bottom (compression) flange, the section must develop a factored moment resistance of at least 540 kN·m over the unbraced length of 2500 mm.

The dimensions and section properties for the W530×82 section are listed in the CISC Handbook:

$d = 528 \text{ mm}$ $\qquad\qquad$ $t = 13.3 \text{ mm}$

$b = 209 \text{ mm}$ $\qquad\qquad$ $w = 9.5 \text{ mm}$

$Z_x = 2060 \times 10^3 \text{ mm}^3$ $\qquad\qquad$ $J = 518 \times 10^3 \text{ mm}^4$

$I_y = 20.3 \times 10^6 \text{ mm}^4$ $\qquad\qquad$ $C_w = 1340 \times 10^9 \text{ mm}^6$

The length of the member between points of lateral support is 2500 mm. The critical moment, based on the assumption that failure will be associated with elastic lateral-torsional buckling of the unbraced length, is calculated from Equation 5.25:

$$M_u = \frac{\omega_2 \pi}{L} \sqrt{E I_y G J + \left(\frac{\pi E}{L}\right)^2 I_y C_w}$$

$$= \frac{1.69 \times \pi}{2500 \text{ mm}} \sqrt{F + H}$$

$$= \frac{1.69 \times \pi}{2500 \text{ mm}} \sqrt{1619 \times 10^{20} \text{ MPa}^2 \text{ mm}^8 + 17182 \times 10^{20} \text{ MPa}^2 \text{ mm}^8}$$

$$= 2910 \times 10^6 \text{ N} \cdot \text{mm} = 2910 \text{ kN} \cdot \text{m}$$

where

$$F = 200\ 000 \text{ MPa} \times 20.3 \times 10^6 \text{ mm}^4 \times 77\ 000 \text{ MPa} \times 518 \times 10^3 \text{ mm}^4$$

$$= 1619 \times 10^{20} \text{ MPa}^2 \text{ mm}^8$$

$$H = \left(\frac{\pi \times 200\ 000 \text{ MPa}}{2500 \text{ mm}} \right)^2 \times 20.3 \times 10^6 \text{ mm}^4 \times 1340 \times 10^9 \text{ mm}^6$$

$$= 17\ 182 \times 10^{20} \text{ MPa}^2 \text{ mm}^8$$

The value of ω_2 has been obtained from Equation 5.26. In this example, the unbraced length of 2500 mm is terminated at one end by attachment of the beam to the column and this connection will provide adequate lateral support to the compression flange of the beam. A brace located at the level of the bottom flange or diaphragm bracing will be introduced at the other end. Because there is no bending moment at any point within the unbraced length greater than the larger end moment and since the segment is bent in single curvature, the moment ratio term will be negative and is $\kappa = -34/540 = -0.63$. The value of ω_2 (Equation 5.26) is therefore 1.69.

For a Class 2 section, if $M_u > 0.67 M_p$ the factored moment resistance must be based on Equation 5.23, which accounts for the effects of inelastic action.

$$M_p = Z_x F_y = 2060 \times 10^3 \text{ mm}^3 \times 350 \text{ MPa}$$

$$= 721 \times 10^6 \text{ N} \cdot \text{mm} = 721 \text{ kN} \cdot \text{m}$$

$$0.67 M_p = 0.67 \times 721 = 483 \text{ kN} \cdot \text{m}$$

Since $2910 > 483$, Equation 5.23 must be used:

$$M_r = 1.15 \ \phi \ M_p \left(1 - \frac{0.28 \ M_p}{M_u} \right)$$

$$= 1.15 \times 0.90 \times 725 \left(1 - \frac{0.28 \times 724}{2910} \right) = 698 \text{ kN} \cdot \text{m}$$

Since this value is greater than that predicted using Equation 5.7, the smaller value governs the design and, finally:

$$M_r = 649 \text{ kN} \cdot \text{m}$$

Since the factored moment resistance is greater than the actual maximum bending moment, the W530×82 will be satisfactory without additional bracing in this region. By inspection (Figure 5.8), the right-hand region of the beam, where the unsupported length is also 2500 mm, is less critical than that just examined.

In accordance with the assumptions made, lateral bracing will have to be supplied to brace the lower flange at the two inflection points in this beam.

The use of the tabulated values in the CISC Handbook [5.14] would greatly aid in the solution of this problem. The value, L_u, tabulated in these tables (L_u = 2660 mm for the W530× 82) represents the greatest unbraced length over which the moment resistance based on local buckling can be developed. Thus, since the actual unbraced length is less than L_u, no reduction in strength is anticipated.

5.12   Concentrated Loads and Reactions

Beams subjected to concentrated loads (including reactions) may require special consideration. In the usual framing schemes, concentrated loads are transferred to a beam through web connections. A typical situation is illustrated in Figure 5.1, which shows a beam framing into a column member. The reaction from the beam is resisted as a concentrated load by the column. However, in the beam itself, the reaction is distributed over the depth of the web.

In other situations, however, a concentrated load may be delivered to one of the flanges and provision must be made for its transfer into the web. The condition shown in Figure 5.14 illustrates two such cases; the concentrated load, P, delivered to the top flange and the reaction, R, which is resisted by the bottom flange at the support point. The issue here is that a large compressive force in the web may lead to (1) local yielding of the web in the region where it joins the flange, or (2) overall buckling of the web over most of its depth. The first problem can result if stresses in the web-to-flange region exceed the yield strength of the material and occur over a significant length. The second problem is simply a consequence of overall buckling of the web because it is too slender.

The problem of local yielding is addressed by assuming that the load or reaction is distributed uniformly over the length of the bearing plate, N, and then spreads out. The area available to resist the load effect in the region of the flange-to-web junction is taken as w (N+ 10t) for the interior load and w (N+ 4t) for the reaction, where t is the flange thickness and w the web thickness [5.20]. According to Clause 14.3.2 of S16–01, the factored compressive resistance at interior locations will be

$$B_r = \phi_{bi} \ w \ (N + 10t) \ F_y \tag{5.27a}$$

and, at end locations

$$B_r = \phi_{be} \ w \ (N + 4t) \ F_y \tag{5.27b}$$

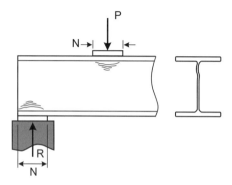

Figure 5.14 – Concentrated Loads and Reactions

In Equation 5.27(a) the resistance factor, ϕ_{bi}, for bearing at an interior location is taken as 0.80. In equation 5.27(b) the resistance factor, ϕ_{be}, for bearing at an end location is taken as 0.75.

To account for the possibility of overall buckling, Clause 14.3.2 provides the following rules, which are based largely upon empirical evidence [5.20].

At interior points—

$$B_r = 1.45\, \phi_{bi}\, w^2\, \sqrt{F_y\, E} \tag{5.28a}$$

At an exterior reaction—

$$B_r = 0.60\, \phi_{be}\, w^2\, \sqrt{F_y\, E} \tag{5.28b}$$

The resistance factors ϕ_{bi} and ϕ_{be} used in equation 5.28 are the same as for Equation 5.27.

The designer must evaluate both Equations 5.27 and 5.28 in any given case and use the lower result as the capacity of the beam in resisting the application of a load directly to a beam flange.

If the factored compressive resistance is exceeded (Equation 5.27), the length of the bearing plate could be increased (provided web yielding governs the web capacity) or a pair of bearing stiffeners might be provided to help carry the load. The detailed design of bearing stiffeners is covered in Chapter 7. The design of the beam bearing plate itself is discussed in Chapter 9.

In the case of extremely slender webs, failure can be accompanied by a buckling motion of the web. To guard against this possibility, Clause 14.4.1 of S16–01 requires that the unframed ends of girders having h/w ratios greater than $1100/\sqrt{F_y}$ must be provided with pairs of bearing stiffeners.

Example 5.8

Given

The end of a W460×74 member of G40.21 350W steel ($F_y = 350$ MPa) is supported on a bearing plate 200 mm long. The reaction is 265 kN. Are bearing stiffeners required?

Solution

The required dimensions for the W460×74 section are listed in the CISC Handbook [5.14]:

$d = 457$ mm $\qquad\qquad$ $t = 14.5$ mm $\qquad\qquad$ $w = 9.0$ mm

The factored compressive resistance of the web in the bearing area is given by Equations 5.27(b) and 5.28(b):

From Equation 5.27(b)

$$B_r = \phi_{be}\, w\, (N + 4t)\, F_y$$

$$= 0.75 \times 9.0\ \text{mm}\ (200\ \text{mm} + (4 \times 14.5\ \text{mm})) \times 350\ \text{MPa}$$

$$= 610 \times 10^3\ \text{N} = 610\ \text{kN}$$

From Equation 5.28(b)

$$B_r = 0.60\, \phi_{be}\, w^2\, \sqrt{F_y\, E}$$

$$= 0.6 \times 0.75 \times 9.0^2\ \text{mm}^2 \times \sqrt{350\ \text{MPa} \times 200\,000\ \text{MPa}}$$

$$= 305 \times 10^3\ \text{N} = 305\ \text{kN} \qquad\qquad \text{(Governs)}$$

Since the governing factored resistance is greater than the reaction produced by the factored loads, the member support is satisfactory for bearing. For this member, the web slenderness is well below $1100/\sqrt{F_y}$, and thus bearing stiffeners are not required to satisfy Clause 14.4.1 of S16–01.

5.13   Beams Subjected to Combined Bending and Torsion

Torsion problems are generally avoided in steel structures by ensuring that beams are loaded through their shear centre. In this way, the externally applied torque is zero. However, there are cases where torsion cannot be avoided, and this is the case, for example, for crane runway girders. Although the moving vertical load is usually applied through the shear centre, the crane bridge also transmits a transverse horizontal load at the top flange of the girder where the crane rail is located, and this creates torsion about the shear centre. Another example of beams subjected to torsion are spandrel beams. In this case, however, the rotation about the axis of the member is restrained by the transverse beams framing into the spandrel beam and also by the floor slab. The torsional effects are therefore significantly reduced because of the restraint forces that counteract the applied torsional moments.

One of the best approaches when dealing with members subjected to torsion is to use a closed cross-section. A circular tube is the structural shape that offers the most resistance to torsion. Although somewhat less favourable than circular tubes, tubes of other cross-sections, such as square or rectangular, also offer a large resistance to torsion. In many applications, however, I-shaped cross-sections must be used even if the member is subject to torsion. The design procedure for these sections is outlined following.

When beams are subjected to combined bending and torsion, both ultimate limit states and serviceability limit states should be checked. Serviceability criteria will often govern the design of beams loaded in torsion. The S16–01 Standard has two serviceability criteria that may be applicable for beams subject to flexure and torsion. A deflection limit may be imposed as for beams in bending and, depending on the nature of the building elements supported on the member, a limitation may be placed on the angle of twist so that non-structural elements are not damaged. In addition, Clause 14.10.4 of the Standard imposes a serviceability limit state based on the attainment of first yield of the cross-section as the result normal stresses. This prevents inelastic deformations under specified loads.

A method that uses an interaction diagram has been proposed to check the ultimate limit state [5.21]. An examination of the proposed method for ultimate limit states indicates that the serviceability limit state based on the attainment of first yield is often the governing case. The ultimate limit state design check is therefore not covered in this text. The reader can refer to the work in Reference [5.21] for guidance on the ultimate limit state check.

When an external torsional moment is applied simultaneously with a bending moment, the combination of the shear and normal stresses caused by the bending and torsional moments must be considered. Figure 5.15 illustrates the shear stresses and normal stresses developed in a beam subjected to flexural bending and torsion. The elastic flexural shear stress, τ_b, is obtained from basic mechanics of materials [5.3]:

$$\tau_b = \frac{V Q}{I t} \tag{5.29}$$

where V is the applied shear, obtained using unfactored loads when calculating the elastic stresses, Q is the first moment of area about the centroid of the cross-section, I is the moment of inertia about the bending axis, and t is the thickness of the plate element of the cross-section in which the shear stress is calculated.

The St. Venant shear stress, τ_{SV}, which is the only type present if a member is in pure torsion (no warping restraint at either end), varies linearly through the wall thickness and the maximum value on the wall surface is obtained as:

$$(\tau_{SV})_{max} = G t \frac{d\phi}{dx} \tag{5.30}$$

where G is the shear modulus of elasticity, t is the wall thickness, and $d\phi/dx$ is the rate of change of the angle of twist along the length of the beam.

Pure torsion never occurs if the member is loaded in combined bending and torsion. The restrained warping, resulting either from the support boundary conditions or from non-uniform torsional moment along the span length, introduces flexural shear stresses and normal stresses in the flanges of the section. The resulting warping shear, τ_w, and warping normal stresses, σ_w, in the flanges are obtained as

$$\tau_w = -E S_w \frac{d^3 \phi}{dx^3} \tag{5.31}$$

$$\sigma_w = -E W_n \frac{d^2 \phi}{dx^2} \tag{5.32}$$

where S_w is the warping statical moment for the cross-section ($= b^2 h/16$ for an I-shaped section) and W_n is the normalized unit warping for the cross section ($= b h/4$ for an I-shaped section).

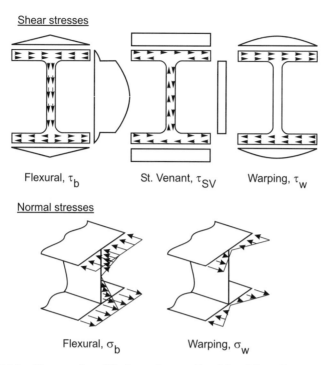

Shear stresses

Flexural, τ_b St. Venant, τ_{SV} Warping, τ_w

Normal stresses

Flexural, σ_b Warping, σ_w

Figure 5.15 – Stresses in a W-shape due to Combined Bending and Torsion

The angle of twist, ϕ, is obtained from the solution of the differential equation obtained when the external couple is equilibrated by the internal force couple describing the resisting torque of a beam. The angle of twist, and hence the stresses from the general solution, are determined from the support conditions at the ends of the member. The exact solution of this problem is classic and all the details can be found elsewhere [5.22, 5.23, 5.24].

An approximate solution to the torsion problem is to consider the applied torsional moment as a couple acting in the plane of the two flanges. The flanges are then treated as loaded in their plane, thus transforming the torsion problem into a simple beam flexure problem. The stresses in the flanges are computed from beam theory, assuming that the flanges act as rectangular beams bending about their strong axis. If torsion results from an eccentric vertical force, the flanges are subjected to equal lateral forces H, which produce lateral bending of the flanges. This is illustrated in Figure 5.16(a). When torsion results from an eccentric lateral load, a statically equivalent system consists of a biaxial bending component and lateral forces in the flanges, Figure 5.16(b).

Because the simple flexure analogy assumes that the applied torque is entirely carried by warping, i.e., the pure torsion contribution is negligible, the flexure analogy is always conservative, i.e., it overestimates the bending normal stresses introduced in the flange plates. For sections with a large ratio of pure torsion stiffness (G J) to warping torsion stiffness (E C_w), the pure torsion component can be important compared to the warping component. The simplifying assumption of the simple flexure analogy can therefore greatly overestimate the stresses due to warping. In order to circumvent this problem, Lin [5.25] proposed a modification to the flexure analogy whereby a correction factor, β, is applied to reduce the effect of the equivalent lateral loads. The resulting reduced stresses become very close to the values calculated using the exact elastic method. The value of this correction factor depends on the support conditions, the nature of the load causing the torsion, the length of the member, and the cross-section properties. Some values of the correction factor are presented in Table 5.2 for a beam simply supported in torsion at both extremities and for two load cases: a concentrated torque, and a uniformly distributed torque.

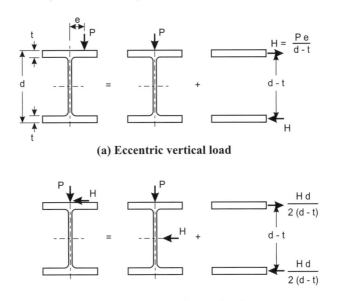

(a) Eccentric vertical load

(b) Vertical and horizontal loads

Figure 5.16 – Flexure Analogy

The values presented in the table represent the maximum load effect, namely, at the point of the applied torque for concentrated torque cases, and at midspan (a = 0.5) for the uniform torque case. The factor μ in Table 5.2 represents the ratio of the pure torsion stiffness to the warping torsion stiffness and is given as

$$\mu = \sqrt{\frac{G\,J}{E\,C_w}} \tag{5.33}$$

As expected, when the factor μ is small, i.e., the warping torsion stiffness is large compared to the pure torsion stiffness, a larger portion of the torque is carried by warping and the error in the simplified flexural analogy is small. This is reflected by a value of β close to 1.0 (i.e., all the torque carried by warping) as the value $\mu\,L$ decreases.

Table 5.2 – Correction factor β for the modified flexure analogy

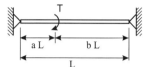 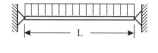

| μ L | Concentrated torque | | | | | Uniform Torque |
	a = 0.1	a = 0.2	a = 0.3	a = 0.4	a = 0.5	(β at midspan)
0.5	0.99	0.99	0.98	0.98	0.98	0.97
1.0	0.97	0.95	0.94	0.93	0.92	0.91
2.0	0.91	0.84	0.80	0.77	0.76	0.70
3.0	0.83	0.72	0.65	0.62	0.60	0.51
4.0	0.76	0.62	0.54	0.50	0.48	0.37
5.0	0.70	0.54	0.45	0.41	0.39	0.27
6.0	0.65	0.47	0.39	0.34	0.33	0.20
8.0	0.55	0.37	0.30	0.26	0.25	0.12
10.0	0.48	0.31	0.24	0.21	0.20	0.08

Example 5.9

Given

The simply supported beam shown in Figure 5.17 consists of a W460×106 with a span length of 7400 mm. It is loaded at midspan with a concentrated gravity load of 90 kN and a concentrated lateral load of 12 kN applied 150 mm above the top flange of the section. The ends of the beam are simply supported with respect to torsional restraint (i.e., $\phi = 0$). Compute the stresses due to bending and torsion. The steel is of grade G40.21M 350W.

Solution

The problem is going to be solved in two different ways: (1) using the flexure analogy, and (2) using the modified flexure analogy proposed in Reference [5.25].

The required dimensions and section properties for the W460×106 are listed in the CISC Handbook [5.14]:

$d = 469$ mm $\qquad$ $b = 194$ mm $\qquad$ $t = 20.6$ mm $\qquad$ $w = 12.6$ mm

$S_x = 2080 \times 10^3$ mm^3 $\qquad$ $S_y = 259 \times 10^3$ mm^3 $\qquad$ $I_x = 488 \times 10^6$ mm^4

138

$$I_y = 25.1 \times 10^6 \text{ mm}^4 \qquad J = 1460 \times 10^3 \text{ mm}^4 \qquad C_w = 1260 \times 10^9 \text{ mm}^6$$

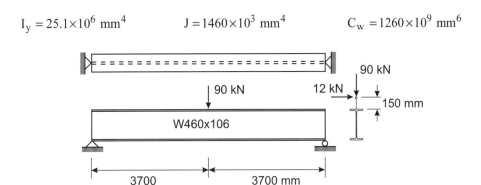

Figure 5.17 – Beam Under Combined Bending and Torsion — Example 5.9

Flexural analogy

The simply supported beam is subjected to a concentrated torque caused by the 12 kN lateral load applied at 384.5 mm (d/2 + 150 mm) above the shear centre of the section. A system of equivalent forces that create the same bending moment about the strong and weak axes and the same torque can be calculated, as shown in Figure 5.18. The lateral load of 12 kN is moved to the shear centre and the torque is replaced by a force couple on the flanges.

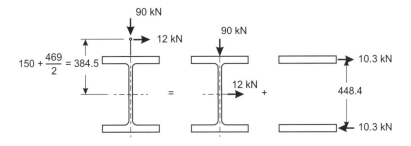

Figure 5.18 – Equivalent Forces on Beam Cross-Section

The problem consequently becomes a combined stress problem, where the first component consists of the beam subjected to the gravity and lateral loads applied at the shear centre, causing bending about the strong and the weak axes, respectively, and the second component consists of the flanges subjected to the equivalent force couple. Both normal and shear stresses can be calculated using simple beam theory.

Normal Stresses

Normal stresses are maximum where the bending moments are maximum, namely, at midspan. Three flexural moments are obtained, namely, the bending moment on the full cross-section caused by the gravity load, M_x, the bending moment on the full cross-section caused by the lateral load, M_y, and the bending moment resulting from the force couple and carried by the flanges, M_{fl}. The first two moments represent the biaxial bending effect, whereas the third moment represents the warping effect. Assuming that conditions remain elastic, the combined normal stress, which is maximum at the flange tips, can be expressed as:

$$\sigma = \frac{M_x}{S_x} + \frac{M_y}{S_y} + \frac{M_{fl}}{S_y/2}$$

where $S_y/2$ is approximately equal to the elastic section modulus of one flange about the axis of symmetry of the cross-section, which can also be taken as $t\,b^2/6$. Since the beam is simply supported at its ends,

$$M_x = \frac{P\,L}{4} = \frac{90\ kN \times 7.4\ m}{4} = 166.5\ kN \cdot m$$

$$M_y = \frac{12\ kN \times 7.4\ m}{4} = 22.2\ kN \cdot m$$

$$M_{fl} = \frac{10.3\ kN \times 7.4\ m}{4} = 19.1\ kN \cdot m$$

Applying the above equation for combined normal stresses, we obtain

$$\sigma = \frac{166.5 \times 10^6\ N \cdot mm}{2080 \times 10^3\ mm^3} + \frac{22.2 \times 10^6\ N \cdot mm}{259 \times 10^3\ mm^3} + \frac{19.1 \times 10^6\ N \cdot mm}{259 \times 10^3\ mm^3/2}$$

$$\sigma = 80.1\ MPa + 85.7\ MPa + 147.5\ MPa = 313\ MPa\ (Compression)$$

A summary of the calculated normal stresses is presented in Figure 5.19. The calculated warping stress, 147.5 MPa, represents 47 percent of the total combined normal stress. Since the maximum normal stress, 313 MPa, is less than the yield strength of the material, 350 MPa, the section is considered to be adequate under service load.

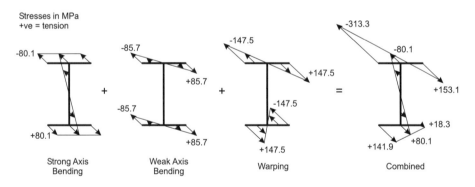

Figure 5.19 – Combination of Normal Stresses

Shear Stresses

The shear stresses consist of four components, namely, flexural shear stresses for bending about the strong axis, flexural shear stresses for bending about the weak axis, St. Venant shear stresses, and warping shear stresses.

For bending about the strong axis, the shear force over half the span is given as:

$$V = 90\ kN\,/\,2 = 45\ kN$$

The resulting shear stress in the flange is maximum at the flange-to-web junction and is obtained as

$$\tau_{bx\ flange} = \frac{V\,Q}{I\,t} = \frac{45\,000\ \text{N} \times 448 \times 10^3\ \text{mm}^3}{448 \times 10^6\ \text{mm}^4 \times 20.6\ \text{mm}} = 2.2\ \text{MPa}$$

The corresponding shear stress in the web, which is maximum at the centroid of the cross-section, is given as

$$\tau_{bx\ web} = \frac{V\,Q}{I\,t} = \frac{45\,000\ \text{N} \times 1.189 \times 10^6\ \text{mm}^3}{448 \times 10^6\ \text{mm}^4 \times 12.6\ \text{mm}} = 9.5\ \text{MPa}$$

For bending about the weak axis, the shear force over half span and the resulting maximum shear stress in the flanges are given as:

$$V = 12\ \text{kN} / 2 = 6\ \text{kN}$$

$$\tau_{by} = \frac{V\,Q}{I\,t} = \frac{6000\ \text{N} \times 84.7 \times 10^3\ \text{mm}^3}{25.1 \times 10^6\ \text{mm}^4 \times 2 \times 20.6\ \text{mm}} = 0.5\ \text{MPa}$$

The resulting shear stress in the web is negligible.

Warping shear stresses are obtained from the equivalent shear forces in the flanges as shown in Figure 5.17. The shear force over the half span is given as:

$$V = 10.3\ \text{kN} / 2 = 5.2\ \text{kN}$$

The resulting maximum shear stress in the flanges caused by this shear force is given as:

$$\tau_w = \frac{V\,Q}{I\,t} = \frac{5200\ \text{N} \times 96.9 \times 10^3\ \text{mm}^3}{12.5 \times 10^6\ \text{mm}^4 \times 20.6\ \text{mm}} = 2.0\ \text{MPa}$$

The pure torsion stresses can be determined Equation 5.30 and the design charts provided in Reference [5.24]. Figure 5.20 shows the chart applicable to a beam simply supported at both ends and a concentrated torque at midspan. The function $(d\phi/dx)(GJ/T)$ is plotted as a function of the distance along the span. The variable T in the torsion function is the applied torque at midspan $(= 12\ \text{kN} \times 0.3845\ \text{m} = 4.61\ \text{kN} \cdot \text{m})$. The dark solid lines represent the torsion function for values of $\mu\,L$ varying from 0.5 to 6.0. For the beam considered here,

$$\mu\,L = \sqrt{\frac{G\,J}{E\,C_w}}\,L = \sqrt{\frac{77\,000 \times 1460 \times 10^3}{200\,000 \times 1260 \times 10^9}} \times 7400 = 4.94$$

The dotted line in Figure 5.20 represents the torsion function for $\mu\,L = 4.94$. The torsion function is maximum at the end supports and zero at midspan. From Figure 5.20 the maximum value of the torsion function is 0.42, from which:

$$\frac{d\phi}{dx} = 0.42\,\frac{T}{G\,J}$$

Substituting into Equation 5.30, we obtain

$$(\tau_{SV})_{max} = G t \frac{d\phi}{dx} = 0.42 \frac{T t}{J}$$

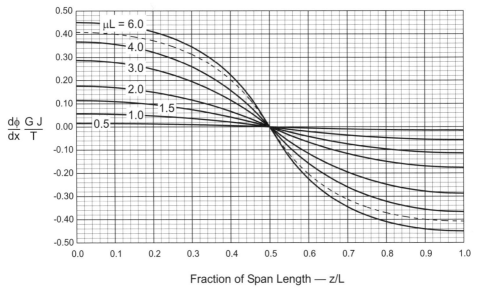

Figure 5.20 – Torsion Function for Concentrated Torque at Midspan

The pure torsion stress is a function of the plate thickness, t, and will therefore be different in the flanges and in the web. The maximum St. Venant shear stress, τ_{SV}, in the flanges is

$$(\tau_{SV})_{max} = 0.42 \times \frac{4.61 \times 10^6 \ N \cdot mm \times 20.6 \ mm}{1460 \times 10^3 \ mm^4} = 27.3 \ MPa$$

Similarly, the maximum St. Venant shear stress in the web is

$$(\tau_{SV})_{max} = 0.42 \times \frac{4.61 \times 10^6 \ N \cdot mmm \times 12.6 \ mm}{1460 \times 10^3 \ mm^4} = 16.7 \ MPa$$

The variation and magnitude of the shear stresses at the supports are shown in Figure 5.21. The most significant shear stresses are the St. Venant shear stresses. Because these stresses are maximum at the supports and zero at midspan, they cannot simply be added to the normal stresses calculated above. The normal stresses were calculated at midspan, where they are maximum. Since the shear stresses are usually small and because the maximum shear stresses do not occur at the same cross-section as the maximum normal stresses, it is common practice to ignore the shear stresses when checking the cross-section for yielding.

142

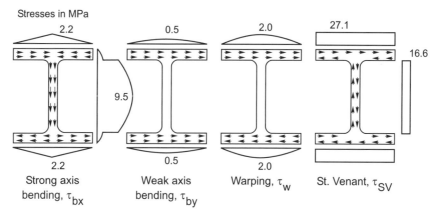

Figure 5.21 – Shear Stresses

Modified flexure analogy

The calculation of the warping normal stress given above is based on the assumption that torsion is resisted entirely by warping. The method of Reference [5.26] proposes a correction factor β based on the ratio of the pure torsion to warping stiffness given as

$$\mu L = \sqrt{\frac{G J}{E C_w}} L = \sqrt{\frac{77\,000 \times 1460 \times 10^3}{200\,000 \times 1260 \times 10^9}} \times 7400 = 4.943$$

From Table 5.2, the correction factor β is approximately 0.4. The adjusted warping normal stress thus becomes 0.4×147.5 MPa (see Figure 5.19), or 59 MPa. The adjusted warping shear stress is 0.4×2.0 MPa (see Figure 5.21), or 0.8 MPa. The exact stresses are 56 MPa and 1.8 MPa, respectively. All the other stresses are as calculated above. The maximum normal stress is therefore 225 MPa, which is well below the yield strength of the material. The section is therefore adequate under the combined action of bending and torsion.

5.14   Special Topics in Beam Design

In this chapter, the basic problems associated with beam design have been discussed. Throughout, it has been assumed that the loading and restraint conditions on the member are such that the cross-section is bent about the major (x–x) axis.

Cases may arise in practice in which the cross-section is bent biaxially, that is, components of bending moments are produced about both principal axes. Such a condition arises, for example, if the member is used as a purlin on a sloping roof. A general discussion of these problems is included in References [5.5] and [5.9], and a detailed design example is included in Reference [5.26].

In almost every phase of design, the computer can be used to facilitate the process. The Canadian Institute of Steel Construction, together with the Canadian Steel Construction Council, has developed a program called Gravity Frame Design 4 (GFD V4.0) to assist in the selection of the most economical floor system for particular situations. Commercial design software such as S–FRAME/S–STEEL®, STAAD®, RAM®, and others are also available to perform this task. Electronic spreadsheets

143

provide also a powerful tool for the design of steel members. Use of any design software never replaces the need for a solid understanding of the behaviour of the members and the design rules, however.

5.15 Beams in Plastically Designed Structures

In a structure designed to resist moments and forces calculated on the basis of a plastic analysis, the beams are required to deliver a moment capacity equal to M_p. In addition, however, portions of the beams must be able to act as plastic hinges, that is, they must be able to resist a moment of M_p while at the same time undergoing considerable inelastic rotation. The required behaviour of a plastic hinge region is illustrated by the curve for Class 1 sections in Figure 5.6.

The additional inelastic rotation requirement means that the flange plate will be subjected to larger average strains than will the flange of a Class 2 section. The limiting flange and web slenderness ratios are correspondingly reduced to those appropriate for a Class 1 section. As given in Equations 5.8 and 5.14, the respective limits are:

$$\frac{b_o}{t} \leq \frac{145}{\sqrt{F_y}} \quad \text{and} \quad \frac{h}{w} \leq \frac{1100}{\sqrt{F_y}}$$

Members in plastically designed structures must also be braced laterally so that the full M_p value can be delivered by the beam and also to ensure that the member can deform inelastically (at plastic hinge locations), as shown by curve B of Figure 5.9.

There is a distinct difference between the behaviour of a beam subjected to a uniform bending moment (Figure 5.9) and one subjected to a moment gradient (Figure 5.6). In the uniform moment case, yielding extends over a considerable length of the member as the beam moment approaches M_p and this weakens the beam significantly with respect to lateral-torsional buckling [5.4]. To achieve the desired behaviour, the distance from a plastic hinge (which must be braced laterally) to the adjacent braced point, L_{cr}, is limited in Clause 13.7 of S16–01 to:

$$L_{cr} = 550\, r_y\, /\, \sqrt{F_y} \tag{5.34}$$

If the moment gradient on the member segment is not large ($\kappa > 0.5$), then Equation 5.34 is applicable. Otherwise ($\kappa < 0.5$), the situation is less severe and Equation 5.35 can be used.

$$L_{cr} = 980\, r_y\, /\, \sqrt{F_y} \tag{5.35}$$

In regions removed from potential plastic hinge locations, these provisions do not apply. In fact, the bracing spacing would be that specified for the same member in a structure designed on the basis of an elastic analysis [5.4].

References

5.1   Canadian Standards Association, CAN/CSA–S16–01, "Limit States Design of Steel Structures," Toronto, Ontario, 2001.

5.2   Redwood, R.G. and Soon Ho Cho, "Design of Steel and Composite Beams with Web Openings," Journal of Constructional Steel Research, Vol. 25, Nos. 1 and 2, 1993.

5.3   Beer, F. P., Johnston, E. R. and DeWolf, J.T., "Mechanics of Materials," Third Edition, McGraw Hill, New York, 2002.

5.4   WRC-ASCE Joint Committee, "Plastic Design in Steel, A Guide and Commentary," 2nd Edition, American Society of Civil Engineers, New York, 1971.

5.5   Gaylord, E.H., Jr., Gaylord, C.N., and Stallmeyer, J.E., "Steel Structures," Third Edition, McGraw-Hill, New York, 1992.

5.6   Lay, M.G., "Flange Local Buckling in Wide-Flange Shapes," Journal of the Structural Division, American Society of Civil Engineers, Volume 91, No. ST6, December, 1965.

5.7   Lukey, A.F. and Adams, P.F., "Rotation Capacity of Beams Under Moment Gradient," Journal of the Structural Division, American Society of Civil Engineers, Volume 95, ST6, June, 1969.

5.8   Canadian Standards Association, CSA–S136–01, "North American Specification for the Design of Cold-Formed Steel Structural Members," Toronto, Ontario, 2001.

5.9   McGuire, W., "Steel Structures," Prentice-Hall Inc., Englewood Cliffs, N.J., 1968.

5.10   Dawe, J.L. and Kulak, G.L., "Plate Instability of W-Shapes," Journal of the Structural Division, American Society of Civil Engineers, Volume 110, ST6, June, 1984.

5.11   Dawe, J.L. and Kulak, G.L., "Local Buckling of W Shape Columns and Beams," Journal of the Structural Division, American Society of Civil Engineers, Volume 110, ST6, June, 1984.

5.12   Galambos, T.V. and Ravindra, M.K., "Properties of Steel for Use in Load and Resistance Factor Design," Journal of the Structural Division, American Society of Civil Engineers, Vol. 104, STB, September, 1978.

5.13   Kennedy, D.J.L. and Gad Aly, M.G., "Limit States Design of Steel Structures – Performance Factors," Canadian Journal of Civil Engineering, Volume 7, Number 1, March 1980.

5.14   Canadian Institute of Steel Construction, "Handbook of Steel Construction," Ninth Edition, Toronto, Ontario, 2006.

5.15   Ricker, D.T., "Cambering Steel Beams," Engineering Journal, American Institute of Steel Construction, Vol. 26, No. 4, Fourth Quarter, 1989.

5.16   Murray, T.M., Allen, D.E., and Ungar, E.E., "Floor Vibrations Due to Human Activity," Steel Design Guide 11, American Institute of Steel Construction and Canadian Institute of Steel Construction, 1997.

5.17   Applied Technology Council, "Minimizing Floor Vibration," ATC Design Guide 1, Applied Technology Council, Redwood City, CA, 1999.

5.18   Structural Stability Research Council, "Guide to Stability Design Criteria for Metal Structures," Fifth Edition, T. V. Galambos Editor, John Wiley and Sons, New York, 1998.

5.19   Nethercot, D.A. "Limit States Design of Structural Steelwork," Third Edition, Spon Press, 2001.

5.20   Kennedy, S.J., Kennedy, D.J.L., Prabha, K.R., Prowse, D., and Ji, X., "The Bearing Resistance of Webs: A Plate Post-Buckling Strength Problem," Structural Stability Research Council, Proceedings of the 1997 Annual Technical Session and Meeting, Toronto, Ontario, June 9-11, 1997.

5.21   Driver, R.G. and Kennedy, D.J.L., "Combined Flexure and Torsion of I-shaped Steel Beams," Canadian Journal of Civil Engineering, Vol. 16, No. 2, 1989.

5.22   Johnston, B.G. "Design of W-shapes for Combined Bending and Torsion," AISC Eng. Journal, Vol. 19, No. 4, 1982.

5.23   Heins, C.P., "Bending and Torsional Design in Structural Members," Lexington Books, Toronto, 1975.

5.24   Seaburg, P. A. and Carter, C.J. "Torsion Analysis of Structural Steel Members," Steel Design Guide 9, American Institute of Steel Construction, 1997.

5.25   Lin, P.H., "Simplified Design for Torsional Loading of Rolled Steel Members," Engineering Journal, American Institute of Steel Construction, Vol. 14, No. 3, Third Quarter, 1977.

5.26   Salmon, C.G. and Johnson, J.E., "Steel Structures – Design and Behavior," Fourth Edition, Harper & Row, New York, 1996.

CHAPTER 6

COMPOSITE DESIGN

6.1   Introduction

A frequent type of construction in both buildings and bridges uses concrete slabs supported by steel beams. The slabs serve to transfer the floor or deck loads to the steel beams. These beams must carry the entire loading, including the dead load of the slab, by themselves. Because the beams and slabs deflect together and since the concrete slabs are normally adjacent to the compression side of the beam cross-section, it was logical to expect that an effort would be made to see if these two elements could be made to act together—a composite cross-section. In the usual situation, this can be accomplished by a mechanical connection between the slab and the steel beam. The resulting system can prove to be both structurally and economically advantageous.

Assuming that adequate interconnection between the slab and the beam can be provided, some of the resulting advantages of the composite cross-section are immediately apparent. The slab will be in compression, a condition particularly suitable for concrete. Since the load is now carried by both the steel and the concrete, the size of the steel beam required will be less than that for a non-composite case. This means a reduction in steel weight, a direct cost saving, and usually a reduction of the overall depth of the beam and slab. This latter reduction may not be important in a low-rise building but it can provide significant savings in a multi-storey building or in a highway overpass. Composite beams will be stiffer than non-composite beams of the same size and they will have better overload capacity. The principal disadvantage of the system is the additional cost of providing the connection between the slab and the beam. Except for short or lightly loaded spans, the saving provided by the reduction in beam size is usually greater than the cost of the necessary connectors.

The principal force that must be transferred if the slab and beam are to act as a unit is the horizontal shear at their interface. The transfer can be accomplished by attaching connectors to the top flange of the steel beam. These connectors will be embedded in the concrete as the slab is placed and will bear against the hardened concrete when loads are applied. Figure 6.1(a) shows short lengths of channel that have been attached to the beam by welding along the toe and heel. Seventy-five, 100, or 130 mm deep channels are used. Adequate cover must be maintained between the top of the channel and the slab surface.

Figure 6.1(b) shows the attachment of welded studs to the beam flange. These are proprietary products, the principal feature being that a welding "gun" is used to simultaneously hold the stud in position and make a weld at its contact with the beam. Studs range in diameter from 14 to 22 mm and normally are about 75 mm long. Installation is rapid and can be done either in the shop or in the field. Studs are the most commonly used type of shear connector at the present time.

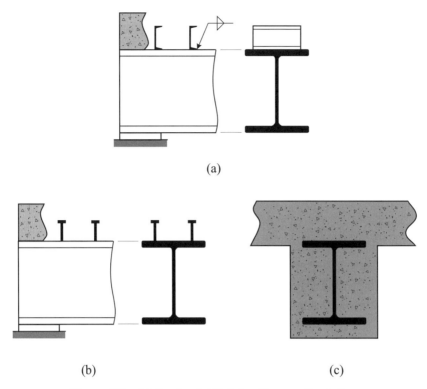

(a)

(b)   (c)

Figure 6.1 – Methods of Attaining Composite Action

A different way of attaining composite action is shown in Figure 6.1(c). Here the steel beam is completely encased in concrete and the load transfer will be by bond between these elements. Although this arrangement does take care of the fireproofing of the steel that is required in many situations, the added dead load of the concrete around the beam is substantial. This system is not often used in modern construction and will not be discussed further here.

6.2   Effective Area of Concrete

In making strength calculations, the area of slab that may be considered tributary to each beam must be established. Theoretically, this will be a function of the span length, the shape of the moment diagram, and Poisson's ratio for the material. Based on these considerations and the results of tests, rules have evolved that provide a sufficiently accurate assessment. The requirements for buildings as given in S16–01 (Clause 17.4.1) can be summarized as [6.1]:

When the slab extends on both sides of the steel beam, the effective slab width b is the lesser of

- One-fourth of the beam span

- Centre-to-centre distance of steel beams.

For slabs extending only on one side of the steel beam, the effective slab width is the width of the top flange of the steel section plus the lesser of

- One-tenth of the beam span

- One-half the clear distance to the adjacent steel beam.

These rules for effective slab width were developed when it was customary to calculate the strength of a composite section on an elastic stress basis. As will be noted subsequently, the strength of a composite section is best described using its ultimate capacity, and it is known that the effective slab widths at ultimate are less than those described above for the case of interior beams and greater for the case of exterior beams [6.2]. Fortunately, even though the elastic design rules can underestimate the effective slab width for an interior beam by a large margin, as much as 20%, the effect on the moment capacity is relatively minor, about 3 to 4%. The S16–01 standard therefore continues to use the rules for effective slab width developed on the basis of elastic analysis.

6.3 Influence of Construction Method

The design of composite sections formerly was differentiated by the method of construction [6.3]. If the steel beams are shored (supported at close intervals) during placement of the slab and if the shores remain in place until the concrete has attained a reasonable amount of its 28-day strength (usually 75%), then the composite section is available to carry all loads upon removal of the shores. This apparently simple situation is complicated, however, by the fact that the hardened concrete will tend to creep under the sustained action of long-term loads. The stresses due to these loads (usually, the dead loads) are thereby increased over their nominal value.

In another method of construction, the forms carrying the wet concrete are supported directly by the steel beam ("unshored construction"). The steel section alone must carry the loads imposed at this time. After the concrete has fully hardened, the composite cross-section is available to carry all subsequently imposed loads.

Despite the differences in these two methods, tests have shown that the ultimate load that can be carried by a given cross-section is independent of the method of construction [6.4, 6.5]. Standard S16–01 assumes therefore that the total load is to be applied to the composite section, regardless of the method of construction. (The adequacy of the steel section under the dead load of the wet concrete plus formwork must be checked, however.) In order to guard against yielding of the bottom flange of an unshored steel beam under the specified loads, a condition that would influence deflections, it is stipulated in Clause 17.11 of the Standard that the stresses in the tension flange of the steel section are not to exceed F_y prior to hardening of the concrete. The loads to be considered are those applied both prior to hardening of the concrete and those applied after. Since this is a service requirement, the loads to be considered are the specified loads. In the form of an equation, this can be expressed as:

$$\frac{M_1}{S_s} + \frac{M_2}{S_t} \leq F_y \tag{6.1}$$

where M_1 =   moment caused by the specified loads that act on the member prior to attainment of 75% of the required concrete strength;

M_2 = moment caused by the specified loads that act on the member subsequent to attainment of 75% of the required concrete strength;

S_s = elastic section modulus, referred to the bottom flange, of the steel section alone;

S_t = elastic section modulus, referred to the bottom flange, of the composite steel–concrete section.

In order to calculate the section modulus of the composite section (S_t), the designer must deal with the combination of the two different structural materials. This is accomplished by transforming the area of the concrete slab into an equivalent area of steel using the ratio of the modulus of elasticity of the two materials. This modular ratio ($n = E_s / E_c$) is usually prescribed in the applicable building code. It is customary to apply the reduction to the slab width, rather than to its thickness or to some proportion of each.

Composite girders are frequently used in bridges

6.4   Strength Calculations

The strength of a beam made of only one material must be evaluated on the basis of its shear and flexural capacities. In addition, a check is usually made of the deflection of the member acting under specified loads. All of these requirements apply equally to the composite beam and, in addition, the designer must ensure that the two parts act as a single unit.

The principles of the strength calculations for composite beams will be illustrated on the basis of a steel beam and a solid concrete slab. In fact, in building construction most composite floors now are constructed using concrete placed on a formed metal deck. The differences that arise when this method of construction is used are discussed in Section 6.7.

In the case of steel beams, it was assumed that the beam web carried all of the vertical shear force. The same approach is appropriate for composite beams and, as outlined in Section 5.8, the shear resistance can therefore be expressed as:

$$V_r = \phi \, A_w \, F_s \qquad\qquad (6.2)$$

where A_w = shear area ($d \times w$ for rolled steel shapes)

and $F_s = 0.66 \, F_y$ (when Equation 5.20 is satisfied, otherwise see Section 7.4).

The flexural capacity of a composite beam is evaluated on the basis that the concrete does not resist tension. Two cases must be considered, one in which the neutral axis falls within the concrete slab and one in which it falls within the steel section. Which of the two possibilities is applicable must be determined by trial.

Neutral Axis in the Slab—The stress conditions for a cross-section in which the neutral axis lies in the slab are shown in Figure 6.2. In accordance with the ultimate strength evaluation of concrete [6.5], the ultimate compressive stress in the concrete is taken as $0.85 \, f'_c$, where f'_c is the 28-day compressive strength. The corresponding compressive force is

$$C'_c = \phi_c \, 0.85 \, f'_c \, b \, a$$

The dimensions b and a are shown in Figure 6.2. The resistance factor for concrete, ϕ_c, is to be taken as 0.60. Calling the cross-sectional area of the steel A_s, an equilibrium equation for horizontal forces can be written as:

$$0.85 \, \phi_c \, f'_c \, b \, a = \phi \, A_s \, F_y$$

Solving for the unknown quantity a:

$$a = \frac{\phi \, A_s \, F_y}{0.85 \, \phi_c \, f'_c \, b} \qquad\qquad (6.3)$$

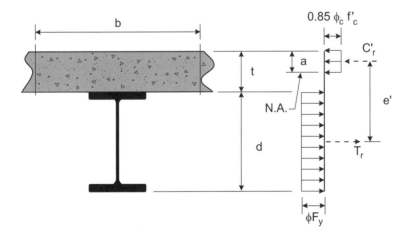

Figure 6.2 – Composite Cross-Section — Neutral Axis in Slab

If the calculated value of a is not equal to or less than the slab thickness t, then the assumption that the neutral axis lies in the slab is not valid and the other alternative must be examined. If the neutral axis does lie in the slab, the ultimate moment resistance can now be evaluated as (S16–01 Clause 17.9.3(a)):

$$M_{rc} = \phi A_s F_y e' \qquad (6.4)$$

Equation 6.4 is obtained by summing moments about the location of the resultant compressive force in the slab. The lever arm between the compressive and tensile forces (e') is shown in Figure 6.2. It can be calculated using the known value of a (Equation 6.3) and the cross-sectional dimensions t and d (Figure 6.2).

The shear connectors must transfer the total force at the interface of the concrete slab and the steel section. This is given by either the total compressive force, C'_r, or the total tensile force, T_r. Since they are equal, either can be used. For the situation shown in Figure 6.2, it is convenient to calculate the tensile force as representing the horizontal shear force to be transferred, V_h.

$$V_h = \phi A_s F_y \qquad (6.5)$$

This factored shear force is to be compared with the factored resistance of the shear connectors. The proportioning and spacing requirements of the connectors are discussed in Section 6.5.

Example 6.1

Given

Determine the flexural capacity of the cross-section shown in Figure 6.3. The effective slab width has been established as 2250 mm, the 28-day strength of the concrete is 25 MPa and the steel is G40.21 350W.

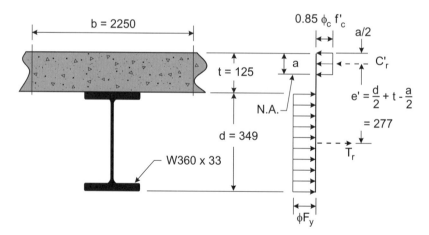

Figure 6.3 – Composite Cross-Section — Example 6.1

Solution

From the CISC Handbook [6.7], the cross-sectional area of a W360 x 33 is 4170 mm^2 and its depth is 349 mm. Assume that the neutral axis of the composite section lies in the slab. Using Equation 6.3;

$$a = \frac{0.90 \times 4170 \text{ mm}^2 \times 350 \text{ MPa}}{0.85 \times 0.60 \times 25 \text{ MPa} \times 2250 \text{ mm}} = 45.8 \text{ mm}$$

152

Since this is less than the slab thickness of 125 mm, the neutral axis does lie in the slab. As shown in Figure 6.3, the distance between the centroids of the two forces can now be determined. Using Equation 6.4, the flexural resistance of the cross-section is

$$M_{rc} = 0.90 \times 4170 \text{ mm}^2 \times 350 \text{ MPa} \times 277 \text{ mm} = 364 \times 10^6 \text{ N} \cdot \text{mm} = 364 \text{ kN} \cdot \text{m}$$

Neutral Axis in the Steel Section—If the neutral axis lies in the steel section, the full depth of the concrete slab is in compression and the steel section is fully yielded in compression above the neutral axis and fully yielded in tension below the neutral axis. This condition is shown in Figure 6.4.

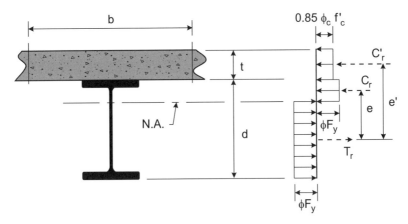

Figure 6.4 – Composite Cross-Section — Neutral Axis in Steel Section

The location of the neutral axis again can be obtained by considering equilibrium of the horizontal forces. For this case,

$$T_r = C_r + C'_r \qquad (6.6)$$

where $T_r =$ the tensile force in the steel section below the neutral axis

$C_r =$ the compressive force in the steel section above the neutral axis

$C'_r =$ the compressive force in the concrete.

Another expression for the tensile force can be written:

$$T_r = \phi \, A_s \, F_y - C_r \qquad (6.7)$$

Equations 6.6 and 6.7 can be used to solve for the value of the compressive force in the steel:

$$C_r = \frac{\phi \, A_s \, F_y - C'_r}{2} \qquad (6.8)$$

Substituting for C'_r the value of $0.85 \, \phi_c \, f'_c \, b \, t$:

$$C_r = \frac{\phi \, A_s \, F_y - 0.85 \, \phi_c \, f'_c \, b \, t}{2} \qquad (6.9)$$

Taking moments of forces about the centroid of the tensile force and using the moment arms shown in Figure 6.4, the flexural resistance of the cross-section is given by (or, see also S16 Clause 17.9.3b):

$$M_{rc} = C_r \ e + \ C'_r \ e' \qquad (6.10)$$

Whenever the neutral axis lies in the steel section, it is implicit that the steel section must accommodate plastic strains in both tension and compression. Therefore, the section chosen should be a Class 1 or Class 2 section, in order that it is capable of developing its plastic moment capacity.

As was the situation when the neutral axis lay in the slab, the shear connectors must transfer the total force at the slab–steel section interface. When the neutral axis falls in the steel section, this is conveniently described using the compressive force above the interface, C'_r. The requirement is (S16 Clause 17.9.5):

$$V_h = 0.85 \ \phi_c \ b \ t \ f'_c \qquad (6.11)$$

Example 6.2

Given

Determine the flexural capacity of the cross-section shown in Figure 6.5. The effective slab width has been established as 1830 mm, the 28-day compressive strength of the concrete is 25 MPa and the steel is G40.21 350W.

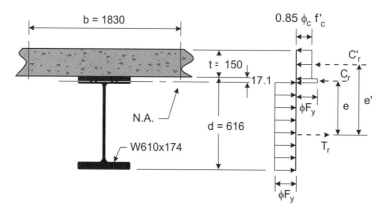

Figure 6.5 – Composite Cross-Section — Example 6.2

Solution

From Table 3 in Appendix A, it is found that the W610×174 is a Group 2 section, for which the yield strength is 350 MPa. The cross-sectional properties needed are, from the CISC Handbook:

$$d = 616 \text{ mm}, \quad b = 325 \text{ mm}, \quad t = 21.6 \text{ mm}, \quad A = 22\ 200 \text{ mm}^2$$

Assume that the neutral axis is in the slab. Using Equation 6.3,

$$a = \frac{0.90 \times 22\,200\ \text{mm}^2 \times 350\ \text{MPa}}{0.85 \times 0.60 \times 25\ \text{MPa} \times 1830\ \text{mm}} = 300\ \text{mm}$$

Since this is greater than the slab thickness (150 mm), the neutral axis is not in the slab and the assumption was incorrect.

Because it is now established that the slab is entirely in compression, the resultant compressive force in the concrete can be calculated:

$$C'_r = 0.85 \times 0.60 \times 1830\ \text{mm} \times 150\ \text{mm} \times 25\ \text{MPa}$$

$$= 3500 \times 10^3\ \text{N} = 3500\ \text{kN}$$

The compressive force in the steel (Equation 6.9) is therefore

$$C_r = \frac{(0.90 \times 22\,200\ \text{mm}^2 \times 350\ \text{MPa}) - 3500 \times 10^3\ \text{N}}{2}$$

$$= 1747 \times 10^3\ \text{N} = 1747\ \text{kN}$$

Assuming that the flange (or only a portion of the flange) of the W610×174 will be sufficient to carry this force, the depth of flange necessary is

$$d_f = \frac{1747 \times 10^3\ \text{N}}{0.9 \times 350\ \text{MPa} \times 325\ \text{mm}} = 17.1\ \text{mm}$$

Since this is less than the total flange thickness (21.6 mm), the assumption was correct. The centroid of the area below the neutral axis can be obtained by summing area moments about the bottom of the section as

$$\bar{y} = \frac{22\,200\ \text{mm}^2 \times 308\ \text{mm} - 17.1\ \text{mm} \times 325\ \text{mm} \times 607\ \text{mm}}{22\,200\ \text{mm}^2 - 17.1\ \text{mm} \times 325\ \text{mm}} = 208\ \text{mm}$$

and now, $e = 616 - (17.1/2) - 208 = 399\ \text{mm}$

$$e' = 616 + 75 - 208 = 483\ \text{mm}$$

Finally, the resisting moment is

$$M_{rc} = (1747\ \text{kN} \times 399\ \text{mm}) + (3500\ \text{kN} \times 483\text{mm})$$

$$= 2388 \times 10^3\ \text{kN} \cdot \text{mm} = 2388\ \text{kN} \cdot \text{m}$$

A check will show that this section meets the local buckling requirements for a Class 2 section.

6.5 Shear Connectors

The strength of the shear connectors necessary to transmit the forces at the slab-steel section interface has been established from tests. Values based on these results are given in the Standard for most commonly encountered situations. For an end-welded stud with a height to diameter ratio of at least four, Clause 17.7.2.1 of the Standard specifies a factored shear resistance (q_{rs}) as the lesser of:

$$q_{rs} = 0.5 \, \phi_{sc} \, A_{sc} \, \sqrt{f'_c \, E_c} \qquad\qquad (6.12)$$

$$q_{rs} = \phi_{sc} \, A_{sc} \, F_u \qquad\qquad (6.13)$$

In these equations, the results will be expressed in newtons per stud with A_{sc} the cross-sectional area (mm^2) per stud, E_c the modulus of elasticity of concrete (MPa), f'_c the 28-day compressive strength of the concrete (MPa), F_u the tensile strength of the stud material, and ϕ_{sc} the resistance factor for the studs. The latter is to be taken as 0.80. For commonly available studs, F_u will be 415 MPa. The expression given in Equation 6.12 is based mainly on test results [6.8] and is valid for studs fully embedded in solid slabs of normal or lightweight concrete. It represents the stud capacity as achieved when the concrete adjacent to the stud fails by crushing. The same tests showed that if the stud itself failed, failure occurred only after considerable bending of the stud. Equation 6.13 is, therefore, an expression for the tensile capacity of the stud.

The Standard also gives an expression for the strength of the less frequently used channel shear connector.

The required number of shear connectors, as established using the force to be transferred (Equation 6.5 or 6.11) and the prescribed resistance per connector (Equation 6.12 or 6.13), can be uniformly distributed between the point of maximum moment and an adjacent zero moment location. The flexibility of the shear connectors permits this uniform spacing to be used. When concentrated loads are present, certain other restrictions are placed on the number of shear connectors (S16–01 Clause 17.9.8).

Example 6.3

Given

The beam and column layout of an interior bay assuming an office occupancy is shown in Figure 6.6. The beam B1 is to be designed as a composite steel-concrete member using G40.21 300W steel and concrete with a 28-day compressive strength of 20 MPa and a modulus of elasticity of 20.1×10^3 MPa (refer to Clause 2.1 of S16-01). The section will not be shored during construction. Use a dead load factor of 1.25 and a live load factor of 1.50, as appropriate.

Solution

The superimposed specified loads are

Dead Load	125 mm concrete slab, forms	3065 Pa
	tile flooring	50
	hung ceiling, lights, etc.	95
	movable partitions	190
	TOTAL	3400 Pa
Live Load (National Building Code)		2400 Pa

A trial section must be chosen and the capacity checked with respect to:

- strength of the steel section with regard to loads applied before the concrete hardens;

- strength of the composite section in flexure;

- shear capacity of the section;

- behaviour of the section under specified loads;

- proportioning of the shear connectors.

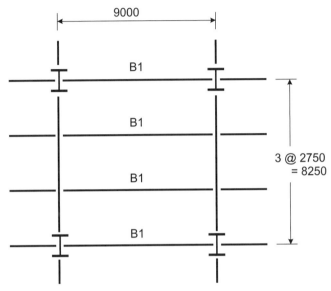

Figure 6.6 – Beam and Girder Layout — Example 6.3

Assuming simple support conditions and adequate lateral support, a suitable non-composite beam would be a W410×54. The composite section will be lighter and a W360×33 will be tried. This is a Class 2 section with $F_y = 300$ MPa for G40.21 300W steel. The cross-sectional properties that will be required are (from the CISC Handbook):

$A = 4170$ mm^2	$S = 474 \times 10^3$ mm^3	$J = 85.9 \times 10^3$ mm^4
$w = 5.8$ mm	$Z_x = 542 \times 10^3$ mm^3	$C_w = 84.3 \times 10^9$ mm^6
$d = 349$ mm	$I_x = 82.7 \times 10^6$ mm^4	
$b = 127$ mm	$I_y = 2.91 \times 10^6$ mm^4	

Design the steel section to carry loads prior to hardening of concrete. Provide lateral bracing to the compression flange at $L/4 = 2250$ mm.

Load: slab + forms = 3065 Pa × load factor
= 3065 × 1.25 = 3831 Pa

or, per metre of beam, 2.75 m × 3831 Pa = 10.54 × 10^3 N/m = 10.54 kN/m

plus estimated beam dead load = 0.32 kN/m × 1.25 = 0.40 kN/m = 0.40 kN/m

Total factored load = 10.94 kN/m, say, 10.9 kN/m

$$M_f = \frac{10.9 \text{ kN/m} \times (9\text{m})^2}{8} = 110 \text{ kN} \cdot \text{m}$$

For the W360×33

$$M_p = Z_x \, F_y = 542 \times 10^3 \times 300 \text{ MPa} = 163 \times 10^6 \text{N} \cdot \text{mm} = 163 \text{ kN} \cdot \text{m}$$

$$M_u = \frac{\omega_2 \, \pi}{L} \sqrt{E \, I_y \, G \, J + \left(\frac{\pi \, E}{L} \right)^2 I_y \, C_w} \qquad \text{(Clause 13.6 of S16)}$$

Taking $\omega_2 = 1.0$ (slightly conservative), $L = 2250$ mm, and the cross-sectional properties listed above, we obtain $M_u = 212 \times 10^6 \text{N} \cdot \text{mm} = 212 \text{ kN} \cdot \text{m}$.

Since $M_u > \dfrac{2}{3} M_p = 109 \text{kN} \cdot \text{m}$, then

$$M_r = 1.15 \, \phi \, M_p \left(1 - \frac{0.28 \times M_p}{M_u} \right)$$

$$= 1.15 \times 0.90 \times 163 \left(1 - \frac{0.28 \times 163}{212} \right) = 132 \text{ kN} \cdot \text{m} \qquad \text{(Governs)}$$

or, $M_r = \phi \, M_p = 0.90 \times 163 = 147 \text{ kN} \cdot \text{m}$

Thus, the resistance of the section under these conditions is 132 kN·m, whereas the factored moment is 110 kN·m. Therefore, the W360×33 is satisfactory with respect to non-composite action. (Although the W360×33 has excess capacity for this loading condition, no adjustment should be made until all the other load cases have been examined.)

Establish the capacity of the composite section —

Loads: Factored dead load — 3400 Pa×1.25 = 4250 Pa

Factored live load — 2400 Pa×1.5 = 3600 Pa

Total = 7850 Pa

or, per metre of beam,

2.75 m×7850 Pa = 21.6×10³ N/m = 21.6 kN/m

plus factored beam dead load of 0.40 kN/m

Total = 22.0 kN/m

and then $M_f = \dfrac{22.0 \text{ kN/m} \times (9 \text{ m})^2}{8} = 223 \text{ kN} \cdot \text{m}$

Effective slab width of composite section
- 1/4×9000 mm = 2250 mm (Governs)

158

- or, 2750 mm

Using the procedure presented in Example 6.1, the factored moment resistance of the composite beam is $M_{rc} = 310 \text{ kN} \cdot \text{m}$.

The W360×33 therefore is satisfactory when acting compositely with the concrete slab in resisting the total factored moment.

The capacity of the section in resisting the maximum vertical shear is (Equation 6.2)

$$V_r = 0.90 \times (349 \times 5.8) \text{ mm}^2 \times 0.66 \times 300 \text{ MPa}$$

$$= 361 \times 10^3 \text{ N} = 361 \text{ kN}$$

The maximum factored shear is

$$V_f = \frac{22.0 \text{ kN/m} \times 9 \text{ m}}{2} = 99 \text{ kN} \qquad \text{(Satisfactory)}$$

Behaviour of the section under specified loads—Assume that the neutral axis for elastic conditions will lie in the steel and the slab therefore will be fully effective. Take area-moments about the base of the steel beam.

Steel section: $A = 4170 \text{ mm}^2$; $y = d/2 = 175 \text{ mm}$;

and $A \cdot y = 730 \times 10^3 \text{ mm}^3$

Slab: Use a modular ratio (E_s/E_c) of $200\,000 \text{ MPa}/20\,100 \text{ MPa} = 9.9$ and transform the concrete area into an equivalent steel area—

$$A = \frac{2250 \text{ mm}}{9.9} \times 125 \text{ mm} = 28\,410 \text{ mm}^2 \qquad y = (349 + (125/2)) = 411 \text{ mm}$$

and $A \cdot y = 11\,680 \times 10^3 \text{ mm}^3$

Now, $\Sigma A = 32\,580 \text{ mm}^2$ and $\Sigma A \cdot y = 12\,410 \times 10^3 \text{ mm}^3$

and thus $\bar{y} = \dfrac{\Sigma A \cdot y}{\Sigma A} = \dfrac{12\,410 \times 10^3 \text{ mm}^3}{32\,580 \text{ mm}^2} = 381 \text{ mm}$ $(> d = 349 \text{ mm})$

Since the neutral axis does not fall below the slab, the assumption that the concrete is fully effective was incorrect. The location of a neutral axis that falls in the slab can be determined conveniently by trial. (It can be determined explicitly, of course: solution of a quadratic equation will be required.) Following an initial trial, not shown here, assume that the neutral axis is located 37 mm above the steel beam. Again take moments about the base of the steel beam.

Steel section: $A = 4170 \text{ mm}^2$, $y = 349 \times 0.5 \text{ mm} = 175 \text{ mm}$

$A \cdot y = 730 \times 10^3 \text{ mm}^3$

Slab: $A = \dfrac{2250 \text{ mm}}{9.9} \times 88 \text{ mm} = 20\,000 \text{ mm}^2$

and then
$$y = (349 + 37 + (125-37)/2) = 430 \text{ mm}$$
$$A \cdot y = 8600 \times 10^3 \text{ mm}^3$$
$$\Sigma A = 24\,170 \text{ mm}^2, \quad \Sigma A \cdot y = 9330 \times 10^3 \text{ mm}^3$$

Finally,
$$\bar{y} = \frac{\Sigma A \cdot y}{\Sigma A} = \frac{9330 \times 10^3 \text{ mm}^3}{24\,170 \text{ mm}^2} = 386 \text{ mm}$$

or, 37 mm above the steel beam, as assumed.

Next, calculate the moment of inertia—

Steel Section: about own centre of gravity plus parallel axis theorem shift to composite section neutral axis

$$= 82.7 \times 10^6 \text{ mm}^4 + 4170 \times \left[\frac{349}{2} + 37 \right]^2 \text{ mm}^4 = 269.2 \times 10^6 \text{ mm}^4$$

Slab: about own centre of gravity plus shift to composite section neutral axis (all dimensions in mm)

$$= \frac{1}{12} \times \frac{2250}{9.9} \times (125-37)^3 + \frac{2250}{9.9} \times 88 \times \left[\frac{125-37}{2} \right]^2 = 51.6 \times 10^6 \text{ mm}^4$$

Moment of inertia of composite section (total of above) $\qquad = 321 \times 10^6 \text{ mm}^4$

The section modulus of the composite section, referred to the bottom flange, is

$$S_t = \frac{321 \times 10^6 \text{ mm}^4}{(349+37) \text{ mm}} = 831 \times 10^3 \text{ mm}^3$$

The specified load acting prior to hardening of the concrete is:

slab + forms $= 3065$ Pa

or, per metre of beam, $2.75 \text{ m} \times 3065 \text{ Pa} = 8429 \text{ N/m} = 8.43 \text{ kN/m}$

plus estimated beam dead load 0.32 kN/m

$$\text{Total} = 8.75 \text{ kN/m}$$

from which the moment M_1 can be calculated as

$$M_1 = \frac{8.75 \text{ kN/m} \times (9 \text{ m})^2}{8} = 88.6 \text{ kN} \cdot \text{m} = 88.6 \times 10^6 \text{ N} \cdot \text{mm}$$

The specified load acting subsequent to hardening of the concrete:

tile, ceiling, partitions, live load $= 2735$ Pa

or, per metre of beam $\quad 2.75 \text{ m} \times 2735 \text{ Pa} = 7521 \text{ N/m} = 7.52 \text{ kN/m}$

from which, $M_2 = \dfrac{7.52 \text{ kN}/\text{m} \times (9 \text{ m})^2}{8} = 76.1 \text{ kN} \cdot \text{m} = 76.1 \times 10^6 \text{ N} \cdot \text{mm}$

Now, checking Equation 6.1

$$\frac{M_1}{S_s} + \frac{M_2}{S_t} = \frac{88.6 \times 10^6 \ \text{N} \cdot \text{mm}}{474 \times 10^3 \ \text{mm}^3} + \frac{76.1 \times 10^6 \ \text{N} \cdot \text{mm}}{831 \times 10^3 \ \text{mm}^3} = 278 \ \text{MPa}$$

The limit is F_y, which is 300 MPa for the steel used. This section is therefore satisfactory.

Shear Connectors — Try 19 mm diameter studs × 75 mm long. These will have adequate cover in the slab and the ratio h/d is approximately 4. The cross-sectional area per stud is 284 mm^2. Checking Equation 6.12—

$$q_{rs} = 0.5 \times 0.80 \times 284 \ \text{mm}^2 \times \sqrt{20 \ \text{MPa} \times 20 \ 100 \ \text{MPa}} = 72 \ 026 \ \text{N} = 72.0 \ \text{kN}$$

or, from Equation 6.13 and taking F_u as 415 MPa

$$q_r = 0.80 \times 415 \ \text{MPa} \times 284 \ \text{mm}^2 = 94 \ 288 \ \text{N} = 94.3 \ \text{kN}$$

The value calculated by Equation 6.12 governs (72.0 kN).

The load to be transferred (Equation 6.5) is

$$V_h = 0.90 \times 4170 \ \text{mm}^2 \times 300 \ \text{MPa} = 1126 \times 10^3 \ \text{N} = 1126 \ \text{kN}$$

Number of connectors required between midspan and ends;

$$N = \frac{1126 \ \text{kN}}{72.0 \ \text{kN/stud}} = 15.6 \ \text{studs}$$

Place 16 studs between midspan and each end of the beam.

For this beam span of 9 m, the studs could be installed in a single line at a spacing of 280 mm. This arrangement provides a total of 32 studs, as required, assuming that the first and last studs are located 160 mm from the column centrelines. The actual detail at the column-to-beam connection would have to be known in order to establish whether or not the 160 mm is suitable.

The W360×33 that was used here is probably the lightest section that would be satisfactory. It represents a saving of 11 kg/m over the least-weight non-composite section. If a reduction in depth were considered important, a 250 mm or 310 mm deep section could be investigated. The result would be a heavier section than the one selected in the example.

Attachment of a coverplate on the bottom flange of the steel beam could be used to bring the neutral axis down below the level of the slab. This provides better utilization of the concrete and the resulting steel section. The steel weight would likely be less than the 33 kg/m obtained in the example, but there would be an additional cost in attaching the coverplate. Economically, it would probably not be advantageous in a lightly loaded span such as this one.

The deflection of this beam is calculated in Example 6.5.

The design of composite beams can be aided considerably by the use of computer programs such as CISC's GFD4 [1.9] or composite beam-trial selection tables contained in the CISC Handbook. More information is also available in Reference [6.9].

6.6 Partial Shear Connection

In many cases, full shear connection is either not necessary or is not economical. In the first instance, design may be controlled by deflections; there would be no advantage, therefore, in providing all the shear connectors required for full shear transfer. In the second case, it might be more economical to reduce the number of shear connectors from 100% of that required for full shear transfer and accept the penalty of reduced flexural capacity. A shear transfer of even 50% will usually produce ultimate flexural capacities of about 80% of that corresponding to full composite action [6.10]. Today, practically all composite construction in buildings in Canada is done on the basis of partial shear connection.

If partial shear connection is used, it is required (S16, Clause 17.9.4) that the number of shear connectors be at least 40% of that needed for full composite action if flexural strength controls the design. This is to ensure that the member will behave compositely throughout its full loading history. If design is controlled by deflection considerations, the degree of shear transfer is permitted to be as low as 25%.

Strength Calculations—The number of shear connectors supplied will identify the force actually transferred at the slab–steel section interface. Calling this force Q_r, it will be given by

$$Q_r = \Sigma q_r \tag{6.14}$$

where q_r is the capacity of an individual connector, as given by Equation 6.12 or Equation 6.13.

Assume that the neutral axis is in the slab. The shear force transferred if full composite action were present would be given by Equation 6.5, that is, $V_h = \phi A_s F_y$. However, since by definition the amount of shear force transferred is less than 100%, it follows that the actual force transferred is less than 100%. This in turn means that, for all cases of shear transfer less than 100%, the neutral axis must lie within the steel section, not in the slab.

The resulting stress block model is shown in Figure 6.7. The compressive force in the concrete is given by

$$C'_r = Q_r = \Sigma q_r \tag{6.15}$$

Alternatively,

$$C'_r = 0.85 \ \phi_c \ f'_c \ b \ a \tag{6.16}$$

Equating these two expressions for C'_r, the depth of concrete slab required to accommodate the shear force actually transferred can be obtained as

$$a = \frac{Q_r}{0.85 \ \phi_c \ f'_c \ b} \tag{6.17}$$

An expression for C_r can be developed in exactly the same way as Equation 6.8 was derived. That equation was

$$C_r = \frac{\phi A_s F_y - C'_r}{2}$$

(Eq. 6.8)

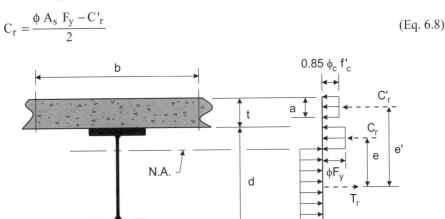

Figure 6.7 – Composite Cross-Section — Partial Shear Connection

The location of the neutral axis within the steel section can now be determined such that equilibrium of horizontal forces is satisfied (Equation 6.6). When this is known, the moment arms e and e' (Figure 6.7) can be determined and the resisting moment written as

$$M_{rc} = C_r e + C'_r e'$$

(Eq. 6.10)

where C'_r is given by Equation 6.15 or 6.16 and C_r is given by Equation 6.8.

Example 6.4

In Example 6.3, the factored moment on the composite cross-section was calculated to be $M_f = 223$ kN·m. However, the resistance of the cross-section used was $M_{rc} = 364$ N·mm. (Recall also that the stress in the bottom flange under the specified loads was very close to the limiting value, 278 MPa vs. 300 MPa). Since we do not need all of the flexural capacity provided, we do not need to provide 100% shear connection in this case. There are other reasons to not provide 100% shear connection, however. The most important one is simply that it is usually more economical to provide less than 100% and to then accept the penalty of reduction in moment capacity.

Given

Redesign the composite cross-section in Example 6.3 on the basis of partial shear connection.

Solution

The ratio of M_f to M_{rc} is 223/364 = 0.61. Try a design in which the shear connection provided will be 70% of that required to produce full flexural capacity.

For 100% shear connection, $V_h = 1126$ kN (Example 6.3). Therefore, for the 70% shear transfer case:

$1126 \text{ kN} \times 0.70 = 788 \text{ kN} \equiv C'_r = \Sigma q_r$

This force is shown in Figure 6.8.

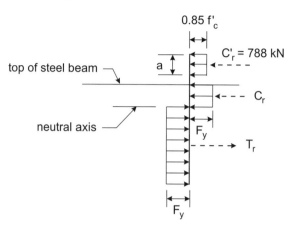

Figure 6.8 – Example 6.4

From the equilibrium requirement, that is, Equation 6.17, the depth of the concrete in compression is:

$$a = \frac{Q_r}{0.85 \; \phi_c \; f'_c \; b} = \frac{788 \times 10^3 \text{ N}}{0.85 \times 0.60 \times 20 \text{ N/mm}^2 \times 2250 \text{ mm}} = 34.3 \text{ mm}$$

Using Equation 6.8, the value of the compressive force in the steel (see Figure 6.8) can now be calculated:

$$C_r = \frac{\phi \; A_s \; F_y - C'_r}{2}$$

$$C_r = \frac{0.90 \times 4170 \text{ mm}^2 \times 300 \text{ N/mm}^2 - 788 \times 10^3 \text{ N}}{2} = 169 \times 10^3 \text{ N}$$

Locate the neutral axis. Assume that the neutral axis is in the flange of the steel beam (see Figure 6.9).

$$0.90 \times (127 \times d_f) \text{ mm}^2 \times 300 \text{ MPa} = 169 \times 10^3 \text{ N}$$

$$d_f = \frac{169 \times 10^3 \text{ N}}{0.90 \times 127 \text{ mm} \times 300 \text{ MPa}} = 4.9 \text{ mm}$$

Since d_f is less than the flange thickness ($t = 8.5 \text{ mm}$), the neutral axis is in the flange.

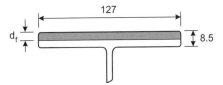

Figure 6.9 – Location of Neutral Axis

Next, locate the force T_f and calculate the moment arms between the forces (refer to Figure 6.10). Taking area moments about the base (and with all dimensions in millimetres):

$$\bar{y} = \frac{\left(4170\times\frac{349}{2}\right)-(127\times4.9)\left(349-\frac{4.9}{2}\right)}{4170-(127\times4.9)} = 144.3 \text{ mm}$$

from the base about which moments were taken, i.e., bottom flange.

Calculate the moment arms relative to the location of T_r (see Figure 6.10) as

$$e' = 349 + 125 - \frac{34.3}{2} - 144.3 = 312.6 \text{ mm}$$

$$e = 349 - \frac{4.9}{2} - 144.3 = 202.3 \text{ mm}$$

And, finally, from Figure 6.10 (or Equation 6.10)

$$M_{rc} = 788 \text{ kN}\times312.5 \text{ mm} + 169 \text{ kN}\times202.3 \text{ mm}$$

$$= 280\times10^3 \text{ kN}\cdot\text{mm} = 280 \text{ kN}\cdot\text{m}$$

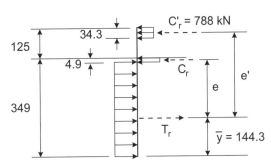

Figure 6.10 – Location of Forces — Example 6.4

Since the value of the factored moment is $M_f = 223$ kN·m, this is satisfactory, although obviously a further reduction could be made in the number of shear connectors.

6.7 Use of Formed Metal Deck

In the discussion of the strength principles so far, it has been assumed that the underside of the concrete has been formed with temporary forms, usually plywood. Permanent sheet steel forms with a modest corrugation (less than 0.25 times the slab thickness) to provide form strength are also used. In either of these cases, the overall thickness of the slab is used in the strength calculations. However, it has already been noted that it is common to use steel deck containing relatively large corrugations as the formwork for the concrete. The resulting system, usually called hollow composite construction, is discussed in this section.

The steel deck, which is made from zinc-coated sheet steel, may be placed either parallel to the steel supporting member or transversely to it (Figure 6.11). If placed transversely, the steel deck itself will act compositely with the slab to transfer slab loads to the beams. The sidewalls and bottom of the trough of the steel deck usually have some kind of embossment in order to provide an interlock with the concrete. This provides for composite action between the steel deck sheet and the concrete slab as it spans from beam to beam.

After the steel deck has been placed on the supporting beams, the studs are attached by welding through the sheet steel. Reinforcement for the slab is then placed and the concrete is placed. It is required that the minimum thickness of concrete above the top of the steel deck be 65 mm (S16–01 Clause 17.2). The shape of the profile of the steel deck and the conditions under which the stud welding can be done are also subject to limitations described in S16.

The strength calculations for vertical shear proceed as described earlier for solid slabs since it has been assumed that the entire shear is carried by the web of the steel section. For calculation of flexural strength, the effective slab thickness is to be taken as the thickness of the concrete between the top of the steel deck and the top of the slab. The calculations then proceed as described earlier for solid slabs, recognizing that there is now a portion of the cross-section (between the top of the steel section and the top of the profile of the steel deck) that is assumed to be totally ineffective [6.11].

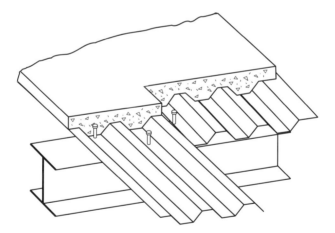

Figure 6.11 – Hollow Composite Construction

The requirements noted under Section 6.10 should also be reviewed, particularly with respect to checks for longitudinal shear strength.

6.8 Behaviour Under Negative Moment

Under the action of a negative bending moment, the concrete slab in a composite section will be subjected to tension and is therefore considered ineffective. However, the steel reinforcement in the slab that runs parallel to the beam and which is within the effective slab width can be considered to carry a share of the negative moment, provided certain conditions are met. These are that shear connectors be provided in this region and that the reinforcement has adequate embedment in a zone of positive moment [6.12]. Theoretically, shear connectors should not be necessary in this region since the concrete has been assumed to be cracked and ineffective. However, the short portions of uncracked concrete that inevitably will be present, if anchored to the steel beam, will serve to transfer load more gradually into the reinforcement than if the embedment length of the bars alone were expected to transfer load. This is illustrated in Figure 6.12.

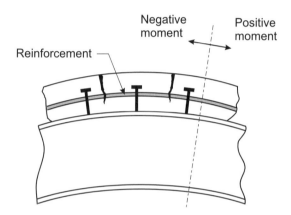

Figure 6.12 – Behaviour Under Negative Moment

If the conditions described above are met, an ultimate strength analysis can be applied to the cross-section. Assuming that the neutral axis will fall somewhere in the steel beam, the ultimate capacity can be calculated by considering the reinforcing bars acting in tension, a portion of the steel beam also acting in tension, and the remainder of the steel beam acting in compression. It should be noted that, in the usual situation, more of the beam cross-section will be in compression than in a non-composite steel beam. The buckling tendency is therefore increased (both local and lateral buckling) and the rotation capacity is also likely to be reduced.

In parallel with the ultimate strength considerations used to proportion the shear connectors in a positive moment region, a similar approach is taken here. A conservative estimate of the number required is obtained by considering that there must be sufficient shear connectors to produce yielding in the longitudinal slab reinforcement. In S16, this requirement is expressed as (Clause 17.9.7);

$$V_h = \phi_r \, A_r \, F_{yr} \qquad\qquad (6.18)$$

where $\phi_r = 0.85$

A_r = area of longitudinal reinforcement contained within the effective slab width

167

F_{yr} = minimum specified yield strength of the longitudinal reinforcing steel.

The number of shear connectors required between any maximum negative moment and an adjacent zero moment location can now be determined.

6.9 Deflections

The deflections of a composite beam under the action of the specified loads will be affected by creep and shrinkage of the concrete, and by the effects of increased flexibility resulting from partial shear connection and from interface slip. The situation is further complicated by the presence (usually) of a slab that is continuous over beam-to-girder connections and around columns. This continuity will reduce deflections as compared to those occurring in a system that has truly simple connections.

The calculation of deflections should start with an identification of those that result from the loads that are applied before composite action is attained. In this condition, the steel beam alone is effective.

Deflections due to short-term live loads applied after the concrete has hardened should be calculated using the moment of inertia of the composite section. The modular ratio n is used to transform the concrete into an equivalent amount of steel. If partial shear connection is present, this must also be recognized. To take this effect into account, it is recommended in Clause 17.3.1(a) of S16 that an adjustment be made to the moment of inertia of the composite section. Based on the results of tests, it is suggested that [6.13]

$$I_e = I_s + 0.85 \, (p)^{0.25} \, (I_t - I_s) \tag{6.19}$$

where

I_e = effective moment of inertia

p = fraction of full shear connection (use $p = 1.0$ for full shear connection)

I_t = transformed moment of inertia of composite section

I_s = moment of inertia of steel section alone.

Note that an adjustment will apply even for the case of full shear transfer. This reflects the observation that the inherent (and desirable) flexibility of the shear connectors will increase beam deflections over those calculated using elastic beam theory.

Dead load and long-term live loads will produce plastic flow (creep) in the concrete. In Clause 17.3.1(b) of S16, it is suggested that these deflections be calculated as though they were elastic and then a 15% increase applied in order to account for the effect of the plastic flow. Because the deflection due to creep is usually a small part of the total deflection of a composite beam, this simple solution to a complex problem seems to give satisfactory results [6.14].

As the concrete in the slab of a composite section cures, volumetric changes occur. This shrinkage of the concrete takes place in a system in which the other component, the steel section, does not change length. The continuity of the two parts of the system, enforced by the shear connectors, requires that curvatures take place, and the resulting deflection can be a significant part of the total deflection of the composite beam [6.14].

168

The force induced in the concrete as a result of the slab shrinkage (see Figure 6.13) is:

$$F = \sigma_c \, A_c \tag{6.20}$$

$$\text{but,} \quad \sigma_c = E_{ct} \, \varepsilon_f \tag{6.21}$$

where ε_f is the free shrinkage strain. This force acts at the centroid of the concrete slab. It produces a moment about the elastic neutral axis of the cross-section (Figure 6.14) of

$$M = F \cdot y = E_{ct} \, \varepsilon_y \, A_c \, y \tag{6.22}$$

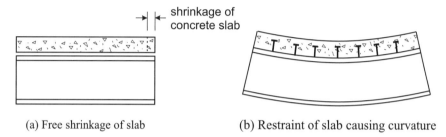

(a) Free shrinkage of slab   (b) Restraint of slab causing curvature

Figure 6.13 – Deflection of Composite Beam Resulting from

Shrinkage of Concrete Slab

In Equation 6.22, E_{ct} is the time-dependent value of the modulus of elasticity of the concrete. If it is assumed that this effect is uniform along the length of the member, then the deflection that will occur in a simply-supported beam of length L is given by

$$\Delta = \frac{M \, L^2}{8 \, E \, I_t} \tag{6.23}$$

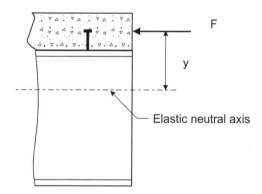

Figure 6.14 – Force Due to Shrinkage

In Equation 6.23, which can be obtained using moment–area theorems, the modulus E is that for steel and the moment of inertia is that of the transformed section. Upon substitution of the value of M obtained using Equation 6.22 and using n_t for the ratio of E/E_{ct}, this deflection resulting from shrinkage of the concrete can be written as

$$\Delta = \frac{\varepsilon_f \, A_c \, L^2 \, y}{8 \, n_t I_t} \qquad (6.24)$$

The S16–01 Standard (Appendix H) suggests that appropriate values for the modular ratio n_t are in the range 40 to 60.

The application of Equation 6.24 is complicated by the question of what value to use for the shrinkage strain and the time dependent nature of the modulus of elasticity of concrete in tension, E_{ct}. The selected value for the free shrinkage strain is dependent on properties of the concrete such as water/cement ratio, percent fines, entrained air, and curing conditions. Appendix H of S16 suggests a value for free shrinkage ε_f of 800×10^{-6} in the absence of better data.

The modulus of elasticity of concrete in tension is time dependent—the tensile strain due to the reducing volumetric change increases, the modulus of the concrete decreases. The shrinkage deflection induced by this tensile strain is not, however, time sensitive to the modulus of elasticity: both the effective moment of inertia and the distance y vary with modulus of elasticity. Again, Appendix H of S16 provides guidance on appropriate values to be used, and, thereby, also corresponding values for the modular ratio n_t. For the purpose of Example 6.5, a value of $n_t = 50$ will be used.

Because deflections are usually accommodated, at least in part, by cambering or by adjustments in slab thickness, it is important to try to estimate the effects of structural continuity. A slab that is "bowed" upward is as unattractive to the observer as one that "sags" downward. The designer customarily will make the deflection calculations using the assumption that members are simply-supported. Calculations made in this way will result in an overestimate of actual deflection by a rather large amount. This is the consequence of two major factors. Firstly, neither beam-to-girder nor girder or beam-to-column connections are truly simple, even though the member may have been analyzed on that basis. Secondly, the concrete slab in the composite system likely will be continuous over all beam-to-girder regions and around the columns. Thus, the resulting system will be much stiffer than calculation on the basis of simple supports would indicate. The only practical way for the designer to handle this is to calculate the deflections on the basis of an assumption of simple connections and then apply a reduction based on experience or judgment. Reference [6.14] has indicated that a reduction based on the application of negative end moments equal to 25% of the mid-span moment of a uniformly loaded beam will give a good estimate of the continuity effect for the type of framing usually found in office building construction.

The continuity of the slab will create regions of unintentional negative moment and the concrete will tend to develop undesirable cracks at the top surface. Extra reinforcing steel should be placed near the top of the slab in such locations so that this cracking will be minimized. Reference [6.9] discusses placement of reinforcing steel for crack control in composite floor systems.

Finally, the designer should be alert to recognize situations in which the effect of shear upon the deflections is significant. Because the shear capacity of a composite beam is generally reduced as compared to that which would have been provided by a non-composite beam, the contribution of shear to the total deflection may be important if the loads are high or the spans are short.

Example 6.5

Given

Calculate the deflection of the composite beam designed in Example 6.3.

Solution

Non-composite beam: The steel beam acts alone to carry the slab load, formwork, plus its own dead weight. This is

$$3065 \text{ Pa} \times 2.75 \text{ m} = 8428 \text{ N/m} = 8.43 \text{ kN/m}$$

plus beam dead load = 0.32 kN/m

Therefore, for a simply-supported beam,

$$\Delta_t = \frac{5}{384} \frac{wL^4}{EI} = \frac{5}{384} \times \frac{8.75 \text{ N/mm} \times (9000 \text{ mm})^4}{200\ 000 \text{ MPa} \times 82.7 \times 10^6 \text{ mm}^4} = 45.2 \text{ mm}$$

Composite beam, short-term loads: It will be assumed that half the specified live load acts on a long-term basis and half on a short-term basis. Since the total live load was 2400 Pa, the short-term load per millimeter of the beam length is

$$2400 \text{ Pa} \times 1/2 \times 2.75 \text{ m} = 3300 \text{ N/m} = 3.30 \text{ N/mm}$$

The transformed moment of inertia of this composite section was calculated in Example 6.3 as 321×10^6 mm^4. The effective moment of inertia can be calculated using Equation 6.19 and setting $p = 1.0$ for this case of full shear transfer:

$$I_e = I_s + 0.85 \ (p)^{0.25} \ (I_t - I_s)$$

$$= 82.7 \times 10^6 + 0.85 \ (1.0)^{0.25} \ (321 - 82.7) \times 10^6 = 285 \times 10^6 \text{ mm}^4$$

$$\Delta_2 = \frac{5}{384} \times \frac{3.30 \text{ N/mm} \times (9000 \text{ mm})^4}{200\ 000 \text{ MPa} \times 285 \times 10^6 \text{ mm}^4} = 4.9 \text{ mm}$$

Composite beam, long-term loads: The assumed long-term load has been established as 1200 Pa. To this must be added the weight of the tile, hung ceiling, lights, and partitions, as listed in Example 6.3. These add up to 335 Pa, so that the long-term load per millimeter of beam length is

$$(1200 + 335) \text{ Pa} \times 2.75 \text{ m} = 4221 \text{ N/m} = 4.22 \text{ N/mm}$$

The deflection due to this load acting on the composite section, and including the 15% allowance for long-term load effect, is

$$\Delta_3 = 1.15 \times \frac{5}{384} \times \frac{4.22 \text{ N/mm} \times (9000 \text{ mm})^4}{200\ 000 \text{ MPa} \times 285 \times 10^6 \text{ mm}^4} = 7.3 \text{ mm}$$

The deflection resulting from the shrinkage of the concrete can be obtained using Equation 6.24. For this calculation, the transformed moment of inertia I_t is based on the modular ratio n_t, taken here as 50. Therefore I_t can be calculated following the procedure used in Example 6.3

Taking area moments about the base of the steel beam:

Steel section: $A = 4170$ mm^2 $y = 349 \times 0.5$ mm $A \cdot y = 730 \times 10^3$ mm^3

Slab: $A = \dfrac{2250 \text{ mm}}{50} \times 125$ mm $= 5625$ mm^2

$y = (349 + (125/2))$ mm $= 412$ mm

$A \cdot y = 2318 \times 10^3$ mm^3

Now, $\Sigma A = 9795$ mm^2 and $\Sigma A \cdot y = 3048 \times 10^3$ mm^3

Hence $y = \dfrac{\Sigma A \cdot y}{\Sigma A} = \dfrac{3048 \times 10^3 \text{mm}^3}{9795 \text{ mm}^2} = 311$ mm $(< d = 349$ mm$)$

Calculate the moment of inertia:

Steel Section: about own centre of gravity + shift to composite section neutral axis

$$= 82.7 \times 10^6 \text{ mm}^4 + 4170 \times \left[311 - \frac{349}{2} \right]^2 \text{mm}^4 = 160.4 \times 10^6 \text{ mm}^4$$

Slab: about own centre of gravity + shift to composite section neutral axis (all dimensions in mm)

$$= \frac{1}{12} \times \frac{2250}{50} \times (125)^3 + \frac{2250}{50} \times 125 \times \left[349 - 311 + \frac{125}{2} \right]^2 = 64.1 \times 10^6 \text{ mm}^4$$

Moment of inertia of composite section (total of above) $= 224.5 \times 10^6$ mm^4

Finally, and using a free shrinkage strain of 800×10^{-6}, the deflection due to shrinkage is (Equation 6.24):

$$\Delta_s = \frac{800 \times 10^{-6} \times (2250 \times 125) \text{ mm}^2 \times (9000 \text{ mm})^2 \times 100.5 \text{ mm}}{8 \times 50 \times 224.5 \times 10^6 \text{ mm}^4} = 20.4 \text{ mm}$$

In this calculation, the information contained in Example 6.3 was used to calculate the eccentricity as $y = 449 + (125/2) - 311 = 100.5$ mm. Note also that the area of concrete is taken as the effective area.

Now, the total deflection from all sources can be calculated as $45.2 + 4.9 + 7.3 + 20.4 = 77.8$ mm. However, as has been discussed, the continuity of the system will have the effect of reducing this theoretical deflection. It can be shown that the application of negative end moments equal to 25% of the mid-span moment of a uniformly loaded beams reduces the maximum deflection of the simple span by 30%. This will be used to adjust the first three terms of the calculated deflection. The application of end moments of 25% of fixed end moment provides a direct reduction of

25% to the calculated shrinkage deflection. (It was obtained by applying a uniform moment.) Thus, an estimate of the deflection of this beam as adjusted for the effects of continuity is—

$$(45.2 + 4.9 + 7.3) \, 0.70 + (20.4 \times 0.75) = 55.5 \text{ mm} \, .$$

At least the major part of this would have to be accounted for in the construction of the beam. This could be handled by

- Cambering of the steel beam: or
- Control of the slab thickness: or
- Shoring of the steel beam at the time of placing of the concrete.

If the latter control were used, the deflections on the non-composite section could be substantially reduced. At the same time, the amount of long-term load would be increased and the calculation of deflections for this effect must be adjusted accordingly.

6.10   Shear Strength of Longitudinal Planes

A check of forces or stresses acting along longitudinal shear planes in the concrete should be made (Clause 17.9.10 of the Standard). Figure 6.15(a) shows these forces in a solid slab composite beam. Another possible shear-out for solid slab composite beams is shown in Figure 6.15(b) and a hollow composite beam is illustrated in Figure 6.15(c).

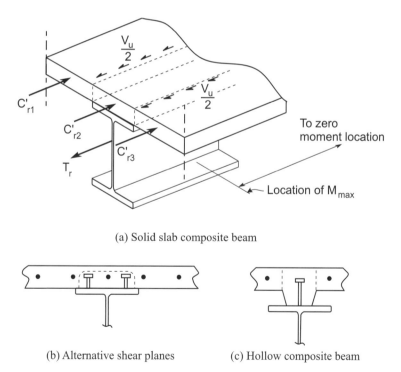

(a) Solid slab composite beam

(b) Alternative shear planes   (c) Hollow composite beam

Figure 6.15 – Longitudinal Shear in Composite Beams

In Figure 6.15(a), the total compressive force in the slab has been broken down into components according to the assumed location of the longitudinal shear planes. The directions of the longitudinal shear forces shown in this figure are those associated with compressive forces C'_{r1} and C'_{r2}. The central section of the slab shown in Figure 6.15(a) is isolated further and is shown in Figure 6.16. The horizontal surface has been taken through the shear connectors, either at the level of the neutral axis if it is within the slab, or at the steel section-to-slab interface otherwise. The longitudinal shear forces in the slab must be equal and opposite to those shown in Figure 6.15(a). For equilibrium

$$V_u + C'_{r2} - Q_u = 0$$

or, $\quad V_u = Q_u - C'_{r2}$ \hfill (6.25)

The compressive force C'_{r2} in Equation 6.25 can be expressed as

$$C'_{r2} = 0.85 \, f'_c \, A_{c2} + A_{r2} \, F_{yr} \hfill (6.26)$$

where

$\quad A_{c2} = $ area of concrete in compression within the region containing the shear connectors

$\quad A_{r2} = $ the area of longitudinal slab reinforcement with the area A_{c2}

$\quad F_{yr} = $ specified minimum yield strength of the reinforcing steel.

Using Equation 6.25, the total ultimate shear force acting on the two longitudinal planes shown in Figure 6.15(a) can be expressed as

$$V_u = Q_u - 0.85 \, \phi_c \, f'_c \, A_{c2} - A_{r2} \, F_{yr} \hfill (6.27)$$

The corresponding resistance, given in Clause 17.9.10 of the Standard using slight different nomenclature, is that suggested in Reference [6.15], namely, the lesser of

$$V_r = 0.80 \, \phi \, A_{r2} \, F_{yr} + 2.76 \, \phi_c \, A_{cv} \hfill (6.28)$$

$$V_r = 0.50 \, \phi_c \, f'_c \, A_{cv} \hfill (6.29)$$

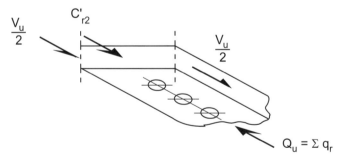

Figure 6.16 – Longitudinal Shear — Free-body Diagram

All of these terms have been defined previously except for A_{cv}, which is the total area of the two longitudinal shear planes extending from the point of maximum moment to an adjacent location of zero moment. Reference [6.9] can be consulted for resistance expressions to be used when semi-low or low density concrete is used.

If the potential planes of longitudinal shear are like those shown in Figure 6.15(b) or 6.15(c), adjustments obviously have to be made to the foregoing development. When metal deck is present (Figure 6.15(c)), the steel in the metal deck will provide some shear resistance. Research work is not available that would help to quantify this contribution and a conservative solution is to neglect it.

6.11   Other Composite Floor Members

While composite beams and composite girders are the most frequently used steel floor framing system in multi-storey commercial buildings, as the span is increased so also is the depth of the member increased. This increases the depth of the floor-ceiling sandwich and may necessitate passing the mechanical ducts through the girder web, thus increasing the fabrication costs. In these situations, where structural-mechanical integration is required, two other types of composite floor members have been used successfully: the composite truss and the stub-girder system.

By reason of its configuration, a truss provides openings through which mechanical and other under-floor services can pass easily. Trusses have been found to be economical for spans from about 10 m to 23 m, and they have often been used to span from the central core of a building to the perimeter columns. The truss chords will usually consist of structural T sections or hollow structural sections, with angle or hollow structural section web members in a Warren or modified Warren configuration.

Composite stub-girder floor system

The truss acting non-compositely must be designed to carry the construction loads (wet concrete, forms, etc.), as is done for unshored girders. Once composite action has been achieved ($f_c \geq 0.75 f'_c$), the moment resistance of the composite truss is determined in a similar manner to that for a girder [6.16]. However, as prescribed in Clause 17.9.2 of S16–01, the cross-section of steel comprising the top chord is to be neglected in the calculations. This represents a conservative simplification. As with beams, the vertical shear must be taken entirely by the steel truss, specifically, by the web members. A detailed explanation of the design of composite trusses can be found in Chapter 5 of Reference [6.9].

A stub girder is a form of truss, in particular a Vierendeel truss wherein the top chord is the deck slab and the bottom chord is a rolled steel section. The top and bottom chords are interconnected using short lengths of a beam section, usually from about 310 to 460 mm deep. The gaps between these short lengths of beam provide the openings for passage of mechanical services. The stub-girder chords are subject to axial loads, bending moments, and shears resulting from the Vierendeel action of the girder. Methods of analysis for stub-girders using hand computations or computer modeling are given in Chapter 6 of Reference [6.9].

The Motorola Building in Toronto consists of steel–concrete composite beams supported on steel columns. (Photo courtesy of Michael I. Gilmor)

References

6.1   Canadian Standards Association, CAN/CSA–S16–01, "Limit States Design of Steel Structures," Toronto, Ontario, 2001.

6.2   Heins, C.P., and Fan, H.M., "Effective Composite Beam Width at Ultimate Load," Journal of the Structural Division, ASCE, Vol. 102, No. ST11, November, 1976.

6.3   Viest, I.M., Fountain, R.S., and Singleton, R.C., "Composite Construction in Steel and Concrete," McGraw-Hill, New York, 1958.

6.4   "Tentative Recommendations for the Design and Construction of Composite Beams and Girders for Buildings," Progress Report of the Joint ASCE-ACI Committee on Composite Construction, Journal of the Structural Division, ASCE, Vol. 85, No. ST12, December, 1960.

6.5   Slutter, R.G., and Driscoll, G.C. Jr., "Ultimate Strength of Composite Members," Conference on Composite Design in Steel and Concrete for Bridges and Buildings Proceedings, ASCE, Pittsburgh, 1962.

6.6   Canadian Standards Association, CAN/CSA–A23.3–04 "Design of Concrete Structures," Toronto, Ontario, 2004.

6.7   Canadian Institute of Steel Construction, "Handbook of Steel Construction," Ninth Edition, Toronto, Ontario, 2006.

6.8   Ollgaard, J.G., Slutter, R.G., and Fisher, J.W., "Shear Strength of Stud Connectors in Lightweight and Normal-Weight Concrete," AISC Engineering Journal, April, 1971.

6.9   Chien, E.Y.L., and Ritchie, J.K., "Design and Construction of Composite Floor Systems," Canadian Institute of Steel Construction, Toronto, Ontario, August, 1984.

6.10   Slutter, R.G., and Driscoll, G.C. Jr., "Flexural Strength of Steel-Concrete Composite Beams," Journal of the Structural Division, ASCE, Vol. 91, No. ST2, April, 1965.

6.11   Fisher, J.W., "Design of Composite Beams with Formed Metal Deck," Engineering Journal, AISC, Vol. 7, No. 3, July, 1970.

6.12   Davison, J.H., and Longworth, J., "Composite Beams in Negative Bending," Structural Engineering Report No. 7, Department of Civil Engineering, University of Alberta, May, 1969.

6.13   Grant, J.A., Fisher, J.W., and Slutter, R.G., "Composite Beams with Formed Steel Deck," Engineering Journal, AISC, Vol. 14, No. 1, First Quarter, 1977.

6.14   Montgomery, C.J., Kulak, G.L., and Shwartsburd, G., "Deflection of a Composite Floor System," Canadian Journal of Civil Engineering, Vol. 10, No. 2, June, 1983.

6.15   Mattock, A.H., "Shear Transfer in Concrete Having Reinforcement at an Angle to the Shear Plane," Special Publication 42, Shear in Reinforced Concrete, American Concrete Institute, 1974.

6.16   Kennedy, D.J.L., and Brattland, A., "Shrinkage Tests of Two Full-Scale Composite Trusses," Canadian Journal of Civil Engineering, Vol. 19, No.2, April, 1992.

CHAPTER 7

PLATE GIRDERS

7.1   Introduction

A plate girder is generally defined as a built-up flexural member having a slender web. It is particularly the presence of the slender web that requires further attention when designing a plate girder. The fundamental concepts that were developed in Chapter 5 to describe the behaviour of beams are equally applicable to plate girders.

Plate girders are used extensively in highway bridges

Members that carry loads acting perpendicular to their longitudinal axis are generally most efficient when the largest proportion of the cross-section is placed at the extremities, that is, in the flanges. As spans and/or loads increase, the distance between flanges should be increased for economical placement of material within the cross-section. When the range of rolled shapes has been exceeded, the designer turns to the built-up shapes that will be discussed in this Chapter. These, in turn, give way to trusses as the economical depth of the plate girders is exceeded. Plate girders have generally found their greatest application in spanning distances in the order of 25 to 45 m. Modern fabrication methods have increased the upper limit considerably, however, and in bridges plate girders exceeding 120 m are not uncommon.

In the past, the most economical built-up sections were generally those with webs so thin that they had to be stiffened at intervals. More recently, improvements in fabrication techniques and reductions in both material and fabrication costs, means that the use of relatively thicker webs, unstiffened, will often be more economical. A cost evaluation will be necessary in order to decide which type to use. In the case of the stiffened web, the stiffening elements will most often be placed transversely to the length of the girder,

179

but longitudinal stiffeners may also be used. Highway bridges often use transverse stiffeners on one side of a plate girder web and a longitudinal stiffener on the other. Such an arrangement is shown in Figure 7.1.

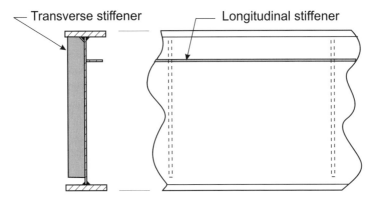

Figure 7.1 – Plate Girder with Longitudinal and Transverse Stiffeners

Present-day fabrication of plate girders will almost always be done by welding, although field splices are usually made with high-strength bolts. As well as providing economic advantages, the welded girder is less cluttered and is more pleasing in appearance than one made using bolts or rivets. It is also relatively easy in welded construction to make cross-sectional or material property changes with length as the strength requirements vary. Both of these techniques are used extensively in plate girder design.

The discussion of the design requirements for plate girders will proceed in accordance with the requirements set forth in S16–01, Limit States Design of Steel Structures [7.1]. The standard governing highway bridge design, CAN/CSA–S6–00, follows the underlying principles developed here but differs in detail [7.2]. Attention will be focused on I-shaped girders although other configurations are often used. In particular, box girders are frequently used in highway bridges.

7.2   Preliminary Proportioning

The selection of the most economical girder depends on a number of variables, but it will be principally a function of the weight of steel used and the amount of fabrication. A preliminary estimate of an economical girder depth can be made on the basis of the optimum depth for resisting moment. Adapting a suggestion made for allowable stress design [7.3]:

$$h \approx 540 \left[\frac{M_f}{F_y} \right]^{1/3} \tag{7.1}$$

where

h =   web depth, mm

M_f =   maximum factored moment, $kN \cdot m$

F_y =   yield strength, MPa

Whether Equation 7.1 is used at the starting point or whether some architectural, clearance, deflection, or other criterion is used, the choice of a girder depth means that an approximate flange size can be chosen. If it is assumed that the flange material will be able to reach yield, that the contribution of the web to bending resistance can be neglected, and that lateral-torsional buckling will not govern the design, then a preliminary flange area, A_f, can be obtained from

$$A_f = \frac{M_f}{F_y \, h} \tag{7.2}$$

Equation 7.2 also assumes that the flange areas are concentrated at the top and bottom of the web. For plate girders, the differences between the overall depth d, the web height h, and the distance between the flange centroids are not large.

As was explained in Chapter 5, the designer must examine whether the section is a Class 1, 2, 3, or 4 cross-section and evaluate conditions of lateral support for the compression flange. Because of the slender web, it will be seen that plate girder cross-sections will almost always fall in the Class 3 category. Also, it generally will be advantageous to provide lateral support at intervals close enough that lateral-torsional buckling will not govern the design. Equation 7.2 therefore gives a reasonable starting point for choosing a preliminary flange size.

The flange selected should meet the plate slenderness requirements (b/t) outlined in Chapter 5.

Once a trial web depth has been established, an assumption that the web carries all the shear (as in rolled shapes) will enable the web thickness, w, to be established from the expression

$$A_w = \frac{V_f}{\phi \, F_s} = w \, h \tag{7.3}$$

As will be discussed in Section 7.4, the ultimate shear strength, F_s, is a function of web slenderness and of whether or not transverse stiffeners are present. If stiffeners are used F_s also depends upon the ratio of the stiffener spacing to web depth. In either case, stiffened or unstiffened, the maximum shear strength (S16–01) will be $0.66 \, F_y$ and the maximum web slenderness for statically loaded girders (corresponding to a minimum shear stress) is $83\,000 / F_y$. Although the range of shear strength is rather large for unstiffened girders, there is less variation for stiffened girders. For example, the ultimate shear stress will be between 231 MPa and 135 MPa for stiffened girders of 350 MPa yield steel in which the stiffener spacing is equal to the girder depth. As a first approximation, a value of F_s for use in Equation 7.3 can be obtained by considering the upper limit of web slenderness, that is, $h \, / \, w \le 83\,000 / F_y$, and an assumed stiffener spacing in the range of one to two times the girder depth. Other considerations, such as the minimum thickness of web required for corrosion protection, must also be included when establishing preliminary proportions for the web. All these aspects are illustrated in the Design Example, Section 7.8.

Box girders are frequently used in highway bridges.

7.3   Design of Cross-Section for Bending

Once the preliminary dimensions for the web and flanges have been determined, the section can then be checked to see whether the flexural capacity of the cross-section is equal to or greater than the factored moment. Since failure can be either by buckling or by yielding, both of these possibilities must be examined.

Web Buckling under Pure Flexure — The application of a bending moment to the cross-section will, according to conventional beam theory, give a distribution of stress under specified loads such as shown in Figure 7.2(a). The thin web is relatively unstable, however, and will also have an initial out-of-flatness. Consequently, it is to be expected that at higher loads the web will not resist the stresses indicated but will throw off some of its load onto the stiffer flange [7.4]. Thus, the web will be less effective than expected and the flange will receive a higher stress than that calculated using ordinary beam theory. Tests have verified this intuitive concept and qualitative results are shown in Figure 7.3.

The effect of the "soft" web upon the load-carrying capacity of the flange is treated by simply considering a portion of the web on the compression side to be ineffective. In accordance with the development of the resistance of the compression flange of a beam (Section 5.10), the cross-section effective in resisting lateral or lateral-torsional buckling is taken as the flange plus one-sixth of the web area adjacent to the flange (see Figure 7.3).

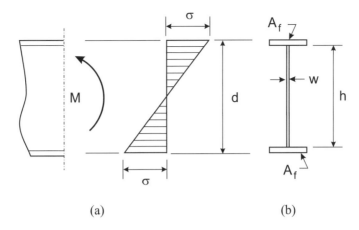

(a)   (b)

Figure 7.2 – Plate Girder Notation

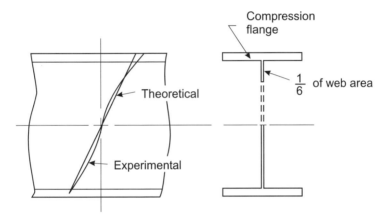

Figure 7.3 – Theoretical and Experimental Distribution of Bending Stress

In treating the problem of the increased stress in the flange as a result of unloading of the web, it is assumed that the maximum moment that can be carried is that corresponding to the yield moment, M_y: the thin web will not permit the attainment of the theoretical plastic moment of the section. A linear reduction to this maximum attainable value is then applied. It is a function of the web slenderness, the relative proportions of the flange and web, and the buckling load of the web (including the restraint provided to the web by the flanges). The requirement specified by S16–01 is (Clause 14.3.4)

$$M'_r = M_r \left[1.0 - 0.0005 \frac{A_w}{A_f} \left(\frac{h}{w} - \frac{1900}{\sqrt{M_f / \phi S}} \right) \right] \tag{7.4}$$

where M'_r =   reduced factored moment resistance

M_r =   basic factored moment resistance ($\leq \phi M_y$)

M_f =   bending moment in the member under factored loads

h   =   web depth

w   =   web thickness

183

$$A_w = \text{web area}$$

$$A_f = \text{compression flange area}$$

$$S = \text{elastic section modulus}$$

In most cases, the reduction in moment resistance will not be large, and there will be no reduction at all for web slenderness values less than $1900/\sqrt{M_f/\phi S}$. For a girder made of steel with 350 MPa yield and for a Class 3 cross-section, this corresponds to a web slenderness (h/w) of 102, for example.

Vertical Buckling of Web — As the curvature that accompanies bending occurs, a vertical force is transmitted from the flanges into the web. Conditions on the compression side of the girder are illustrated in Figure 7.4. A similar situation exists on the tension side but, as no possibility of buckling will be present there, only the condition shown needs to be examined. The vertical force applied over the length dx is

$$F = 2C\sin(\kappa/2) \approx 2C(\kappa/2) = C\kappa$$

Noting that the compressive force (C) is equal to the product of the stress in the compressive flange and its area $(A_f \sigma_f)$

$$F = A_f \sigma_f \kappa$$

The angle change (κ) occurring over the length dx is

$$\kappa = \frac{\varepsilon_f \, dx}{h/2}$$

and now

$$F = (2A_f \sigma_f \varepsilon_f \, dx)/h$$

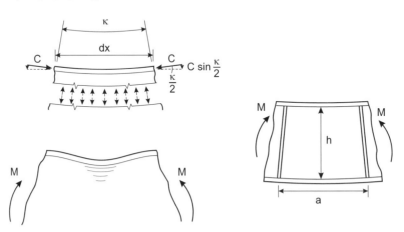

Figure 7.4 – Vertical Buckling of Web

The resisting force of the web will be the web area (w dx) times the Euler buckling stress of this element. The buckling equations for plates take the same general form as those developed in Chapter 4 for long columns. In terms of load, the expression is

$$P_{cr} = \frac{\pi^2 EI}{(KL)^2} \qquad \text{or, in terms of stress} \qquad \sigma_{cr} = \frac{\pi^2 E}{\left(\dfrac{KL}{r} \right)^2}$$

The term K is a factor introduced in Chapter 4 to permit the equations to be applied to columns with various end conditions. The critical stress equation can be rewritten as

$$\sigma_{cr} = k \frac{\pi^2 E}{(L/r)^2}$$

where $k = (1/K)^2$

If a thin plate of thickness w and a height h which is large compared to its width b is subjected to a compressive force (Figure 7.5), the buckling stress is given by

$$\sigma_{cr} = k \frac{\pi^2 E}{(1 - v^2)(b/r)^2}$$

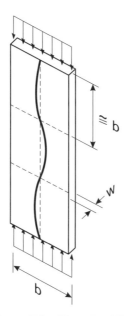

Figure 7.5 – Plate Buckling

The inclusion of Poisson's ratio, v, takes into account that, unlike column buckling, two-way action is occurring here. The radius of gyration is $r = w/\sqrt{12}$. Upon substitution, this gives

$$\sigma_{cr} = k \frac{\pi^2 E}{12 \left(1 - v^2 \right)\left(\dfrac{b}{w} \right)^2}$$

The value of k is determined by the longitudinal boundary conditions and the ratio a/h. If the dimensions are such that $a \geq h$, as would be expected in the constant moment region pictured in Figure 7.4(b), the expression becomes

$$\sigma_{cr} = k \; \frac{\pi^2 E}{12 \left(1 - v^2\right) \left(\dfrac{h}{w}\right)^2} \tag{7.5}$$

For this case, k can conservatively be taken as unity.

The resisting force of the web subjected to the compressive load pictured in Figure 7.4 will be equal to the web area (w dx) times the buckling stress given by Equation 7.5. Equating the applied and resisting forces,

$$2 A_f \, \sigma_f \, \varepsilon_f \, \frac{dx}{h} = \left[\frac{\pi^2 E}{12 \left(1 - v^2\right) \left(\dfrac{h}{w}\right)^2} \right] w \, dx$$

or, solving for the web slenderness ratio

$$\frac{h}{w} = \sqrt{\frac{\pi^2 E}{12 \left(1 - v^2\right)} \; \frac{A_w}{A_f} \; \frac{1}{2\sigma_f \, \varepsilon_f}}$$

where $A_w = w\,h$

In order to provide a design requirement, this expression will be put in terms of an inequality and two assumptions will be made:

(1) Residual stresses are distributed linearly, as shown in Figure 4.5(a). Thus,

$$\varepsilon_f = \left(\sigma_y + \sigma_r\right)/E$$

(2) The limit of web area to compression flange area will be taken as 0.5. This will generally give conservative results for plate girders but some welded wide flange shapes with relatively high web slenderness have web to flange area ratios of almost unity [7.5].

It is also noted that the stress in the compression flange, σ_f, should reach σ_y before buckling occurs. Making these substitutions and using a value of 0.3 for Poisson's ratio;

$$\frac{h}{w} \leq \frac{0.48 E}{\sqrt{\sigma_y (\sigma_y + \sigma_r)}} \tag{7.6}$$

Assuming the residual stress to be approximately one-third of the yield stress, using the notation F_y instead of σ_y and using $E = 200\,000\,\text{MPa}$, Equation 7.6 becomes

$$\frac{h}{w} \leq \frac{83\,138}{F_y} \tag{7.7}$$

where F_y is expressed in units of MPa. This is the requirement (approximately) given by S16–01 in Clause 14.3.1 as the maximum permissible web slenderness.

7.4   Design of Cross-Section for Shear

Although bending can be present unaccompanied by shear, a transversely loaded beam will always have shear combined with moment. In regions where shear predominates, it can be considered to act alone, however [7.6]. The resulting behaviour will be discussed in this section. Regions in which both shear and moment are present in significant amounts will have to be examined for the resulting interaction. This will be treated in Section 7.6.

Unstiffened Girder Web — One limit of usefulness of an unstiffened girder web acting primarily under shear is given by the stress corresponding to the buckling condition. The general expression for this case takes a form similar to Equation 7.5. (As shown in Figure 7.6, pure shear on an element is equivalent to tension and compression on adjacent faces at 45°.) Using the notation of Figure 7.5

$$\tau_{cr} = k \ \frac{\pi^2 \, E}{12 \left(1 - v^2\right) \left(\dfrac{b}{w}\right)^2} \tag{7.8}$$

For $a/b \geq 1.0$, for simply supported edges, it is found that [7.7]

$$k = 5.34 + \frac{4.0}{\left(a/b\right)^2}$$

and for fixed edges

$$k = 8.98 + \frac{5.6}{\left(a/b\right)^2}$$

Taking the aspect ratio (a/b) of an unstiffened web to be infinity and using $v = 0.3$ and $E = 200\,000$ MPa , a girder "h" deep will have

$$\tau_{cr} = \frac{180\,760}{\left(h/w\right)^2} \, k \tag{7.9}$$

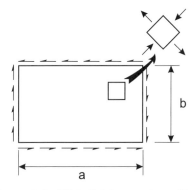

Figure 7.6 – Web Subject to Pure Shear

187

This is the requirement covered in Clause 13.4.1.1 of the Standard, where the symbol F_{cre} is used instead of τ_{cr}, and the numerical value is rounded down to 180 000. The plate buckling coefficient, called k_v in the Standard, will be either 5.34 (simply supported edges) or 8.98 (fixed edges) for an unstiffened girder. The larger value, which would be appropriate when the compression flange of the girder is in continuous contact with a concrete slab for example, is not acknowledged by the Standard.

The Standard provides the shear strength statements for both stiffened and unstiffened girders in one combined section, Clause 13.4.1.1. The statements are written in terms of the aspect ratio a/h, which is the ratio of stiffener spacing a to girder depth h. In order to extract the requirements for unstiffened girders, the user must recognize that $a = \infty$, i.e., the stiffener spacing is infinite for an unstiffened girder. Thus, the parameter k_a used in the expressions given in Clause 13.4.1.1 is $k_a = 1/\sqrt{1+(a/h)^2} = 0$ for unstiffened girders.

The other limit for this case of the unstiffened web will be that corresponding to the load that will cause shear yielding. As indicated in Chapter 5, this will occur at a stress approximately equal to $F_y/\sqrt{3}$. Considering the beneficial effects of strain-hardening, the Standard permits a somewhat higher value (Clause 13.4.1.1(a)) and specifies the ultimate shear stress as

$$F_s = 0.66\, F_y \tag{7.10}$$

The ultimate shear stresses for unstiffened girder webs as given by Equations 7.9 and 7.10 are shown in Figure 7.7. Principally because of the presence of residual stresses, it is to be expected that one curve cannot be directly run into the other. A transition curve between the two limiting cases, chosen mainly on the basis of test results, is shown on the figure. It is given by

$$F_s = \frac{290\sqrt{F_y\, k_v}}{(h/w)} \tag{7.11}$$

and it applies for web slenderness values in the range $h/w = 439\sqrt{k_v/F_y}$ to $h/w = 621\sqrt{k_v/F_y}$. (In the Standard, these are Clauses 13.4.1.1(b) and (c). The use of two clauses is to accommodate the stiffened girder requirements in this region. For unstiffened girders, Equation 7.11 applies throughout the range.)

With the ultimate shear stress now established as that given by Equation 7.9, 7.10, or 7.11, the capacity of the section can be calculated as:

$$V_r = \phi\, A_w\, F_s \tag{7.12}$$

where A_w is the shear area. The shear area customarily would be taken as the product of the total depth of the section times the web thickness for rolled shapes (d× w) and the product of the web depth times the web thickness for built-up sections (h× w).

Stiffened Girder Webs – The upper limit of the strength of a girder web stiffened by vertical supports will be the same as that of the unstiffened girder, that is, the strength corresponding to shear yielding. Thus, one expression for ultimate shear stress in stiffened girders is the same as that given by Equation 7.10.

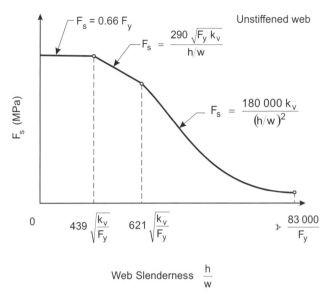

Figure 7.7 – Web Shear Strength — Unstiffened Web

Buckling of the stiffened web can precede yielding, however, just as was the case in unstiffened girders. It is found here that significant additional amounts of shear past the theoretical buckling load can be carried [7.8]. Figure 7.8(a) shows a portion of a stiffened plate girder and Figure 7.8(b) shows the shear forces acting on an element in the panel. Another orientation of the element (Figure 7.8(c)) shows the compressive force that develops in the one direction and the tensile force in the other. It is this tensile component, analogous to the force in the diagonal members of a Pratt truss, that enables the girder web to carry additional shear past the point of theoretical buckling. It is referred to as tension field action, and it is assumed that the corresponding contribution to the shear capacity (V_t) will be additive to the shear capacity as supplied by normal beam action (V_b). The latter is simply that capacity attained at the point of theoretical web buckling—

$$V_b = \tau_{cr} \, h \, w \tag{7.13}$$

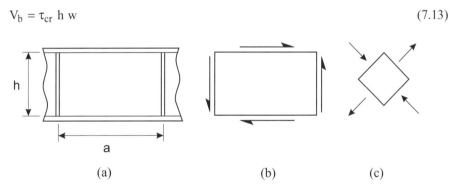

Figure 7.8 – Stiffened Plate Girder Web

A necessary requirement for the additional contribution provided by the tension field action is the presence of the vertical stiffeners. They are necessary in order that the vertical components of the inclined web forces have a reaction point.

189

Because the girder flanges offer little bending resistance transverse to their longitudinal axis, it has to be assumed that the tension field will develop only through the strip of the web shown in Figure 7.9(a). Using the notation shown in that figure, the vertical component of the force developed by the tension field can be described as

$$V_t = \sigma_t \, w \, (h \cos\theta - a \sin\theta) \sin\theta \tag{7.14}$$

It is reasonable to expect that the direction of the tension field will assume the most efficient orientation. Differentiating Equation 7.14 with respect to θ and setting it equal to zero gives the optimum angle as

$$\theta = \tan^{-1}\left(\sqrt{1+(a/h)^2} - a/h \right) \tag{7.15}$$

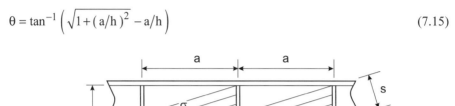

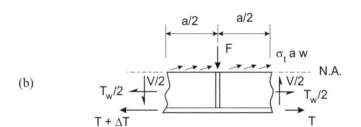

Figure 7.9 – Web Tension Field

Another expression for the shear due to the tension field action can be obtained by applying the equations of equilibrium to the free-body diagram shown in Figure 7.9(b). Using this and the result obtained in Equation 7.15 gives

$$V_t = \sigma_t \, w \, h \, \frac{1}{2\sqrt{1+(a/h)^2}} \tag{7.16}$$

The total shear force that can be carried now can be written as

$$V_u = V_b + V_t = \tau_{cr} \, h \, w \, + \, \sigma_t \, \frac{w \, h}{2} \, \frac{1}{\sqrt{1+(a/h)^2}} \tag{7.17}$$

The criterion of failure will again be established as the yield condition. For any element subjected to pure shear, pure tension, or any combination, this can be approximated by a linear relationship. It also will be assumed, with only small error, that the result will be applied for $\theta = 45^\circ$, rather than the actual angle of inclination of the tension field. The yield condition, as described, is:

190

$$\frac{\sigma_t}{\sigma_y} = 1 - \frac{\tau_{cr}}{\tau_y} \tag{7.18}$$

Now, Equation 7.17 can be written:

$$V_u = \tau_{cr} \, h \, w + \frac{\sigma_y \, w \, h}{2} \frac{1}{\sqrt{1+(a/h)^2}} - \frac{\tau_{cr}}{\tau_y} \frac{\sigma_y}{2} \frac{h \, w}{\sqrt{1+(a/h)^2}} \tag{7.19}$$

The value of τ_{cr} is given by Equation 7.8. Using the notation associated with plate girders (Figure 7.8), this can be rewritten as

$$\tau_{cr} = k_v \frac{\pi^2 E}{12\left(1-v^2\right)\left(\dfrac{h}{w}\right)^2} \tag{7.20}$$

where $k_v = 5.34 + \dfrac{4.0}{(a/h)^2}$ when $a/h \geq 1.0$ \hfill (7.21a)

or $k_v = 4.0 + \dfrac{5.34}{(a/h)^2}$ when $a/h < 1.0$ \hfill (7.21b)

As before, the shear yield stress is taken as $\sigma_y/\sqrt{3}$, $E = 200\,000$ MPa, and $v = 0.30$. Using these values and dividing by the web area ($h \times w$), an expression for the ultimate shear stress in MPa can be obtained from Equations 7.5, 7.19 and 7.20 as

$$F_s = \frac{180\,760\,k_v}{(h/w)^2} + \frac{0.50\,F_y}{\sqrt{1+(a/h)^2}} - \frac{156\,544\,k_v}{(h/w)^2\,\sqrt{1+(a/h)^2}} \tag{7.22}$$

Equation 7.22 is a more fundamental form of S16–01 Clause 13.4.1.1(d). Like any other problem associated with elastic buckling, a limit on the applicability of Equation 7.22 must be established. Based on test results, it is observed that the proportional limit in shear is about 0.80 times the shear yield value. Equation 7.22 can be set equal to this value (or its equivalent in terms of F_y) and substitutions made for E and v in order to establish the limit of applicability of the equation. In addition, the contribution of the tension field (the second and third terms on the right-hand side of the equation) will be neglected in establishing the limit. It is considered that in the inelastic region the shear capacity of the web is not significantly augmented by the presence of the tension field. The limit for which Equation 7.22 is valid is thereby established as:

$$\frac{h}{w} \geq 621 \sqrt{\frac{k_v}{F_y}} \tag{7.23}$$

The upper limit of Equation 7.22 will be taken as $83\,000/F_y$, as developed in Section 7.3. These limits, and Equation 7.22, are shown in Figure 7.10.

The upper limit of the applicability of Equation 7.10 ($F_s = 0.66\,F_y$) is taken at the same relative location as chosen for unstiffened girder webs. This is 70% of the value established by Equation 7.22, or

$$\frac{h}{w} \le 439 \sqrt{\frac{k_v}{F_y}} \qquad\qquad (7.24)$$

In the transition region (see Figure 7.10), two expressions for F_v, linear with respect to web slenderness, are used:
For

$$439 \sqrt{\frac{k_v}{F_y}} < \frac{h}{w} \le 502 \sqrt{\frac{k_v}{F_y}}$$

$$F_s = 290 \frac{\sqrt{k_v F_y}}{h/w} \qquad\qquad (7.25)$$

and for

$$502 \sqrt{\frac{k_v}{F_y}} < \frac{h}{w} \le 621 \sqrt{\frac{k_v}{F_y}}$$

$$F_s = 290 \frac{\sqrt{k_v F_y}}{h/w} - \frac{251\sqrt{k_v F_y}}{h/w\sqrt{1+(a/h)^2}} + \frac{0.50 F_y}{\sqrt{1+(a/h)^2}} \qquad\qquad (7.26)$$

All of the requirements listed above are contained in Clause 13.4.1.1 of S16–01, where they are expressed in a slightly different format.

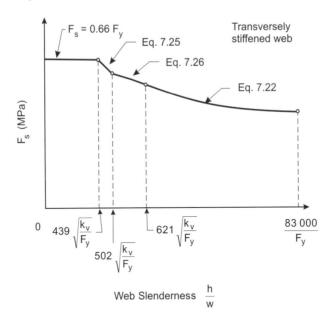

Figure 7.10 – Web Shear Strength – Stiffened Web

A plot of ultimate shear stress as a function of web slenderness is given in Part 2 of the CISC Handbook [7.9], where a Commentary to the S16–01 Standard is provided. In that figure, both unstiffened webs and stiffened webs are shown on the same plot. Of course, the differences in shear carrying capabilities of the two cases will depend on the actual proportions involved, particularly on the stiffener spacing in the stiffened girder

192

case. In general, the difference can be appreciable. However, as was pointed out in Section 7.1, the extra cost of fabrication introduced when a stiffened girder is selected must be considered.

As was the case for unstiffened webs, the factored shear resistance of the stiffened girder web can now be calculated using Equation 7.12.

7.5 Stiffener Requirements

The role of transverse stiffeners in acting as posts to provide tension field action was indicated in Section 7.4. In addition, the application of concentrated loads to the girder will usually require the use of stiffeners to prevent local instability. The latter are termed bearing stiffeners.

Intermediate Transverse Stiffeners – Summation of the vertical components of the tension field action over one panel width (Figure 7.9(b)) gives the force that must be resisted by each stiffener as

$$F = \frac{\sigma_t \, h \, w}{2} \left[\frac{a}{h} - \frac{(a/h)^2}{\sqrt{1+(a/h)^2}} \right] \tag{7.27}$$

Assuming that yielding of the stiffener will not be preceded by its buckling, Equation 7.27 can be divided by the yield strength of the stiffener material (F_{ys}) and the value of σ_t given by Equation 7.18 used to provide a requirement for stiffener area (S16–01 Clause 14.5.3):

$$A_s \geq \frac{a \, w}{2} \left[1 - \frac{a/h}{\sqrt{1+(a/h)^2}} \right] \left[1 - \frac{310\,000 \, k_v}{F_y \, (h/w)^2} \right] \frac{F_y}{F_{ys}} \tag{7.28}$$

The development of this equation assumes that the placement of stiffeners will be symmetrical about the web, that is, the stiffeners will be axially loaded. It is sometimes expedient to put stiffeners only on one side of the web. To account for the additional stress that will thereby result [7.8], the S16–01 Standard modifies its form of Equation 7.28 by multiplying by another factor D, where;

D = 1.0 for stiffeners furnished in pairs

D = 1.8 for stiffeners composed of angles placed on one side of the web only

D = 2.4 for stiffeners composed of plates placed on one side of the web only.

The stiffener area expressed by Equation 7.28, as modified above, is based on the requirement that full tension field action will be developed. The area may be reduced in girders, or portions of girders, where moment predominates and the full ultimate shear force will not be attained. Conservatively, the area of stiffener required (Equation 7.28) can be reduced in the ratio of V_f / V_r, where

V_f = actual factored shear force in panel adjacent to stiffener

V_r = maximum factored shear resistance in panel adjacent to stiffener.

The force in the stiffener must be transferred into and out of the web from top to bottom. The exact manner in which this occurs is indeterminate. The assumption upon which the Standard requirement is based is that the force F described in Equation 7.27 must be transferred in one-third of the web depth. Rather than compute each actual stiffener force, an approximation of the maximum possible value is used to establish the shear flow (newtons per mm) at each location of a transverse stiffener as (Clause 14.5.4)

$$v = 1 \times 10^{-4} \, h \left(F_y \right)^{1.5} \tag{7.29}$$

Plate girders are used in buildings for long spans.

Fasteners (usually, fillet welds) should be provided to meet this shear flow requirement. Customarily, they would be provided to meet the requirements of Equation 7.29 over the full depth of the stiffener.

In addition to being able to resist the force imposed upon it by the tension field action, an intermediate transverse stiffener should have sufficient rigidity so that the web does not move out-of-plane at this location. With some theoretical justification and much evidence of practical satisfactory behaviour, the S16–01 requirement is (Clause 14.5.3):

$$I_s \geq \left(\frac{h}{50} \right)^4 \tag{7.30}$$

in which I_s = moment of inertia of stiffener (single or pair) about an axis in the plane of the web, mm^4. Naturally, there is the concomitant requirement that the b/t ratio of the stiffener be established as for any element under compression.

The horizontal component of the tension field stress is resisted mainly by the flanges, but also partly by the girder web. At the ends of the girder, the horizontal force component in the web must either be taken out of the member or resisted internally. It is generally not convenient to provide an external reaction and experience shows that, if the

194

force is resisted by internal action only, considerable distortion of the girder occurs in the vicinity of the free end. The usual solution is simply to establish an end panel in which tension field action is not permitted to develop.

Looking at Equation 7.22, the general expression for the ultimate shear stress in a stiffened girder, it has already been pointed out that the second and third terms in this expression represent the tension field contribution. The first term is the elastic shear buckling contribution. In order to establish an end panel in which tension field action does not take place, the factored resistance, ϕF_s, can be set equal to (or greater than) the effect of the factored shear force, f_s.

$$\phi F_s = \phi \frac{180\,000}{(h/w)^2} k_v \geq f_s \tag{7.31}$$

Equation 7.31 uses the Standard value of 180 000 instead of the corresponding value of 180 760 derived for use in Equation 7.22. The expression for F_s given by Equation 7.31 is designated as F_{cre} in Clause 13.4.1.1 of the Standard.

The choice of stiffener spacing and the factored shear resistance in the resulting panels are, of course, interdependent. The increased factored shear resistance that will result from an increased number of stiffeners must be compared to the additional cost of these stiffeners. The S16–01 Standard does place limits on maximum stiffener spacing, however. These are (Clause 14.5.2)

$$\text{for} \quad h/w \leq 150, \quad a/h \leq 3 \tag{7.32a}$$

$$\text{and for} \quad h/w > 150, \quad a/h \leq \frac{67\,500}{(h/w)^2} \tag{7.32b}$$

The first restriction reflects the fact that when the stiffener spacing to web depth ratio exceeds about 3, the effectiveness of the tension field is minor. The second restriction is related to ease in handling and fabrication.

The stiffener requirements as outlined in this section have been promulgated on the basis that a node point in the web be established and that the vertical reaction of the tension field force be accommodated. The required size, stiffness, and spacing of the stiffeners have been established. The only outstanding question concerns the detail of the stiffener in the vicinity of the flanges.

In addition to the requirements already discussed, the stiffener serves to maintain the shape of the cross-section as loads are applied and the girder distorts. Formerly, this was accomplished by fitting the stiffeners closely against both flanges and providing a light weld at the junctions. This is an expensive fabrication technique and it also introduces residual stresses and minute cracks that can affect the fatigue life of the girder. Studies have shown, however, that since the tension flange will be self-aligning, the stiffener can safely be stopped short of this flange [7.8]. This detail is shown in Figure 7.11. To prevent a local buckle in the girder web in what will be a region of high strain, the amount of this cut-back should not exceed six times the web thickness, but it should be greater than four times the web thickness in order to provide a reasonable strain gradient.

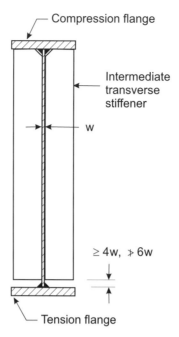

Figure 7.11 – Intermediate Transverse Stiffener

The stiffener should be fitted against the underside of the compression flange, as also shown in Figure 7.11. If the stiffener is present on both sides of the web, no weld is needed between the flange and stiffener. When a stiffener is placed only on one side of the web, a nominal weld should be placed between the web and flange. A weld should be present in either case if lateral bracing is attached to the stiffener, frequently the situation. The inside corners of the stiffener should be clipped to clear the flange-to-web weld.

Bearing Stiffeners — The possibility of local failure of the web under application of a concentrated load was discussed in Chapter 5. It was pointed out that if the bearing resistance of the web (Equations 5.27 and 5.28) was exceeded, bearing stiffeners could be introduced to help carry the load. The relatively thin web in plate girders means that bearing stiffeners are generally needed at points of concentrated load. If the girder end does not frame into another beam or into a column, they are mandatory when the web slenderness exceeds $1100/\sqrt{F_y}$ (Clause 14.4.1).

It is customary to design bearing stiffeners as axially loaded columns, considering the cross-section to consist of the stiffener plus a strip of web with a width equal to 25 times the web thickness at interior stiffeners or 12 times the web thickness at end stiffeners. The effective column length is taken as 3/4 of the actual stiffener length. As well as checking the capacity of this equivalent column, the bearing capacity of the area of stiffener outside the web-flange girder weld and the capacity of the gross area of the stiffeners must be checked. The stiffeners should extend out as far as practicable toward the edge of the flange. They must meet the width-thickness ratios required to prevent local buckling. Bearing stiffeners can be stopped short of the flange opposite to the one through which the load is being delivered. The detailed design of both intermediate and bearing stiffeners is part of the Design Example presented in Section 7.8.

7.6   Combined Shear and Moment

The presence of significant shear and moment together can occur, for example, at the interior supports of a continuous beam. In such cases, the effect of the interaction between these two force effects upon girder strength must be examined [7.6].

The yield moment as carried by the flanges alone can be expressed as

$$M_{fl} = \sigma_y \, d \, A_f \tag{7.33a}$$

If the web is considered to contribute to the moment capacity, the yield moment can be expressed as [7.10]

$$M_y = \sigma_y \, d \left(A_f + \frac{1}{6} A_w \right) \tag{7.33b}$$

Similarly, the plastic moment of the section can be put in the form

$$M_p = \sigma_y \, d \left(A_f + \frac{1}{4} A_w \right) \tag{7.33c}$$

As outlined in Section 7.5, the ultimate shear strength of a plate girder is considered to be independent of any contribution from the flanges. Therefore, for the region in which the flanges are assumed to provide the total moment capacity, the shear strength will not be reduced because of the presence of moment. Using the terminology of Equation 7.33, this can be written as

$$\frac{V_f}{V_u} = 1.0 \qquad \text{for the condition} \qquad 0 < \frac{M_f}{M_y} < \frac{M_{fl}}{M_y}$$

where V_f and M_f are the factored shear and moment, respectively.

If the shear is zero, the maximum moment that can be carried (theoretically) is the plastic moment. Thus,

$$\frac{V_f}{V_u} = 0 \qquad \text{for the condition} \qquad \frac{M_f}{M_y} = \frac{M_p}{M_y}$$

These portions of the interaction curve are shown in Figure 7.12. The only portion over which true interaction occurs then is over the range

$$0 \le \frac{V_f}{V_u} \le 1.0 \qquad \text{and} \qquad \frac{M_{fl}}{M_y} \le \frac{M_f}{M_y} \le \frac{M_p}{M_y}$$

A parabolic curve, tangent at the lower end, is found to be in good agreement with the test results in this region. This takes the form

$$\left(\frac{V_f}{V_u} \right)^2 + \frac{M_f - M_{fl}}{M_p - M_{fl}} = 1.0 \tag{7.34}$$

It was noted earlier that girders with slender webs will not be able to attain the plastic moment. The curve is therefore cut off by the vertical line $M_f / M'_r = 1.0$, where

M'_r is the moment evaluated from Equation 7.4. The remaining curved portion can be closely approximated by a straight line.

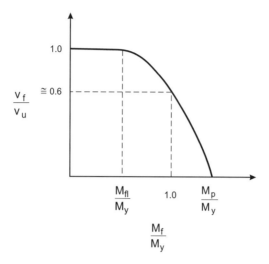

Figure 7.12 – Shear–Moment Interaction

The end points of the straight line can be established by using the parabolic equation, Equation 7.34. The abscissa

$$\frac{M_f}{M_y} = \frac{M_{fl}}{M_y}$$

can be obtained using Equation 7.33 as

$$\frac{M_f}{M_y} = \frac{A_f}{A_f + \dfrac{A_w}{6}}$$

It is found in practice that the ratio A_w/A_f usually ranges between about 0.5 and 2.0. A conservative result will be obtained by using the higher value. Thus

$$\frac{M_f}{M_y} = 0.75$$

The ordinate for the abscissa $M_f/M_y = 1.0$ can likewise be obtained from Equation 7.34 and use of the lower value (0.50) of A_w/A_f as

$$\frac{V_f}{V_u} \approx 0.6$$

The equation of the straight line joining these end points gives the S16–01 interaction check (Clause 14.6):

$$0.727\frac{M_f}{M_r} + 0.455\frac{V_f}{V_r} \leq 1.0 \tag{7.35}$$

198

The interaction check is required only if the factored shear force at the section being considered exceeds 60% of the shear resistance of the section and if the girder proportions are such that the tension field action develops, that is, when $h/w > 502\sqrt{k_v/F_y}$.

7.7   Application of Concentrated Loads

The application of concentrated loads to the flange of a beam can result in local failure. As described in Section 5.12, this can be either by local buckling of the web in the region where it joins the flange or by overall buckling of the web throughout its depth. For an interior location, the governing equations for these two situations, respectively, are (S16–01 Clause 14.3.2(a))

$$B_r = \phi_{bi} \, w \, (N + 10t) \, F_y \tag{7.36}$$

$$B_r = 1.45 \, \phi_{bi} \, w^2 \, \sqrt{F_y \, E} \tag{7.37}$$

where   N = length of bearing

w = web thickness

t = flange thickness

$\phi_{bi} = 0.80$

For end reactions, the numerical modifier 10 in Equation 7.36 is reduced to 4, the value 1.45 in Equation 7.37 is reduced to 0.60, and the resistance factor to be used is $\phi_{be} = 0.75$.

7.8   Design Example

Given

Design the plate girder for which the span and loading are shown in Figure 7.13. The uniformly distributed load is applied through a concrete slab while the concentrated load is applied to the top flange of the girder through a 300 mm × 300 mm baseplate. Assume that sufficient lateral bracing will be supplied to the top flange such that lateral-torsional buckling need not be considered. Use G40.21 350W throughout ($F_y = 350$ MPa).

Solution

Use Equation 7.1 to obtain an estimated web depth –

$$h = 540 \left(\frac{6200}{350} \right)^{1/3} = 1408 \ mm$$

Try h = 1400 mm

Approximate flange area (Equation 7.2) –

$$A_f = \frac{6200 \times 10^6 \ N \cdot mm}{350 \ MPa \times 1400 \ mm} = 12\,650 \ mm^2$$

Try 500×25 flange plates

Check slenderness: b/t = 250/25 = 10.0   (b = half flange width).

For a Class 3 section, allowable $b/t = 200/\sqrt{350} = 10.7$ (Satisfactory)

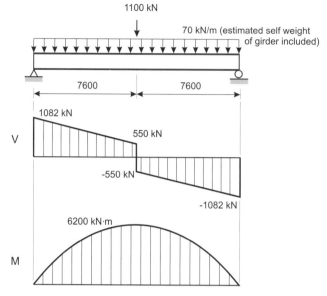

Figure 7.13 – Design Example

Trial web thickness:

Maximum slenderness (Equation 7.7) $\dfrac{h}{w} \le \dfrac{83\,000}{350} = 237$

or, for h = 1400 mm, minimum w = 5.9 mm.

For protection against corrosion, the minimum w is 4.5 mm (S16–01 Clause 6.5.7).

For no reduction in flange stress (Equation 7.4) $\dfrac{h}{w} = \dfrac{1900}{\sqrt{350}}$

or, for h = 1400 mm, w = 13.8 mm.

Considering all of the above requirements, try w = 10 mm ($A_w = 1400 \times 10 = 14\,000$ mm^2, h/w = 140).

The trial section consists of a 10×1400 web plate with 25×500 flanges. The moment of inertia of this cross-section is $14\,980 \times 10^6$ mm^4. It has already been established that the trial flange section meets the requirement for a Class 3 section. A comparison of the actual slenderness of the web with the upper limit prescribed by the Standard (Clause 11.2) will show that the web chosen here exceeds the limit. This is almost always the case for plate girders. The bending capacity of the section will therefore be governed by Equation 7.4. The basic capacity, M_r, will be calculated first:

$$M_r = \phi\, S\, F_y = 0.90 \times \frac{14\,980 \times 10^6 \text{ mm}^4}{725 \text{ mm}} \times 350 \text{ MPa} = 6500 \times 10^6 \text{ N} \cdot \text{mm}$$

Now, using Equation 7.4 (the term under the radical sign is to be expressed in newtons and mm units)

$$M'_r = 6500 \left[1.0 - 0.0005 \times \frac{14\,000}{500 \times 25} \left(140 - \frac{1900}{\sqrt{\dfrac{6200 \times 10^6}{0.90 \times 20.66 \times 10^6}}} \right) \right] = 6370 \text{ kN} \cdot \text{m}$$

This is about 3% over the actual factored moment of $6200 \text{ kN} \cdot \text{m}$. The trial cross-section will therefore be taken as satisfactory with respect to bending.

The section just chosen and checked is needed only at the location of maximum moment. It is usual to reduce the cross-section of a welded girder at least once as the moment decreases. Assume here that the flange size will be changed once only. Try a cross-section consisting of 25×300 flange plates and the 10×1400 web. For this section;

$$I = 9902 \times 10^6 \text{ mm}^4$$

$$M_r = 0.90 \times \frac{9902 \times 10^6 \text{ mm}^4}{725 \text{ mm}} \times 350 \text{ MPa} = 4300 \times 10^6 \text{ N} \cdot \text{mm} = 4300 \text{ kN} \cdot \text{m}$$

$$M'_r = 4300 \left[1.0 - 0.0005 \times \frac{14\,000}{300 \times 25} \left(140 - \frac{1900}{\sqrt{\dfrac{4300 \times 10^6}{0.90 \times 13.66 \times 10^6}}} \right) \right] = 4146 \text{ kN} \cdot \text{m}$$

(In this calculation for M'_r, the value $M_r = 4300 \text{ kN} \cdot \text{m}$ has been used instead of M_f in the term under the square root sign. This is convenient since the location at which M_f must be calculated is not known yet, and it provides a conservative answer.)

This moment is found to occur approximately 3.1 m from centreline. Figure 7.14 shows the detail at the location where the 500 mm wide plate meets the 300 mm wide plate. The transition allows for the gradual flow of stress from one section to the other. A complete joint penetration groove weld (CP) would be used to join the two plates.

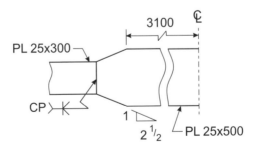

Figure 7.14 – Flange Plate Transition

In order to have an unstiffened web, the actual shear would have to be less than that given by Equation 7.9. Using the form of that equation provided by the Standard (13.4.1.1(d)) and $k_v = 5.34$,

$$F_s = \frac{180\,000 \times 5.34}{140 \times 140} = 49.0 \text{ MPa}$$

The actual shear at the end of the beam is

$$f_s = \frac{1082 \text{ kN}}{14\,000 \text{ mm}^2} = 77.3 \times 10^{-3} \text{ kN/mm}^2 = 77.3 \text{ MPa} \quad > F_s$$

Stiffeners are therefore needed.

Establish end panel spacing for no tension field action in this panel (Equation 7.31)

$$0.9 \times \frac{180\,000}{140^2} \, k_v \quad \geq \quad 77.3 \text{ MPa}$$

from which $k_v \geq 9.35$

Assuming that a/h > 1, Equation 7.21(a) can be used to obtain the end panel spacing as a = 1400 mm.

Intermediate Stiffeners:

Shear at 1400 mm from end = 984 kN

$$f_s = \frac{984 \times 10^3 \text{ N}}{14\,000 \text{ mm}^2} = 70.3 \text{ MPa}$$

Maximum allowable stiffener spacing (Equation 7.32(a)) is

a = 3×1400 = 4200 mm

Use a = 4200 mm as a trial stiffener spacing. From Equation 7.21(a)

$$k_v = 5.34 + \frac{4.0}{3^2} = 5.78$$

Checking Equation 7.23

$$\frac{h}{w} \geq 621 \sqrt{\frac{5.78}{350}} = 80$$

Actual h/w = 140. Therefore, the ultimate shear stress is given by Equation 7.22:

$$F_s = \frac{180\,760 \times 5.78}{140^2} + \frac{0.50 \times 350}{\sqrt{1+3^2}} - \frac{156\,544 \times 5.78}{140^2 \sqrt{1+3^2}} = 94.0 \text{ MPa}$$

Since the maximum shear stress in this region (between the end panels) is only 70.3 MPa, intermediate stiffeners placed even at the maximum permissible spacing will provide sufficient shear-carrying capacity. The exact stiffener layout will be determined after it has been established whether a bearing stiffener is needed under the concentrated load.

The effect of combined shear and moment should be examined. At centreline, $V_f = 550$ kN, $F_s = 94.0$ MPa and, using Equation 7.12

$$V_r = 0.90 \times 14\,000 \text{ mm}^2 \times 94.0 \text{ MPa} = 1184 \times 10^3 \text{ N} = 1184 \text{ kN}$$

As explained in Section 7.6, interaction of shear and moment is critical only when V_f equals or exceeds 60% of V_r. Since 60%$\times$1184 is greater than V_f, the interaction is not critical at this location.

The location of 60% V_r (710 kN) is 2.3 m from centreline. At this point, $M_f = 4750$ kN$\cdot$m. The resistance of the section in bending is still 6370 kN$\cdot$m. Checking the interaction relationship (Equation 7.35)

$$0.727 \times \frac{4750}{6370} + 0.455 \times \frac{710}{1184} = 0.81 \quad < 1.0 \qquad \text{(Satisfactory)}$$

The location where the cross-section is reduced should also be checked for shear–moment interaction. At the end of the transition, 3.3 m from centreline (see Fig. 7.14), the factored moment is 4005 kN$\cdot$m and the factored shear is 781 kN. The shear resistance is still 1184 kN and the resisting moment of this section was calculated as 4146 kN$\cdot$m. Checking Equation 7.35

$$0.727 \times \frac{4005}{4146} + 0.455 \times \frac{781}{1184} = 1.00 \qquad \text{(Satisfactory)}$$

Design of Bearing Stiffeners – In order that bearing stiffeners not be required, the factored concentrated load must be less than the web buckling capacities prescribed in Clause 14.3.2 of S16–01, that is

Local web buckling capacity (Equation 7.36)

$$B_r = \phi_{bi} \, w \, (N + 10t) \, F_y = 0.80 \text{ x } 10 \text{ mm } (300 + (10 \times 25)) \times 350 \text{ MPa}$$

$$= 1540 \times 10^3 \text{ N} = 1540 \text{ kN}$$

Overall web buckling (Equation 7.37)

$$B_r = 1.45 \, \phi_{bi} \, w^2 \, \sqrt{F_y \, E} = 1.45 \times 0.80 \times 10^2 \text{ mm}^2 \sqrt{350 \text{ MPa} \times 200\,000 \text{MPa}}$$

$$= 970 \times 10^3 \text{ N} = 970 \text{ kN} \qquad \text{(Governs)}$$

Since the factored concentrated load (1100 kN) is in excess of the latter value, a stiffener will be required under the load. Bearing stiffeners will also be required at each end of the girder since the actual web slenderness (140) exceeds the prescribed limit of $1100/\sqrt{350} = 58.8$.

At the ends, try two 125$\times$12 plates $(F_y = 350 \text{ MPa})$, as shown in Figure 7.15. These extend nearly to the edge of the flange. In the calculations following, the requirements of Clause 14.4 of S16–01 are used.

$$\frac{b}{t} = \frac{125}{12} = 10.4 \quad < \quad \frac{200}{\sqrt{350}} = 10.7$$

$$A = (125 \times 12) \times 2 + (120 \times 10) = 4200 \text{ mm}^2$$

$$I = \frac{1}{12} \times 12 \times 260^3 = 17.58 \times 10^6 \text{ mm}^4$$

$$r = \sqrt{17.58 \times 10^6 \text{ mm}^4 / 4200 \text{ mm}^2} = 64.7 \text{ mm}$$

$$\frac{KL}{r} = \frac{0.75 \times 1400 \text{ mm}}{64.7 \text{ mm}} = 16.2$$

Using Equations 4.20 and 4.21 (Clause 13.3.1 of the Standard) with n = 1.34,

$$\lambda = \frac{KL}{r} \sqrt{\frac{F_y}{\pi^2 E}} = 16.2 \sqrt{\frac{350 \text{ MPa}}{\pi^2 \times 200\,000 \text{ MPa}}} = 0.216$$

$$C_r = \phi A F_y \left(1 + \lambda^{2n}\right)^{-1/n}$$

$$= 0.90 \times 4200 \text{ mm}^2 \times 350 \text{ MPa} \left(1 + 0.216^{2 \times 1.34}\right)^{-1/1.34}$$

$$= 1307 \times 10^3 \text{ N} = 1307 \text{ kN}$$

Since this is greater than the actual factored load at the ends (1082 kN), the behaviour of the trial section as a column is satisfactory.

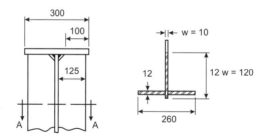

Figure 7.15 – Bearing Stiffener

Bearing on contact area – assume 100 mm bearing on the stiffeners (see Figure 7.15). The bearing resistance (Clause 13.10(a) of the Standard) is

$$B_r = 1.50 \, \phi \, F_y \, A = 1.50 \times 0.90 \times 350 \text{ MPa} \times (100 \times 12) \times 2$$

$$= 1134 \times 10^3 \text{ N} = 1134 \text{ kN} > 1083 \text{ kN} \qquad \text{Satisfactory}$$

It can be noted that it is implicit in this calculation for bearing resistance that none of the load is carried into the girder directly by the web. Such an assumption is very conservative. In the calculation just completed, the bearing resistance of the stiffener plates alone was sufficient to carry the load, and so the issue of just how much load could be transferred directly by the web did not arise. In other circumstances, the designer must exercise judgment if it is wished to include some web capacity. The load distribution procedure suggested in Section 9.12 for beam bearing plates could be used.

Bearing stiffener at centreline – The bearing stiffener at centreline must accommodate a superimposed load of 1100 kN. (See Figure 7.13.) The calculation just completed shows that the two 125×12 plates at the girder ends can transfer 1134 kN by bearing on the contact area and provide an overall column strength of 1306 kN. Thus, the capacities provided by the two 125×12 plates are sufficient also for the stiffener forces at the centreline. However, the choice will be to use two 140×16 plates at this location. The 140 mm dimension is selected in order to support more of the flange width at this location (500 mm). The plate slenderness limit $200/\sqrt{F_y}$ will be met for the width of 140 mm if the thickness is increased from 12 mm to 16 mm.

Welding of bearing stiffener – transfer load of 1100 kN.

Try a 6 mm fillet, E49xx electrode. Along the fusion face, the strength of the base metal (Equation 9.11) is

$$V_r = 0.67\,\phi_w\,A_m\,F_u\ = 0.67\times0.67\times6\text{ mm}\times450\text{ MPa}$$

$$= 1212\text{ N/mm} = 1.21\text{ kN/mm}$$

The strength of the weld itself (Equation 9.12(b) and taking $\theta = 0^o$) is

$$V_r = 0.67\,\phi_w\,A_w\,X_u\ = 0.67\times0.67\,(\,6\text{ mm}\times0.7071\,)\times490\text{ MPa}$$

$$= 933\text{ N/mm} = 0.933\text{ kN/mm} \qquad\qquad\qquad\text{Governs}$$

Total weld length required $= \dfrac{1100\text{ kN}}{0.933\text{ kN/mm}} = 1180\text{ mm}$

Use an intermittent weld –

Minimum length (CSA–W59–03) = 40 mm or 4 times the fillet weld size

Maximum clear spacing (Clause 19.1.3(b) of S16–01) = 300 mm

or $\quad\dfrac{330\times16\text{ mm}}{\sqrt{350\text{ MPa}}} = 282\text{ mm}$

Try 6 mm fillet welds, 60 mm long at 250 mm c/c. This will provide a total of 1200 mm of weld within the maximum possible length of the stiffener. (See Fig. 7.17.) Use this weld detail at the bearing stiffeners at both ends and at the centreline of the girder. (See Fig. 7.16.)

Design of Intermediate Stiffeners – Now that it has been established that bearing stiffeners are required both at the girder ends and at centreline, the spacing of the intermediate stiffeners can be finalized and the stiffeners designed. Since the spacing of the end panel has been established at 1400 mm, the remaining distance to centreline is 6200 mm. The maximum permissible spacing for the intermediate stiffeners is 4200 mm. It will be convenient to subdivide the 6200 mm into two equal spaces by placing an intermediate stiffener as shown in Figure 7.16. This gives an actual aspect ratio a/h = 3100/1400 = 2.21, for which $k_v = 6.16$. Assuming that plates will be provided in pairs, the stiffener area required (Equation 7.28) is

$$A_s \geq \frac{a\,w}{2}\left[1 - \frac{a/h}{\sqrt{1+(a/h)^2}}\right]\left[1 - \frac{310\,000\,k_v}{F_y\,(h/w)^2}\right]\frac{F_y}{F_{ys}}$$

$$= \frac{3100\ \text{mm}\times10\ \text{mm}}{2}\left[1 - \frac{2.21}{\sqrt{1+2.21^2}}\right]\left[1 - \frac{310\,000\times6.16}{350\times140^2}\right] = 995\ \text{mm}^2$$

Also, from Equation 7.30, $\ I \geq \left(\dfrac{h}{50}\right)^4 = \left(\dfrac{1400}{50}\right)^4 = 615 \times 10^3\ \text{mm}^4$

Try two 80×8 plates, for which

$A = 1280\ \text{mm}^2 \quad \text{and} \quad I = 3275 \times 10^3\ \text{mm}^4$

Shear to be transferred (Equation 7.29) –

$$v = 1 \times 10^{-4}\,h\left(F_y\right)^{1.5}$$

$$= 1 \times 10^{-4} \times 1400\,(350)^{1.5} = 917\ \text{N/mm} = 0.92\ \text{kN/mm}$$

Try a 6 mm fillet weld.

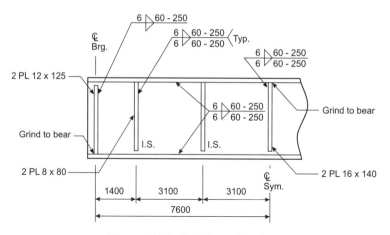

Figure 7.16 – Stiffener Spacing

From the calculations for the bearing stiffener welds, the strength of the weld metal will govern at 0.933 kN/mm. As for those welds, try an intermittent 6 mm fillet weld of minimum length (40 mm). In accordance with Clause 14.5.4 of the Standard, the clear distance required between welds is not to exceed the lesser of

$16 \times$ web thickness $= 16 \times 10\ \text{mm} = 160\ \text{mm}$

$4 \times$ weld length $= 4 \times 40\ \text{mm}$ Governs

Try 6 mm fillet welds, 60 mm long, spaced at 190 mm c/c (130 mm clear between welds). The shear transfer available is

$$v = (0.933\ \text{kN/mm} \times 60\ \text{mm})/190\ \text{mm} = 0.29\ \text{kN/mm}$$

at each web to stiffener junction. Since stiffeners have been provided in pairs, this gives four such weld locations and the total shear transfer provided is 1.16 kN/mm. This is greater than the shear transfer required.

The detail of the intermediate stiffener is shown in Figure 7.17. It should be remembered that the girder design proceeded on the basis that adequate lateral bracing for the compression flange would be provided. The calculations for location, size and connection of the lateral bracing are not included here. (Generally, it will be convenient to attach the bracing to the intermediate stiffeners. In this case, a weld between the stiffener and the compression flange of the girder would be provided to transfer the force in the bracing to the girder.)

Welds between the flange and the web will be necessary to transfer the horizontal shear at this junction. At the end of the span, the shear flow is:

$$q = \frac{V\,Q}{I} = \frac{1082 \times 10^3 \text{ N} \times (25 \times 300) \text{ mm}^2 \times 712.5 \text{ mm}}{9902 \times 10^6 \text{ mm}^4} = 584 \text{ N/mm}$$

and at the location where the cross-section changes

$$q = \frac{781 \times 10^3 \text{ N} \times (25 \times 500) \text{ mm}^2 \times 712.5 \text{ mm}}{14\,980 \times 10^6 \text{ mm}^4} = 464 \text{ N/mm}$$

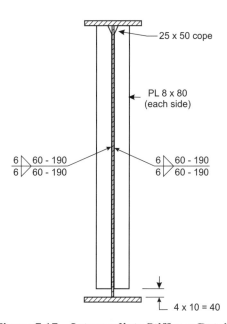

Figure 7.17 – Intermediate Stiffener Details

A weld suitable for the larger shear flow will be chosen and this will be used throughout.

The minimum fillet weld that can be used against the 25 mm thick flange plate is 8 mm (CSA W59-M1989 (R1998)). Thus, use the lesser of

$$V_r = 0.67 \, \phi_w \, A_m \, F_u \; = 0.67 \times 0.67 \times 8 \; mm \times 450 \; MPa = 1616 \; N/mm$$

$$V_r = 0.67 \, \phi_w \, A_w \, X_u \; = \; 0.67 \times 0.67 \, (8 \; mm \times 0.7071) \times 490 \; MPa = 1244 \; N/mm$$

Recognizing that the fillet welds will be placed in pairs, an intermittent weld will be suitable.

Minimum length = 40 mm or 4 times weld size.

Maximum clear spacing = 300 mm or

$$\frac{330 \times 10 \; mm}{\sqrt{350 \; MPa}} = 176 \; mm$$

Try an 8 mm weld 50 mm long spaced at 240 mm on centres. The resistance provided is

$$q = \frac{(1244 \; N/mm \times 50 \; mm) \times 2 \; welds}{240 \; mm} = 518 \; N/mm \qquad \text{Satisfactory}$$

Although use of intermittent fillet welds has been illustrated here, it is probably more common now to use continuous submerged arc welds deposited with semi-automatic welding equipment. This reduces labour costs.

The design of this girder is now complete but it must be emphasized that the usual procedure would be to repeat the process for several other trial cross-sections. An examination would then be made as to which design is the most economical in terms of material, fabrication, and erection costs.

References

7.1 Canadian Standards Association, CAN/CSA–S16–01, "Limit States Design of Steel Structures," Toronto, Ontario, 2001.

7.2 Canadian Standards Association, CAN/CSA–S6–00 (R2005), "Canadian Highway Bridge Design Code," Toronto, Ontario, 2005.

7.3 Bresler, B., Lin, T. Y., and Scalzi, J. B., "Design of Steel Structures," Second Edition, John Wiley and Sons, New York, 1968.

7.4 Basler, K., Yen, B. T., Mueller, J. A., and Thurlimann, B., "Web Buckling Tests on Welded Plate Girders," Bull. No. 64. Welding Research Council, New York, 1960.

7.5 Basler, K., and Thurlimann, B., "Strength of Plate Girders in Bending," Journal of the Structural Division, ASCE, Vol. 87, No. ST6, August, 1961.

7.6 Basler, K., "Strength of Plate Girders Under Combined Bending and Shear," Journal of the Structural Division, ASCE, Vol. 87, No. ST7, October, 1961.

7.7 Galambos, T.V., Editor, "Guide to Stability Design Criteria for Metal Structures," Fifth Edition, John Wiley, New York, 1998.

7.8 Basler, K., "Strength of Plate Girders in Shear," Journal of the Structural Division, ASCE, Vol. 87, No. ST7, October, 1961.

7.9 Canadian Institute of Steel Construction, "Handbook of Steel Construction," Ninth Edition, Toronto, Ontario, 2006.

7.10 Salmon, C. G., and Johnson, J. E., "Steel Structures – Design and Behavior," Harper Collins, Fourth Edition, New York, 1996.

Notes

CHAPTER 8

BEAM-COLUMNS

8.1   Introduction

Beam-columns are those members in a structure that are subjected to both significant axial load and bending moment. Although there are many structural steel members that are loaded only axially, for example truss members and bracing members, probably the majority of the elements in a structure have both axial force and bending moment present. Generally speaking, members that are loaded principally transversely ("beams") have small levels of axial force and are usually designed on the basis that the axial force can be neglected. In a building structure, the vertical elements almost always have significant axial force combined with significant bending moments, however. These are termed "beam-columns." Beam-columns can also result when lateral forces are applied transversely to an axially loaded member, as for example in the case of a column on the exterior wall of a building. It receives transverse loading due to wind in addition to the vertical forces it must carry.

Beam-columns can be subjected to either axial tensile force or axial compressive force combined with moment. In this chapter, emphasis will be placed on the latter case because it represents both the more common occurrence and it presents the more difficult technical issues.

In a building structure, the vertical elements are generally beam-columns that derive their axial force and bending moments as a result of the action of adjacent members. A typical situation is shown in Figure 8.1(a), where a portion of the framing for an office building is shown. The members are joined using moment-resisting connections. If the spans or the loading are not symmetrical, then the beam loading will induce bending moments at the column ends in addition to the axial force induced by the beam shears and the loads from the column segment. The resulting free-body diagram is shown in Figure 8.1(b).

The forces and bending moments on individual structural elements are determined through the structural analysis process briefly discussed in Chapter 1. Throughout this text it is implied that the analysis procedure can be separated from the member selection procedure within the total design process. Such is never really the case, however, and in the design of beam-columns it is particularly important that the designer appreciate the implications of the analysis procedure.

The member selection process for a beam-column is based on the ultimate strength of the member [8.1]. Depending on the member proportions, the ultimate strength may be limited by overall stability of the member or by the bending strength of a particular cross-section, usually at a load or reaction point. As was the case for beams and for columns, the possibility of premature plate buckling must be eliminated by satisfying the pertinent width-to-thickness limitations [8.1]. The overall stability of the member may be limited by in-plane stability or by lateral-torsional buckling. For this reason, both overall failure modes and the local bending strength must be checked for any given member. Overall stability issues play an important role in the design of beams and of columns. These stability issues, however, did not have any effect on the magnitude of the design bending moments and axial loads. This is not the case, however, for beam-columns. Because of the significant interaction between stability and the magnitude of the moments and forces for which the beam-columns need to be designed, it is important that the stability issues be considered in the calculation of the design force effects. For this reason, it is appropriate to look first at stability of members and frames and their effect on the design moments and axial forces. Design considerations for beam-columns will follow.

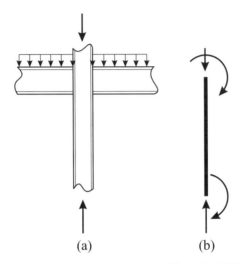

(a)   (b)

Figure 8.1 – Beam-Column Loading Condition

8.2   Stability of Members and Frames

In many situations, the attainment of the moment capacity at the critical section marks the ultimate strength of the member. For example, consider the beam-column of length L subjected to an axial load C and equal end moments M_0 as shown in Figure 8.2. The member has pinned ends and it is assumed that translation does not occur.

For low values of M_0 the member behaves in a linear elastic manner, but as the moment is increased, the extreme fibres will yield. When columns are short, the behaviour of the member is governed by the strength of the cross-section, i.e., as governed by the slenderness of the flanges and web that form the cross-section. As the member becomes more slender, the behaviour of the member is no longer governed by the strength of the cross-section because failure by overall instability becomes more critical. If axial load predominates over bending, and depending on the support conditions on the member, failure can be by flexural buckling about one of the principal axes, by torsional buckling, or by flexural-torsional buckling. However, if bending prevails, the member may either bend under the combined action of the bending moments and the axial load that acts on the deformed member until the capacity of the member is reached, or it could fail by what is termed lateral-torsional instability. The lateral-torsional buckling capacity is a function of the lateral support conditions, end conditions, the unsupported length, and loading conditions, as discussed in Chapter 5. These modes of failure will be discussed further in Section 8.3.

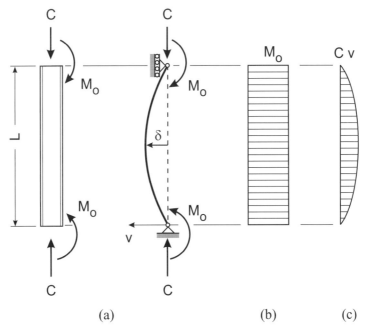

(a)   (b)   (c)

Figure 8.2 – Primary and Secondary Bending Moments

The effect of the axial load acting on the deformed shape of the member and the resulting secondary moment shown in Figure 8.2(c) is termed the P–δ effect. Its effect can be very significant but it is not usually accounted for in the analysis of the structure. It must therefore be accounted for in the design stage. Secondary moments also result when the top of the beam-column sways relative to its base. The resulting secondary moment, termed the P–Δ moment, is also important and must also be accounted for in the design process. Both secondary effects are discussed below.

8.2.1   P–δ Effects

Consider the member shown in Figure 8.3, which is subjected to a distributed load q_f, end moments M_{f1}, and M_{f2}, and an axial load C_f. The applied moments and loads M_{f1}, M_{f2} and q_f cause first-order moments in the member, M_o, as shown in Figure 8.3(b). These first-order moments are obtained by considering equilibrium of the member in its undeformed shape. They cause the beam to deform by an amount v, which varies along the beam length. Under the action of the axial load, C_f, on the deformed shape of the member, so-called second-order moments are present. These moments are designated second-order moments because they are moments that do not exist in the beam in its undeformed configuration. The second-order moments create additional deflections, which in turn create additional moments. This action will gradually stabilize when the deformed shape is consistent with the applied moments, both first and second-order, or may lead to failure of the member. This effect, resulting from the deformation of a member between its ends, is called the P–δ effect, and it affects individual members in a frame. The total bending moment and final deflection are given as $M = M_o + C_f v$ and $v = v_o + v_{II}$.

In order to design the beam-column, the maximum moment, M_{max}, somewhere along the length of the member must be determined. It is therefore necessary to solve the differential equation that describes the behaviour of the member for given boundary conditions. However, to facilitate the calculations, consider the particular and critical case of a sinusoidal second-order moment and a maximum deflection at midspan. The differential equation for this case is [8.2]:

$$-EI\frac{d^2 v_{II}}{dz^2} = C_f \delta \sin\frac{\pi z}{L}$$

(8.1)

where z is the distance along the member and δ is the maximum deflection of the member, assumed to be at midspan ($z = L/2$) for the condition assumed in Equation 8.1.

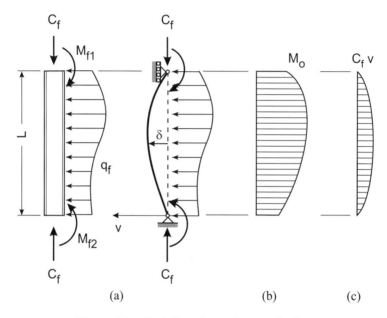

(a)   (b)   (c)

Figure 8.3 – Stability of member: P–δ effect

If Equation 8.1 is integrated twice with respect to z, an expression is obtained for the second-order deflection, v_{II}, along the length of the member

$$v_{II} = \frac{L^2}{\pi^2\, EI} C_f \delta \sin\frac{\pi z}{L}$$

(8.2)

According to the earlier assumption, the maximum second-order deflection, δ_{II} occurs at midspan and is given as

$$\delta_{II} = \frac{L^2}{\pi^2\, EI} C_f \delta = \delta\frac{C_f}{C_e}$$

(8.3)

where C_e is the elastic buckling load of a pin ended column of length L, given as

214

$$C_e = \frac{\pi^2 \, E \, I}{L^2} \tag{8.4}$$

The total deflection at midspan is equal to the sum of the first-order deflection, δ_I and the second-order deflection, δ_{II}, expressed as

$$\delta = \delta_I + \delta_{II} \tag{8.5}$$

Substituting Equation 8.3 into 8.5 and solving for the total midspan deflection,

$$\delta = \frac{1}{1 - \dfrac{C_f}{C_e}} \, \delta_I \tag{8.6}$$

If it is now assumed that the maximum first-order moment, M_{Imax}, occurs at midspan or close to midspan, the maximum bending moment in the member is

$$M_{max} = M_{Imax} + C_f \, \delta \tag{8.7}$$

Substituting Equation 8.6 into Equation 8.7 and rearranging the terms gives

$$M_{max} = \left(\frac{1 + \psi \dfrac{C_f}{C_e}}{1 - \dfrac{C_f}{C_e}} \right) M_{Imax} \tag{8.8}$$

where the parameter ψ is equal to

$$\psi = \frac{\delta_I \, C_e}{M_{Imax}} - 1 \tag{8.9}$$

The numerator of the term in brackets in Equation 8.8 is an equivalent moment factor and is denoted ω_1.

$$\omega_1 = 1 + \psi \frac{C_f}{C_e} \tag{8.10}$$

Equation 8.8 can thus be rewritten as

$$M_{max} = \left(\frac{\omega_1}{1 - C_f/C_e} \right) M_{Imax} = U_1 \, M_{Imax} \tag{8.11}$$

The term in brackets in Equation 8.11 is the amplification factor used to evaluate the maximum bending moment in the beam-column, taking into account the P–δ effects. For load cases where lateral loads are applied between the end supports, the parameter ψ given by Equation 8.9 is negative. This results in a value of ω_1 less than unity. Clause 13.8.5 of S16–01 uses a more conservative value of $\omega_1 = 1.0$ for a distributed load or a series of point loads applied between the supports. For a concentrated load or moment between the supports, S16–01 suggests $\omega_1 = 0.85$.

A simpler load case consists of end moments only, M_{f1} and M_{f2}, with the axial load: beam-columns in buildings are seldom loaded laterally between the supports. For this case, an expression for ω_1 proposed in Reference [8.3] gives a generally conservative value of the equivalent moment factor that has been adopted in S16–01 as follows:

$$\omega_1 = 0.6 - 0.4\,\kappa \geq 0.4 \tag{8.12}$$

were κ is the end moment ratio, M_{f1}/M_{f2}, with $|M_{f1}| \leq |M_{f2}|$. When M_{f1} and M_{f2} are applied in the same direction, the moment ratio is positive and the member is bent in double curvature. Conversely, when the end moments are applied in opposite directions, the moment ratio is negative and the member is bent in single curvature.

8.2.2   P–Δ Effects

The vertical forces on a structure acting through sway displacements produce additional moments and displacements, termed sway effects, or P–Δ effects. In the calculation of the load effects, design standards require that the effect of the loads acting on the deformed shape of the structure be taken into account. These second-order effects can be determined either by performing a second-order analysis or by modifying the effects of a first-order analysis.

A second-order analysis can be used to determine the additional force effects caused by the effect of the gravity loads acting on the deformed structure. The lateral displacements can be caused either by applied lateral loads such as wind, or they can be due to initial out-of-plumb of the structure.

The P–Δ effect is illustrated in Figure 8.4 for a simple portal frame. If the moments at joints B and C of the portal frame are obtained from a first-order analysis (on the underformed frame), they are equal to H h/2. However, because of the sway in the frame, there are P–Δ effects and the moment at these joints is actually equal to H h/2 + PΔ.

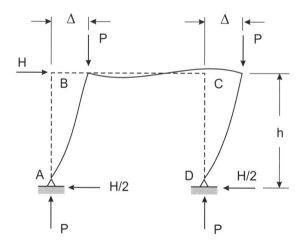

Figure 8.4 – P–Δ Effects in a Sway Frame

Second-order analyses can include various types of non-linearities, including non-linear joint behaviour to account for semi-rigid connections (connections for which the angle between the connected members changes with a change in moment), non-linear

216

material behaviour taking into account residual stresses and material yielding, and geometric non-linearities (P–δ and P–Δ effects).

Most of the analyses performed on building structures assume that the members behave elastically, even under the factored loads. Thus, these analyses neglect the changes in force and moment distributions that could be caused by localized yielding at loads approaching the factored levels.

Conceptually, the analysis incorporates the member behaviour within a relationship between the end forces on a member segment and the deformations of the ends of the segment. The slope-deflection equations provide an example of this type of relationship. These relationships are organized into a set of equations relating the loads on the structure to the overall deformations (and thus to the deformations and forces appropriate to each individual member) by enforcing the equations of equilibrium.

For the simple frame shown in Figure 8.4, equilibrium requires that at each joint the member end moments sum to zero and that, for the structure as a whole, the forces balance in both the vertical and horizontal directions.

Since the equations of equilibrium are satisfied for the analysis of the structure, the possible changes in the distribution of forces among the individual structural elements are not considered to be significant. In fact, a distribution based on the assumption of elastic behaviour provides a safe lower bound and can be used in combination with member selection processes that do, in fact, account for yielding in assessing the ultimate member resistances.

The curved members supporting this canopy are subjected to combined axial force and bending (Photo courtesy of Michael I. Gilmor)

8.3 Methods of Frame Analysis

8.3.1 Introduction

An overview of frame response predicted using various methods of analysis is presented in Figure 8.5 for a simple portal frame. The plots illustrate the relationship between the magnitude of the applied loads, expressed as the load factor μ, and the lateral displacement of the frame, Δ. The fundamental differences between the analysis methods used to obtain the curves presented in Figure 8.5 are whether the analysis considers equilibrium on the deformed or the undeformed structure, and whether the effect of material yielding is included in the analysis. In this respect, four types of analysis are illustrated in the figure, and they are briefly described following.

First-order elastic analysis. This is the simplest level of analysis—the material is assumed to be linear elastic and equilibrium is considered on the undeformed shape. Consequently, the predicted structure behaviour is linear. A multitude of methods have been developed for first-order analysis of frames [8.4]. These methods comprise, for example, slope-deflection, virtual work, moment distribution and stiffness methods based on matrix algebra. The effect of the axial force and the shear force on the stiffness of the members is usually neglected.

This level of analysis is deficient in several ways. The most significant are that yielding of the material, likely to happen at factored load level, is ignored, and the effect of axial loads on the moments is also ignored. First-order elastic analysis therefore provide no direct measure of frame stability. Although this type of analysis is acceptable by S16–01 for design purposes, the Standard requires that the moments obtained from such an analysis subsequently be adjusted to account for second-order effects.

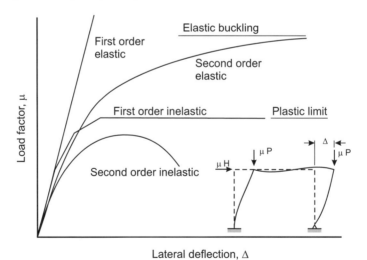

Figure 8.5 – Effect of Analysis on Load–Deflection Behaviour

Second-order elastic analysis. In this level of analysis the material is still assumed to remain linear elastic, but equilibrium is formulated on the deformed structure, i.e., the moments in the members are magnified by the effect of the axial load acting on a deformed member. Deflections obtained in this manner are larger than the deflections

218

obtained from a first-order elastic analysis and the relationship between load and deflection is non-linear. As the load magnitude is increased, moments and deflections increase at an increasing rate due to the action of the gravity loads on the deflected structure. As the load is increased incrementally, a load level at which the structure becomes unstable is reached. This load level represents a limiting load that approaches the elastic buckling load level for the structure.

First-order inelastic analysis. Common to the two methods of analysis presented so far is the assumption that the material remains linear elastic over the full range of loading. However, under factored loads it is expected that part of the frame would yield. In a first-order inelastic analysis plastification of the members in the frame is considered, but equilibrium is formulated on the undeformed shape. The inelastic effects can be handled by techniques ranging from the formation of discrete plastic hinges (development of the plastic moment at a cross-section) to the spread of plasticity over a portion of the length of the members. As the load on the structure is increased, successive plastic hinges form until a sufficient number have been created to produce a mechanism. When the material stress versus strain curve is assumed to be elastic-plastic (i.e., strain-hardening of the material is ignored) the formation of a mechanism represents a limit load, one at which deformations keep increasing without any increase in load. This limiting load is designated as the *plastic limit*.

Second-order inelastic analysis. This type of analysis accounts for the decrease in stiffness due to material inelasticity and deformation of the structure. The second-order inelastic analysis accounts for most of the behavioural aspects of frames, and the limit load obtained by this analysis is the most accurate representation of the true strength of a frame. Since the computational effort is considerably greater than that involved in linear elastic analyses, the second-order inelastic analysis is not widely used in design practice.

8.3.2   Second-Order Analysis Methods

Although some highly advanced analysis software (e.g., *ANSYS, ABAQUS, NISA* and few others) have the capability of conducting a second-order inelastic analysis, these are used mainly for research purposes or for the solution of specialized problems. The capability of performing second-order inelastic analysis is not yet available in most commonly used analysis software used by design engineers. Consequently, it is usual in design practice to conduct either a first or a second-order analysis with a linear elastic material model. The assumption of linear elastic material is usually sufficient for most practical design situations provided that allowance is made for inelastic behaviour at the design stage. It is often acceptable to use simplified methods to account for second-order effects for elastic analysis of building frames where deformations are usually small. Some of these methods are described below. It should be noted that simplified P–Δ analysis methods do not include P–δ effects and, given the assumption of small deflections, they are limited in their ability to model very slender structures.

(a) Amplification factor method

Calculation of second-order moments using the amplification factor method requires decomposition of the first-order moments into sidesway and nonsidesway components. The nonsidesway moments, M_{fg}, are obtained from a first-order analysis under gravity loads only and the frame considered as braced. The sidesway moments, M_{ft}, are obtained from an analysis of the frame in an unbraced condition and where only lateral loads are applied to the frame (see Figure 8.6). These lateral loads are the applied factored load plus the lateral reaction required to prevent sway in the gravity load analysis The amplified sidesway moments are then added to the factored gravity load moments. Thus, the factored design moment is obtained as

$$M_f = M_{fg} + U_2 \, M_{ft} \tag{8.13}$$

where

U_2 is an amplification factor that accounts for P–Δ effects. It is calculated as:

$$U_2 = \frac{1}{1 - \dfrac{\Sigma C_f \, \Delta_f}{\Sigma V_f \, h}} \tag{8.14}$$

Δ_f : the lateral displacement at the level considered relative to the level below.

h : the height of the storey between these two levels.

ΣC_f : sum of the columns axial load at the storey considered.

ΣV_f : storey shear.

M_{fg} : factored first-order moment resulting from gravity loads.

M_{ft} : factored first-order moment resulting from lateral loads.

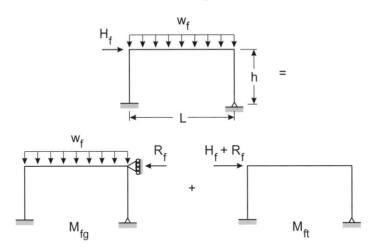

Figure 8.6 – Analysis Using the Amplification Factor Method

(b) Fictitious horizontal loads method

The fictitious horizontal load method is based on the assumption that the effect of a vertical (gravity) load C acting on a column of length h with the top displaced laterally relative to the base by an amount Δ can be simulated by a fictitious horizontal load equal to C Δ/h applied at the top of the column. This is illustrated by the free body diagrams shown in Figure 8.7.

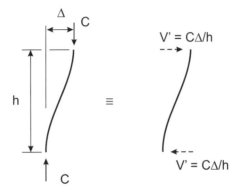

Figure 8.7 – Equivalent Fictitious Horizontal Loads

The procedure to obtain the second-order moments can be described as follows:

1) Perform a first-order analysis of the structure subjected to the factored loads to obtain the lateral displacement at each level, Δ_i.

2) Calculate the fictitious shears that produce at the extremities of the column the same moments as the moments due to gravity loads acting on the displaced structure. This is calculated as follows:

$$V'_i = \frac{\sum C_i}{h_i} \ (\Delta_{i+1} - \Delta_i) \tag{8.15}$$

where the summation sign applies to all the columns in the storey. The quantities h_i, Δ_i, and Δ_{i+1} are shown in Figure 8.8.

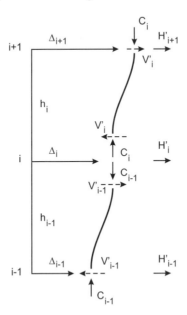

Figure 8.8 – Sway Forces Due to Vertical Loads

3) Calculate the fictitious horizontal force at each level as follows.

$$H'_i = V'_{i-1} - V'_i \qquad (8.16)$$

4) Add H'_i to the lateral load applied to level i and repeat the analysis.

5) When the lateral displacements obtained at the end of one cycle are almost the same as those obtained in the previous cycle, the method has converged and the resulting force effects include the P–Δ effects.

A slow convergence indicates that the structure is too flexible and a lack of convergence indicates that the structure is not stable.

The method is iterative and may be time consuming. Simplifications, aimed at accelerating the process, have been proposed [8.5]:

1) Start at step 2 using estimated lateral displacements. If the lateral displacements calculated under the actual plus fictitious lateral loads are smaller than those assumed, the results can be conservatively used for design.

2) Use $V'_i = V'_i \times U_2$

where

$$V'_i = \frac{\Sigma C_i}{h_i} (\Delta_{i+1} - \Delta_i)$$

and

$$U_2 = \frac{1}{1 - \dfrac{(\Delta_{i+1} - \Delta_i) \Sigma C_i}{\Sigma V_i\, h_i}}$$

(c) Negative Area Brace Method

It is possible to simulate P–Δ effects by inserting a bracing member of negative area at each level of the frame [8.5]. These fictitious members, placed diagonally and pinned at both extremities, cause additional lateral displacements equal to those created by the P–Δ effects.

The area of the fictitious bracing member is taken as:

$$A_o = - \frac{\Sigma C_f}{h} \frac{L_o}{E \cos^2 \alpha} \qquad (8.17)$$

where

ΣP_f : sum of column forces at the level considered

h : storey height

E : modulus of elasticity of the columns

L_o : length of the fictitious member

α : angle of inclination of the fictitious bracing element

The braced frame is analyzed using a first-order analysis. The results obtained from this analysis include the P–Δ effects. It can be shown [8.5] that the horizontal component of the force in the fictitious diagonal is the fictitious shear given by $V'_i = V'_i \times U_2$. Therefore, the technique gives the same result as the amplification factor method.

An advantage of the negative brace technique is that it can be used with software that does not have built-in features for second-order analysis. However, when using non-iterative procedures to determine P–Δ effects it may be difficult to tell whether the frame is too flexible.

(d) Finite Element Method

The methods of second-order analysis described above are all approximate methods of analysis. As such, their formulation accounts for the P–Δ (frame stability) effects, but not the P–δ (member stability) effects. Accurate methods of second-order analysis have been developed and are becoming more widespread. One of the most powerful methods of analysis is the finite element method, which has gained wide acceptance in the engineering profession because it allows engineers to solve increasingly complex problems for which closed-formed solutions are not obtainable. Based on energy principles, the finite element method is used to formulate the stiffness matrix relating joint forces and joint displacements. Although finite element formulations have been developed to account for material yielding, large deformations, and P–δ and P–Δ effects, not all these effects are implemented in commonly used design software. The general procedure for finite element formulation is available in a number of textbooks [8.6] and will not be discussed here.

8.3.3   Notional Load Concept

Geometric imperfections such as initial out-of-plumb of columns and out-of-straightness of axially loaded members will increase the second-order effects. Initial imperfections can be incorporated directly into the frame model through the geometrical description of the frame. This procedure is time consuming and impractical, however.

A shortcoming in common to all the methods of second-order analysis described above is that none consider the effect of material yielding in the formulation. As the factored load level is reached, material is expected to yield, leading to a reduction of stiffness of the structure and larger deflections. The larger deflections will have the effect of increasing the second-order effects.

In order to account for the effect of initial imperfections and partial yielding of frames at factored load level, artificial lateral loads are applied to the structure to create increased sway in the structure. These artificial loads, called notional loads, are used to account indirectly for effects not otherwise considered in the analysis [8.7]. Clause 8.7.2 of S16–01 [8.8] recommends notional lateral loads, applied at each storey, equal to 0.005 times the factored gravity loads contributed by the storey. These notional loads are added to the lateral loads that may already exist on the building and are therefore included in the second-order analysis.

Example 8.1

Given

Calculate the design moments and axial loads in members AB and CD of the frame shown in Figure 8.9. The gravity load of 50 kN/m and lateral load of 35 kN applied at E are factored loads. Since member EF is pinned at both ends, it is not able to resist any of the lateral loads. It is therefore called a leaning member because it is relying on the rigid frame ABCD to provide stability. The design moments will be calculated using the various methods discussed above.

Solution

Since the following P–Δ analysis will make use of first-order elastic analysis results, the results of such an analysis are presented in Figure 8.10. Figure 8.10(a) presents the results of a gravity load analysis. In order to prevent sway moments from developing, a lateral support is placed at E. The reaction at E becomes part of the lateral load in the lateral load analysis. In addition, Clause 8.7.2 of S16–01 specifies that a notional load of 0.005 times the factored gravity load contributed by a given storey shall be applied for all load cases.

Notional Load $= 0.005 \times 50$ kN / m $\times 22$ m $= 5.5$ kN

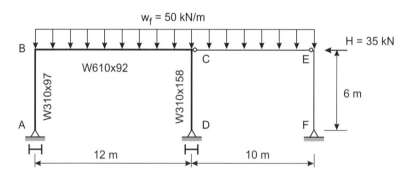

Figure 8.9 – Frame of Example 8.1

Since the reaction force at E for the gravity load case is 21.6 kN, the total lateral load applied at E is

$H_t = 35$ kN $+ 5.5$ kN $+ 21.6$ kN $= 62.1$ kN

In the present case, all three lateral load components are applied in the same direction. The sway force is applied in the direction opposite to that of the reaction force found in the gravity load analysis. The notional load, on the other hand, is applied in the same direction as the resultant of the sway force and the lateral load.

The results of a first-order analysis for the lateral load case are presented in Figure 8.10(b). The corresponding storey sway of 55.3 mm is indicated in the figure.

224

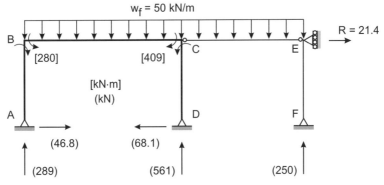

(a) First-Order Analysis – Gravity Loads

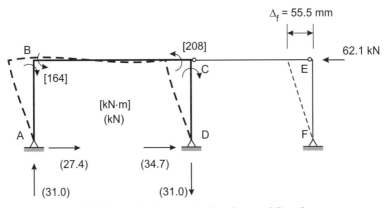

(b) First-Order Analysis – Lateral Load

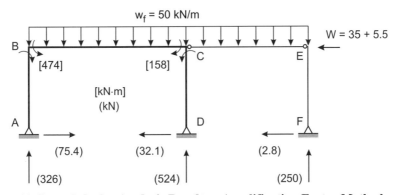

(c) Second-Order Analysis Results – Amplification Factor Method

Figure 8.10 – Analysis Results for Frame of Example 8.1 — Amplification Factor Method

(a) Amplification Factor Method

The amplification factor U_2 is given as

$$U_2 = \cfrac{1}{1 - \cfrac{\sum C_f \, \Delta_f}{\sum V_f \, h}}$$

where,

$$\sum C_f = 50 \text{ kN/m} \times (12 \text{ m} + 10 \text{ m}) = 1100 \text{ kN}$$

$\cfrac{\Delta_f}{\sum V_f}$ is the flexibility of the storey, obtained from the results of the first-order

analysis.

$$\frac{\Delta_f}{\sum V_f} = \frac{55.5 \text{ mm}}{62.1 \text{ kN}} = 0.894 \text{ mm/kN}$$

h is the storey height

$$U_2 = \cfrac{1}{1 - \cfrac{\sum C_f \, \Delta_f}{\sum V_f \, h}} = \cfrac{1}{1 - \cfrac{1100 \text{ kN}}{6000 \text{ mm}} \, 0.894 \text{ mm/kN}} = 1.196$$

The second-order moments at B and C can be obtained from Equation 8.13,

$$M_f^B = M_{fg}^B + U_2 \, M_{ft}^B = 278 \text{ kN} \cdot \text{m} + 1.196 \times 164 \text{ kN} \cdot \text{m} = 474 \text{ kN} \cdot \text{m}$$

$$M_f^C = M_{fg}^C + U_2 \, M_{ft}^C = 408 \text{ kN} \cdot \text{m} + 1.196 \times (-209 \text{ kN} \cdot \text{m}) = 158 \text{ kN} \cdot \text{m}$$

A summary of the second-order analysis results using the amplification factor method is presented in Figure 8.10(c). The lateral load is shown as the applied load of 35 kN plus the notional load of 5.5 kN. It should be noted that column EF would be designed for an axial load 250 kN. To satisfy equilibrium of horizontal forces, it is noted that column EF must develop a small shear force. Although column EF is pinned at both ends, a shear force can develop in the column. This shear force can develop while maintaining equilibrium of moments in the pin ended column only because, in a second-order analysis, equilibrium is considered on the deformed shape.

(b) Fictitious Horizontal Loads Method

A first-order analysis of the structure with the factored loads, including the notional load of 5.5 kN, is performed, from which the storey drift is obtained. The results of this analysis are presented in Figure 8.11(a). Fictitious column shear and horizontal force are calculated using Equations 8.15 and 8.16, respectively.

A first-order analysis of the frame with only gravity load shows that the lateral deflection at the top of the frame is 19.3 mm. With a unit lateral load applied at E, the calculated lateral deflection is 0.894 mm. (This information is used following for the iterative process.)

Iteration 1

Using Equation 8.15,

$$V_i^{'1} = \frac{\sum C_i}{h_i} \ (\Delta_{i+1} - \Delta_i) = \frac{1100 \ kN}{6000 \ mm} (55.3 \ mm - 0) = 10.1 \ kN$$

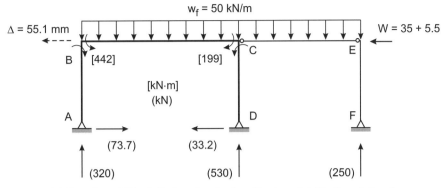

(a) Results of First-Order Analysis – Factored + Notional Loads

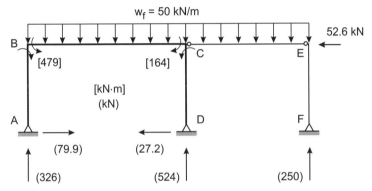

(b) Final Results of Iterative Analysis

Figure 8.11 – Analysis Results for Frame of Example 8.1 — Fictitious Lateral Load Method

Since the frame consists of only one storey, the fictitious horizontal force obtained using Equation 8.16 is equal to the fictitious shear, namely, 10.1 kN. This fictitious lateral load is added to the applied lateral load, including the notional load of 5.5 kN. The new lateral load is therefore 50.6 kN. Since the deflection is obtained from a first-order analysis, the results of the first-order analyses presented above can be used to determine the lateral deflection at E as follows:

$$\Delta_{top}^1 = 19.3 \ mm + (0.894 \ mm \ / \ kN \times 50.6 \ kN) = 64.5 \ mm$$

Iteration 2

Using the deflection calculated in the first iteration, the fictitious shear and lateral load are updated.

$$V_i^{'2} = \frac{1100 \ kN}{6000 \ mm} (64.5 \ mm - 0) = 11.8 \ kN$$

227

$H'^2_i = 11.8$ kN

The total lateral load is 40.5 kN + 11.8 kN = 52.3 kN

$\Delta^2_{top} = 19.3$ mm $+ (0.894$ mm$/$kN$\times 52.3$ kN$) = 66.1$ mm

Iteration 3

Using the deflection calculated in the first iteration, the fictitious shear and lateral load are updated.

$$V'^3_i = \frac{1100 \text{ kN}}{6000 \text{ mm}}(66.1 \text{ mm} - 0) = 12.1 \text{ kN}$$

$H'^3_i = 12.1$ kN

The total lateral load is 40.5 kN + 12.1 kN = 52.6 kN

$\Delta^3_{top} = 19.3$ mm $+ (0.894$ mm$/$kN$\times 52.6$ kN$) = 66.3$ mm

This deflection is within <1.0 % of the deflection calculated in the second iteration, and the problem has converged. The second-order effects are now obtained from a first-order analysis with a lateral load of 52.6 kN applied as shown in Figure 8.11(b). The results are in very close agreement with those obtained using the amplification factor method. It should be noted that some of the reaction forces are not in complete agreement because the reaction forces shown in Figure 8.11(b) were determined from a first order analysis with the amplified lateral load, i.e., equilibrium was considered on the undeformed structure rather than on the deformed structure.

(c) Negative Brace Area Method

The negative brace area is obtained from Equation 8.17.

$$A_o = -\frac{\sum C_f}{h} \frac{L_o}{E \cos^2 \alpha}$$

where L_o is equal to 13.42 m, the length of the diagonal from B to D.

$$A_o = -\frac{1100 \times 10^3 \text{ N}}{6000 \text{ mm}} \times \frac{13\,420 \text{ mm}}{200\,000 \text{ MPa} \left(\dfrac{12 \text{ m}}{13.42 \text{ m}}\right)^2} = -15.4 \text{ mm}^2$$

A first-order analysis of the modified frame with the factored loads and the notional load leads to the same results as those presented in Figure 8.11(b).

(d) Finite Element Method

Several commercially available structural analysis software will perform a P–Δ analysis. Although different software developers have implemented the stiffness method slightly differently for P–Δ analysis, the results are similar for most practical problems. The P–Δ analysis is performed with the factored loads and the notional load applied simultaneously on the structure. The results of an analysis conducted using the commercial software S-FRAME are presented in Figure 8.12.

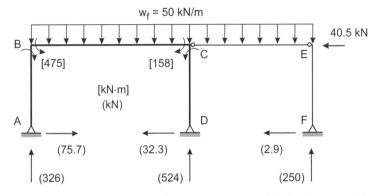

$w_f = 50$ kN/m

B

[475]

[158]

C

40.5 kN

E

[kN·m]
(kN)

A

D

F

(75.7)

(32.3)

(2.9)

(326)

(524)

(250)

Figure 8.12 – Results of Second-Order Analysis — Finite Element Method

A comparison of the results obtained using different methods of P–Δ analysis indicates that all approximate methods lead to approximately the same end results. Obviously, the use of commercial software to perform an exact elastic second-order analysis is the least time consuming. However, when second-order analysis software is not available to the design engineer any of the approximate methods will provide the accuracy required for design purpose.

Example 8.2

Given

Calculate the design moments and axial loads in the rigid frame of the two-storey structure shown in Figure 8.13. The loads indicated in the figure are factored loads. The exterior column are pinned to the beams and are also pinned at their base. Therefore, they are leaning columns and do not contribute to the lateral stability of the frame. The design moments will be calculated using the various methods discussed above.

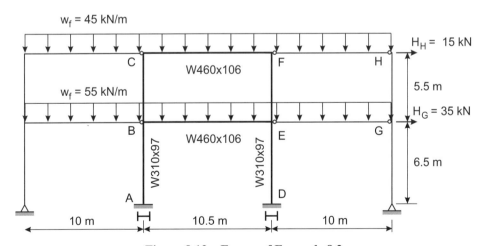

$w_f = 45$ kN/m

C

W460x106

F

H

$H_H = 15$ kN

5.5 m

$w_f = 55$ kN/m

B

W460x106

E

G

$H_G = 35$ kN

W310x97

W310x97

A

D

6.5 m

10 m

10.5 m

10 m

Figure 8.13 – Frame of Example 8.2

Solution

The results of a first-order elastic analysis are presented in Figure 8.14. Figure 8.14(a) presents the results of a gravity load analysis. Because of the symmetry of the frame and the gravity loads, the frame does not have a natural tendency to sway. Therefore, the reaction forces at E and F, which are points of lateral support required for the gravity load analysis, are both zero. For unsymmetrical structures or loads horizontal reactions would develop at these supports, as illustrated in Example 1.

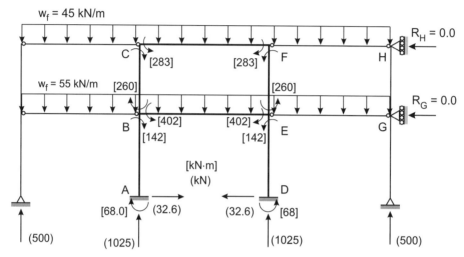

(a) First-Order Analysis – Gravity Loads

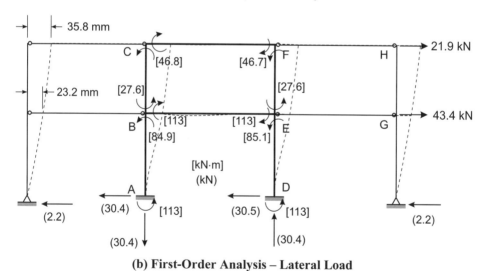

(b) First-Order Analysis – Lateral Load

Figure 8.14 – Analysis Results for Frame of Example 8.2 — Amplification Factor Method

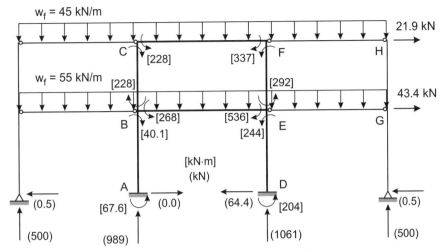

(c) Second-Order Analysis Results – Amplification Factor Method

Figure 8.14 – (cont'd)

The lateral load analysis includes both the applied lateral loads and notional forces, where the notional forces are

at G $= 0.005 \times 55$ kN / m $\times 30.5$ m $= 8.4$ kN

at H $= 0.005 \times 45$ kN / m $\times 30.5$ m $= 6.9$ kN

The total lateral loads applied at G and H is the sum of the applied factored load, the notional load, and the reaction force obtained from the gravity load analysis shown in Figure 8.14(a).

$H_{Gt} = 35.0$ kN $+ 8.4$ kN $+ 0.0 = 43.4$ kN

$H_{Ht} = 15.0$ kN $+ 6.9$ kN $+ 0.0 = 21.9$ kN

The results of a first-order analysis for the lateral load case are presented in Figure 8.14(b). The corresponding first storey sway is 23.2 mm and the second storey sway, that is, the difference between the deflections at the roof level and second floor level, is 12.6 mm.

(a) Amplification Factor Method

The amplification factor, U_2, is calculated for each storey using

$$U_2 = \frac{1}{1 - \dfrac{\Sigma C_f \, \Delta_f}{\Sigma V_f \, h}}$$

where, for the first storey

$$\Sigma C_f = (55 \text{ kN} / \text{m} + 45 \text{ kN} / \text{m}) \times (10 \text{ m} + 10.5 \text{ m} + 10 \text{ m}) = 3050 \text{ kN}$$

231

This value can also be obtained by adding the axial force in all the columns of the first storey.

$\dfrac{\Delta_f}{\sum V_f}$ is the flexibility of the storey, obtained from the results of the first-order analysis.

$$\frac{\Delta_f}{\sum V_f} = \frac{23.2 \text{ mm}}{21.9 \text{ kN} + 43.4 \text{ kN}} = 0.355 \text{ mm/kN}$$

h is the storey height (= 6500 mm)

$$U_2 = \frac{1}{1 - \dfrac{\sum C_f \ \Delta_f}{\sum V_f \ h}} = \frac{1}{1 - \dfrac{3050 \text{ kN}}{6500 \text{ mm}} 0.355 \text{ mm/kN}} = 1.200$$

Similarly, for the second storey,

$$\sum C_f = (45 \text{ kN/m}) \times (10 \text{ m} + 10.5 \text{ m} + 10 \text{ m}) = 1372 \text{ kN}$$

$$\frac{\Delta_f}{\sum V_f} = \frac{(35.8 - 23.2) \text{ mm}}{21.9 \text{ kN}} = 0.575 \text{ mm/kN}$$

For a storey height of 5500 mm,

$$U_2 = \frac{1}{1 - \dfrac{\sum C_f \ \Delta_f}{\sum V_f \ h}} = \frac{1}{1 - \dfrac{1372 \text{ kN}}{5500 \text{ mm}} 0.575 \text{ mm/kN}} = 1.167$$

The second-order moments for the beam-columns located in the first storey can be obtained from Equation 8.13. When adding moments, a clockwise moment is taken as a positive moment.

$$M_f^{AB} = M_{fg}^{AB} + U_2 \ M_{ft}^{AB} = 68 \text{ kN} \cdot \text{m} + 1.200 \times (-113 \text{ kN} \cdot \text{m}) = -67.6 \text{ kN} \cdot \text{m}$$

$$M_f^{BA} = M_{fg}^{BA} + U_2 \ M_{ft}^{BA} = 142 \text{ kN} \cdot \text{m} + 1.200 \times (-84.9 \text{ kN} \cdot \text{m}) = 40.1 \text{ kN} \cdot \text{m}$$

$$M_f^{DE} = M_{fg}^{DE} + U_2 \ M_{ft}^{DE} = -68 \text{ kN} \cdot \text{m} + 1.200 \times (-113 \text{ kN} \cdot \text{m}) = -204 \text{ kN} \cdot \text{m}$$

$$M_f^{ED} = M_{fg}^{ED} + U_2 \ M_{ft}^{ED} = -142 \text{ kN} \cdot \text{m} + 1.200 \times (-85.1 \text{ kN} \cdot \text{m}) = -244 \text{ kN} \cdot \text{m}$$

Similarly, for the columns in the second storey,

$$M_f^{BC} = M_{fg}^{BC} + U_2 \ M_{ft}^{BC} = 260 \text{ kN} \cdot \text{m} + 1.167 \times (-27.6 \text{ kN} \cdot \text{m}) = 228 \text{ kN} \cdot \text{m}$$

$$M_f^{CB} = M_{fg}^{CB} + U_2 \ M_{ft}^{CB} = 283 \text{ kN} \cdot \text{m} + 1.167 \times (-46.8 \text{ kN} \cdot \text{m}) = 228 \text{ kN} \cdot \text{m}$$

$$M_f^{EF} = M_{fg}^{EF} + U_2 \ M_{ft}^{EF} = -260 \text{ kN} \cdot \text{m} + 1.167 \times (-27.6 \text{ kN} \cdot \text{m}) = -292 \text{ kN} \cdot \text{m}$$

$$M_f^{FE} = M_{fg}^{FE} + U_2 \, M_{ft}^{FE} = -283 \text{ kN} \cdot \text{m} + 1.167 \times (-46.7 \text{ kN} \cdot \text{m}) = -337 \text{ kN} \cdot \text{m}$$

A summary of the second-order analysis results using the amplification factor method is presented in Figure 8.14(c). The lateral loads are shown as the applied load plus the notional loads. The reaction forces are determined from equilibrium consideration on the deformed structure.

(b) Fictitious Horizontal Loads Method

A first-order analysis of the structure with the factored loads, including the notional loads, is performed to obtain the storey drift. The results of this analysis are presented in Figure 8.15(a). Fictitious column shears and horizontal forces are calculated using Equations 8.15 and 8.16, respectively.

A first-order analysis of the frame with only lateral loads shows that the lateral deflection at level 2 is 23.2 mm and 36.0 mm at the top of the frame.

Iteration 1

Using Equation 8.15,

$$V'_1 = \frac{\Sigma C_1}{h_1} \left(\Delta_{1+1} - \Delta_1 \right) = \frac{3050 \text{ kN}}{6500 \text{ mm}} (23.2 \text{ mm} - 0) = 10.9 \text{ kN}$$

$$V'_2 = \frac{\Sigma C2}{h2} \left(\Delta_{2+1} - \Delta_2 \right) = \frac{1372 \text{ kN}}{5500 \text{ mm}} (36.0 \text{ mm} - 23.2 \text{ mm}) = 3.2 \text{ kN}$$

The fictitious horizontal forces at levels 2 and 3 are obtained using Equation 8.16. At level 2, the fictitious lateral load is equal to the difference between the shear force in the first storey and the shear force in the second storey, namely,

$$H'_2 = V'_1 - V'_2 = 10.9 - 3.2 = 7.7 \text{ kN}$$

$$H'_3 = V'_2 - V'_3 = 3.2 - 0 = 3.2 \text{ kN}$$

These fictitious lateral loads are now added to the applied lateral loads, including the notional loads. The new lateral loads are therefore 51.1 kN and 25.1 kN for levels 2 and 3, respectively. Since the deflections are obtained from a first-order analysis, the principle of superposition can be used to obtain the resulting deflections. Alternatively, the structure can be re-analyzed with the incremented lateral loads. The resulting lateral deflections are:

$$\Delta_2 = 27.0 \text{ mm}; \qquad \Delta_3 = 41.6 \text{ mm}$$

Iteration 2

Using the deflections calculated in the first iteration, the fictitious shears and lateral loads are updated.

$$V'_1 = \frac{3050 \text{ kN}}{6500 \text{ mm}} (27.0 \text{ mm} - 0) = 12.7 \text{ kN}$$

233

$$V'_2 = \frac{1372 \text{ kN}}{5500 \text{ mm}} (41.6 \text{ mm} - 27.0 \text{ mm}) = 3.6 \text{ kN}$$

$$H'_2 = 9.1 \text{ kN}; \qquad H'_3 = 3.6 \text{ kN}$$

The total lateral load at level 2 is 43.4 kN + 9.1 kN = 52.5 kN and the total load at level 3 is 21.9 kN + 3.6 kN = 25.5 kN. The resulting deflections are:

$$\Delta_2 = 27.6 \text{ mm}; \qquad \Delta_3 = 42.6 \text{ mm}$$

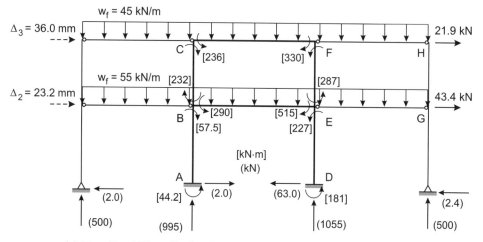

(a) Results of First-Order Analysis – Factored + Notional Loads

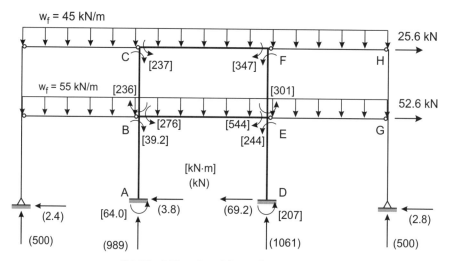

(b) Final Results of Iterative Analysis

Figure 8.15 – Analysis Results for Frame of Example 8.2 — Fictitious Lateral Load Method

234

Iteration 3

Using the deflection calculated in the first iteration, the fictitious shear and lateral load are updated.

$$V'_1 = \frac{3050 \text{ kN}}{6500 \text{ mm}} (27.6 \text{ mm} - 0) = 13.0 \text{ kN}$$

$$V'_2 = \frac{1372 \text{ kN}}{5500 \text{ mm}} (42.6 \text{ mm} - 27.6 \text{ mm}) = 3.7 \text{ kN}$$

$$H'_2 = 9.2 \text{ kN}; \qquad H'_3 = 3.7 \text{ kN}$$

The total lateral loads for this iteration are 52.6 kN and 25.6 kN for levels 2 and 3, respectively. The resulting lateral deflections are:

$$\Delta_2 = 27.7 \text{ mm}; \qquad \Delta_3 = 42.7 \text{ mm}$$

The deflections are within 1.0 % of the deflections calculated in the second iteration. The problem has therefore converged. The second-order effects can now be obtained from a first-order analysis with the lateral loads calculated in iteration 3. The results, shown in Figure 8.15(b), are in very close agreement with those obtained using the amplification factor method. The reader is reminded that the reaction forces shown in Figure 8.15(b) were determined considering equilibrium on the undeformed structure rather than on the deformed structure.

(c) Negative Brace Area Method

A brace member with a negative area is inserted in the structure in each storey. The area of each brace is obtained from Equation 8.17.

$$A_o = -\frac{\sum C_f}{h} \frac{L_o}{E \cos^2 \alpha}$$

where L_o is equal to 13.35 m for the first storey and 11.85 m for the second storey.

For the first storey, the area of the fictitious bracing member is equal to:

$$A_o = -\frac{3050 \times 10^3 \text{ N}}{6500 \text{ mm}} \times \frac{12\,350 \text{ mm}}{200\,000 \text{ MPa} \left(\dfrac{10.5 \text{ m}}{12.35 \text{ m}}\right)^2} = -40.08 \text{ mm}^2$$

The area of the fictitious bracing member for the second storey is equal to:

$$A_o = -\frac{1372 \times 10^3 \text{ N}}{5500 \text{ mm}} \times \frac{11\,850 \text{ mm}}{200\,000 \text{ MPa} \left(\dfrac{10.5 \text{ m}}{11.85 \text{ m}}\right)^2} = -18.83 \text{ mm}^2$$

A first-order analysis of the modified frame with the factored loads and the notional load leads to the same results as those presented in Figure 8.15(b).

(d) Finite Element Method

A P–Δ analysis for the frame of Figure 8.13 was performed with the factored loads and the notional load applied simultaneously on the structure. The results of this analysis, conducted using commercial software, are presented in Figure 8.16.

A comparison of the results obtained using different methods of P–Δ analysis indicates that all methods lead to approximately the same end results.

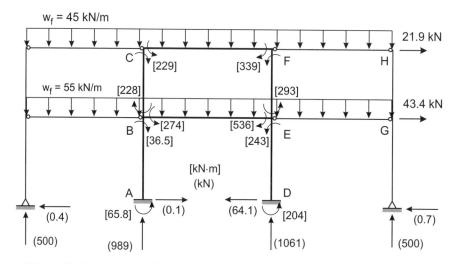

Figure 8.16 – Results of Second-Order Analysis — Finite Element Method

8.4   Design of Beam-Columns

Limit states design of beam-columns comprises four ultimate limit states: 1) local buckling; 2) yielding of the cross-section under the action of axial compression and bending (including second-order effects); 3) overall member instability, which consists of buckling of the beam-column in the plane of bending when the member is subjected to bending about one principal axis only; and, 4) lateral-torsional buckling, implying an out-of-plane behaviour.

8.4.1   Local Buckling Consideration

The design philosophy employed by almost all specifications for the design of steel structures of hot rolled sections is that local buckling must not take place until the member has reached its capacity as controlled by the strength of the cross-section. As developed later in this Chapter, it will be seen that the capacity corresponding to the overall strength of the member is always equal to or less than the capacity based on the strength of the cross-section. Hence, the philosophy adopted by the S16–01 standard for proportioning the cross-section of the beam-column will generally be conservative.

The cross-sectional strength of beams (Chapter 5) was established based on local buckling requirements. In that respect, the cross-sectional proportions were established to provide the desired behaviour, namely, sections of Class 1 can attain the plastic moment capacity and have some additional rotation capability; sections of Class 2 can attain the plastic moment but with no additional rotation capability; sections of Class 3 can attain the yield moment; and sections of Class 4 local buckle elastically. The same general requirements apply to beam-columns, except that each slenderness requirement has to reflect the presence of combined axial force and bending moment.

The limits on plate slenderness for a flange will be the same for a beam-column as for a beam since that element will be under uniform compression in both instances. Thus, the limits given in S16–01 are identical for both types of members. Table 8.1 contains the slenderness provisions for the flanges of I–shaped cross-sections of Classes 1, 2, and 3 used as beam-columns. As noted in the table and as developed in Section 5.4, these limits are b_o/t maximum of $145/\sqrt{F_y}$, $170/\sqrt{F_y}$, or $200/\sqrt{F_y}$ for Class 1, Class 2, or Class 3, respectively.

Table 8.1 – Width-Thickness Ratios: Compression Elements

Element	Section Classification		
	Class 1	Class 2	Class 3
Flanges of I-sections	$\dfrac{b_o}{t} \leq \dfrac{145}{\sqrt{F_y}}$	$\dfrac{b_o}{t} \leq \dfrac{170}{\sqrt{F_y}}$	$\dfrac{b_o}{t} \leq \dfrac{200}{\sqrt{F_y}}$
Webs of I-sections	$\dfrac{h}{w} \leq \dfrac{1100}{\sqrt{F_y}}\left(1 - 0.39\dfrac{C_f}{\phi\,C_y}\right)$	$\dfrac{h}{w} \leq \dfrac{1700}{\sqrt{F_y}}\left(1 - 0.61\dfrac{C_f}{\phi\,C_y}\right)$	$\dfrac{h}{w} \leq \dfrac{1900}{\sqrt{F_y}}\left(1 - 0.65\dfrac{C_f}{\phi\,C_y}\right)$

The slenderness provisions for the web element of the cross-section are not so simple because the amount of the web plate that is under compression will depend upon the amount of the axial compressive force present. If the level of axial force approaches zero, the beam-column is really just a beam and the web slenderness limit should be the same as that for a beam. In this case, only one-half of the web plate is in compression. On the other hand, if the level of axial force is very high, then the beam-column approaches the behaviour of a column, that is, almost the entire web is in compression. Obviously, in this case the slenderness limit for the beam-column web should be the same as that for the web of a column. Table 8.1 lists the web slenderness limits for these limiting cases. As developed in Section 5.4, the h/w ratios for beam webs are limited to $1100/\sqrt{F_y}$, $1700/\sqrt{F_y}$, or $1900/\sqrt{F_y}$, for Class 1, Class 2, or Class 3, respectively. For webs entirely under compression, the limit is $670/\sqrt{F_y}$ (Section 4.1). Note that, for this case, the same value of web slenderness applies to all situations; the terms Class 1, Class 2, and Class 3 have no meaning, since, by definition, bending is not present.

The rules for the slenderness of the webs of beam-columns must lie between the limiting cases of beams (negligible axial force) and columns (negligible bending moment). In order to reflect the level of axial force present, the S16–01 standard provides the slenderness limitations listed in Table 8.1.

The equations for the web slenderness limits are straight line representations of the results that are considered to be the best representations of the actual interaction curves, which were developed on the basis of both numerical and experimental studies [8.9].

As was also the case for beams and for columns, it must be remembered that both the flange slenderness limit (b_o /t) and the web slenderness limit (h/w) must be met in order that a particular beam-column cross-section be designated as Class 1, Class 2, or Class 3. Finally, if it is desired to use a shape in which one or both limits do not meet at least those for Class 3, then the capacity of the cross-section (now Class 4) must be established on the basis of its actual dimensions. Some of the implications of this are discussed in Chapters 5 and 7.

Example 8.3

Given

Check a W250×73 section of G40.21 grade 350W steel ($F_y = 350$ MPa) subject to axial load and moments as shown in Figure 8.1(b) to ensure that the member meets the requirements of a Class 2 section. The factored axial load is 900 kN.

Solution

The cross-section dimensions and properties for the W250×73 section are listed in the CISC handbook:

d = 253 mm   t = 14.2 mm   b = 254 mm   w = 8.6 mm

A = 9280 mm^2 r_x = 110 mm

The flange slenderness is computed as:

$$\frac{b_o}{t} = \frac{b/2}{t} = \frac{254/2}{14.2} = 8.9$$

The allowable flange slenderness ratio for a section of Class 2 is given by Equation 5.9 as:

$$\frac{170}{\sqrt{F_y}} = \frac{170}{\sqrt{350}} = 9.1$$

Since the actual flange slenderness is less than the specified limit, the flange plate meets the requirements for a Class 2 section. The actual web slenderness ratio is calculated as:

$$\frac{h}{w} = \frac{d - 2t}{w} = \frac{253 - (2 \times 14.2)}{8.6} = 26.1$$

The web slenderness limit is calculated using the expression given in Table 8.1. In this expression, $C_f = 900$ kN and $C_y = F_y \times A = 350$ MPa× 9280 mm^2 = 3248 kN. Thus, the slenderness limitation becomes

$$\frac{h}{w} \leq \frac{1700}{\sqrt{F_y}}\left(1 - 0.61\frac{C_f}{\phi\, C_y}\right) = \frac{1700}{\sqrt{350}}\left(1 - 0.61\frac{900}{0.9 \times 3248}\right) = 73.8$$

Since the actual web slenderness ratio is less than the limit, the web plate meets the requirements for Class 2. It has now been established that both the flange and the web meet the Class 2 limits, and it can be concluded that the section meets the local buckling requirements for a Class 2 beam-column.

8.4.2 Cross-Sectional Strength

A short element of the member shown in Figure 8.1 is shown to a larger scale in Figure 8.17(a). The element is subjected to an axial force, C, applied at the centroid of the cross-section and to a bending moment, M, applied about the strong axis of the section. For small values of the bending moment, the strain distribution is shown in Figure 8.17(b), along with the corresponding stress distribution, determined by applying Hooke's law to the strain distribution. In this situation, the neutral axis is shifted (relative to the centroid of the cross-section) such that the net compressive force produced by the internal stresses is sufficient to balance the applied force, C. It is assumed that at this stage the total strains, including the residual strains, are low enough so that yielding does not occur.

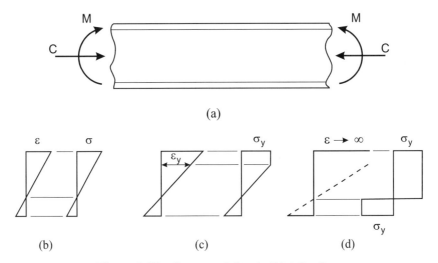

Figure 8.17 – Stress and Strain Distributions

As the bending moment is increased, the location of the neutral axis remains at the same location until the stress in the extreme fibres reaches yield, as shown in Figure 8.17(c). The strain distribution due to the applied moment and axial load is shown in this figure, along with the corresponding stress distribution. The neutral axis has moved up slightly from the position shown in Figure 8.17(b) since the stress distribution is no longer linear. The residual strain distribution (not shown) will modify the progression of yielding slightly but will not affect the results [8.1].

As bending continues, plane sections are assumed to remain plane, which leads to the observation that the strain distribution remains linear. In the final stages, the strains would approach infinite values and yielding of all the fibres of the cross-section, except those immediately adjacent to the neutral axis, would take place, as shown by the stress distribution in Figure 8.17(d). Although the stress distribution shown is not attainable in fact, the resisting moment computed on the basis of this stress distribution gives an excellent estimate of the ultimate capacity of the cross-section [8.1]. The error from the simplifying assumption of the entire cross-section yielding is minimal because the elastic portion of the cross-section is located close to the neutral axis and its effect is compensated by strain-hardening of the material at the extreme fibres, which is ignored in the calculation of the plastic moment.

The ultimate moment capacity, reduced to account for the presence of an axial force, is denoted by M_{pc}. The solid lines in Figure 8.18 show representative dimensionless interaction curves obtained for bending about the strong and weak axes for sections of Class 1 and Class 2. The interaction curves were derived for a flange area to web area ratio, A_f / A_w, varying from 1.0 to 2.0, which covers most commonly used wide flange sections. Points on the interaction curves are obtained assuming a stress distribution as shown in Figure 8.17(d) and equilibrium considerations. For a given axial load, equilibrium of forces is invoked to determine the location of the neutral axis and equilibrium of moments is used to determine the corresponding reduced plastic moment, M_{pc}. The dotted lines show the approximate curves used for design [8.8]. For Class 1 and Class 2 sections bent about the strong axis and when the axial force, C, is less than approximately $0.15\,C_y$ (C_y denotes the yield load $A\,F_y$), Figure 8.18(a) shows that M_{pc} can be taken as equal to the full plastic moment capacity, M_p. For larger values of the axial force, M_{pc} about the strong axis of I–shaped members is given by [8.1]:

$$M_{pcx} = 1.18\,M_{px}\left(1-\frac{C}{C_y}\right) \le M_{px} \tag{8.19}$$

For weak axis bending, Figure 8.18(b) shows that a straight line does not approximate the interaction curves as well as for strong axis bending. Nevertheless, it is seen that a conservative estimate of the exact interaction curves can be obtained by a straight line interaction curve of the form of Equation 8.19 where the constant 1.18 is replaced by 1.67.

$$M_{pcy} = 1.67\,M_{py}\left(1-\frac{C}{C_y}\right) \le M_{py} \tag{8.20}$$

In order to prevent failure of the cross-section, the maximum moment about the strong axis or the weak axis of the member must be less than the value M_{pcx} or M_{pcy} given by Equation 8.19 and Equation 8.20, respectively. In Clause 13.8.2 of S16–01, a general expression is written that covers all the required checks of beam-column strength for Class 1 and Class 2 I–shaped members. The capacity of the cross-section is one of those cases. This general expression, but considering bending about one axis at a time, is:

$$\frac{C_f}{C_r} + \frac{0.85\,U_{1x}\,M_{fx}}{M_{rx}} \le 1.0 \ \text{ for strong axis (x-axis) bending} \tag{8.21a}$$

$$\frac{C_f}{C_r} + \frac{0.6\,U_{1y}\,M_{fy}}{M_{ry}} \le 1.0 \ \ \text{ for weak axis (y-axis) bending} \tag{8.21b}$$

where the load effects, C_f, M_{fx} and M_{fy}, have been factored and the axial load resistance, C_r, and moment resistances, M_{rx} and M_{ry}, are factored resistances. The factors U_{1x} and U_{1y}, applicable to bending about the strong and the weak axis, respectively, account for the P–δ effect and are defined by Equation 8.11. When considering cross-sectional strength, the Standard limits the value of U_{1x} and U_{1y} to values greater than or equal to 1.0.

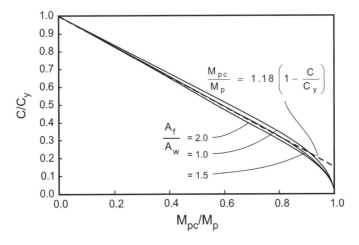

(a) Strong Axis Bending

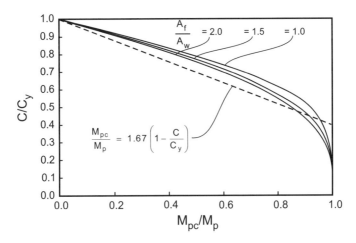

(b) Weak Axis Bending

Figure 8.18 – Interaction Curves for Combined Bending and Axial Compression in Class 1 and Class 2 Sections

With the exception of U_{1x} and U_{1y}, Equations 8.21(a) and 8.21(b) are essentially the same as Equations 8.19 and 8.20 but with M_{pcx} and M_{pcy} replaced by the factored load effects, M_{fx} and M_{fy}, and the plastic moments M_{px} and M_{py} replaced by the factored moment resistance M_{rx} and M_{ry}, respectively. The limits of validity of these equations are that the ratios M_{fx}/M_{rx} and M_{fy}/M_{ry} cannot exceed 1.0. This latter condition governs when bending is predominant.

In Equation 8.19, M_{rx} is the resisting moment of the cross-section about the strong axis (or, M_{px} in Equation 8.19 multiplied by the resistance factor, ϕ), C_f is the axial force due to factored loads (the equivalent of C in Equation 8.19), and C_r must be taken as the factored yield capacity, $\phi A F_y$, of the cross-section. Similarly, M_{ry} is the resisting moment of the cross-section about the weak axis (or, M_{py} in Equation 8.18 multiplied by the resistance factor, ϕ).

In addition to Equation 8.21, I–shaped members of Class 1 and Class 2 sections subjected to biaxial bending must also satisfy the following requirement,

$$\frac{M_{fx}}{M_{rx}} + \frac{M_{fy}}{M_{ry}} \leq 1.0 \tag{8.22}$$

For I–shaped members of Class 3 bent about their strong axis, the strength of the cross-section is described by a similar interaction relationship. The expression used in the Standard (again, showing only the uniaxial bending case) is given in Clause 13.8.2.

$$\frac{C_f}{C_r} + \frac{U_{1x} M_{fx}}{M_{rx}} \leq 1.0 \tag{8.23}$$

For a Class 3 section, it is required that the cross-section proportions (h/w, b/t) be sufficiently stocky such that the combination of axial force and moment up to the level that produces yielding at the most highly strained fibre can be sustained. The local buckling rules for beam-columns take these demands into account.

Example 8.3

Given

A W250×73 member of G40.21 350W steel ($F_y = 350$ MPa) is subjected to the axial force and bending moments shown in Figure 8.19(a). The bending moments and force are those corresponding to the application of the factored loads to the structure and account for P–Δ effects. Is the member adequate with regard to the strength of the cross-section?

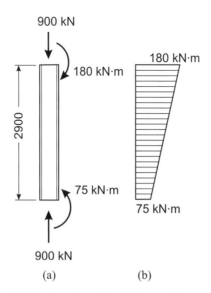

Figure 8.19 – Loading Condition — Example 8.3

Solution

The cross-section properties for the W250×73 section are listed in the CISC handbook:

$$A = 9280 \text{ mm}^2 \qquad I_x = 113 \times 10^6 \text{ mm}^4 \qquad Z_x = 985 \times 10^3 \text{ mm}^3$$

As was established in Example 8.3, the section meets the Class 2 local buckling requirements when this section is used as a beam-column.

The bending moment diagram is shown in Figure 8.19(b). The largest bending moment is at the upper end of the column. At this location the axial load is $C_f = 900 \text{ kN}$ and the bending moment is $M_f = 180 \text{ kN} \cdot \text{m}$.

The factored compressive resistance of the cross-section is:

$$C_r = \phi A F_y = 0.90 \times 9280 \text{ mm}^2 \times 350 \text{ MPa} = 2920 \times 10^3 \text{ N} = 2920 \text{ kN}$$

and the factored moment resistance is (Equation 5.7):

$$M_{rx} = \phi Z_x F_y = 0.90 \times 985 \times 10^3 \text{ mm}^3 \times 350 \text{ MPa} = 310 \times 10^6 \text{ N} \cdot \text{mm}$$

$$= 310 \text{ kN} \cdot \text{m}$$

Since M_{rx} is greater than the maximum factored moment, M_{fx}, Equation 8.22 is satisfied.

From Equation 8.11,

$$U_{1x} = \frac{\omega_1}{1 - \dfrac{C_f}{C_{ex}}}$$

where

$$C_{ex} = \frac{\pi^2 E I_x}{L^2} = \frac{\pi^2 \times 200\,000 \text{ MPa} \times 113 \times 10^6 \text{ mm}^4}{2900^2}$$

$$= 26\,520 \times 10^3 \text{ N} = 26\,520 \text{ kN}$$

ω_1 is given by Equation 8.12 as

$$\omega_1 = 0.6 - 0.4 \kappa = 0.6 - 0.4 \times \left(-\frac{75 \text{ kN} \cdot \text{m}}{180 \text{ kN} \cdot \text{m}} \right) = 0.767$$

Substituting into the equation for U_{1x},

$$U_{1x} = \frac{\omega_1}{1 - \dfrac{C_f}{C_{ex}}} = \frac{0.767}{1 - \dfrac{900 \text{ kN}}{26\,520 \text{ kN}}} = 0.794$$

Since U_{1x} is less than 1.0, it is taken as 1.0 for the cross-section strength check.

The interaction equation to determine the cross-sectional strength of a Class 2 beam-column is (Equation 8.21(a)):

$$\frac{C_f}{C_r} + \frac{0.85 \, U_{1x} \, M_{fx}}{M_{rx}} \le 1.0$$

$$\frac{900}{2920} + \frac{0.85 \times 1.0 \times 180}{310} = 0.31 + 0.49 = 0.80 \le 1.0$$

The cross-sectional capacity of the W250×73 is therefore satisfactory.

8.4.3   Overall Member Strength – In-Plane Stability

The member shown in Figure 8.2(a) is subjected to an axial load, C, and to equal and opposite end moments, M_o, about its strong axis. Because the member is subjected to a symmetrical loading condition, the maximum deflection, and therefore the maximum second-order moment, occurs at mid-height. Each element along the length of the member is then subjected to an axial thrust, C, and to a bending moment, M, that is the total of the primary and secondary bending moments at the location considered. Under the action of these forces, the element will develop curvatures in accordance with the relationship shown in Figure 8.20 for the particular C/C_y ratio of the member. The solid lines in Figure 8.20 ignore the presence of residual stresses whereas the dotted lines are based on residual stresses initiating early yielding of the member.

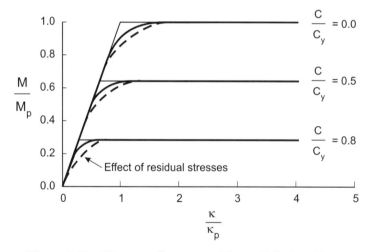

Figure 8.20 – Moment–Curvature–Thrust Relationships *y*

The end rotation corresponding to a given end moment value can be determined by summing the curvatures along half the length of the member. In this manner, moment vs. rotation (M–θ) relationships may be developed, similar to the one shown schematically in Figure 8.21 [8.10]. The M–θ relationship describes the response of a particular member to increasing end moments while the axial force is held constant.

When the end moments are first applied, the member behaves elastically. Under increasing moments, the strains at various locations in the member reach the yield level, and the corresponding curvatures increase at a more rapid rate, in accordance with the relationships for Figure 8.20. The deflections also increase rapidly since the deflection is a function of the magnitude and distribution of the curvatures along the length of the member. The rapid increases in deflections are accompanied by corresponding increases in the P–δ moments. As yielding progresses, the deflections increase at an increasing rate, whereas the moment resistance, given in Figure 8.20, increases at a decreasing rate until the maximum moment, M_{max}, is reached. Beyond this, a further increase in end rotation must be accompanied by a decrease in primary moment, M_o, in order to satisfy equilibrium. The attainment of the maximum member strength in this situation is not uniquely related to the ultimate capacity of the cross-section, but depends on the overall stiffness of the member, its length, the axial load, and the loading and support conditions.

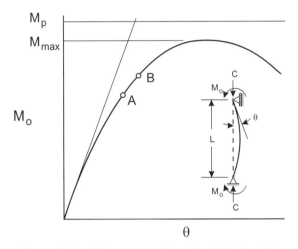

Figure 8.21 – Moment vs. Rotation Relationship

Because of the many factors involved in the failure, the ultimate strength of a beam-column cannot be determined directly. Instead, the complete moment vs. rotation relationship must be predicted so that the peak value (M_{max} in Figure 8.21) can be obtained [8.10]. This is the ultimate strength. The initial portion of the moment vs. rotation relationship can be predicted by solving the appropriate differential equation, since the moment and curvature are related through the flexural rigidity, EI, of the member.

As the end moments are increased, however, yielding occurs in the central portion of the member and the curvature increases more rapidly as the stiffness of the yielding section decreases. At this stage, a numerical procedure must be used to determine the shape of the moment vs. rotation relationship. The deflected shape of the member is first assumed, and the primary and secondary bending moments are then computed at several locations along the member length. Using moment vs. curvature relationships derived from a plane section analysis (the effect of residual stresses can be incorporated in the formulation at this stage), the corresponding curvatures are determined and these are then integrated to determine the end rotation of the member and the deflected shape. The process is repeated until the final deflected shape agrees with that assumed initially.

This procedure must be repeated for increasing values of the end moment, up to the ultimate strength. The procedure is also repeated for different values of axial load. A plot of axial load ratio, C/C_y, versus maximum moment ratio, M/M_p, is thus obtained.

This interaction curve is applicable for only one column slenderness and, therefore, the full procedure must be repeated for different slenderness and end moment conditions.

Using a modification of the above procedure to incorporate both the effect of residual stresses and initial out-of-straightness, interaction curves have been derived for wide flange beam-columns bent about their strong axis [8.11]. The interaction curves for slenderness ratios, L/r_x, varying from 0 to 120, are presented as solid lines in Figure 8.22, where the amplified moment ratio $U_1 M_x / M_{px}$ is plotted on the horizontal axis. The factor U_1 is the elastic moment amplification factor given by Equation 8.11.

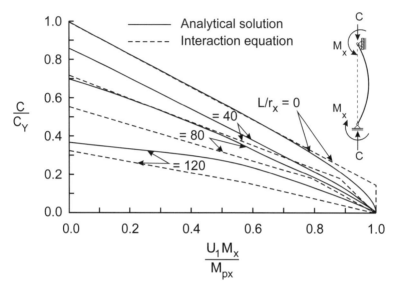

Figure 8.22 – In-Plane Strength Interaction — Strong Axis Bending

The determination of the ultimate strength for a particular member is a tedious process and not suited to design office use. For design purposes, interaction equations have been fitted to the results, as shown by the dashed curves in Figure 8.22 [8.12]. The S16–01 Standard provides the necessary interaction expressions in Clause 13.8.2 (Classes 1 and 2 I–shaped members) and in Clause 13.8.3 (Class 3, I–shaped members). The equations for Class 1 and Class 2 members will be illustrated here: the rules for Class 3 follow a similar development. Also, the expressions given in the Standard include bending about both major axes: only the case of bending about a principal axis will be treated here.

The general expression given in the Standard for Class 1 or Class 2 sections is

$$\frac{C_f}{C_r} + 0.85 \frac{U_{1x} M_{fx}}{M_{rx}} \leq 1.0 \tag{8.24}$$

For the particular case of overall member strength, the terms in this equation are to be established as follows:

M_{fx} = maximum moment on the member produced by the factored loads, including

the P–Δ effects.

246

C_f = axial load on the member produced by the factored loads.

C_r = the factored compressive resistance developed by the member if subjected to an axial load. The factored compressive resistance is based on Equation 4.21 for buckling about the strong axis (the plane of bending) with K = 1.0 and reflects the overall behaviour of the member.

$$U_{1x} = \frac{\omega_1}{1 - \left(\dfrac{C_f}{C_e}\right)}$$ for members in braced frames and $U_{1x} = 1.0$ for members in

sway frames.

C_e = $\pi^2 E I / L^2$, the elastic (Euler) buckling strength of the member. The moment of inertia to be used is that corresponding to the axis about which bending takes place.

ω_1 = equivalent moment factor given by Equation 8.12 and discussed in Section 8.2.

M_{rx} = the factored moment resistance developed by the member if subjected to loads causing bending moments and with sufficient lateral bracing to prevent lateral-torsional buckling. For Class 1 and 2 sections Equation 5.7 is applicable, and for Class 3 sections Equation 5.12 should be used.

The factored axial load resistance, C_r, is calculated for an effective length factor, K, of 1.0 since the effect of column sway in reducing the column capacity is taken into account in the P–Δ analysis.

The parameter U_{1x} accounts for P–δ effects and was derived in Section 8.2 based on the assumption that the member is not swaying. The same parameter is used in S16–01 for braced frames so that the assumptions made to derive U_{1x} are satisfied. It has been shown in Reference [8.11] that in sway frames the maximum moments usually occur at the ends of the members, where the P–δ effects are zero. For this reason, the value of U_{1x} is set at 1.0 in sway frames. If the frame does not have moment-resisting connections and is stabilized by direct-acting bracing, the frame is designed as a braced frame and the direct-acting bracing must be designed to resist the applied horizontal loads and the P–Δ effects. If the frame does not have any direct-acting bracing, the moment connections are designed to resist both the horizontal loads and P–Δ effects. When both direct-acting bracing and moment resisting frames co-exist in the same structure, it is important to determine whether the direct-acting bracing provides sufficient stiffness to brace the frame. Clause 13.8.1 of S16–01 indicates that a frame with direct acting bracing is classified as braced when its sway stiffness is at least five times that of the frame without direct acting bracing.

The form of Equation 8.24 is for uniaxial bending (strong axis) alone. The curves of Figure 8.22 and the above discussion also require that the member under consideration be braced to prevent premature failure by lateral-torsional buckling.

The interaction equation for all sections except Class 1 and Class 2 sections of I–shaped members is similar to Equation 8.24 except for the deletion of the factor 0.85

(Clause 13.8.3 of S16–01) so that the correct end point (Equation 8.23) is obtained for members of zero length, and M_{rx} is to be calculated in accordance with Equation 5.7.

The in-plane behaviour of beam-columns bent about the weak axis can be investigated using the same approach outlined above. Interaction curves for this case are also available [8.11]. The curves are presented as solid lines in Figure 8.23. For design purposes, interaction equations have been fitted to the results, as shown by the dashed curves in Figure 8.23. The proposed interaction equation for Classes 1 and 2 I–shaped members is

$$\frac{C_f}{C_r} + \frac{\beta\, U_{1y}\, M_{fy}}{M_{ry}} \le 1.0 \qquad\qquad (8.25)$$

where C_f, C_r, and M_{fy} are as defined for bending about the strong axis. Here, however, C_r is calculated for buckling about the y-axis.

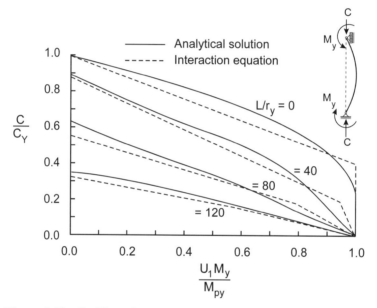

Figure 8.23 – In-Plane Strength Interaction — Weak Axis Bending

$U_{1y} = \dfrac{\omega_1}{1 - \left(\dfrac{C_f}{C_e}\right)}$ for members in braced frames and $U_{1y} = 1.0$ for members in sway

frames. C_e and ω_1 are as defined for bending about the strong axis.

M_{ry} = the factored weak axis factored moment resistance ($= \phi\, Z_y\, F_y$ for Classes 1 and 2 sections).

$\beta = 0.6 + 0.4\, \lambda_y \le 0.85$

$\lambda_y = \dfrac{L}{\pi\, r_y} \sqrt{\dfrac{F_y}{E}}$

Where L is the unsupported length of the member and r_y the radius of gyration about the weak axis.

A comparison of Equations 8.25 and 8.21(b) indicates that the value of the β parameter takes the value of 0.6 for the specific case of cross-section strength interaction.

Example 8.5

Given

A W250×73 member of G40.21 350W steel ($F_y = 350$ MPa) is subjected to an axial force of 900 kN and end moments of 180 kN·m (strong axis bending) as shown in Figure 8.24. The moments and forces are those caused by the factored loading condition. The member is 3600 mm long and is pinned at both ends. The moments are applied so as to bend the member in symmetrical single curvature. Is the member adequate to resist the moments and force shown? The member is known to be braced so that lateral-torsional buckling cannot occur, and the frame in which the member is located is also known to be braced.

The cross-sectional member strength at the support point has been checked in Example 8.3 and was found to be adequate. This example will check the member capacity with respect to overall in-plane member strength.

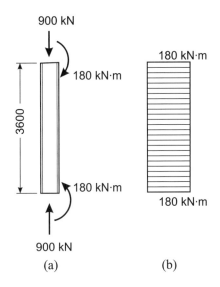

Figure 8.24 – Loading Condition — Example 8.5

Solution

The required cross-section properties for the W250×73 section are listed in the CISC handbook:

$$I_x = 113 \times 10^6 \text{ mm}^4 \qquad Z_x = 985 \times 10^3 \text{ mm}^3 \qquad r_x = 110 \text{ mm}$$

$$A = 9\,280 \text{ mm}^2$$

The axial force and bending moment caused by the factored loads are:

$$C_f = 900\,\text{kN} \quad \text{and} \quad M_f = 180\,\text{kN}\cdot\text{m}$$

The section was determined in Example 8.3 to be a Class 2 beam-column.

Since in-plane strength behaviour is considered, M_{rx} is calculated as:

$$M_{rx} = \phi Z_x F_y = 0.90 \times 985 \times 10^3\,\text{mm}^3 \times 350\,\text{MPa}$$

$$= 310 \times 10^3\,\text{N}\cdot\text{mm} = 310\,\text{kN}\cdot\text{m}$$

Since the factored moment resistance is greater than the maximum factored applied moment, Equation 8.22 is satisfied.

For in-plane strength check, the factored compressive resistance depends on the strong axis slenderness ratio, which is

$$\left(\frac{KL}{r}\right)_x = \frac{1.0 \times 3600}{110} = 33$$

In beam-column design check, K is conservatively taken as unity. The non-dimensional slenderness factor is calculated from Equation 4.20 as:

$$\lambda = \frac{KL}{r}\sqrt{\frac{F_y}{\pi^2 E}} = 33\sqrt{\frac{350\,\text{MPa}}{\pi^2 \times 200\,000\,\text{MPa}}} = 0.44$$

The factored compressive resistance is determined from Equation 4.21. The appropriate value of n for this case (a W-shape) is 1.34. Thus:

$$C_r = \phi A F_y \left(1 + \lambda^{2n}\right)^{-1/n}$$

$$= 0.90 \times 9280\,\text{mm}^2 \times 350\,\text{MPa} \left(1 + 0.44^{2 \times 1.34}\right)^{-1/1.34}$$

$$= 2700 \times 10^3\,\text{N} = 2700\,\text{kN}$$

The elastic (Euler) buckling strength of the member is to be calculated using the slenderness ratio for the axis of bending under consideration. In this case, this is the strong axis and hence

$$C_e = \frac{\pi^2 \times 200\,000\,\text{MPa} \times 113 \times 10^6\,\text{mm}^4}{(1.0 \times 3600)^2\,\text{mm}^2} = 17\,210 \times 10^3\,\text{N} = 17\,210\,\text{kN}$$

The equivalent moment factor $\omega_1 = 1.0$ because the end moments are equal and produce single curvature bending. Therefore, U_{1x} can be calculated as follows:

$$U_{1x} = \frac{\omega_1}{1 - \left(\dfrac{C_f}{C_e}\right)} = \frac{1.0}{1 - \left(\dfrac{900}{17210}\right)} = 1.06$$

It should be noted that if the member was part of a sway frame, U_{1x} would be taken as 1.0 and the factored moment M_{fx} would include P–Δ effects. All the terms required for Equation 8.24 have now been computed and the calculation is:

$$\frac{C_f}{C_r} + \frac{0.85 \, U_{1x} \, M_{fx}}{M_{rx}} \le 1.0$$

$$\frac{900}{2700} + \frac{0.85 \times 1.06 \times 180}{310} = 0.33 + 0.52 = 0.85 \le 1.0$$

Since the left hand side of the interaction equation is less than unity, the member is adequate with regard to its overall in-plane member strength. In Example 8.3 the same member was shown to be adequate with regard to the attainment of the ultimate cross-sectional strength. Thus, the W250×73 is satisfactory for this structural application.

The CISC Handbook [8.12] contains tabulated values of C_e/A, ω_1, and the amplification factor $[1/1-(C_f/C_e)]$. These tables may be used to reduce the computational effort. In addition, tabulated quantities relating to beam and column action, discussed in Chapters 4 and 5, can also be applied to the design of beam-columns.

Example 8.6

Given

The W250×73 member of G40.21 350W steel, ($F_y = 350$ MPa) used for Example 8.5 is subjected to an axial force of 900 kN and to a bending moment of 180 kN·m applied at the top of the member. The member and its corresponding primary bending moment diagram is shown in Figure 8.25. Is the member adequate to resist the moments and force shown?

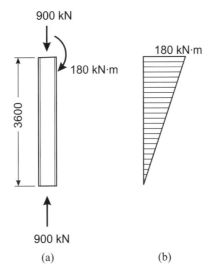

Figure 8.25 – Loading Condition — Example 8.6

251

Solution

The cross-sectional strength of the member was checked in Example 8.3 and will still be satisfactory under this new loading condition because the maximum moment has not increased. This example can therefore address the adequacy of the member as governed by overall in-plane strength. Quantities already computed in Example 8.5 can be used here. The member is assumed to be braced laterally to prevent premature lateral-torsional buckling.

The applied axial force and maximum end moment are the same as those of Example 8.5. In this example, the maximum moment occurs at the upper end of the member.

$$C_f = 900 \text{ kN} \qquad M_{fx} = 180 \text{ kN} \cdot \text{m}$$

The resistances are also the same as those computed in Example 8.5. Thus,

$$M_{rx} = 310 \text{ kN} \cdot \text{m} \qquad C_r = 2700 \text{ kN} \qquad C_e = 17\,210 \text{ kN}$$

In Example 8.5, the equivalent moment factor was unity because the member was subjected to equal end moments. In this example, however, the equivalent moment factor must be calculated using Equation 8.12.

$$\omega_1 = 0.6 - 0.4\,\kappa \geq 0.4$$

$$\kappa = -0/180 = 0$$

Since $\omega_1 = 0.6$ is greater than 0.4, use $\omega_1 = 0.6$.

Therefore

$$U_{1x} = \frac{0.6}{1 - \left(\dfrac{900}{17\,210}\right)} = 0.63$$

The interaction equation, Equation 8.24, is now checked using the calculated quantities:

$$\frac{C_f}{C_r} + \frac{0.85\,U_{1x}\,M_{fx}}{M_{rx}} \leq 1.0$$

$$\frac{900}{2700} + \frac{0.85 \times 0.63 \times 180}{310} = 0.33 + 0.31 = 0.64 \leq 1.0$$

The W250× 73 is adequate to resist the applied moment and force.

8.4.4 *Lateral–Torsional Buckling*

The previous examples have examined beam-columns whose behaviour is in-plane. This is the case for members that have sufficient lateral support such that the deflection of the member is restricted to the plane of the applied bending moments. This is also the case for members subjected to an axial load and a bending moment about its weak axis. There is yet one more mode of failure to which a beam-column may be susceptible, however, and this arises when the member is bent about the strong axis and is free to deflect out of the plane of the applied moments. In this case, failure by lateral-torsional buckling may take place. When the beam-column fails in this mode, it first bends about the strong axis, then suddenly deflects about the weak axis and twists—this is lateral-torsional buckling and it marks the ultimate capacity of the member for this condition.

The interaction expressions, Equation 8.21 for Class 1 and Class 2 sections and Equation 8.23 for Class 3 sections, must reflect the failure mode now under consideration, i.e., out-of-plane behaviour. This means, first, that in determining the axial compressive resistance, C_r, the maximum slenderness ratio must be used, $(KL/r)_x$ or $(KL/r)_y$. In the majority of practical cases, the y-axis conditions will govern. Second, when calculating the resistance to bending about the x-axis, M_{rx}, lateral-torsional buckling must be included.

In Equation 8.21 or 8.23, compensation for non-uniform bending moment will now be present in both the numerator and in the denominator. The term ω_1, which is part of the modifier U_{1x}, appears in the numerator. As explained in Section 8.2, its purpose is to transform a non-uniform moment into an equivalent uniform moment. The expression for moment resistance, M_{rx}, contains the modifier ω_2 (see Section 5.2), which transforms the resistance of a beam under uniform moment into a resistance to a non-uniform moment. Although there seems to be inconsistency between the term in the numerator and the moment resistance in the denominator, this inconsistency disappears when U_1 is limited to a value greater than unity. This is demonstrated in some detail in Reference [8.13]. Thus, it is required that:

$$U_{1x} = \frac{\omega_1}{1 - \left(\dfrac{C_f}{C_e}\right)} \geq 1.0 \tag{8.26}$$

Because bending about the weak axis of an I–shaped member does not initiate lateral-torsional buckling, the lateral-torsional buckling interaction check is not required when bending is about the weak axis only.

Example 8.7

Given

The W250×73 member of G40.21 350W steel $(F_y = 350 \text{ MPa})$ considered in Example 8.5 is again to be checked under the loads and moments shown in Figure 8.24. In this example, however, it is assumed that lateral bracing is provided only at the ends of the member.

Solution

A check to ensure that the member was adequate with regard to the attainment of the cross-sectional capacity was performed in Example 8.3 and the fact that the member is now braced only at the member ends does not change that examination. The member was found to be adequate with regard to its cross-sectional strength.

The cross-section properties for the W250×73 section are listed in the CISC Handbook:

$$A = 9\,280 \text{ mm}^2 \qquad\qquad r_x = 110 \text{ mm} \qquad\qquad J = 575 \times 10^3 \text{ mm}^4$$

$$Z_x = 985 \times 10^3 \text{ mm}^3 \qquad\qquad r_y = 64.7 \text{ mm} \qquad\qquad I_y = 38.8 \times 10^6 \text{ mm}^4$$

$$C_w = 553 \times 10^9 \text{ mm}^6$$

Equation 8.21(a) is the governing interaction equation for this Class 2 beam-column. The component parts will be identified individually, followed by application of the equation.

The axial force and maximum moment caused by the factored loads are the same as those calculated in Example 8.3, that is:

$$C_f = 900 \text{ kN}, \qquad\qquad M_{fx} = 180 \text{ kN} \cdot \text{m}$$

Since the member may fail by bending about either principal axis, the factored compressive resistance C_r will depend on the larger slenderness ratio:

$$\left(\frac{KL}{r} \right)_x = \frac{1.0 \times 3600}{110} = 33$$

$$\left(\frac{KL}{r} \right)_y = \frac{1.0 \times 3600}{64.6} = 56$$

For G40.21 350W steel $\left(F_y = 350 \text{ MPa} \right)$, the governing slenderness factor is calculated from Equation 4.20 as:

$$\lambda = \frac{KL}{r} \sqrt{\frac{F_y}{\pi^2 E}} = 56 \sqrt{\frac{350 \text{ MPa}}{\pi^2 \times 200\,000 \text{ MPa}}} = 0.75$$

The factored compressive resistance is determined from Equation 4.21, with the appropriate value of $n = 1.34$, as:

$$C_r = \phi A F_y \left(1 + \lambda^{2n} \right)^{-1/n}$$

$$= 0.90 \times 9280 \text{ mm}^2 \times 350 \text{ MPa} \left(1 + 0.75^{2 \times 1.34} \right)^{-1/1.34}$$

$$= 2200 \times 10^3 \text{ N} = 2200 \text{ kN}$$

Next, calculate the term $U_{1x} = \omega_1 / (1 - C_f / C_e)$. The equivalent moment factor, ω_1, is equal to 1.0 because the moment diagram is uniform. The denominator in the expression for U_{1x} is the magnifier to account for the $P - \delta$ moments. As discussed in Section 8.2, the elastic buckling load must be calculated for the axis about which bending is taking place, the x-axis in this example. This calculation is:

$$C_e = \frac{\pi^2 \times 200\,000 \times 113 \times 10^6 \text{ mm}^4}{\left(1.0 \times 3600 \right)^2 \text{ mm}^2} = 17\,210 \times 10^3 \text{ N} = 17\,210 \text{ kN}$$

and the modifier U_{1x} can now be calculated as:

$$U_{1x} = \frac{\omega_1}{1 - \left(\dfrac{C_f}{C_e}\right)} = \frac{1.0}{1 - \left(\dfrac{900}{17\,210}\right)} = 1.06$$

Since the term U_{1x} has turned out to be greater than 1.0 (Equation 8.26), the calculated value of U_{1x} is valid. It can also be noted that the same value for U_{1x} was calculated in Example 8.5, although there the stipulation that the result be greater than unity did not apply.

The computation of the factored moment resistance for a laterally unbraced beam was illustrated in detail in Chapter 5. Only the results are shown below. Using Equation 5.25 and for a length $L = 3600$ mm :

$$M_u = \frac{\omega_2\,\pi}{L}\sqrt{E\,I_y\,G\,J + \left(\frac{\pi E}{L}\right)^2 I_y\,C_w}$$

$$= \frac{\omega_2\,\pi}{L}\sqrt{A + B}$$

$$= \frac{1.0 \times \pi}{3600 \text{ mm}}\sqrt{3436 \times 10^{20}\ \text{MPa}^2\text{mm}^8 + 6536 \times 10^{20}\ \text{MPa}^2\text{mm}^8}$$

$$= 871 \times 10^6\ \text{N} \cdot \text{mm} = 871\ \text{kN} \cdot \text{m}$$

in which:

$$A = 200\,000\ \text{MPa} \times 38.8 \times 10^6\ \text{mm}^4 \times 77\,000\ \text{MPa} \times 575 \times 10^3\ \text{mm}^4$$

$$= 3436 \times 10^{20}\ \text{MPa}^2\ \text{mm}^8$$

$$B = \left(\frac{\pi \times 200\,000\ \text{MPa}}{3600\ \text{mm}}\right)^2 \times 38.8 \times 10^6\ \text{mm}^4 \times 553 \times 10^9\ \text{mm}^6$$

$$= 6536 \times 10^{20}\ \text{MPa}^2\ \text{mm}^8$$

For the W250× 73 section:

$$M_p = Z_x\,F_y = 985 \times 10^3\ \text{mm}^3 \times 350\ \text{MPa} = 345 \times 10^6\ \text{N} \cdot \text{mm} = 345\ \text{kN} \cdot \text{m}$$

Since $M_u > 0.67\,M_p$, the factored moment resistance must be calculated using Equation 5.23:

$$M_r = 1.15\,\phi\,M_p\left(1 - \frac{0.28\,M_p}{M_u}\right)$$

$$= 1.15 \times 0.9 \times 345\left(1 - \frac{0.28 \times 345}{871}\right) = 317\ \text{kN} \cdot \text{m}$$

The factored moment resistance M_r as computed by Equation 5.23 (i.e., 317 kN $\cdot$ m) is greater than the capacity computed on the basis of the strength of the cross-section

(310 kN · m , see Example 8.5). Therefore, the latter governs. The interaction expression, Equation 8.21, can now be checked.

$$\frac{C_f}{C_r} + \frac{0.85\ U_{1x}\ M_{fx}}{M_{rx}} \le 1.0$$

$$\frac{900}{2200} + \frac{0.85 \times 1.06 \times 180}{310} = 0.41 + 0.52 = 0.93 \le 1.0$$

Since the interaction equation is satisfied, the member is adequate with regard to lateral-torsional buckling capacity.

Example 8.8

Given

The W250× 73 member of G40.21 350W steel, ($F_y = 350$ MPa) used for Example 8.6 is again to be checked under the loading conditions of Example 8.6. However, in this example the member is not restrained against lateral-torsional buckling, as was the case in Example 8.6. Is the member adequate to resist the moments and force shown in Figure 8.25?

Solution

The axial load and the maximum end moment are the same as those in Example 8.5. The strength of the cross-section was checked in that example and found to be adequate.

$$C_f = 900\ kN \qquad\qquad M_f = 180\ kN \cdot m$$

Since the member is not braced between its ends, the factored axial compressive resistance must be based on weak axis buckling. Therefore, $(KL/r)_y$ is the appropriate slenderness ratio to be used. In Example 8.7, the slenderness ratio $(KL/r)_y$ was calculated for the same member as 56, from which the factored axial compressive resistance was determined to be $C_r = 2200\ kN$.

In determining the factored moment resistance for the laterally unbraced member subject to non-uniform moments along the unbraced length, the value for ω_2 must be computed. According to Equation 5.26, this is:

$$\kappa = -0/180 = 0$$

$$\omega_2 = 1.75 + 1.05\ \kappa + 0.3\ \kappa^2 \le 2.5$$

$$\omega_2 = 1.75 \le 2.5 = 1.75$$

Using Equation 5.25 and L = 3600 mm

$$M_u = \frac{\omega_2\ \pi}{L} \sqrt{E I_y\ G J + \left(\frac{\pi E}{L}\right)^2 I_y\ C_w}$$

$$= \frac{\omega_2\ \pi}{L} \sqrt{A + B}$$

$$= \frac{1.75 \times \pi}{3600 \text{ mm}} \sqrt{3436 \times 10^{20} \text{ MPa}^2\text{mm}^8 + 6536 \times 10^{20} \text{ MPa}^2\text{mm}^8}$$

$$= 1\,525 \times 10^6 \text{ N} \cdot \text{mm} = 1\,525 \text{ kN} \cdot \text{m}$$

where the terms A and B have been calculated in Example 8.7.

For the W250× 73 section:

$$M_p = Z_x \, F_y = 985 \times 10^3 \text{ mm}^3 \times 350 \text{ MPa} = 345 \times 10^6 \text{ N} \cdot \text{mm} = 345 \text{ kN} \cdot \text{m}$$

Since $M_u > 0.67 \, M_p$, the factored moment resistance must be calculated using Equation 5.23:

$$M_r = 1.15 \, \phi \, M_p \left(1 - \frac{0.28 \, M_p}{M_u} \right)$$

$$= 1.15 \times 0.9 \times 345 \left(1 - \frac{0.28 \times 345}{1525} \right) = 334 \text{ kN} \cdot \text{m}$$

The factored moment resistance M_r as computed by Equation 5.23 (i.e., $334 \text{ kN} \cdot \text{m}$) is greater than the capacity computed on the basis of the strength of the cross-section ($310 \text{ kN} \cdot \text{m}$; see Example 8.5). Therefore, the latter governs and the value of M_r to be used in interaction Equation 8.21 is $310 \text{ kN} \cdot \text{m}$.

Because the member is subjected to a varying moment distribution, ω_1 must be determined using Clause 13.8.5. In Example 8.6, the value of ω_1 for the same moment distribution was found to be 0.6 and the corresponding U_{1x} was calculated to be 0.63. Since U_{1x} is limited to a value ≥ 1.0 for the lateral-torsional buckling interaction check, the value $U_{1x} = 1.0$ is used in the interaction equation,

The interaction Equation 8.21 is now checked using the above quantities.

$$\frac{C_f}{C_r} + \frac{0.85 \, U_{1x} \, M_{fx}}{M_{rx}} \leq 1.0$$

$$\frac{900}{2200} + \frac{0.85 \times 1.0 \times 180}{310} = 0.41 + 0.49 = 0.90 \leq 1.0$$

The section is therefore satisfactory.

Example 8.9

A beam-column frequently encountered is one supporting both the roof of a building and the girders of a traveling crane in a manufacturing or maintenance facility. Crane columns may utilize a single structural steel shape, commonly a W-shape, or it may be composed of several interconnected shapes, depending upon the class of crane supported. Some commonly used configurations are illustrated in Figure 8.26.

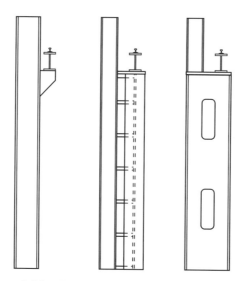

Figure 8.26 – Crane Beam-Column Configurations

Crane columns differ from the beam-columns discussed to this point in that they have loads applied at locations other than the ends of the member. These additional loads can be both vertical and horizontal, and they are applied in a manner that usually creates bending moments within the member about the strong axis.

Given

The beam-column illustrated in Figure 8.27 has an overall length of 12 000 mm and supports a load from the roof framing system of 180 kN and vertical and horizontal loads of 220 kN and 22 kN, respectively, due to the passage of a crane. The crane loads are applied at a bracket located at a height of 8 000 mm and at a 500 mm offset from the centreline of the column. The column is fixed at its base and is assumed to be simply supported at the top. The W250×73 member of G40.21 350W steel of Example 8.7 is to be checked for the moments and forces shown in Figure 8.27.

Solution

For beam-columns that are used as crane columns, Clause 13.8.5 of S16–01 states that the beam-column can be treated as having two segments, broken at the level of the lateral force. Of the two segments, the lower segment has the longer length and is subjected to larger moments and forces. It is therefore the critical segment in this example.

(i) Cross-sectional strength check

The cross-sectional strength for the member is checked according to Clause 13.8.2(a) as follows.

As determined in Examples 8.3 and 8.4, the W250×73 is a Class 2 beam-column section, the factored compressive resistance is $C_r = 2920$ kN, and the factored moment resistance is $M_{rx} = 310$ kN·m. It should be noted that a change in factored axial load from 900 kN (Example 8.3) to 400 kN does not change the web slenderness limit significantly.

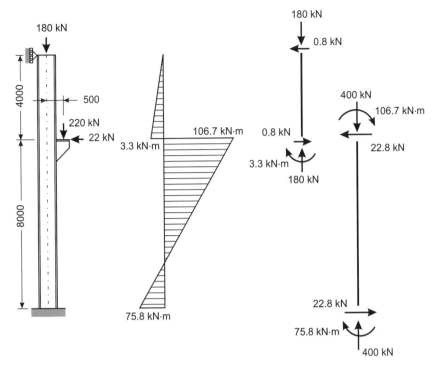

Figure 8.27 – Moments and Forces — Example 8.9

The interaction equation to determine the cross-sectional strength of the lower segment, Equation 8.21, then becomes:

$$\frac{C_f}{C_r} + \frac{0.85\, U_{1x}\, M_{fx}}{M_{rx}} \leq 1.0$$

where.

$$U_{1x} = \frac{\omega_1}{1 - \left(\dfrac{C_f}{C_e}\right)}$$

Since the column is subjected to a concentrated moment between the supports, Clause 13.8.5(c) specifies that $\omega_1 = 0.85$.

The elastic buckling strength is computed using the slenderness ratio for the axis about which the bending occurs, the strong axis in this case, to reflect the plane in which secondary moments are developed. Since the column is restrained at the top and bottom only, the effective length is taken as the full length of the column. Note that the bracket on which the crane girder rests does not provide support against buckling in the plane of the applied moments. Thus:

$$C_e = \frac{\pi^2 \times 200\,000 \text{ MPa} \times 113 \times 10^6 \text{ mm}^4}{\left(1.0 \times 12\,000\right)^2 \text{ mm}^2} = 1550 \times 10^3 \text{ N} = 1550\,\text{kN}$$

therefore,

$$U_{1x} = \cfrac{0.85}{1-\left(\cfrac{400}{1550}\right)} = 1.15$$

The interaction equation can now be evaluated as follows

$$\frac{400}{2\,920} + \frac{0.85 \times 1.15 \times 107}{310} \leq 1.0$$

$$0.14 + 0.34 \leq 1.0$$

$$0.48 \leq 1.0 \qquad \text{Cross-section strength is satisfactory.}$$

(ii) Overall in-plane strength check.

For the overall in-plane member strength check, the entire member length is used to determine the slenderness ratio when checking each segment. For the strong axis, x–x, the slenderness ratio is:

$$\left(\frac{KL}{r}\right)_x = \frac{1.0 \times 12\,000}{110} = 109$$

In this calculation K is taken conservatively as unity. The non-dimensional slenderness factor is calculated from Equation 4.20 as:

$$\lambda = \frac{KL}{r}\sqrt{\frac{F_y}{\pi^2\,E}} = 109\sqrt{\frac{350\ \text{MPa}}{\pi^2 \times 200\,000\ \text{MPa}}} = 1.45$$

From Equation 4.21 and with n = 1.34, C_r is

$$C_r = \phi\,A\,F_y\left(1 + \lambda^{2n}\right)^{-1/n}$$

$$= 0.9 \times 9\,280\ \text{mm}^2 \times 350\ \text{MPa}\left(1 + 1.45^{2 \times 1.34}\right)^{-1/1.34}$$

$$C_r = 1100\ \text{kN}$$

$$U_{1x} = 1.15 \text{ from the cross-section strength check}$$

All the terms required for use in the interaction equation have now been computed and the equation is:

$$\frac{C_f}{C_r} + \frac{0.85\,U_{1x}\,M_{fx}}{M_{rx}} \leq 1.0$$

$$\frac{400}{1100} + \frac{0.85 \times 1.15 \times 107}{310} \leq 1.0$$

$$0.36 + 0.34 \leq 1.0$$

$$0.70 \leq 1.0$$

Since the left hand side of the interaction expression is less than unity, the section is adequate for overall in-plane member strength.

(iii) Lateral-torsional buckling strength check

For this check, the crane column is considered braced from out-of-plane buckling at both ends of the member and at the location of the applied crane loads. Although the crane girder does not provide much restraint to the column in the plane of bending, it generally provides adequate restraint in the out-of-plane direction. Therefore, the unbraced length for computing the factored axial compressive resistance (for buckling about the weak axis) and the bending resistance is taken as 8 000 mm.

The slenderness ratio about the weak axis:

$$\left(\frac{KL}{r}\right)_y = \frac{1.0 \times 8000}{64.6} = 124$$

The non-dimensional slenderness parameter is based on the larger slenderness ratio, in this case 124.

$$\lambda = \frac{KL}{r}\sqrt{\frac{F_y}{\pi^2 E}} = 124\sqrt{\frac{350 \text{ MPa}}{\pi^2 \times 200\,000 \text{ MPa}}} = 1.65$$

From Equation 4.21 and with n = 1.34, C_r is

$$C_r = \phi\, A\, F_y \left(1 + \lambda^{2n}\right)^{-\frac{1}{n}}$$

$$= 0.9 \times 9280 \text{ mm}^2 \times 350 \text{ MPa} \left(1 + 1.65^{2 \times 1.34}\right)^{-\frac{1}{1.34}}$$

$$C_r = 903 \times 10^3 \text{ N} = 903 \text{ kN}$$

The lower segment of the crane column is subject to unequal end moments, and the value for ω_2 must be determined from Equation 5.26 as:

$$\kappa = \frac{75.8}{107} = 0.708$$

$$\omega_2 = 1.75 + 1.05\,\kappa + 0.3\,\kappa^2 \leq 2.5$$

$$\omega_2 = 1.75 + (1.05 \times 0.708) + (0.3 \times 0.708^2) \leq 2.5$$

$$\omega_2 = 2.64$$

Since the value calculated for ω_2 is greater than the limit 2.5, it is set equal to 2.5.

Using Equation 5.25

$$M_u = \frac{\omega_2\,\pi}{L}\sqrt{E\,I_y\,G\,J + \left(\frac{\pi E}{L}\right)^2 I_y\,C_w}$$

$$= \frac{\omega_2 \, \pi}{L} \sqrt{A + B}$$

$$= \frac{2.5 \times \pi}{8000} \sqrt{3436 \times 10^{20} \text{ MPa}^2 \text{ mm}^8 + 1324 \times 10^{20} \text{ MPa}^2 \text{ mm}^8}$$

$$= 677 \times 10^6 \text{ N} \cdot \text{mm} = 677 \text{ kN} \cdot \text{m}$$

where:

$$A = 200\,000 \text{ MPa} \times 38.8 \times 10^6 \text{ mm}^4 \times 77\,000 \text{ MPa} \times 575 \times 10^3 \text{ mm}^4$$

$$= 3436 \times 10^{20} \text{ MPa}^2 \text{ mm}^8$$

$$B = \left(\frac{\pi \times 200\,000 \text{ MPa}}{8000 \text{ mm}} \right)^2 \times 38.8 \times 10^6 \text{ mm}^4 \times 553 \times 10^9 \text{ mm}^6$$

$$= 1324 \times 10^{20} \text{ MPa}^2 \text{ mm}^8$$

For the W250 x 73 section:

$$M_p = Z_x \, F_y = 985 \times 10^3 \text{ mm}^3 \times 350 \text{ MPa}$$

$$= 345 \times 10^6 \text{ N} \cdot \text{mm} = 345 \text{ kN} \cdot \text{m}$$

Since $M_u > 0.67 \, M_p$, the factored moment resistance must be calculated using Equation 5.23:

$$M_r = 1.15 \, \phi \, M_p \left(1 - \frac{0.28 \, M_p}{M_u} \right)$$

$$= 1.15 \times 0.9 \times 345 \left(1 - \frac{0.28 \times 345}{677} \right)$$

$$= 306 \text{ kN} \cdot \text{m}$$

Unlike the case in Example 8.8, M_r is less than the capacity computed on the basis of local buckling ($M_r = 310 \text{ kN} \cdot \text{m}$). Thus, the factored moment resistance for the member is governed by Equation 5.23 and $M_r = 306 \text{ kN} \cdot \text{m}$.

The value for U_{1x} has been determined previously for the cross-section strength interaction expression as 1.15. Since this value is greater than 1.0, the value $U_{1x} = 1.15$ is used in the interaction check. Thus, the interaction expression can be evaluated as follows:

$$\frac{C_f}{C_r} + \frac{0.85 \, U_{1x} \, M_{fx}}{M_{rx}} \leq 1.0$$

$$\frac{400}{903} + \frac{0.85 \times 1.15 \times 107}{306} \leq 1.0$$

$0.44 + 0.34 \le 1.0$

$0.78 \le 1.0$

Since the interaction values for cross-sectional, overall member, and lateral-torsional member strength are all less than 1.0, the W250×73 is adequate for this crane column. The investigation of a lighter section may be warranted, however.

Beam columns are common in industrial buildings

(Photo courtesy of Empire Iron Works Ltd.)

Example 8.10

Given

This example considers the analysis and design check of the beam-columns in the frame shown below. The frame is part of a building subjected to combination of wind load, W, dead load, w_D, and live load, w_L. The adequacy of the selected shapes (shown in Figure 8.28) must be checked. The frame is pin supported at A and D. The members are oriented so that their webs are parallel to the plane of the frame. The steel is of grade G40.21 350W.

Solution

Using the limit state design Equation 1.1, a total of three load combinations must be checked as follows:

Load Case 1: $1.4\,w_D$

Load Case 2: $1.25\,w_D + 1.5\,w_L + 0.4\,W$

Load Case 3: $1.25 \, w_D + 1.4 \, W + 0.5 \, w_L$

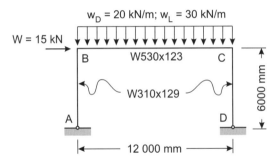

$w_D = 20 \text{ kN/m}; \, w_L = 30 \text{ kN/m}$

$W = 15 \text{ kN}$

B   W530x123   C

W310x129

A   D

6000 mm

12 000 mm

Figure 8.28 – Loaded Frame — Example 8.10

The importance factor for wind load is taken as 1.0. The factored loads for each one of the load cases described above are as follows:

Load Case 1 ($1.4 \, w_D$)

Gravity load, $w_f = 1.4 \times 20 \text{ kN/m} = 28 \text{ kN/m}$

Notional load $= 0.005 \times w_f \times L = 0.005 \times 28 \text{ kN/m} \times 12 \text{ m} = 1.7 \text{ kN}$

Load Case 2 ($1.25 \, w_D + 1.5 \, w_L + 0.4 \, W$)

Factored gravity load, $w_f = 1.25 \times 20 \text{ kN/m} + 1.5 \times 30 \text{ kN/m} = 70 \text{ kN/m}$

Factored wind load $= 0.4 \times 15 \text{ kN} = 6.0 \text{ kN}$

Notional load $= 0.005 \times w_f \times L = 0.005 \times 70 \text{ kN/m} \times 12 \text{ m} = 4.2 \text{ kN}$

Total lateral load $= 6.0 \text{ kN} + 4.2 \text{ kN} = 10.2 \text{ kN}$

Load Case 3 ($1.25 \, w_D + 1.4 \, W + 0.5 \, w_L$)

Factored gravity load,

$$w_f = 1.25 \times 20 \text{ kN/m} + 0.5 \times 30 \text{ kN/m} = 40.0 \text{ kN/m}$$

Factored wind load $= 1.4 \times 15 \text{ kN} = 21 \text{ kN}$

Notional load $= 0.005 \times w_f \times L = 0.005 \times 40 \text{ kN/m} \times 12 \text{ m} = 2.4 \text{ kN}$

Total lateral load $= 21.0 \text{ kN} + 2.4 \text{ kN} = 23.4 \text{ kN}$

All three load cases are illustrated in Figure 8.29, along with the results of a first-order analysis of the frames. From a close examination of the three load cases, it is obvious that load case 2 will be the governing load case because both the axial force and the bending moment in columns AB and CD are significantly larger than for the other two load cases.

Load Case 2 – Fictitious horizontal load method

For illustration purpose, the method of fictitious horizontal loads will be used to conduct the P–Δ analysis for this load case. A notional load of 0.005 times the factored

264

gravity load will be applied to the top of the frame. This was calculated above as 4.2 kN. Since the frame is loaded with a wind force as shown in Figure 8.28, the notional load is applied in the same direction as the wind force. A first-order analysis indicated that the combined lateral load causes a lateral deflection at the top of the frame of 8.4 mm.

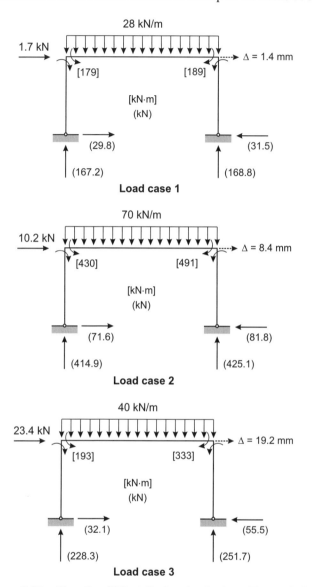

Figure 8.29 – Results of First-Order Analysis — Example 8.10

The fictitious storey shear is obtained from Equation 8.15 as

$$V'_i = \frac{\sum C_i}{h_i} \left(\Delta_{i+1} - \Delta_i \right)$$

where $\sum C_i = 414.9 + 425.1 = 840$ kN

$$V' = \frac{840 \text{ kN}}{6000 \text{ mm}} \times (8.4 \text{ mm} - 0 \text{ mm}) = 1.18 \text{ kN}$$

The fictitious lateral load, including the notional load, thus becomes

$$H' = 10.20 + 1.18 = 11.38 \text{ kN}$$

From a first-order analysis,

$$\Delta' = 9.35 \text{ mm}$$

2nd iteration

$$V' = \frac{840 \text{ kN}}{6000 \text{ mm}} \times 9.35 \text{ mm} = 1.31 \text{ kN}$$

$$H' = 11.51 \text{ kN}$$

From a first-order analysis of the frame with $H' = 11.51 \text{ kN}$,

$$\Delta' = 9.45 \text{ mm}$$

Since the resulting deflection in this iteration is about 1% from the previous iteration, the analysis could be stopped at this stage without significant loss of accuracy.

3rd iteration

$$V' = \frac{840 \text{ kN}}{6000 \text{ mm}} \times 9.45 \text{ mm} = 1.32 \text{ kN}$$

$$H' = 11.52 \text{ kN}$$

$$\Delta' = 9.47 \text{ mm}$$

The calculated deflection at this stage is less than 1% away from the value in the previous iteration. The problem has therefore converged and the P–Δ effects are found by applying a fictitious lateral load at the top of the frame and performing a first-order analysis of the frame. The results are summarized in Figure 8.30.

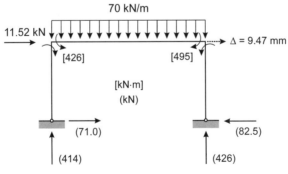

Load case 2

Figure 8.30 – Results of Second-Order Analysis – Load Case 2

Load Case 2 – Amplification factor method

The P–Δ analysis will be repeated for load case 2 using the amplification factor method. In order to implement this method, two separate first-order analyses will be needed, namely, one with only the gravity loads and the frame supported laterally to prevent sway, and a second case with the lateral loads (wind plus notional) and the frame free to sway. The results of these two analyses are summarized in Figure 8.31.

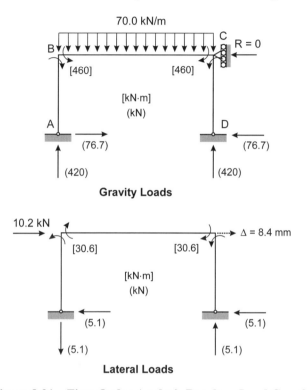

Figure 8.31 – First-Order Analysis Results – Load Case 2

Using the amplification factor method and the analysis results for the lateral load case shown in Figure 8.31,

$$U_2 = \frac{1}{1 - \dfrac{\sum C_f \, \Delta_f}{\sum V_f \, h}}$$

where

$$\frac{\Delta_f}{\sum V_f} = \frac{8.4 \text{ mm}}{10.2 \text{ kN}} = 0.824 \text{ mm} / \text{kN} \text{ is the flexibility of the storey. Since the analysis}$$

used to determine the storey flexibility is linear, any magnitude of lateral load can be applied to the frame to determine Δ_f.

$$\sum C_f = 840 \text{ kN}$$

$$U_2 = \frac{1}{1 - 0.824 \text{ mm} / \text{kN} \times \dfrac{840 \text{ kN}}{6000 \text{ mm}}} = 1.13$$

From the results of the first-order analysis presented in Figure 8.31, the moment at the top of column AB is

$$M_f^B = M_{fg}^B + U_2 \ M_{ft}^B = 460 \text{ kN} \cdot \text{m} - (1.13 \times 30.6 \text{ kN} \cdot \text{m}) = 425 \text{ kN} \cdot \text{m}$$

The moment at the top of column CD is

$$M_f^C = M_{fg}^C + U_2 \ M_{ft}^C = 460 \text{ kN} \cdot \text{m} + (1.13 \times 30.6) = 495 \text{ kN} \cdot \text{m}$$

The results of the P–Δ analysis using the amplification factor method are almost identical to those obtained using the method of fictitious horizontal loads. Column CD is the most critical (larger moment and axial load). Although this column is critical for this load case, if the lateral load, including the notional load, were reversed, column AB would become the critical column. It is therefore logical that both columns be designed for the same set of axial load and bending moment ($C_f = 426 \text{ kN}$, $M_f = 495 \text{ kN} \cdot \text{m}$).

The cross-section dimensions and properties for the W310× 129 section are listed in the CISC handbook:

$d = 318 \text{ mm}$ $t = 20.6 \text{ mm}$ $b = 308 \text{ mm}$ $w = 13.1 \text{ mm}$

$A = 16\ 500 \text{ mm}^2$ $I_x = 308 \times 10^6 \text{ mm}^4$ $Z_x = 2160 \times 10^3 \text{ mm}^3$

$r_x = 137 \text{ mm}$ $I_y = 100 \times 10^6 \text{ mm}^4$ $r_y = 78.0 \text{ mm}$

$J = 2\ 130 \times 10^3 \text{ mm}^4$ $C_w = 2\ 220 \times 10^9 \text{ mm}^6$

(i) Local buckling check

The flange slenderness is computed as:

$$\frac{b_o}{t} = \frac{b/2}{t} = \frac{308/2}{20.6} = 7.5$$

The allowable flange slenderness ratio for a section of Class 1 is given by Equation 5.9 as:

$$\frac{145}{\sqrt{F_y}} = \frac{145}{\sqrt{350}} = 7.8$$

Since the actual flange slenderness is less than the specified limit, the flanges meet the requirements for a Class 1 section. The actual web slenderness ratio is calculated as:

$$\frac{h}{w} = \frac{d - 2t}{w} = \frac{318 - (2 \times 20.6)}{13.1} = 21.1$$

The web slenderness limit is calculated from the expression given in Table 8.1. In this expression, $C_f = 426 \text{ kN}$ and $C_y = F_y \times A = 350 \text{ MPa} \times 16\ 500 \text{ mm}^2 = 5\ 775 \text{ kN}$. Thus, the slenderness limitation becomes

$$\frac{h}{w} \leq \frac{1100}{\sqrt{F_y}} \left(1 - 0.39 \frac{C_f}{\phi C_y}\right) = \frac{1100}{\sqrt{350}} \left(1 - 0.39 \frac{426}{0.9 \times 5\,775}\right) = 56.9$$

Since the actual web slenderness ratio is less than the limit, the web plate meets the requirements for Class 1. It has now been established that both the flange and the web meet the Class 1 limits, and it can be concluded that the section meets the local buckling requirements for a Class 1 beam-column.

(ii) Cross-sectional strength check

Since the section satisfies the requirements for Class 1, the factored compressive resistance is

$$C_r = \phi\, A\, F_y = 0.9 \times 16\,500 \text{ mm}^2 \times 350 \text{ MPa} = 5\,200 \times 10^3 \text{ N} = 5\,200 \text{ kN}$$

and the factored moment resistance is

$$M_{rx} = \phi\, Z_x\, F_y = 0.9 \times 2\,160 \times 10^3 \text{ mm}^3 \times 350 \text{ MPa} = 680 \times 10^6 \text{ N} \cdot \text{mm}$$
$$= 680 \text{ kN} \cdot \text{m}$$

The interaction equation for the cross-sectional strength interaction check, Equation 8.21, then becomes:

$$\frac{C_f}{C_r} + \frac{0.85\, U_{1x}\, M_{fx}}{M_{rx}} \leq 1.0$$

where $U_{1x} = 1.0$ because the beam-column is part of a sway frame and the P–δ effects and the P–Δ effects cannot be added together.

The interaction equation becomes

$$\frac{426}{5200} + \frac{0.85 \times 1.0 \times 495}{680} \leq 1.0$$

$$0.08 + 0.62 \leq 1.0$$

$$0.70 \leq 1.0 \qquad \text{Cross-section strength is satisfactory.}$$

(iii) Overall in-plane strength check

For the overall in-plane member strength check, the entire member length is used to determine the slenderness ratio when checking the beam-column. For the strong axis, x–x, the slenderness ratio is:

$$\left(\frac{KL}{r}\right)_x = \frac{1.0 \times 6000}{137} = 43.8$$

The non-dimensional slenderness factor is calculated from Equation 4.20 as:

$$\lambda = \frac{KL}{r} \sqrt{\frac{F_y}{\pi^2\, E}} = 43.8 \sqrt{\frac{350 \text{ MPa}}{\pi^2 \times 200\,000 \text{ MPa}}} = 0.58$$

From Equation 4.21 and with n = 1.34, C_r is

$$C_r = \phi\, A\, F_y \left(1 + \lambda^{2n}\right)^{-1/n}$$

$$= 0.9 \times 16\ 500\ \text{mm}^2 \times 350\ \text{MPa}\ \left(1 + 0.58^{2 \times 1.34}\right)^{-1/1.34}$$

$C_r = 4\ 450$ kN

$U_{1x} = 1.0$ for a beam-column in a sway frame

The interaction equation can now be evaluated.

$$\frac{C_f}{C_r} + \frac{0.85\, U_{1x}\, M_{fx}}{M_{rx}} \le 1.0$$

$$\frac{426}{4450} + \frac{0.85 \times 1.0 \times 495}{680} \le 1.0$$

$$0.10 + 0.62 \le 1.0$$

$$0.72 \le 1.0$$

Since the left hand side of the interaction expression is less than unity, the section is adequate for overall in-plane member strength.

(iv) Lateral-torsional buckling strength check

For this check, the beam-column is considered braced from out-of-plane buckling at both ends of the member. The unbraced length for computing the factored axial compressive resistance (for buckling about the weak axis) and the bending resistance is taken as 6 000 mm.

The slenderness ratio about the weak axis:

$$\left(\frac{KL}{r}\right)_y = \frac{1.0 \times 6\ 000}{78.0} = 76.9$$

The non-dimensional slenderness parameter is based on the larger slenderness ratio, in this case 76.9.

$$\lambda = \frac{KL}{r}\sqrt{\frac{F_y}{\pi^2\, E}} = 76.9 \sqrt{\frac{350\ \text{MPa}}{\pi^2 \times 200\ 000\ \text{MPa}}} = 1.024$$

From Equation 4.21 and with n = 1.34, C_r is

$$C_r = \phi\, A\, F_y \left(1 + \lambda^{2n}\right)^{-1/n}$$

$$= 0.9 \times 16\ 500\ \text{mm}^2 \times 350\ \text{MPa}\ \left(1 + 1.024^{2 \times 1.34}\right)^{-1/1.34}$$

$C_r = 3\,020 \times 10^3$ N = 3 020 kN

The lower end of the beam-column is pinned, yielding a triangular moment distribution in the beam-column, for which $\omega_2 = 1.75$ from Equation 5.26.

Using Equation 5.25,

$$M_u = \frac{\omega_2\,\pi}{L} \sqrt{E\,I_y\,G\,J + \left(\frac{\pi\,E}{L}\right)^2 I_y\,C_w}$$

$$= \frac{\omega_2\,\pi}{L} \sqrt{A + B}$$

$$= \frac{1.75 \times \pi}{6\,000} \sqrt{328.0 \times 10^{22}\ \text{MPa}^2\ \text{mm}^8 + 243.4 \times 10^{22}\ \text{MPa}^2\ \text{mm}^8}$$

$$= 2\,190 \times 10^6\ \text{N} \cdot \text{mm} = 2\,190\ \text{kN} \cdot \text{m}$$

where:

$$A = 200\,000\ \text{MPa} \times 100 \times 10^6\ \text{mm}^4 \times 77\,000\ \text{MPa} \times 2\,130 \times 10^3\ \text{mm}^4$$

$$= 328.0 \times 10^{22}\ \text{MPa}^2\ \text{mm}^8$$

$$B = \left(\frac{\pi \times 200\,000\ \text{MPa}}{6\,000\ \text{mm}}\right)^2 \times 100 \times 10^6\ \text{mm}^4 \times 2\,220 \times 10^9\ \text{mm}^6$$

$$= 243.4 \times 10^{22}\ \text{MPa}^2\ \text{mm}^8$$

For the W310 × 129 section:

$$M_p = Z_x\,F_y = 2160 \times 10^3\ \text{mm}^3 \times 350\ \text{MPa}$$

$$= 756 \times 10^6\ \text{N} \cdot \text{mm} = 756\ \text{kN} \cdot \text{m}$$

Since $M_u > 0.67\,M_p$, the factored moment resistance must be calculated using Equation 5.23:

$$M_r = 1.15\,\phi\,M_p \left(1 - \frac{0.28\,M_p}{M_u}\right)$$

$$= 1.15 \times 0.9 \times 756 \left(1 - \frac{0.28 \times 756}{2\,190}\right)$$

$$= 707\ \text{kN} \cdot \text{m}$$

M_r is greater than the capacity computed on the basis of local buckling ($M_r = 680\ \text{kN} \cdot \text{m}$). Thus, the factored moment resistance for the member is governed by Equation 5.23 and $M_r = 680\ \text{kN} \cdot \text{m}$.

The value for U_{1x} remains at 1.0 for the lateral-torsional buckling check. Thus, the interaction expression can be evaluated as follows:

$$\frac{C_f}{C_r} + \frac{0.85 \, U_{1x} \, M_{fx}}{M_{rx}} \le 1.0$$

$$\frac{426}{3\,020} + \frac{0.85 \times 1.0 \times 495}{680} \le 1.0$$

$$0.14 + 0.62 \le 1.0$$

$$0.76 \le 1.0$$

Since the interaction values for cross-sectional, overall member, and lateral-torsional member strength are all less than 1.0, the W310×129 is adequate for the two columns.

8.5   Summary: Axial Compression and Bending

Members subjected to a compressive axial force and bending moments reach their ultimate capacity by attaining 1) the ultimate strength of the cross-section; 2) the overall in-plane strength, or 3) the lateral-torsional buckling strength. Empirical interaction equations are used in design to provide a consistent margin of safety against failure by any of these modes.

Clauses 13.8.2 and 13.8.3 of S16–01 detail the basic beam-column expressions used to ensure that the smallest of the resistances will exceed the effects of the applied forces.

The design of beam-columns is a time-consuming task. Their design is intrinsically related to the analysis of the frame in which the beam-columns are used. Because of the many different factors that must be considered, design aids in chart or table form are generally not effective. Spreadsheets are effective tools when combined with the Steel Section Table (SST) electronic database available from the Canadian Institute of Steel Construction.

8.6   Axial Tension and Bending

In most practical cases, the beam-column is subjected to axial compression and bending, and that has been the member treated so far in this Chapter. Occasionally, however, the combination is axial tension and bending. The rules provided by the Standard for this case are in S16-01 Clause 13.9. The interaction equation given in part (a) of the clause is a check on the cross-section strength of the member under this type of loading. It is expressed as follows:

$$\frac{T_f}{T_r} + \frac{M_f}{M_r} \le 1.0 \tag{8.27}$$

The moment resistance, M_r, to be used is that of the cross-section. However, when the member is subject mostly to bending and with just a small amount of axial tensile force present, then failure may occur by lateral-torsional buckling. Thus, a second interaction equation check is required (one for Class 1 and 2 sections or a different one for Class 3 sections, as appropriate). Consider the first of these equations (Clause 13.9(b)):

$$\frac{M_f}{M_r} - \frac{T_f}{M_r} \frac{Z}{A} \le 1.0$$

where Z is the plastic section modulus of the cross-section and A is the cross-sectional area.

This equation can be re-written as

$$\frac{M_f - T_f \,(Z/A)}{M_r} \le 1.0 \qquad \text{and then further as}$$

$$\frac{\dfrac{M_f}{Z} - \dfrac{T_f}{A}}{\dfrac{M_r}{Z}} \le 1.0 \qquad \text{or, finally,} \qquad \frac{M_f}{Z} - \frac{T_f}{A} \le \frac{M_r}{Z}$$

In the last form, it can be recognized that the interaction equation states that the net stress on the compression side of the beam-column must be less than or equal to the permissible compressive stress for the member. The moment resistance, M_r, must be based on overall member behaviour, taking lateral-torsional buckling into account.

References

8.1   WRC-ASCE Joint Committee, "Plastic Design in Steel, A Guide and Commentary," 2nd Edition, American Society of Civil Engineers, New York, 1971.

8.2   Galambos, T.V., "Structural Members and Frames," Prentice-Hall, Inc. Englewood Cliffs, N.J., 1968.

8.3   Austin, W.J., "Strength and Design of Metal Beam-Columns," Journal of the Structural Division, American Society of Civil Engineering, Vol. 87, ST7, July 1987.

8.4   French, S.E., "Fundamentals of Structural Analysis," West Publishing Company, New York, N.Y., 1995.

8.5   Nixon, D., Beaulieu, D. and Adams, P.F., "Simplified Second Order Frame Analysis," Canadian Journal of Civil Engineering, Vol. 2, No. 4, 1975.

8.6   Cook, R. D., Malkus, D. S., and Plesha, M. E., "Concepts and Applications of Finite Element Analysis," 3rd edition, John Wiley & Sons, New York, 1989.

8.7   Clarke, M. and Bridge, R., "The Design of Steel Frames Using the Notional Load Approach," Proceedings of the 5th Colloquium on Stability of Metal Structures, Structural Stability Research Council, 1996.

8.8   Canadian Standards Association, CAN/CSA–S16–01, "Limit States Design of Steel Structures," Toronto, Ontario, 2001.

8.9   Dawe, J.L. and Kulak, G.L. "Local Buckling Behavior of Beam-Columns," Journal of the Structural Division, American Society of Civil Engineers, Vol. 112, ST11, November 1986.

8.10   Galambos, T.V. and Ketter, R.L., "Columns Under Combined Bending and Thrust," Journal of the Engineering Mechanics Division, American Society of Civil Engineers, Vol. 84, EM2, April 1959.

8.11   Essa, H.E. and Kennedy, D.J.L., "Proposed Provisions for the Design of Steel Beam-Columns in S16-2001," Canadian Journal of Civil Engineering, Vol. 27, No. 4, August 2000.

8.12   Canadian Institute of Steel Construction, "Handbook of Steel Construction," Ninth Edition, Toronto, Ontario, 2006.

8.13   Kennedy, D.J.L., Picard, A., and Beaulieu, D., "New Canadian Provisions for the Design of Steel Beam-Columns," Canadian Journal of Civil Engineering, Vol. 17, No.6, Dec. 1990.

CHAPTER 9

CONNECTIONS

9.1 Introduction

There are very few structural steel members for which the designer does not have to provide connections. In most common types of framing, one member adjoins another—beam to column, for example—and a connection between the members is necessary to transfer the forces. Safety is paramount, but an important component of the economy of a fabricated steel structure resides in the selection of connections that are inexpensive to make and which permit easy erection. Continuing research in this area has resulted in a better understanding of connection performance and more economical design of joints.

The common fastening elements for structural steel are bolts and welds. Although rivets were widely used in the past, they are not used now in North America for new work. After a brief discussion of their characteristics, emphasis will be placed on bolts and welds.

9.2 Rivets

Bar stock was used for rivets, with a head formed on one end by either hot or cold-driving in the manufacturing process. After the rivet was inserted in a hole in the connection, this end was held while a second head was formed against the gripped material. Generally, the rivet was hot while this was being done.

It generally is assumed that, as a result of the driving process, the rivet fills the hole and that a joint results in which there will be no relative movement of the parts under load. In fact, the degree to which such hole-filling occurs is uncertain. Tests have shown that there is less movement (or, slip) in a comparable joint using high-strength bolts wherein a nominal 2 mm clearance between bolt and hole is provided [9.1]. Additionally, the properties of the rivet material are probably changed somewhat during the driving process.

Although the cost per rivet was less than that of an equal diameter high-strength bolt, the rivet had less load-carrying capacity and required more labor to install.

9.3 Bolts

Unfinished (or, common) bolts are usually known by their ASTM designation, A307 [9.2]. They are made of low-carbon steel and are generally supplied with square heads and nuts. The specified minimum tensile strength is 414 MPa. These bolts are installed by turning the nut on against the gripped parts with a hand wrench, using only the ordinary effort of the worker. As such, the amount of any initial tension in the bolt can be expected to be both small and variable. This can affect the load transfer mechanism, as will be described subsequently. This type of fastener may be economical when used in light framing work and where vibration and load reversal are not a problem.

Riveted connections are often encountered in older structures

The type of bolt most frequently used in structural steel work is the high-strength bolt. These are made from heat-treated steel, either carbon steel (ASTM A325 bolts) or high-strength alloy steel (ASTM A490 bolts). The specified minimum tensile strengths are 825 MPa for A325 bolts [9.3] and 1035 MPa for A490 bolts [9.4]. These specifications cited are written in US Customary units. Equivalent SI standards are available for both types. These are A325M [9.5] and A490M bolts [9.6], where the specified minimum tensile strengths are 830 MPa and 1040 MPa, respectively. The fasteners most readily available through bolt supply warehouses conform to Imperial sizes, but the major North American bolt manufacturers now produce high-strength bolts according to the SI specifications as well. The metric series bolts, A325M and A490M, will be cited in this Chapter for specific references or examples.

Installation of both ordinary bolts and high-strength bolts is normally done in holes that are 2 mm greater in diameter than the fastener. Oversize or slotted holes may be used with the high-strength bolts in certain circumstances [9.7].

Obviously, the use of bolts with such high strengths will have a direct effect on the capacity of joints in which they are used. Additionally, the bolts may be intentionally pretensioned during the installation process: this will also have implications respecting the behaviour of the joint. Depending upon the intended function of the joint, the S16–01 Standard [9.8] permits the use of either non-pretensioned or pretensioned bolts. The bolt installation procedure required for each of these two possibilities will be described in the remainder of this section. Section 9.5 and later sections of this chapter will describe the load transfer mechanisms of a bolted joint and identify whether non-pretensioned bolts may be used or whether pretensioned bolts will be required.

The installation of high-strength bolts that are not required to be pretensioned simply requires that the holes be properly aligned, the bolts inserted, and then the nuts turned on until all the plies in a joint are in firm contact. This is referred to as the "snug-tight" - condition for the bolts, and it can usually be attained by the ordinary effort of a worker using a spud wrench.[1] If an air-driven impact wrench is being used, snug-tight usually corresponds to the first impact of the wrench as the nut is run down the threads. However, the governing condition is that the connected parts be in firm contact with one another.

For those cases where the bolts are required to be pretensioned, the Standard requires that the minimum installed fastener tension be equal to 70% of the specified minimum tensile strength of the bolts. This pretension is induced as the nut is turned on against the gripped material and the bolt elongates. Although two methods of attaining the desired preload were used in the past, the calibrated wrench method and the turn-of-nut method, only the latter is permitted by the S16 Standard for use in Canada. As well as being simpler, the turn-of-nut method provides better control of the pretension than did the calibrated wrench method.

The turn-of-nut procedure of bolt installation is a method that uses elongation control to induce the desired bolt pretension. The holes in the parts to be connected are first aligned, then a sufficient number of bolts are inserted and taken to the snug-tight condition so that the parts of the joint are brought into full contact with each other. Bolts are then placed in the remaining holes and brought up to the snug-tight condition, that is, the nut is turned on using the ordinary effort of a worker with a spud wrench or the nut turned on to the point of first impact of an impact wrench. Re-snugging of the first bolts installed may be required in large joints. Fortunately, the exact location of "snug" is not critical: what is important is that all parts be in close contact with one another.

After all bolts have been brought to the snug-tight condition and the parts are in firm contact, each nut is given an additional one-half turn if the grip length of the bolt exceeds 4 bolt diameters but does not exceed 8 diameters or 200 mm. For so-called short-grip bolts (less than 4 bolt diameters in the grip), one-third turn is specified, and for long-grip bolts (more than 8 bolts diameters in the grip), two-thirds of a turn is required. The tightening process should be done systematically, moving from the most rigid part of the joint to its free edges.

Since the frictional resistance that is present in the bolt–nut assembly plays no role in the turn-of-nut method of installation, washers are generally not required. However, when A490 bolts are used to connect material with a yield strength of less than 280 MPa washers are necessary under both head and nut in order to prevent galling and indentation of the connected material. (The great majority of steels used today will have a yield strength greater than 280 MPa.) Special requirements for washers apply in cases where oversize or slotted holes are present.

The preloads in the A325 fasteners of a relatively large joint are shown in Figure 9.1 [9.9, 9.10]. Using the histogram at the bottom of the figure in conjunction with the plot of bolt tension vs. bolt elongation, it can be noted that all fasteners in the joint exceeded the specified minimum pretension of 174 kN and that all were loaded well into the inelastic range. Because the load vs. elongation response of the fasteners is relatively flat in the

---

[1] A spud wrench is a tool used by an ironworker. It has an open hexagonal head and a tapered handle that allows the worker to insert it into holes for purposes of initial alignment of parts.

inelastic region, variations in the induced elongation (which includes the influence of the snug condition) produce only minor changes in the individual bolt pretensions.

A comparison of load vs. nut rotation for A325 and A490 bolts is given in Figure 9.2 [9.9, 9.10]. The margin against twisting off can be expected to be between two and three for both types of fastener.

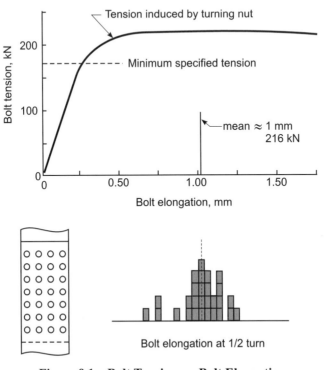

Figure 9.1 – Bolt Tension vs. Bolt Elongation

There are two other ways that can be used to obtain a desired pretension. One is the use of so-called direct tension indicators. These are a washer-type element that is placed under the bolt head or under the nut. As the nut is turned, small arch-shaped protrusions that have been formed into the washer surface compress under the pretension that develops in the bolt. If a suitable calibration has been carried out, the amount of pretension in the bolt can be established by measuring the size of the gap remaining as the protrusions close. This calibration requires that a number of individual measurements be made in a load-indicating device and a feeler gauge used to measure the gap. (In practice, measurements are not performed, but a verifying feeler gauge is used.) Details of the load-indicating washer itself and the procedure necessary for calibration are given in References [9.7] and [9.11].

The direct tension indicator is used with conventional A325 or A490 bolts. The other alternative to obtain pretension is to use a bolt that is specially configured to reflect the pretension [9.12]. This is called a "twist-off" or "tension-control" bolt. A tension-control bolt is a fastener that meets the overall requirements of ASTM A325 bolts, but which has special features that pertain to installation. In particular, this bolt has a splined end that extends beyond the threaded portion of the bolt and an annular groove between the threaded portion of the bolt and the splined end. The bolt usually is manufactured with a round head (also called button or dome), but it can also be supplied with the same head as heavy hex structural bolts.

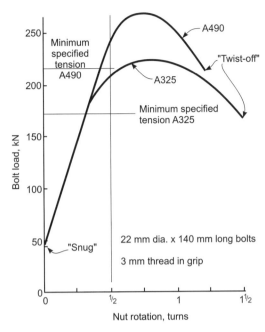

Figure 9.2 – Bolt Load vs. Nut Rotation

The special wrench required to install these bolts has two coaxial chucks—an inner chuck that engages the splined end and an outer chuck that envelopes the nut. The two chucks turn opposite to one another to tighten the bolt. At some point, the torque developed by the friction between the nut and bolt threads and at the nut–washer interface overcomes the torsional shear resistance of the bolt material at the annular groove. The splined end of the bolt then shears off at the groove. If the system has been properly manufactured and calibrated, the target bolt pretension is achieved at this point. Factors that control the pretension are bolt material strength, thread conditions, the diameter of the annular groove, and the surface conditions at the nut–washer interface. The installation process is done by one person and takes place from one side of the joint only, which is often an economic advantage. The wrench used for the installation is electrically powered, and this can be advantageous in the field.

9.4   Welds

Although several welding processes are used for welding of steel and other metals, arc welding is by far the most commonly used process for structural steel. Arc welding consists of generating an intense heat from an electric arc to melt the metal at the joint between two parts. The two parts are fused together, either directly or, more commonly, with an intermediate filler metal (a consumable welding electrode). The electrode is moved along the joint either manually or mechanically, or the work itself can be moved under a stationary electrode.

Several arc welding processes are available for use in the fabrication of steel structures. All are capable of delivering the quality required for safe structures when implemented properly, and economic factors generally determine which one will be used. The design engineer usually allows the fabricator to select the most appropriate process because it is often a reflection of the equipment and manpower availability within a certain shop. However, the structural design engineer should be aware of the various processes, their advantages and limitations, and be sensitive to unique fabrication problems.

The most commonly used arc welding processes in steel fabrication shops are the shielding metal arc welding (SMAW) process, the flux cored arc welding (FCAW) process, the gas metal arc welding (GMAW) process, also called metal inert gas (MIG) process or metal active gas (MAG) process, and the submerged arc welding (SAW) process. Each welding process requires its own specialized equipment, a power source and filler metal, with or without gas shielding or flux.

Shielded Metal Arc Welding (SMAW) — The process, commonly known as "stick" electrode welding or manual welding, makes use of a solid wire covered with a coating called flux. The primary role of the flux is to provide shielding to the molten weld metal pool in order to prevent oxidation of the weld metal and molten base metal. This is achieved by a gas formed during combustion of the flux and by the slag cover. It also contains chemical elements that act as scavengers for the impurities in the weld metal and to provide the weld metal with special properties that may be required under certain conditions (e.g., promotion of rapid solidification of the molten weld metal so that welding can be carried out in the overhead position). The flux can also provide a means of adding iron powder to increase the deposition rate of weld metal. The covered electrodes are typically 225 mm to 450 mm long and therefore frequent replacement is required as the electrodes are consumed. This slows down the rate of welding and produces start and stop locations that are potential sites of weld defects.

SMAW is a versatile, simple, and flexible welding process. It is commonly used for tack welding, fabrication of miscellaneous components, and for repair and maintenance welding since the amount of welding in these cases is relatively small and in-situ locations are most suitable for the SMAW process. Because of the relatively low efficiency of this process, it is seldom used for primary fabrication. Although shielded metal arc welding can deposit high quality welds in a dependable fashion, it is a slower process and more costly than other arc welding processes discussed below.

Designation of shielded metal arc welding electrodes follows the notation specified in CSA-W48-01 [9.13]. A typical electrode classification is E4918, for example. The prefix "E" designates an arc welding electrode. The first two digits of a four digit number indicate the minimum tensile strength of the weld metal in increments of 10 MPa. The last two digits convey important information to the welding engineer regarding the position in which welding can be executed, type of coating and the current to be used.

Flux Cored Arc Welding (FCAW) — This process uses a continuous filler metal electrode, making this process more efficient than the shielded metal arc process. It is suitable for automatic or semi-automatic welding applications because the electrode is fed continuously. The electrode is tubular and inside the metal sheath is a combination of materials that may include metallic powder and flux. Shielding of the molten metal can be provided by the flux (for self-shielded flux cored wire) or by an external source of gas (for the gas shielded flux cored process). Another group of tubular electrode is called metal cored electrode. These electrodes contain a core of metal powders and provide high metal deposition rate.

The flux cored arc welding process is frequently used for tack welding and miscellaneous fabrication. Production welds that are short, change direction, are difficult to access, must be done out-of-position (e.g., vertical or overhead), or are part of a short production run generally will be made with semiautomatic FCAW. The process offers two distinct advantages over the SMAW process—the electrode is continuous, which eliminates built-in starts and stops, and the increased amperages that can be used with flux cored arc welding increase the weld deposition rate.

A typical designation for a flux cored electrode is E491T-1. The prefix "E" designates an arc welding electrode. The first two digits of a three digit number indicates the minimum tensile strength in increments of 10 MPa. The third digit indicates the weld position, followed by a letter "T" indicating that the electrode consists of a flux-cored electrode (the letter C is used for a metal cored electrode) and the last digit indicates specific operational, compositional and mechanical requirements.

Submerged arc welding (SAW) — When an application lends itself to automatic welding, the submerged arc welding process is usually selected. Submerged arc welding differs from other arc welding processes in that a granular flux is used to shield the arc and the molten metal. The arc is struck between the workpiece and the tip of a bare wire electrode. Because the arc is completely submerged, the weld is made without the flash, spatter and sparks that characterize other welding processes. The nature of the flux is such that very few fumes are released, and this makes SAW an ideal welding process for shop fabrication. Welds made using submerged arc welding have an excellent appearance and are spatter-free. The process is best suited for fully mechanized operation, although it can also be used as a semi-automatic process. The high quality of the submerged arc welds, high deposition rates, deep penetration characteristics, and its fully automatic characteristic makes it popular for the fabrication of such components as plate girders and fabricated columns. Because the flux is granular, the process is only suitable for welding in the horizontal or flat position.

An example of a flux and carbon steel electrode classification for submerged arc welding is F49A3-EL8K. The letter "F" designates a flux and the number 49 indicates the minimum tensile strength of 490 MPa. The following letter indicates the heat treatment condition (A for as-welded and P for post weld heat treated condition). The fourth digit indicates the temperature at which the impact strength of the weld metal meets the requirements. The letter E indicates an arc welding electrode. The letter L indicates a low manganese content. The last two digits relate to the chemical composition of the electrode.

Gas Metal Arc Welding (GMAW) — This process is very similar to the flux cored welding process. The major differences are that the GMAW process uses a solid electrode and leaves no appreciable amount of residual slag on the weld surface. Therefore, protection to the molten weld metal is provided by a continuous stream of shielding gas or gas mixture. When the process uses argon-based mixtures as a shielding gas, it is referred to as a metal inert gas (MIG) process. Carbon dioxide can also be used as a shielding gas, and the process is then referred to as a metal active gas (MAG) process. In addition to providing protection during welding, the gas mixture affects the characteristics of the weld metal transfer, thus affecting the weld surface appearance and weld penetration. Since the GMAW process does not use a slag-forming flux, the process is sensitive to impurities on the base metal surface, such as mill-scale and rust. This also makes the GMAW process more sensitive to the loss of shielding since there is no slag to provide protection to the molten weld metal. Because of these problems, the GMAW process is not a popular welding process in structural steel fabrication shops. Metal cored electrodes alleviate some of these problems. A variety of metallic powders are used in the core, making the process less sensitive to surface impurities such as mill scale, but leaves the weld surface virtually free of slag.

An example of an electrode classification for gas metal arc welding is ER49S-2. The letter "E" designates an electrode and the letters "ER" indicates that the filler metal can be used either as an electrode or a rod (straight length). The following two digits indicate the strength of the weld metal in increments of 10 MPa. The following letter designates the type of electrode or rod. A letter "S" designates a solid electrode whereas a letter "C" indicates a metal cored electrode. The suffix following the hyphen indicates the chemical composition of the weld metal.

A considerable range of electrodes is available for each welding process outlined above, so that an electrode can be chosen that is both compatible with the grade of steel being joined, possess the qualities required for the specific application and an economical choice [9.13, 9.14, 9.15].

Within the industry, the term "Welding Procedure Specification" (WPS) is used to signify the combination of variables that are to be used to make a weld. The welding procedure specification consists of specifying the process, the electrode specification and classification, base metal specification, heat input (expressed in terms of welding speed, voltage and amperage) and special considerations such as preheat temperature and post-weld heat treatment requirements, etc. that affect the quality of the final product. The purpose of the welding procedure specification is to communicate to the welder and inspectors the parameters under which welding is to be performed. Welding procedures are usually developed by welding engineers or welding technicians, not the welder. The welders, on the other hand, must be able to read and apply the procedure, although it is not expected that they understand how and why each variable was selected.

A welded connection can be a very satisfactory structural solution since it is relatively easy to maintain full continuity of a section (such as in a beam or girder splice) or to provide full continuity at an abrupt change in cross-section (such as at a beam-to-column connection). Fabrication tolerances generally must be closer than those when bolted connections are used, however. Even under the most ideal conditions, inspection of the finished weld requires considerable expertise and experience, and labor costs for fabrication and inspection reflect the high degree of skill involved in these operations. Nevertheless, welded connections are frequently more economical than bolted connections when made in the fabricator's shop, and may also, in some cases, be more economical in the field.

The main types of structural welds are shown in Figure 9.3, although the plug (or, slot) weld shown in Figure 9.3(d) is used infrequently in structural work. A groove weld may have either complete penetration (Figure 9.3(a)) or partial penetration (Figure 9.3(b)). In either case, if the deposited weld metal is made using a "matching" electrode grade, the deposited weld metal is as effective as the base metal itself. A complete penetration groove weld therefore restores the original base metal. The partial penetration groove weld is less effective only by reason of the fact that it provides less cross-sectional material than was originally provided by the base metal. The groove is generally necessary so that the interior portion of the base metal can be properly reached during the welding process. It can be shaped in a number of different ways, as well as the one shown.

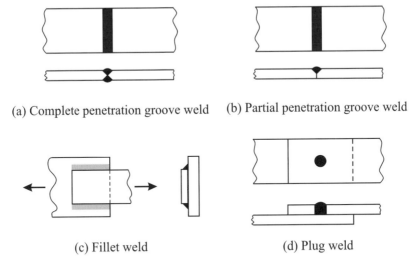

(a) Complete penetration groove weld   (b) Partial penetration groove weld

(c) Fillet weld   (d) Plug weld

Figure 9.3 – Common Weld Types

A fillet weld is another commonly used weld for structural work. Fillet welds are easier to make than groove welds, but they are less effective in carrying stress. The weld may be oriented as shown in Figure 9.3(c) (a longitudinal placement of the weld), located transversely to the direction of the load, or at any angle in between these limits. As shown in Figure 9.4, both the strength and the ductility of the fillet weld are markedly dependent upon this angle of inclination [9.17]. Until recently, specifications did not recognize the strength increase shown. However, this relationship is covered in Clause 13.13.2.2(b) of S16–01. It will still be advantageous to use the weld with the greatest ductility, the longitudinally placed fillet weld, in preference to the other orientations. Some common terminology related to groove welds and fillet welds, which will be used in the following discussions are illustrated in Figure 9.5.

Because of the difficulty in trying to show a weld on an engineering drawing, it is necessary to adopt a set of symbols that will convey the necessary information concerning the size, length, spacing, etc. of the weld. To assist in the identification of weld, the shaper of the symbol is often made to reflect the configuration of the fusion faces of the weld as seen in a vertical section through the joint. A description of standard symbols is presented in Figure 9.6 and their use is illustrated in the design examples in this Chapter.

Further information on welding symbols is available in the CSA Standard W59-03, Welded Steel Construction [9.16].

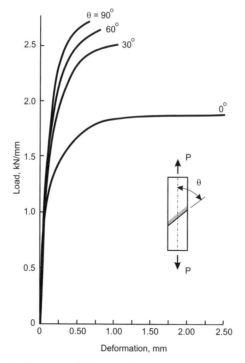

Figure 9.4 – Load vs. Deformation Response of Fillet Welds

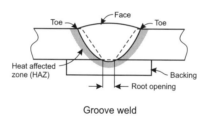

Groove weld

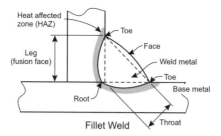

Figure 9.5 – Weld Terminology

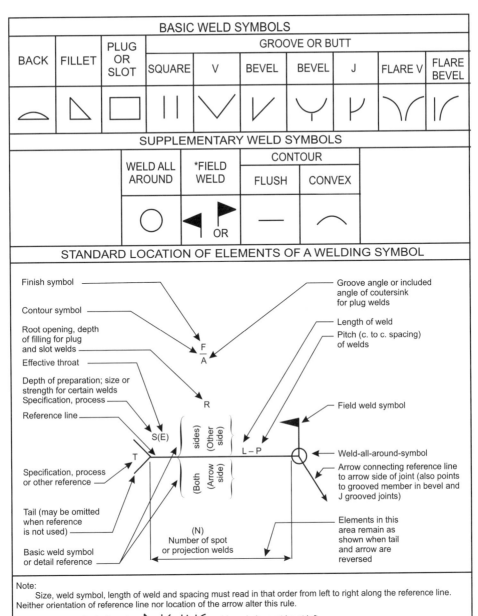

BASIC WELD SYMBOLS

BACK	FILLET	PLUG OR SLOT	GROOVE OR BUTT						
			SQUARE	V	BEVEL	BEVEL	J	FLARE V	FLARE BEVEL

SUPPLEMENTARY WELD SYMBOLS

	WELD ALL AROUND	*FIELD WELD	CONTOUR		
			FLUSH	CONVEX	

OR

STANDARD LOCATION OF ELEMENTS OF A WELDING SYMBOL

Finish symbol

Contour symbol

Root opening, depth of filling for plug and slot welds

Effective throat

Depth of preparation; size or strength for certain welds

Specification, process

Reference line

Specification, process or other reference

Tail (may be omitted when reference is not used)

Basic weld symbol or detail reference

Groove angle or included angle of coutersink for plug welds

Length of weld

Pitch (c. to c. spacing) of welds

Field weld symbol

Weld-all-around-symbol

Arrow connecting reference line to arrow side of joint (also points to grooved member in bevel and J grooved joints)

Elements in this area remain as shown when tail and arrow are reversed

$\frac{F}{A}$

R

S(E)

T

(sides) (Other side)

(Both) (Arrow side)

L – P

(N) Number of spot or projection welds

Note:

Size, weld symbol, length of weld and spacing must read in that order from left to right along the reference line. Neither orientation of reference line nor location of the arrow alter this rule.

The perpendicular leg of ◿, ∨, ⊬, ⌐ weld symbols must be at left.

Size and spacing of fillet welds must be shown on both the Arrow Side and the Other Side Symbol.

Symbols apply between abrupt changes in direction of welding unless governed by the "all around" symbol or otherwise dimensioned.

These symbols do not explicitly provide for the case that frequently occurs in structural work, where duplicate material (such as stiffeners) occurs on the far side of a web or gusset plate. The fabricating industry has adopted this convention; that when the billing of the detail material discloses the identity of far side with near side, the welding shown for the near side shall also be duplicated on the far side.

*Pennant points away from arrow.

Figure 9.6 – Standard Weld Symbols

Example 9.1

Figure 9.7 presents examples of welded details with the appropriate weld symbols for various joint configurations and weld types. Figure 9.7(a) illustrates a cruciform joint made from three plates welded together with four fillet welds. The joints between the plates are horizontal and each weld symbol describes the fillet welds on each side of the joints. The weld symbol below the weld symbol line refers to the weld on the arrow side of the joint. Figure 9.7(b) illustrates a similar joint, except that the joints are now in the vertical position. Figure 9.7(c) illustrates a groove weld in a T-joint. Here the vertical plate is beveled on each face and fillet welds are added to the double groove weld. Combined weld symbols are required to identify both the groove welds and the fillet welds. Finally, figure 9.7(d) illustrates a welded butt joint with a single bevel groove weld and a backing bar. It should be noted that the arrow line is broken to indicate which of the two plates is beveled. This was not required in Figure 9.7(c) since ambiguity was not possible in that case. The angle of the bevel is also indicated. The backing bar, required to support the molten weld, is sometimes removed after the weld is completed.

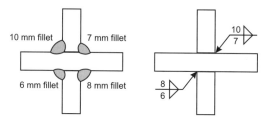

(a) Fillet welds in a cruciform joint (horizontal joints)

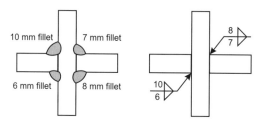

(b) Fillet welds in a cruciform joint (vertical joints)

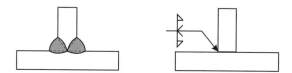

(c) Groove weld in a T-joint with fillet weld reinforcement

(d) Butt joint with single bevel groove weld and backing bar

Figure 9.7 – Examples of weld symbols

9.5   Load Transfer Mechanisms

To design or analyze a connection, the load transfer mechanism through the fasteners must be known. The resulting forces on the fasteners can then be examined and compared with the limiting values. In addition, the strength, stability, and possibly the ductility, of the connected parts must be examined to ensure satisfactory behaviour of the connection. Bolts may be subjected to shearing, tensile, or combined tensile and shearing forces, depending on their location in the joint with respect to external forces. Fillet welds are almost always acting in shear and the forces acting on groove welds are the same as those that act on the connected material.

The bolts in a single lap connection such as shown in Figure 9.8(a) will be subjected to shearing across a single surface as the plates pull up against the fasteners. It cannot be assumed that all of the fasteners in a line share equally in carrying the load. In fact, the fasteners towards the ends of the joint carry the largest portion of the load. This unequal loading of the fasteners is accentuated as the joint becomes longer [9.18]. According to Clause 13.12.1.1 of the Standard, no reduction in basic permissible bolt shear stress is necessary if the joint length L is $\leq 15\,d$ (where d is the bolt diameter). However, for joints longer than this, the shearing resistance must be taken as $1.075 - 0.005\,L/d$ times the basic shear resistance, with a limit of 0.75 on the reduction factor. (The limit becomes operative at $L/d = 65$.)

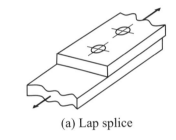

(a) Lap splice

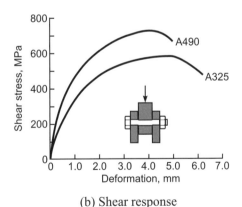

(b) Shear response

Figure 9.8 – Bolts in Shear

The response of single A325 or A490 bolts to a loading producing shear on two planes is shown in Figure 9.8(b). As has been noted, the A490 bolt is a higher strength fastener than the A325 bolt. This higher strength comes at the expense of a slightly reduced ductility. It should also be noted that little, if any, of the response could be said to be elastic for either type of fastener.

As the plates pull up against the fasteners (Figure 9.8(a)), failure can occur in one of four ways. The plate can tear through the net section or fail by a combination of shear and tension, the bolt can shear at the interface of the two plates, the plate can shear out between the end fastener and the end of the plate, or the plate immediately adjacent to a bolt can pile up and/or yield as a result of the contact force between the two. The problem of net section tearing or what is called "tension and shear block" failure is related to the design of the member itself and this has been treated in Sections 3.2 and 3.4, respectively. The shearing of the plate (Figure 9.9) is avoided by limiting the distance between the centreline of the bolt and the end of the plate (S16 Clause 22.3.4). For bolts that act like the one shown in Figure 9.8(b), the two remaining problems are the bolt shear resistance and the bearing capacity of the plate. A joint in which the fasteners act as just described is termed a "bearing-type" connection. This behaviour will be expected either when non-pretensioned bolts are used or when the frictional resistance provided to a joint by pretensioned bolts has been overcome. The latter type of connection is referred to as "slip-critical," and it will be described next.

When high-strength bolts are pretensioned, the high clamping force present mobilizes frictional resistance between the parts that are being joined. This behaviour, which will occur at an earlier stage of loading than the bearing-type behaviour just outlined, is illustrated in Figure 9.10. At some stage of loading the frictional resistance will be overcome, the plates will slip until they bear against the fasteners, and the situation is as has been described for bearing-type joints.

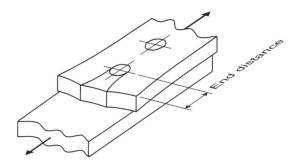

Figure 9.9 – End Failure of Plate

The deformation behaviour of a typical joint that uses pretensioned bolts is shown in Figure 9.11. The amount of the slip can be theoretically twice the hole clearance (i.e., 2×2 mm), but tests show that it is usually in the order of only one-half of the hole clearance [9.9]. The designer should justify the need for slip-critical connections because they will generally be less economical than a bearing-type joint. Appropriate situations would be any connection under repetitive loading (fretting might occur if the parts were allowed to slip cyclically), impact loading, or structures in which slip would produce unacceptable geometrical changes (as in the case of a dish antenna, for example). In most building structures, repeated loading or impact loading is not a consideration and geometry changes are unlikely because the bolts will already be in bearing at the time of installation as a natural consequence of the dead weight of the members themselves.

Thus, for buildings, bearing-type connections should be the norm. On the other hand, joints in bridges will require slip-critical characteristics because of the repetitive loading.

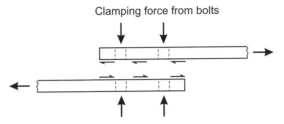

Figure 9.10 – Friction Behaviour Produced by Pretensioned Bolts

In a slip-critical connection, the potential failure mode is simply slip of the connected parts, and examination is to be made at specified load levels. (If slip has been judged to be potentially detrimental to the function of the structure, then slip must not occur under the day-to-day loads, i.e., the specified loads.) Once the slip resistance of a joint has been overcome, the connected parts come into bearing against the fasteners and the joint is now a bearing-type connection. It must meet the requirements for that type of joint, and this examination is to be made at factored load levels. In summary, if a connection is designated as bearing-type, then the examination is made at factored load levels. If the connection has been designated as slip-critical, then the joint must be examined at both specified load levels (against slip) and at factored load levels (as a bearing-type connection).

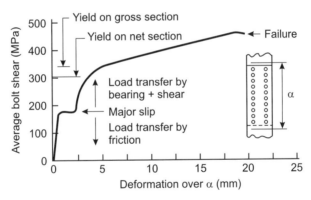

Figure 9.11 – Overall Joint Behaviour

Direct tension loading of bolts results from conditions such as the one shown in Figure 9.12(a). Because the application of the external tensile load produces both an elongation of the bolt and an expansion of the pre-compressed plates, little, if any, change occurs in the preload of pretensioned high-strength bolts [9.9]. After separation of the parts, or in an assembly where the parts are not initially in contact, the external load is taken directly by the bolts. If ordinary bolts are used in a connection like this, the bolts simply act as tension members since there is no preload present.

If the parts in a tension-type connection are not relatively rigid, there is the possibility that additional forces due to prying action will exist, as implied in Figure 9.12(b). These should be taken into account in proportioning the bolts. A conservative estimate [9.9] of the prying force can be obtained by multiplying the nominal force per bolt by the quantity

$$Q = \frac{3}{8}\frac{b}{a} - \frac{t^3}{328 \times 10^3}$$ (9.1)

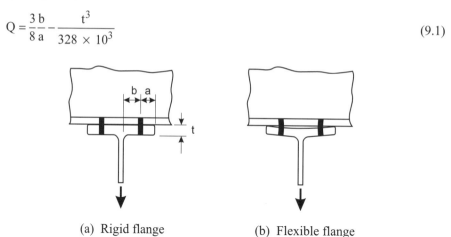

(a) Rigid flange   (b) Flexible flange

Figure 9.12 – Bolts in Tension

The bolts in a connection such as the one illustrated in Figure 9.13 will be subjected to a combination of both tension and shear. An elliptical interaction expression (Clause 13.12.1.3 of S16) combining the resistances for the two single effects is used in this instance.

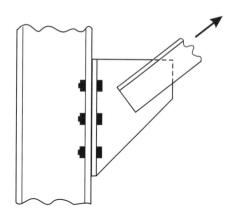

Figure 9.13 – Bolts in Combined Tension and Shear

As was indicated in Section 9.4, a groove weld simply replaces main section material. The forces in such a weld can therefore be calculated on the same basis as for the main material. The reduced cross-sectional area of partial penetration groove welds should be kept in mind when computing the forces in these elements.

Irrespective of the actual loading, fillet welds are usually assumed to be subjected to shearing force, as they would be in the welds shown in Figure 9.3(c). For this case, and for shear loading of groove welds, the resistance of both the weld and the adjacent base metal must be examined. There are a number of rules governing minimum and maximum weld sizes, effective areas of partial penetration groove welds, and certain restrictions on details. The CSA W59 Standard should be consulted on these [9.16].

9.6   Use of Pretensioned Bolts

Pretensioned high-strength bolts are required, of course, in slip-critical connections. As described earlier, slip-critical connections should be used in cases where fatigue or frequent load reversal is present or in structures sensitive to deflections that would be the result of slip in the joints. Other examples in which slip-critical joints should be used (S16 Clause 22.2.2) include connections for supports of running machines or other live loads that produce impact or cyclic load, for all elements resisting crane loads, and in connections using oversize or slotted holes (unless specifically designed to accommodate movement), and in certain connections in structures designed according to the seismic provisions of the Standard. Clause 22.2.2 of the Standard also requires that pretensioned high-strength bolts be used in connections subject to tensile loading. Although the ultimate tensile strength of a pretensioned bolt and non-pretensioned bolt is the same, this is a requirement based on the practical need to have the component parts of a joint loaded in tension stay in close contact at specified load levels.

All connections other than those just described can be made using non-pretensioned high-strength bolts (or, indeed, A307 bolts). Thus, all bearing-type joints can be made using snug-tightened bolts, i.e., the only requirement is that the component parts are brought into firm contact with one another.

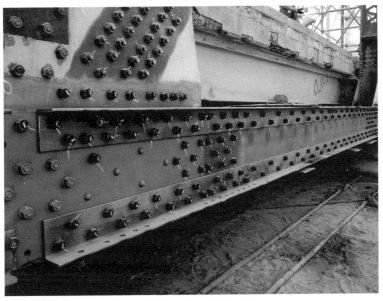

High strength bolts used in the rehabilitation of a highway bridge have to be pretensioned

(Photo courtesy of Cohos Evamy)

9.7   Fastener Resistance—Bolts

The resistances corresponding to the various potential failure modes are given in this section for high-strength bolts and for welds. The provisions for high-strength bolts can also be applied to common bolts (A307) except that, as discussed in Section 9.5, only pretensioned high-strength bolts are suitable for use in slip-critical connections.

In providing rules for evaluating fastener resistances it is the initial premise of S16 that the strength of a structure should be governed by the capacity of the member rather than that of the connections. Hence, the value of the resistance factor is to be taken as $\phi_b = 0.80$, which is less than the resistance factor used for members. This has the effect of providing a higher safety index for the bolts than for the members being connected by the bolts.

In Section 9.5 it was indicated that, for bolts in bearing-type connections, the shear capacity of the bolts and the bearing capacity of the connected material immediately adjacent to the bolts remained to be evaluated. The bearing capacity of a single bolt is really the resistance of the plate adjacent to the bolt, and this can be expressed as

$$B_r = \sigma_b \, d \, t \tag{9.2}$$

where σ_b is the bearing stress that can be sustained by the plate, d is the bolt diameter, and t is the plate thickness. The bearing stress will be some function of the location of the bolt with respect to the end of the plate, e. Tests [9.9] have shown that a reasonable representation of this is given by

$$\frac{\sigma_b}{F_u} = \frac{e}{d}; \quad \text{or,} \quad \sigma_b = \frac{F_u \, e}{d} \tag{9.3}$$

where F_u is the ultimate tensile strength of the plate. Substituting this expression into Equation 9.2, the bearing resistance associated with a single bolt is obtained as

$$B_r = e \, t \, F_u \tag{9.4}$$

The test data show that this estimate of strength is valid only for ratios of e/d up to about 3. Beyond this limit, the failure mode changes gradually from one where the plate material shears out beyond the bolt to one in which large hole and plate deformations occur. For this reason, Clause 13.10 (c) also requires that

$$B_r = 3 \, \phi_{br} \, t \, d \, n \, F_u \tag{9.5}$$

This equation is obtained by substituting the value e = 3 d in Equation 9.4, including all bolts (n) in the joint, and applying the resistance factor ϕ_{br}, taken as 0.67.

It would be reasonable to expect a design requirement to arise from Equation 9.4, as indeed was the case in earlier editions of the Standard (up to 1989). However, the tearing out of material beyond a bolt (Figure 9.9), or a group of bolts, is now treated as part of the design requirements of a tension member. The tension and shear block examination for tension members (Section 3.4) has the same effect as would a requirement arising from Equation 9.4. In the case of a compression member, the phenomenon shown in Figure 9.9 would not occur. Thus, for compression members, only the requirement given by Equation 9.5 (large plate and hole deformations) needs to be considered. In the case of tension members, Equation 9.5 must be satisfied. Good practice also requires that the fasteners be placed so as to satisfy the minimum end distances given in Clause 22.3.4 of the Standard.

Based on extensive testing, it has been established that the shear strength of high-strength bolts is approximately 0.60 times the tensile strength of the bolt material [9.9]. It is important to recognize that this shear strength is independent of whether or not the bolt is pretensioned. As the ultimate capacity of the bolt is approached, the bolt pretension developed by relatively small elongations have been dissipated by the shear deformations. For all practical purposes, the pretension is zero at the time the ultimate load in shear is reached. Thus, to obtain the shear resistance of a group of bolts, whether pretensioned or not pretensioned, the strength parameter $0.60\ F_u$ is multiplied by the cross-sectional area of one bolt (A_b), the number of shear planes in the joint (m), and the total number of bolts present (n), and the performance factor $\phi_b = 0.80$. The result (S16 Clause 13.12.1.1(b)) is:

$$V_r = 0.60\ \phi_b\ n\ m\ A_b\ F_u \tag{9.6}$$

Two modifications are necessary in special circumstances. If the bolt thread is intercepted by a shear plane, then there is less shear area available than that given above. The ratio of the area through the thread root of a bolt to its shank area is about 0.70 for the usual structural sizes and the value of V_r given by Equation 9.6 is to be multiplied by this factor if the bolt thread is intercepted by a shear plane.

The second modification concerns joint length. As was noted in Section 9.5, the strength of a bolted joint is not linearly proportional to joint length (except for the case of two bolts in line). The average resistance per fastener decreases with the number of bolts in line. Clause 13.12.1.1 of the Standard provides the reduction factor (also shown in Section 9.5).

The behaviour of bolts in slip-critical connections, whether loaded in a shear connection or in connections where there is combined shear and tension, must be evaluated first under the specified loads. As noted in Section 9.5, the requirement is that the assembly must not slip as these loads are applied. In addition, however, the designer must also check to ensure that the ultimate factored capacity of the joint (as described above) is equal to or greater than the effect of the factored loads.

The slip resistance of a bolted joint is given by the product of the number of faying surfaces, the coefficient of friction of the parts being joined, and the total clamping force provided by the bolts. In addition to these quantities, the Standard recognizes that the ideal situation of zero probability of slip is not attainable.

Both the slip coefficient and the initial clamping force have considerable variation about their mean values. The necessary frequency distributions for these effects are known for a large number of practical cases and they have been used to evaluate the slip probability levels for various situations [9.9]. The slip probability level corresponding to the rules provided in the Standard is 5%.

The expression for slip resistance as given in S16 (Clause 13.12.2.2) is:

$$V_s = 0.53\ c_1\ k_s\ m\ n\ A_b\ F_u \tag{9.7}$$

In accordance with the recognized way of calculating slip resistance, Equation 9.7 should express the product of the friction coefficient (k_s), the clamping force, and the number of faying surfaces (m). The clamping force is contained within the terms $0.53\ n\ A_b\ F_u$. This can be stated more fundamentally as $0.70 \times 0.75\ n\ A_b\ F_u$, where n is the number of bolts, F_u is the ultimate tensile strength of the bolt material, and A_b is the cross-sectional area of the bolt corresponding to its nominal diameter. The multiplier 0.70 is used to express the requirement that the minimum pretension is to be at least 70% of the specified tensile strength of the bolt material, F_u . Also, it is convenient to use the area of the bolt corresponding to the nominal diameter in Equation 10.7. The area that should be used is the "stress area," a value lying somewhere between the nominal area and the area through the threads. The 0.75 multiplier is a reasonable conversion from nominal area to stress area for most bolt sizes used in structural practice.

All terms in Equation 9.7 have now been defined except for the term c_1. This coefficient is used to relate mean slip coefficient values and the specified initial tension (i.e., 70% F_u) to a 5% probability of slip. Values of both c_1 and the slip coefficient, k_s, are given in Table 3 of the Standard. For slip-critical connections in which a greater probability of slip might be tolerable, information is available for the 10% level [9.9].

The ultimate resistance of a single high-strength bolt loaded in tension by the connected parts is equal to the product of its stress area (as described above) and the ultimate tensile strength of the bolt material. For simplicity, the equation given in Clause 13.12.1.2 of the Standard again uses the nominal area of the bolt (A_b) and the multiplier 0.75 to provide a reasonable conversion to the stress area. For a tensile connection containing n high-strength bolts and where F_u is the ultimate tensile strength of the bolt material, the capacity of the fasteners is therefore given by

$$T_r = 0.75 \, \phi_b \, n \, A_b \, F_u \qquad (9.8)$$

The designer is reminded that when comparing the resistance given by Equation 9.8 to the effect of the factored loads, the latter must reflect the influence of prying action in the joint. Prying action can be calculated using Equation 9.1 or by similar rules [9.9].

When bolts in a bearing-type connection also have a component of tensile load in addition to the shear, they are to be proportioned according to the expression given in Clause 13.12.1.3 of the Standard—

$$\left(\frac{V_f}{V_r} \right)^2 + \left(\frac{T_f}{T_r} \right)^2 \leq 1 \qquad (9.9)$$

This is an elliptical interaction equation developed directly from test results [9.9].

Bolts in a slip-critical shear connection that also have a component of load parallel to the axes of the bolts are covered in Clause 13.12.2.3 of S16. There are no published test results covering this situation and, as a matter of engineering judgment, the following equation has been chosen:

$$\frac{V}{V_s} + 1.9 \, \frac{T}{n \, A_b \, F_u} \leq 1 \qquad (9.10)$$

Taking as a base the case where there is no component of load parallel to the axes of the bolts, it is apparent that the resistance to slip will be reduced as tensile load is applied. This reduction will continue until the parts are on the verge of separation, at which time the slip resistance goes to zero. The interaction relationship given assumes linear response between the end limits of all shear and no tension, and all tension and no shear. All of the terms in Equation 9.10 follow directly from this. The term $n \, A_b \, F_u / 1.9$ is equal to the bolt preload, namely, 70 percent of the bolt tensile strength.

9.8 Fastener Resistance—Welds

There are a number of categories for which the unit resistance of a weld is the same as the calculated unit resistance of the base metal. These cases are (a) tension or compression parallel to axis of complete penetration groove welds, of partial penetration groove welds, and of fillet welds and (b) tension or compression normal to the axis of complete groove welds. For the case of compression normal to the axis of partial penetration groove welds, the same rule applies except that the unit resistance can be applied to both the area of the weld metal and to the area of any unwelded base metal that is in contact bearing. When a partial penetration groove weld is loaded in tension normal to its axis, the resistance of the weld is to be taken as $\phi_w A_n F_u$, where A_n is the area of weld metal normal to the load. The calculation of weld resistances in all of these categories is straightforward.

The remaining category of weld resistance evaluation is the need to determine the shear resistance of complete or partial joint penetration groove welds, of plug and slot welds, and of fillet welds. (The case of tension or compression normal to the axis of a fillet weld is taken to be the same as shear.) S16–01 explicitly recognizes that the shear resistance of a weld must be evaluated on the basis of both the resistance of the weld itself and of the base metal adjacent to the weld. The resistance of the base metal for all these cases is given as (Clauses 13.13.2.1(a) and 13.13.2.2(a)):

$$V_r = 0.67\ \phi_w\ A_m\ F_u \tag{9.11}$$

This is consistent with the shear resistance of connecting elements. The area of metal (A_m) to be used here is the area of the fusion face (see Figure 9.5).

Except for fillet welds, the strength of the weld metal is given as

$$V_r = 0.67\ \phi_w\ A_w\ X_u \tag{9.12a}$$

For fillet welds, it is recognized that the strength is also a function of the angle of the axis of the weld with respect to the line of action of the force (Clause 13.13.2.2):

$$V_r = 0.67\ \phi_w\ A_w\ X_u\ \left(1.00 + 0.50\ \sin^{1.5}\ \theta\right) \tag{9.12b}$$

In Equation 9.12 the term A_w is the effective throat area of the weld, θ is the angle between the axis of the weld and the load vector, and X_u is the ultimate tensile strength of the electrode (as given by the electrode classification number). Conservatively, the term in parentheses in Equation 9.12(b) can be taken as unity.

The value of ϕ_w is to be taken as 0.67. This reduced value (as compared to $\phi = 0.90$ to be used in determining the resistance of the member) is used to ensure that the weld will not fail before the ultimate resistance of the connected parts is reached. The numerical modifier 0.67 in Equation 9.12 relates the shear strength of the weld to the specified electrode tensile strength, X_u . This is known to be a conservative choice [9.19].

9.9 Analysis and Design of Simple Connections

A simple load transfer requirement is shown in Figure 9.14. The load may be either tensile, as indicated, or compressive. The situation could involve transfer between plates, as shown, but more often will be between gusset or splice plates and a main member. As far as the fastening elements are concerned, the principles are the same, however. Attention will be focused here on the connection details, although the complementary design aspects of the member will be introduced in some examples.

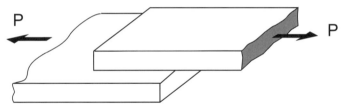

Figure 9.14 – Lap Splice

Example 9.2

Given

The connection for the lap splice illustrated in Figure 9.14 will be proportioned considering the fastening elements to be (a) welds, (b) high-strength bolts, slip-critical connection, (c) high-strength bolts, bearing-type connection. The plate material is G40.21 300W steel, the factored load is 640 kN, and the specified load is 430 kN. The faying surfaces consist of clean mill scale.

Solution (a)

For a welded connection using longitudinal fillet welds, as shown in Figure 9.15(a), the minimum weld size is 8 mm (Table 4-4, CSA W59). A minimum weld size is required to ensure that a small weld does not cool too quickly when used with relatively thick material. Hence, the requirement is a function of the thicker material being joined, 25 mm in this example. The maximum fillet weld size permitted by CSA W59 is 2 mm less than the thickness of the piece against which it will be placed, and the maximum weld size in this example will therefore be 23 mm. (Information on maximum and minimum fillet weld sizes is also contained in the CISC Handbook, Part 6).

Try a 10 mm fillet weld, E49xx electrodes. (Fillet weld may be specified as 5 or 6 mm, but should then increase in 2 mm increments.)

The strength per unit length of the base metal along the fusion face of the weld, i.e., next to the 10 mm leg of the fillet weld, is (Equation 9.11):

$$V_r = 0.67 \times 0.67 \times 10 \text{ mm} \times 450 \text{ MPa} = 2020 \text{ N/mm} = 2.02 \text{ kN/mm}$$

The strength of the weld itself, taking the throat area as given by the shortest distance between the root of the weld and the surface (see Figure 9.5), is (Equation 9.12(b)):

$$V_r = 0.67 \times 0.67 \times (10 \text{ mm} \times 0.707) \times 490 \text{ MPa} \times \left(1 + 0.50 \sin^{1.5} 0\right)$$

$$= 1555 \text{ N/mm} = 1.56 \text{ kN/mm}$$

The strength of the weld metal governs and the weld length required can now be calculated as

$$L = \frac{640 \text{ kN}}{1.56 \text{ kN/mm}} = 410 \text{ mm}$$

Use 410 mm of 10 mm fillet weld arranged as shown in Figure 9.15(a). Note the information contained in the weld symbol. (Half of the weld is placed on each side of the plate.) The reader can verify that the plates selected can carry the factored load of 640 kN (Section 3.2), including a check for shear lag (Section 3.3).

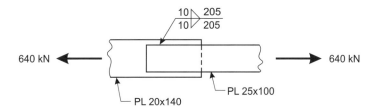

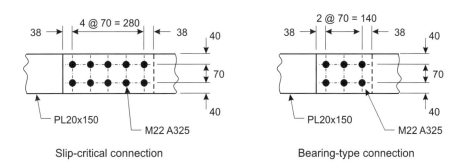

(a) Welded lap splice

Slip-critical connection   Bearing-type connection

(b) Bolted lap splice

Figure 9.15 – Splice Details

Solution (b)

Try using 22 mm diameter A325M bolts ($A_b = 380$ mm^2) and the 20 mm thick plates shown in Figure 9.15(b) for the bolted slip-critical connection. From Table 3 of the S16 Standard, for clean mill scale faying surfaces $k_s = 0.33$ and $c_1 = 0.82$. For one bolt, using Equation 9.7 (Clause 13.12.2.2 of S16):

$$V_s = 0.53 \times 0.82 \times 0.33 \times 1 \text{ shear plane} \times 380 \text{ mm}^2 \times 830 \text{ MPa}$$

$$= 45.2 \times 10^3 \text{ N} = 45.2 \text{ kN}$$

$$\text{Number of bolts required} = \frac{430 \text{ kN}}{45.2 \text{ kN/bolt}} = 9.5$$

Use 10 M22 A325M bolts in two lines.

Details (refer to Figure 9.15(b)):

Minimum bolt pitch 3 diameters = 66 mm. Use 70 mm.

Minimum edge distance 38 mm (Table 6 of S16).

Edge distance provided = 40 mm.   (Satisfactory)

The minimum end distance (in the line of stress), i.e., the distance from the last bolt to the end of the connected part, is set by the requirements of Clause 22.3.4 of S16. Where there are more than two bolts in line, this simply refers to Table 6 of the Standard. Assuming the plate end to have been sheared, this minimum end distance for a 22 mm diameter bolt is given as 38 mm.

As explicitly required by the Standard, it is also necessary to check the ultimate capacity of any connection designed as slip-critical. See the concluding statement in part (c) of this example with respect to this check.

Solution (c)

For the bearing-type connection and again considering 22 mm diameter A325M bolts, for one bolt the shear resistance (Equation 9.6) is:

$$V_r = 0.60 \times 0.80 \times 1 \text{ shear plane} \times 380 \text{ mm}^2 \times 830 \text{ MPa}$$
$$= 151 \times 10^3 \text{N} = 151 \text{ kN}$$

This calculation assumes that the threads are not intercepted by a shear plane, and this must now be checked. The necessary information regarding bolt and nut dimensions can be found in the Handbook (p. 6–158, 159). Helpful tables for the design of bolted connections are also available in the Handbook.

The material that must be accommodated within the bolt grip is a total of $20 + 20 = 40 \text{ mm}$. A 22 mm dia. bolt that is 70 mm long (underside of bolt head to end of bolt) will be a suitable choice. Since the thread length on a 22 mm dia. bolt is 38 mm (for bolts $\leq 100 \text{ mm}$ long), this means that the threads start $70 - 38 = 32 \text{ mm}$ from the underside of the bolt head. The shear plane is 20 mm from the underside of the head, and therefore the threads are not intercepted by the shear plane. The bolt shear capacity calculated above (151 kN) does not have to be adjusted.

The plate capacity in bearing for one bolt is (Equation 9.5):

$$B_r = 3 \times 0.67 \times 20 \text{ mm} \times 22 \text{ mm} \times 450 \text{ MPa} = 398 \times 10^3 \text{ N} = 497 \text{ kN}$$

(If plates of different thickness had been used, the thickness of the thinner plate would be used in this calculation. If a double shear arrangement is present, then the bolt bears against two plate thicknesses in one direction and one thickness in the other. The combination giving the least thickness is used in calculating the bearing resistance.)

The capacity is governed by the resistance in shear. The number of bolts can now be calculated and, once the joint length is known, the need for reduction in bolt shear capacity due to joint length examined.

$$\text{No. req'd.} = \frac{640 \text{ kN}}{127 \text{ kN/bolt}} = 5.0$$

Use six M22 A325M bolts in two lines, as shown in Figure 9.15(b).

Now that the bolt layout has been established, the bolt shear strength reduction with length can be checked. As noted in Section 9.5, a reduction is required only when $L > 15 \text{ d}$. In this example, $L = 140 \text{ mm}$ (see Figure 9.15(b)), which is less than $15 \text{ d} = 15 \times 22 = 330 \text{ mm}$, and no reduction is required.

Next, the tension and shear block capacity of the connected plates (Section 3.4) can be checked according to Equation 3.10. The necessary areas are—

$$A_{nt} = [\,70 \text{ mm} - (22 + 2 + 2)\text{mm}\,] \times 20 \text{ mm} = 880 \text{ mm}^2$$

$$A_{gv} = 2 \times (140 + 38) \text{ mm} \times 20 \text{ mm} = 7120 \text{ mm}^2$$

$$A_{nv} = 7120 \text{ mm}^2 - 2 \times [\,2.5 \times (22 + 2 + 2)\,] \text{ mm} \times 20 \text{ mm} = 4520 \text{ mm}^2$$

and checking Equation 3.10(a) (repeated here for convenience)

$$T_r + V_r = \phi \, A_{nt} \, F_u + 0.60 \, \phi \, A_{gv} \, F_y$$

$$= (0.90 \times 880 \text{ mm}^2 \times 450 \text{ MPa}) + (0.60 \times 0.90 \times 7120 \text{ mm}^2 \times 300 \text{ MPa})$$

$$= 356 \times 10^3 \text{ N} + 1153 \times 10^3 \text{ N} = 1509 \times 10^3 \text{ N} = 1509 \text{ kN}$$

and for Equation 3.10(b)

$$T_r + V_r \leq \phi \, A_{nt} \, F_u + 0.60 \, \phi \, A_{nv} \, F_u$$

$$= 356 \times 10^3 \text{ N} + (0.60 \times 0.90 \times 4520 \text{ mm}^2 \times 450 \text{ MPa})$$

$$= 356 \times 10^3 \text{ N} + 1098 \times 10^3 \text{ N} = 1454 \times 10^3 \text{ N} = 1454 \text{ kN} \qquad \text{Governs}$$

Since the tension plus shear block capacity (1454 kN) is greater than the factored load (640 kN), this requirement has been met. Finally, checking the tensile capacity of the connected material (Equations 3.1 and 3.2)—

$$A_g = 20 \text{ mm} \times 150 \text{ mm} = 3000 \text{ mm}^2$$

$$A_n = A_g - A_{holes} = 3000 \text{ mm}^2 - 2 \times (22 + 2 + 2) \text{ mm} \times 20 \text{ mm} = 1960 \text{ mm}^2$$

$$T_r = \phi \, A_g \, F_y = 0.90 \times (3000) \text{ mm}^2 \times 300 \text{ MPa} = 810 \times 10^3 \text{ N} = 810 \text{ kN}$$

$$T_r = 0.85 \, \phi \, A_n \, F_u = 0.85 \times 0.90 \times 1960 \text{ mm}^2 \times 450 \text{ MPa} = 674.7 \times 10^3 \text{ N} = 675 \text{ kN}$$

The governing value[2] is 675 kN, which is greater than the factored load of 640 kN. In this illustration (part c) all aspects of the tension member design have been covered— tension member capacity, tension plus shear block capacity, and the shear and bearing capacity of the fasteners.

Since six bolts are adequate to carry the factored load, it is obvious now that the ultimate capacity of the ten bolts required when this connection was assumed to be slip-critical (part (b)) will also have adequate capacity at the factored load level.

---

[2] It will be obvious by inspection to many designers that the net section tension strength will be less than the tension plus shear block strength in this example. However, the complete set of calculations has been included for illustrative purposes.

Example 9.3

Given

A beam-to-column connection is illustrated in Figure 9.16. This type of arrangement, which uses web framing angles, is intended to transmit only shear and the beam itself will have been designed accordingly. The fastening elements could be bolts, as shown, welds, or a combination of both. In the latter case, the angles would be shop-welded to either the beam or to the column and the field connection made using bolts. Consider here using 20 mm diameter A325M bolts ($A_b = 314$ mm^2) in a bearing-type connection. The 60 mm dimension shown is the standard gauge for these angles (Table 5 of Appendix A). Such a small eccentricity of load can be neglected in the design of the connection. All steel is G40.21 300W and the factored reaction of the beam is 180 kN.

Solution

Angles to beam web—

Shear resistance per bolt

$V_r = 0.60 \times 0.80 \times 2$ shear planes $\times 314$ mm$^2 \times 830$ MPa

$= 250 \times 10^3$ N $= 250$ kN

The bolts bear against the beam web in one direction (t = 7.6 mm) and the two angles in the other direction (t = 9.5 + 9.5 = 19 mm). Obviously, the former controls.

$B_r = 3 \, \phi_{br} \, t \, d \, n \, F_u$

$= 3 \times 0.67 \times 7.6$ mm $\times \, 20$ mm$\times 1$ bolt$\times 450$ MPa

$= 137 \times 10^3$ N $= 137$ kN

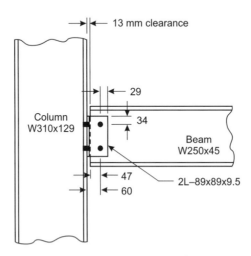

Figure 9.16 – Beam-to-Column Connections

Of these two capacities, the bearing capacity at 137 kN/bolt governs and the number of bolts required is

No. req'd. $= \dfrac{180 \text{ kN}}{137 \text{ kN/bolt}} = 1.3$ bolts

Use two M20 A325M bolts, as shown in Figure 9.16.

Angles to column flange—

Shear resistance per bolt

$V_r = 0.60 \times 0.80 \times 1$ shear plane $\times$ 314 mm^2 $\times$ 830 MPa

$\qquad = 125 \times 10^3$ N $= 125$ kN

The thickness of thinner part (angle thickness is 9.5 mm and column flange thickness is 20.6 mm) will be used to determine the bearing resistance.

$B_r = 3 \times 0.67 \times 9.5$ mm $\times 20$ mm $\times 1$ bolt $\times 450$ MPa

$\qquad = 172 \times 10^3$ N $= 172$ kN

The shear capacity governs and number of bolts required is

No. req'd. $= \dfrac{180 \text{ kN}}{125 \text{ kN/bolt}} = 1.44$ bolts

It is considered good practice to use a minimum of two bolts in any element of a connection. Thus, use four M20 A325M bolts, two in each angle leg.

Now that the number of bolts is known, their layout can be established (see Figure 9.16), and the combined tension and shear resistance of these framing angles established according to Equation 3.10. (Equations 3.10 were repeated in Example 9.1, above.) The necessary areas (for one angle) are

$A_{nt} = [\,29 \text{ mm} - 0.5 \times (20 + 2 + 2) \text{ mm}\,] \times 9.5 \text{ mm} = 162 \text{ mm}^2$

$A_{gv} = [\,(60 + 34) \text{ mm}\,] \times 9.5 \text{ mm} = 893 \text{ mm}^2$

$A_{nv} = 893 \text{ mm}^2 - [\,1.5 \times (20 + 2 + 2) \text{ mm}\,] \times 9.5 \text{ mm} = 551 \text{ mm}^2$

Checking Equation 3.10(a)

$T_r + V_r = (\,0.90 \times 162 \text{ mm}^2 \times 450 \text{ MPa}\,) + (\,0.60 \times 0.90 \times 893 \text{ mm}^2 \times 300 \text{ MPa}\,)$

$\qquad = (\,66 \times 10^3 \text{ N}\,) + (\,145 \times 10^3 \text{ N}\,) = 211 \times 10^3 \text{ N} = 211$ kN

Checking Equation 3.10(b)

$T_r + V_r = (66 \times 10^3) + (0.60 \times 0.90 \times 551 \text{ mm}^2 \times 450 \text{ MPa})$

$\qquad = (66 \times 10^3 \text{ N}) + (134 \times 10^3 \text{ N}) = 200 \times 10^3 \text{ N} = 200$ kN

It is also possible that the angles fail in shear. This is a similar failure mode to the one just checked, except that there is no longer a tension contribution. Since only the shear area contributes to the capacity, the calculations require only the net shear area.

$A_{nv} = [\,(60 + 2 \times 34) \text{ mm} - 2 \times (20 + 2 + 2) \text{ mm}\,] \times 9.5 \text{ mm} = 760 \text{ mm}^2$

Using the second part of Equation 3.10(b)

$$V_r = (0.60 \times 0.90 \times 760 \text{ mm}^2 \times 450 \text{ MPa}) = 185 \times 10^3 \text{ N} = 185 \text{ kN}$$

The capacity of one angle in combined tension and shear is 185 kN, which is in excess of the factored load that must be carried (180 kN for the pair of angles).

In principle, the combined tension plus shear block failure could also take place in the web of the beam, as shown in Figure 9.17. Tests and analysis [9.20] of this type of connection show that it is unlikely to take place, however, unless the top flange has been cut back (coped) for clearance purposes. For the coped beam case, this failure mode could be a governing condition. Figure 9.18 shows the tension plus shear block failure mode for a coped beam.

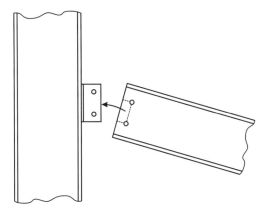

Figure 9.17 – Tear-Out of Web Material

To check the capacity of a coped beam, Clause 13.11(b) of the Standard should be used. The rules given there are similar to Equation 3.10, except that the tensile strength attainable on the net section is reduced. This is done because the tensile stress is not uniform across the length of the net section.

In order that the connection fulfils the design assumption implied for the beam (i.e., simply supported), the detail should provide good rotational capability. In this example, this means primarily that the web framing angles should be kept as short as practicable. If the beam is deep, the angles should be placed toward the top so as to provide lateral support for the compression flange. The need for considering the eccentricity of load on the fasteners should also be kept in mind. This is discussed in the next section.

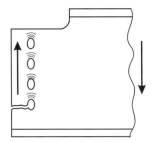

Figure 9.18 – Tension Shear Block Failure of a Coped Beam

9.10 Eccentrically Loaded Connections

Ideally, the line of action of a force should pass through the centroid of the fastening elements. This is not always possible, however, and eccentric forces sometimes have to be accommodated. Typical examples of this type are shown in Figure 9.19.

At one time, the way of treating such connections was to assume that the fastener response to load is elastic. The fastener stresses can then be computed as the vector sum of direct shear stresses and shearing stresses due to torsion. Figures 9.4 and 9.8 show very clearly that neither high-strength bolts nor fillet welds have any appreciable portion over which the relationship between load and deformation can be idealized as elastic. In addition, it is apparent also that the direction of the force on an element of weld is of significance. As a result of an appreciation of these factors, it is recognized that the ultimate strength of eccentrically loaded connections is the proper basis for design.

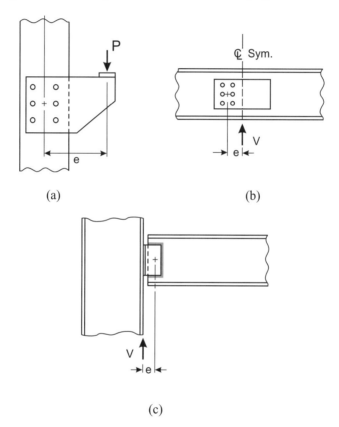

(a)   (b)

(c)

Figure 9.19 – Eccentrically Loaded Connections

The procedure that is used [9.9] starts by assuming some location for the instantaneous center of rotation of the fastener group. (The displacements of a system like that shown in Figure 9.19 are a translation and a rotation of the fastener group. This can be reduced to a rotation-only condition about a point called the instantaneous centre of rotation.) At the time the ultimate load is reached, the fastener furthest from the instantaneous centre will just reach its failure load and deformation. These failure load and deformation conditions have been established by tests on representative numbers of bolts and short lengths of fillet weld. The deformations of the other fasteners are assumed

303

to be proportional to their distance from the instantaneous centre and their corresponding loads can be obtained from load vs. deformation relationships like those in Figures 9.4 and 9.8(b). (It should be noted that a length of weld is broken up into a series of elemental lengths, each of which is then treated like an individual fastener.) A check of the equations of equilibrium will reveal whether or not the trial location of the instantaneous centre of rotation was the correct one.

If these equations are not satisfied, a new location of the instantaneous centre is chosen and the process is repeated.

Example 9.4

Given

Determine the ultimate resistance of the three-bolt eccentrically loaded connection shown in Figure 9.20. The bolts are M22 A325M and they are loaded in double shear. The load versus deformation response will be assumed to be that in Figure 9.8(b), where the maximum deformation is 4.8 mm and the corresponding stress is 592 MPa.

Solution

A trial location of the instantaneous centre is chosen as shown. For bolts 1 and 3, the maximum force will be

$$P_1 = P_3 = 592 \text{ MPa} \times 380 \text{ mm}^2 \times 2 \text{ shear planes}$$
$$= 450 \times 10^3 \text{ N} = 450 \text{ kN}$$

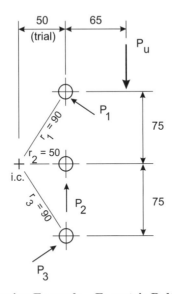

Figure 9.20 – Design Example – Eccentric Bolted Connections

At bolt 2, the amount of deformation will be

$$\Delta_2 = \frac{r_2}{r_1} \times \Delta_1 = \frac{50 \text{ mm}}{90 \text{ mm}} \times 4.8 \text{ mm} = 2.7 \text{ mm}$$

304

From Fig. 9.7(b), it is estimated that the stress corresponding to this deformation is 517 MPa.

Force in bolt 2:

$$P_2 = 517 \text{ MPa} \times 380 \text{ mm}^2 \times 2 \text{ shear planes} = 393 \times 10^3 \text{ N} = 393 \text{ kN}$$

The vertical components of these bolt forces are

Bolts 1 and 3: $P_v = (50/90) \times 450 \text{ kN} = 250 \text{ kN (each)}$

Bolt 2: $P_v = P_2 = 393 \text{ kN}$

and then— $\Sigma F_v = P_u = (250 \text{ kN} \times 2) + 393 \text{ kN} = 893 \text{ kN}$

Summing moments about the instantaneous center—

Counterclockwise: $(450 \text{ kN} \times 90 \text{ mm}) \times 2 + 393 \text{ kN} \times 50 \text{ mm} = 100.6 \times 10^3 \text{ kN} \cdot \text{mm}$

Clockwise: $893 \text{ kN} \times (50 \text{ mm} + 65 \text{ mm}) = 102.7 \times 10^3 \text{ kN} \cdot \text{mm}$

This will be taken as close enough agreement and, finally, $P_u = 893 \text{ kN}$

The method of solution described above is obviously not suitable for direct design purposes. Mathematical expressions are available, however, that describe the results to a reasonable degree of accuracy [9.21, 9.22].

The problem of eccentrically loaded connections can also be solved with the aid of the CISC Handbook [9.23], where tables have been prepared for a large number of cases of both welded and bolted connections. Although the same method is used by the Handbook as has been presented here, the Handbook relates the strength to that tabulated for a single bolt in a relatively long line of fasteners (less than, but close to, 1300 mm). Thus, the individual fastener strength is taken somewhat more conservatively than that used here. Of course, the solution in the Handbook also includes the resistance factor, ϕ.

9.11   Connections Carrying Shear, Thrust, and Moment

Connections occurring at the corners of rigid frames or at the intersections of beams and columns that are to be rigidly framed must be able to transfer all three possible components of force. It is obvious that the connection must be of adequate strength to accomplish this. It must also provide adequate rotation capacity, however, and both of these requirements must be met with economy in mind. Local elements of the connection must also be proportioned carefully so that their premature failure will not result in a lowering of overall connection strength.

Except in the case of prefabricated buildings, rigid frame connections are almost always welded. This gives a clean and compact connection in a region that tends to be otherwise crowded by the intersection of the main framing members as well as by the purlins and bracing. If splices are necessary, they should be made away from this region and at a location of lower shear and moment.

A straight corner connection formed by the intersection of two rolled shapes is shown in Figure 9.21(a). One arrangement is to run the beam through the connection, as shown, and provide extensions of the column flanges.

In proportioning the connection, it is usual to assume that the bending moment and thrust are carried entirely by the flanges and the shear is carried entirely by the web [9.24]. The force system resulting from application of these assumptions is shown in Figure 9.21(b). The value of the force in the beam flange, which is transferred into the web as a shear, is taken as

$$V_b = \frac{M}{d_b} \tag{9.13}$$

The moment to be used (M) is that resulting from the application of the factored loads to the structure.

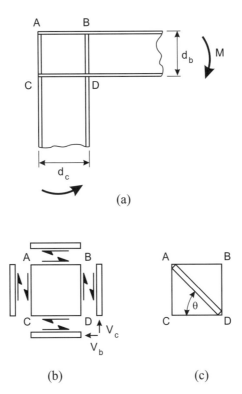

(a)

(b)   (c)

Figure 9.21 – Connection Carrying Shear, Thrust and Moment

If the beam has been extended into the connection as shown, the portions A–B and C–D will be adequate in the connection given that they were adequate in the beam. Nominally, the stress in the connection portion will be a little higher and the flange buckling strength a little lower because of the assumption that all the force is taken by the flanges, but this can be disregarded. Portion A–C is made either as a continuation of the column flange or as an equivalent plate groove welded to the column. Member B–D can be made as a partial or full-depth stiffener. It must transfer the compressive force from the column flange into the beam web.

Equating the shear resistance of the web along A–B (thickness w) to the applied shear force and assuming that the yield in shear is $\tau_y = F_y / \sqrt{3}$

$$d_c \ w \ \frac{F_y}{\sqrt{3}} = \frac{M}{d_b}$$

and solving for the web thickness, $w = \dfrac{\sqrt{3} \ M}{d_c \ d_b \ f_y}$

Applying the resistance factor, and writing as a requirement, this becomes

$$w \geq \frac{\sqrt{3} \ M}{\phi \ d_c \ d_b \ f_y} = \frac{1.9 \ M}{d_b \ d_c \ F_y} \tag{9.14}$$

If the web of the beam supplied is not at least equal to the requirement given by Equation 9.14, doubler plates or a diagonal stiffener can be provided. The selection of a new section size may also be economical. The diagonal stiffener, as shown in Figure 9.21(c), is the usual choice.

The stiffener is proportioned by first considering the equilibrium conditions at point A. The total force to be transmitted (V_b) is assumed to be shared by the stiffener and the web as

$$V_b = \frac{M}{d_b} = d_c \ w \ \frac{F_y}{\sqrt{3}} + F_y \ A_{st} \ \cos \theta \tag{9.15}$$

where A_{st} is the total stiffener area required. Solving for this quantity, assuming that all parts have the same yield strength, and introducing the resistance factor—

$$A_{st} = \frac{1}{\phi \ F_y \ \cos \theta} \left(\frac{M}{d_b} - \frac{\phi \ F_y \ w \ d_c}{\sqrt{3}} \right) \tag{9.16}$$

Since this element is acting under a compressive load, the ratio of its width to thickness (b/t) should be selected so as to avoid the possibility of premature local buckling. (This requirement is discussed in Chapter 4.)

For the corner arrangement that has been discussed, groove welds could be used at the junction of the column flanges and the lower flange of the beam. Fillet welds can be used at the other locations to transfer the necessary forces. The resulting fillet weld at the column web to beam flange may be rather large, however, and a groove weld is often used at this location as well. Details of the weld design are given in Example 9.4.

Example 9.5

Given

Design the corner connection between a column and a beam, both of which are W410×60 sections of G40.21 350W steel ($F_y = 350$ MPa). Use E49xx electrodes. (The notation of Figure 9.21 will be followed and details of the welding selected will be shown in Figure 9.22.) The beam is to act as a Class 2 section.

Solution

The connection will be designed to carry the factored moment on the section, which has been determined to be 375 kN · m. The effects of the axial thrust and shear on the connection web can be neglected. These are small and are of the opposite sign to shears produced by the moment. The factored shear in the column, needed for the design of the weld between the column web and beam flange, is 680 kN.

The web thickness required, using Equation 9.14 is

$$w = \frac{1.9 \times 375 \times 10^6 \ \text{N} \cdot \text{mm}}{407 \ \text{mm} \times 407 \ \text{mm} \times 350 \ \text{MPa}} = 12.3 \ \text{mm}$$

The web thickness provided by a W410×60 is only 7.7 mm. Therefore, diagonal stiffeners (AD) will be provided and, from Equation 9.16

$$A_{st} = \frac{1}{0.90 \times 350 \times 0.707} \left(\frac{375 \times 10^6}{407} - \frac{0.90 \times 350 \times 7.7 \times 407}{\sqrt{3}} \right) = 1578 \ \text{mm}^2$$

Provide 789 mm^2 in each of two stiffeners, one on each side of the beam web.

Try 10 mm × 80 mm plates, area = 800 mm^2 each, F_y = 350 MPa.

Allowable $\dfrac{b}{t} \leq \dfrac{170}{\sqrt{F_y}} = \dfrac{170}{\sqrt{350}} = 9.1$

Actual b/t = 8.0   (Satisfactory)

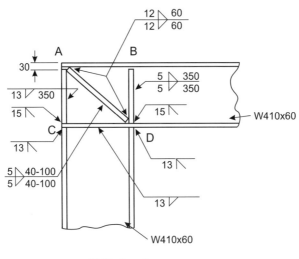

Welds shown for near
side; far side same.

Figure 9.22 – Design Example – Corner Connection

Stiffeners at A–C and B–D: Provide 15 mm × 80 mm plates on each side of beam web. This provides the same area (approximately) as the column flanges. A full-depth stiffener will be used at A–C. At B–D, the stiffener can be either full-depth as shown or based upon the weld length required.

Checking, b/t = 80/15 = 5.3 $\ll$ 9.1 (Satisfactory)

Welds:

Column flanges to beam flange—use complete joint penetration groove welds to develop the full strength of the column flanges.

Column web to beam flange—since it has been assumed that the column flanges carry all the moment in that member, the web will be assumed to carry all the shear (680 kN in this case). For E49xx electrodes, the strength of the weld metal for a 1 mm leg size and for $\theta = 0°$ (weld axis and force vector parallel) is

$$V_r = 0.67 \, \phi_w \, A_w \, X_u$$
$$= 0.67 \times 0.67 \times (1 \text{ mm} \times 0.707) \times 490 \text{ MPa}$$
$$= 156 \text{ N/mm} = 0.156 \text{ kN/mm}$$

The strength of the base metal is

$$V_r = 0.67 \, \phi_w \, A_m \, F_u$$
$$= 0.67 \times 0.67 \times 1 \text{ mm} \times 450 \text{ MPa}$$
$$= 202 \text{ N/mm} = 0.202 \text{ kN/mm}$$

The strength of the weld metal governs. The weld length available is $2 \times 348 = 696$ mm. (The flat portion of the web of a W410 $\times$ 60, tabulated as "T" in the CISC Handbook, is 348 mm.)

$$\text{Leg size required} = \frac{680 \text{ kN}}{696 \text{ mm} \times 0.156 \text{ kN/mm}} = 6.3 \text{ mm}, \quad \text{say 8 mm}$$

Stiffeners—

The forces delivered by the column flanges at C and D by means of the complete joint penetration groove welds between these flanges and the lower beam flange must be transferred into the stiffeners A–C and B–D. This can be accomplished by means of complete joint penetration groove welds at C and D, as shown in Figure 9.22.

The forces now in the stiffeners must be transferred into the beam web, preferably by fillet welds placed along the length of the stiffeners. At either stiffener, this force is (approximately)—

$$F = \frac{375 \times 10^6 \text{ N} \cdot \text{mm}}{407 \text{ mm}} = 921 \times 10^3 \text{ N} = 921 \text{ kN}$$

Weld length available for both stiffeners at A–C $\approx 348 \times 2 = 696$ mm.

Leg size required (weld strength as calculated for column web to beam flange)

$$= \frac{921 \text{ kN}}{696 \text{ mm} \times 0.156 \text{ kN/mm}} = 8.5 \text{ mm}, \quad \text{say, 10 mm}$$

Stiffener B–D must carry the difference between the flange force (921 kN) and the resistance provided by the beam web. The latter is given by Equation 9.18 (development and explanation to follow) as

$$B_r = \phi_{bi} \, w_c \, (t_b + 10t_c) \, F_{yc}$$

$$B_r = 0.80 \times 7.7 \text{ mm} (12.8 + (10 \times 12.8)) \text{ mm} \times 350 \text{ MPa} = 304 \times 10^3 \text{ N} = 304 \text{ kN}$$

Thus, the force in the stiffener is $921 - 304 = 617$ kN.

If stiffener BD is full depth, the length available for welding is 4×348 mm $= 1392$ mm.

$$\text{Leg size required} = \frac{617 \text{ kN}}{1392 \text{ mm} \times 0.156 \text{ kN/mm}} = 2.8 \text{ mm}$$

For convenience, a full-depth stiffener will be used with a 5 mm weld, as shown in Figure 9.22.

Neither stiffener A–C nor B–D needs to extend to meet the underside of the top flange of the beam because all of the stiffener force has already been transferred into the beam web. In this example, both stiffeners will be stopped short by 30 mm, the value of k (CISC Handbook) identifying the location of the start of the web-to-flange fillet. Fitting the stiffeners to the underside of the beam flange is both expensive and unnecessary.

In developing the requirement for the area of steel required for a diagonal stiffener (Equation 9.16), it was assumed that the entire force in the stiffener was applied at its ends. As such, the welding requirement would be to provide sufficient weld at one end of the stiffener to transfer the force from the beam flange into the stiffener and an identical amount at the far end of the same stiffener to take it out. This idealized force transfer is almost certainly not fulfilled, and a conservative solution is to provide sufficient weld at the ends to transfer the force as described above, but also to provide enough weld along the length of the stiffener to transfer that same force into or out of the beam web. This conservative approach will be used in this example.

Using the actual stiffener area, the force in each stiffener at A–D can be as large as

$$F = 800 \text{ mm}^2 \times 350 \text{ MPa} = 280 \times 10^3 \text{ N} = 280 \text{ kN}$$

Length available for welding along the 80 mm wide stiffener plate is $80 - 20 = 60$ mm. (The 20 mm accounts for the flange-to-web fillet at this location; see CISC Handbook.) Thus, at the end of one stiffener, the length available for welding is $2 \times 60 = 120$ mm.

$$\text{Leg size required} = \frac{280 \text{ kN}}{0.156 \text{ kN/mm} \times 120 \text{ mm}} = 15.0 \text{ mm}$$

This is a large fillet weld and it has to be placed into a confined space. The advantage provided by Equation 9.12(b) for a weld transverse to the direction of load will be invoked. For $\theta = 90°$, the increase is a factor of 1.5. Thus, the strength used in the calculation above can be increased from 0.156 kN/mm to 0.234 kN/mm. This makes the base metal strength the governing value at 0.202 kN/mm. Recalculation of the leg size required gives $15.0 \times 0.156/0.202 = 11.6$ mm. Use 12 mm.

Finally, transferring the 280 kN force from either end of stiffener A–D into the beam web can be done by means of a fillet weld along its length of approximately 490 mm. Thus, the length available for welding along the sides of a single stiffener at A–D is $2 \times 490 = 980$ mm. Using a continuous weld of even the smallest permissible size, 5 mm, results in a great deal more capacity than required. Therefore, an intermittent fillet weld of 5 mm leg size will be tried, using the minimum permissible weld length of 40 mm. (CSA W59 should be consulted for minimum fillet weld lengths.) A centre-to-centre spacing of 100 mm will meet the requirements of S16 Clause 19.1.3(b) and will provide a resistance of

$$V_r = \frac{0.156 \text{ kN} \times 5 \text{ mm} \times 40 \text{ mm}}{100 \text{ mm}} = 0.312 \text{ kN/mm}$$

The load to be transferred is

$$V = \frac{280 \text{ kN}}{980 \text{ mm}} = 0.286 \text{ kN/mm} \qquad \text{(Satisfactory)}$$

Use an intermittent fillet weld arrangement as shown in Figure 9.22.

The only other type of connection required to carry all three force components that will be discussed is the interior type connection shown in Figure 9.23. An exaggerated view of the deformed connection (Figure 9.24) shows the two possible failure modes; (a) failure of the column web as the beam flange delivers its compressive load, (b) exhaustion of the ductility of the groove weld in the stiff region at the beam tension flange.

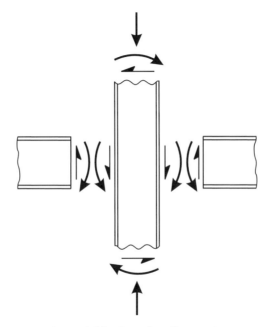

Figure 9.23 – Interior Connection

On the compression side, it will be assumed that the force from the beam flange can be treated as a concentrated load. The design rule for this case was described in Section 5.12. The total factored force from the flange must be less than or equal to the factored web resistance at this point (Equation 5.27(a)). This can be expressed as

$$\frac{M_f}{d_b} \leq B_r \quad \text{or,} \quad \frac{M_f}{d_b} \leq \phi_{bi} \, w_c \, (t_b + 10 t_c) \, F_{yc} \tag{9.17}$$

Some adjustments to the notation have been made as compared with Equation 5.27(a). In the latter, the symbol N is used to represent the length of the bearing plate. In the problem under discussion now, this is simply the thickness of the beam flange, t_b. The web thickness w and the flange thickness t have been expressed more specifically in Equation 9.17 as w_c, and t_c, respectively, and the yield strength has been identified specifically as that of the column, F_{yc}. The resistance factor, ϕ_{bi}, is to be taken as 0.80. If Equation 9.17 is not satisfied, stiffeners are required opposite the beam compression flange.

The requirement given by Equation 9.17 is found in Clause 21.3 of the S16 Standard. In addition, a second requirement is given that pertains when the columns has a Class 3 or 4 web. Since Class 3 or 4 sections are rarely used as columns, that information will not be given here. Consult the Standard if the need arises.

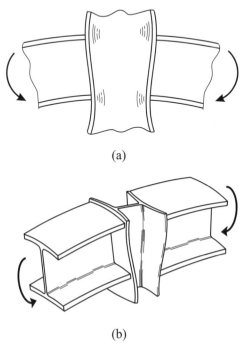

(a)

(b)

Figure 9.24 – Interior Connection — Failure Modes

On a semi-empirical basis [9.24], it has been established that a conservative requirement for stiffeners opposite the beam tension flange is given by

$$T_r = 7\,\phi\,t_c^2\,F_{yc} \geq M_f/d_b \tag{9.18}$$

If Equation 9.18 is not satisfied, stiffeners are required in the column web opposite the tension flange of the beam. From equilibrium considerations, the force that must be transmitted by the stiffener is

$$F_{st} = (M_f/d_b) - B_r \tag{9.19a}$$

$$\text{or,} \quad F_{st} = (M_f/d_b) - T_r \tag{9.19b}$$

A check on the stability of the stiffener chosen should also be made. Horizontally placed stiffeners are usual and they should be used in pairs, one on each side of the column web.

As was the case in the corner connection, the web formed by the intersection of the beams and column must be checked here against excessive shear stress (see Clause 21.3

of S16). The situation is usually less critical than that occurring at a corner because only the unbalanced moment across any given direction of the connection must be carried into the web as a shear force. The direct column or beam shears will again be neglected since they act opposite to shears produced by the flange forces.

Beams of equal depth are shown framing into a column in Figure 9.25. Considering the equilibrium requirements at the top of the panel formed by the intersection, it is seen that

$$V = \frac{M_1 - M_2}{d_b} \tag{9.20}$$

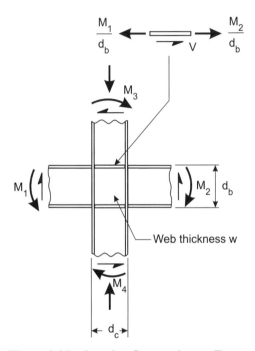

Figure 9.25 – Interior Connection — Forces

In terms of shear stress, and considering the algebraic difference of the factored moments, this can be written as

$$\tau = \frac{\Delta M_f}{d_b \, d_c \, w} \tag{9.21}$$

Setting this equal to the shear yield stress $\left(F_{yc} / \sqrt{3} \right)$, introducing the resistance factor, and solving for the column web thickness w,

$$w = \frac{1.9 \, \Delta M_f}{d_b \, d_c \, F_y} \tag{9.22}$$

The same quantity must also be examined for shears resulting from the column moments. Since the change in moments on opposite sides of the connection will be the only variable in the analysis, this can be examined first in order to establish the governing case. If the actual web thickness is less than that described by Equation 9.22, a diagonal stiffener or doubler plates would be provided, as was discussed for corner connections.

Example 9.6

Given

The connection of example 9.3 is now to be designed to transfer a bending moment of $150 \text{ kN} \cdot \text{m}$, causing compression at the bottom of the connection, in addition to the shear force of 180 kN for which the connection was designed in example 9.3.

The required geometric properties of the column sections are:

$d_c = 318 \text{ mm}$; $w_c = 13.1 \text{ mm}$; $t_c = 20.6 \text{ mm}$

The required geometric properties of the beam section are:

$d_b = 266 \text{ mm}$; $t_b = 20.6 \text{ mm}$

Solution

In example 9.3 the connection was designed to transfer the shear force from the beam to the column. This part of the design does not change when the connection is designed to carry both shear and moment. The transfer of moment between the beam and the column is achieved by connecting the beam flanges to the column flange, either by welding the beam flanges directly to the column flange, or by using moment plates. Both options will be illustrated here.

Alternative 1 – Welding beam flanges directly to the column

The forces transferred by the beam flanges to the column are determined using Equation 9.13:

$$V_b = \frac{M}{d_b} = \frac{150 \times 10^3 \text{ kN} \cdot \text{mm}}{266 \text{ mm}} = 564 \text{ kN}$$

Because there is only one beam connecting into the column, this force also corresponds to the shear force in the column panel zone. The column web thickness required to resist this shear force is obtained from Equation 9.14.

$$w_c \geq \frac{1.9 \, M}{d_b \, d_c \, F_y} = \frac{1.9 \times 50 \times 10^6 \text{ N} \cdot \text{mm}}{266 \text{ mm} \times 318 \text{ mm} \times 350 \text{ MPa}} = 3.2 \text{ mm}$$

The web thickness provided by a W310× 129 is 13.1 mm. The panel zone is therefore adequate. The bearing resistance of the column opposite to the beam compression flange is obtained from Equation 9.17.

$$B_r = \phi_{bi} \, w_c \, (t_b + 10t_c) F_{yc} = 0.80 \times 13.1 \times (13.0 + (10 \times 20.6)) \times 350$$
$$= 803 \times 10^3 \text{ N} = 803 \text{ kN}$$

This is larger than the flange force of 564 kN. The tension resistance of the flange opposite the beam tension flange can be obtained from Equation 9.18.

$$T_r = 7 \, \phi \, t_c^2 \, F_{yc} = 7 \times 0.9 \times 20.6^2 \times 350 = 936 \times 10^3 \text{ N} = 936 \text{ kN}$$

314

This is also larger than the flange force. No stiffeners are therefore required in the connection area.

The connection between the beam flanges and the column flange is design to transfer a force of 564 kN. This can be accomplished by welding the beam flanges directly to the column flange with fillet welds.

The strength per unit weld size of the base metal is given by Equation 9.11:

$$V_r = 0.67 \times 0.67 \times 1 \text{ mm} \times 1 \text{ mm} \times 450 \text{ MPa} = 202 \text{ N/mm/mm}$$

The strength of the weld itself is given by Equation 9.12(b):

$$V_s = 0.67 \times 0.67 \times (1 \text{ mm} \times 0.707) \times 490 \text{ MPa} \times (1 + 0.50\sin^{1.5} 90°)$$
$$= 233 \text{ N/mm/mm}$$

The strength of the transverse weld is therefore governed by the strength of the base metal ($V_r = 0.202 \text{ kN/mm/mm}$). The total weld length available if the flange is welded top and bottom is equal to 288 mm, namely, $2b - w$. The minimum fillet weld size required for transferring the beam flange force to the column flange is:

$$\text{weld size} = \frac{564 \text{ kN}}{288 \text{ mm} \times 0.202 \text{ kN/mm/mm}} = 9.7 \text{ mm}$$

Therefore, use a 10 mm fillet weld all around the flange. The minimum weld size, which is governed by the 20.6 mm column flange, is 8 mm. This is smaller than the required weld size. All this welding would be performed in the field as indicated in Figure 9.26(a). An alternative to the fillet weld all around the beams flanges is a complete penetration groove weld. In this case, a weld access hole would be cut in the beam web below the top flange in order to insert a backing bar to support the molten weld metal during welding. Similarly, a backing bar would be used for the bottom flange weld and a weld access hole is used to ensure a continuous weld over the full width of the flange. This weld detail is illustrated in Figure 9.26(b).

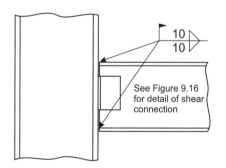

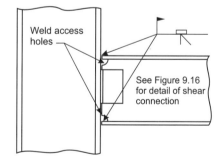

(a) Fillet welded flanges   (b) Full penetration groove welded flanges

Figure 9.26 – Beam–to–column moment connection

Alternative 2 – Use of moment plates shop welded to the column and field bolted to the beam flanges with A325 M22 bolts (see Figure 9.27). Drilled holes will be used.

The plate size required is based either on yielding of the gross section or rupture at the net section. From yielding of the gross section,

$$A_g = \frac{T_f}{\phi\, F_y} = \frac{564 \times 10^3 \text{ N}}{0.9 \times 300} = 2089 \text{ mm}^2$$

Based on rupture at the net section,

$$A_n = \frac{T_f}{0.85\, \phi\, F_u} = \frac{564 \times 10^3 \text{ N}}{0.85 \times 0.9 \times 450} = 1638 \text{ mm}^2$$

Select a 150×16 mm plate ($A_g = 2400$ mm^2; $A_n = 1632$ mm^2)

The number of bolts required is based either on bearing or bolt shear capacity.

From Equation 9.5 and using the flange thickness of a W250x45,

$$B_r = 3\, \phi_{br}\, t\, d\, n\, F_u = 3 \times 0.67 \times 13 \text{ mm} \times 22 \text{ mm} \times 1 \text{ bolt} \times 450 \text{ MPa} = 259 \text{ kN / bolt}$$

Assuming that the bolt threads will be intercepted by the shear plane, the shear resistance given by Equation (9.6) is reduced by 30%, resulting in

$$V_r = 0.7 \times 0.60\, \phi_b\, n\, m\, A_b\, F_u$$
$$= 0.7 \times 0.60 \times 0.80 \times 1 \text{ bolt} \times 1 \text{ shear plane} \times 380 \text{ mm}^2 \times 825 \text{ MPa} = 105 \text{ kN / bolt}$$

The shear capacity of the bolts governs and at least 5.4 bolts are required (564 kN/105 kN per bolt). Six bolts will be used for each of the top and the bottom flanges.

The moment plates will be attached to the column using full penetration groove welds as shown in Figure 9.27. Clause 22.3 of S6-01 is used to determine the bolted joint configuration. From these provisions, bolt spacing is taken as 60 mm, the end and edge distances are taken as 40 and 45 mm, respectively.

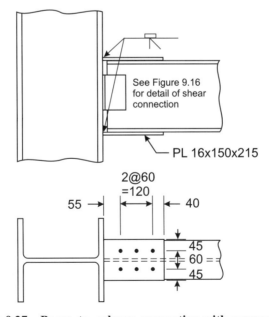

Figure 9.27 – Beam–to–column connection with moment plates

9.12   Beam Bearing Plates, Column Base Plates

The compressive strength of structural steel is substantially greater than the corresponding values in the masonry or reinforced concrete upon which a beam or column may rest. An intermediate component is usually required to "step-down" the high compressive stresses in the steel to a value that is acceptable for the concrete or masonry. This intermediate stage is performed by a bearing plate in the case of beams (Figure 9.28) or by a base plate in the case of columns (Figure 9.29). The same function is carried out by a footing as it spreads out a load over a material of relatively low bearing capacity, the soil.

In the case of the beam bearing plate, it is assumed that the contact stress between the plate and the masonry is uniformly distributed and that the plate bends only about an axis parallel to the length of the beam. The face of bending is taken as the intersection of a 45 degree line from the web-to-fillet junction down to the extremity of the beam flange, a distance k (Figure 9.28).

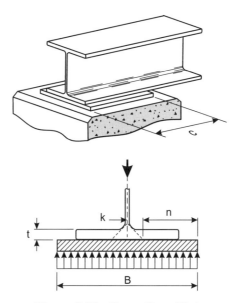

Figure 9.28 – Beam Base Plate

The plate is assumed to act as a cantilever between its free edge and this line. The designer must ensure that (a) sufficient plate area is provided such that the bearing stress on the masonry is within the permissible value for that material; (b) the plate is thick enough to provide the necessary bending resistance. Since there is no possibility here of lateral buckling or a local failure, the resisting bending moment can be taken as the value prescribed for Class 1 and 2 sections (Clause 13.5(a) of S16).

Example 9.7

Given

A W460× 82 beam is to be set on a 150 mm wide concrete wall. Choose a suitable bearing plate of G40.21 300W steel (F_y = 300 MPa) for a factored beam reaction of

345 kN and a permissible bearing stress in the concrete of 12.0 MPa. (CSA–A23.3–04 [9.25] can be consulted for details as to how to obtain permissible bearing stresses.)

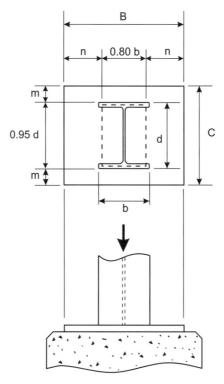

Figure 9.29 – Column Base Plate — Axial Load

Solution

Bearing area required $= \dfrac{345 \times 10^3 \text{ N}}{12.0 \text{ MPa}} = 28\ 750 \text{ mm}^2$

Assuming a 125 mm usable width of wall,

$B = \dfrac{28\ 750 \text{ mm}^2}{125 \text{ mm}} = 230 \text{ mm}$

The W460× 82 has a flange width of 191 mm and a dimension $k = 33$ mm.

The bending length is therefore $n = 230/2 - 33 = 82$ mm , and considering a strip of plate 1 mm wide,

$M_{max} = (12.0 \text{ N/mm})(82 \text{ mm} \times 82 \text{ mm})\ 1/2 = 40\ 344 \text{ N} \cdot \text{mm}$

The resistance of a section of plate 1 mm wide and of thickness t (i.e., ϕM_p) is

$M_r = \dfrac{\phi F_y t^2}{4}$

Using $F_y = 300$ MPa and $\phi = 0.90$ and equating this to the applied factored moment, solve for the required thickness as

$$t = \sqrt{\frac{4 \times 40\ 344}{0.90 \times 300}} = 24.4 \text{ mm} \qquad \text{Use 25 mm.}$$

In order to minimize deflections, it is also considered desirable that the thickness should be greater than about 1/5 of the amount by which the base plate extends beyond the beam flange. In this case, the projection is very small and the requirement will not be checked.

Use a 125 mm $\times$ 25 mm plate $\times$ 230 mm.

A column base plate that is distributing the load from an axially loaded column is treated in substantially the same way as the beam base plate just discussed. It is obvious from Figure 9.29 that the bending of the plate is now not restricted to one direction, however. It is probably not economically worthwhile to attempt any rigorous analysis and the usual procedure it to consider the bending as occurring independently about either principal axis of the column. The details of the design are illustrated in the example following.

Example 9.8

Given

An axially loaded column carries a factored load of 4110 kN onto a concrete footing that is capable of a bearing pressure of 15.0 MPa. The column section used is a W310$\times$143. Select a suitable base plate of G40.21–M 300W steel.

Solution

$$\text{Bearing area required} = \frac{4110 \times 10^3 \text{ N}}{15.0 \text{ MPa}} = 274\ 000 \text{ mm}^2$$

Try C = 560 mm, B = 500 mm. (Notation as in Figure 9.29).

$$\text{Area provided} = 560 \text{ mm} \times 500 \text{ mm} = 280\ 000 \text{ mm}^2 \qquad\qquad \text{(Satisfactory)}$$

$$\text{Actual bearing stress } f_p = \frac{4110 \times 10^3 \text{N}}{280\ 000 \text{ mm}^2} = 14.7 \text{ MPa}$$

Other dimensions—

$$0.95 \text{ d} = 0.95 \times 323 \text{ mm} = 307 \text{ mm}$$

$$m = \frac{560 - 307}{2} = 127 \text{ mm}$$

$$0.80 \text{ b} = 0.80 \times 309 \text{ mm} = 247 \text{ mm}$$

$$n = \frac{500 - 247}{2} = 126 \text{ mm}$$

(The dimensions m and n should be kept nearly equal)

The factored moment on the plate will be that of a cantilever either m or n long acting under the 14.7 MPa loading. In this example, the dimension m is the larger and, considering a strip of plate 1 mm wide—

$$M_{max} = (14.7 \text{ N/mm})(127 \text{ mm} \times 127 \text{ mm}) \ 1/2 = 118 \ 550 \ N \cdot mm$$

The resistance of the plate, as for the beam bearing plate, can be taken as

$$M_r = \frac{\phi \ F_y t^2}{4}$$

Equating these two expressions and using the appropriate values of ϕ and F_y,

$$t = \sqrt{\frac{4 \times 118 \ 550}{0.90 \times 300}} = 41.9 \text{ mm}$$

Use a 500 mm × 40 mm plate × 560 mm .

Strictly speaking, a base plate for an axially loaded column would not require any anchor rods because neither moment nor a horizontal force is present. However, in all practical situations, anchor rods would be provided to assist in locating the column, to provide a means of leveling the base plate (using nuts on threaded rods), and to take care of small values of horizontal force and moment that may occur. The column would probably be shipped with the base plate attached (using a minimum size fillet weld), although many different arrangements are possible.

Column bases required to transfer both axial load and moment will only be discussed here. If the combination of axial load and moment produces a condition wherein compression is maintained over the entire base, it may be assumed that the anchor rods are not effective in transmitting axial forces, either tensile or compressive. McGuire [9.26] suggests that the actual stress distribution in this case, Figure 9.30(a), be replaced by the idealization shown in Figure 9.30(b) for values of $e \leq B/6$. The design can then be carried out on the basis of the procedures developed for base plates under axial load only.

If the combination of the factored axial load and moment does not produce compression over the entire base, then the anchor rods must provide a tensile axial force as shown in Figure 9.30(c). Starting with trial values of the plate width B, the location of the anchor rods d, and their area A, the values of the unknown width of the stress block a and the resisting moment provided by the tensile and compressive forces can be found using the equations of equilibrium. Assuming that the actual bearing stress in the concrete is found to be within the permissible limit, the thickness required for the baseplate can be determined as has been described previously. The trial size and location of the anchor rods can now be checked. Clause 25 of S16 should be consulted for assistance in the proportioning of the anchor rods. Because of the number of variables present, it should be evident that several trials will usually be necessary to produce a satisfactory design.

In Canadian practice, the permissible bearing stress in the concrete should follow the requirements of CSA–A23.3–04 [9.25]. Thus, in Figures 9.30(b) and (c) the stress in the concrete is either $0.85 \ \phi_c \ f'_c$ or an increased value that depends on the ratio of loaded area to footing area.

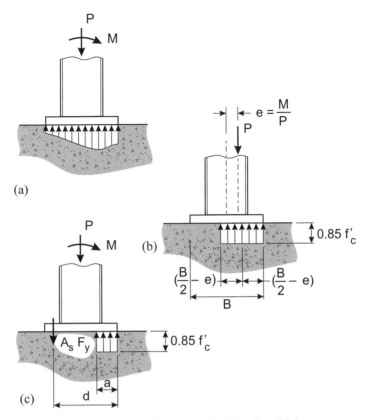

Figure 9.30 – Base Plate — Axial Load and Moment

Connections at the base of the roof arches for the Pearson International Airport

(Photo courtesy of Halcrow Yolles)

References

9.1   Fisher, J.W., and Yoshida, N., "Large Bolted and Riveted Shingle Splices," Journal of the Structural Division, ASCE, Vol. 96, No. ST9, Sept., 1970.

9.2   Standard Specification for Carbon Steel Bolts and Studs, 60 000 psi Tensile Strength, ASTM A307–04.

9.3   Standard Specification for Structural Bolts, Steel, Heat-Treated, 120/105 ksi Minimum Tensile Strength, ASTM A325–04b.

9.4   Standard Specification for Heat-Treated Steel Structural Bolts, 150 ksi Minimum Tensile Strength, ASTM A490–04a.

9.5   Standard Specification for High-Strength Bolts for Structural Steel Joints [Metric], ASTM A325M-05.

9.6   Standard Specification for High-Strength Steel Bolts, Classes 10.9 and 10.9.3, For Structural Steel Joints [Metric], ASTM A490M-04a.

9.7   Specification for Structural Joints Using ASTM A325 or A490 Bolts, Research Council on Structural Connections, 2004.

9.8   Canadian Standards Association, CAN/CSA–S16–01, "Limit States Design of Steel Structures," Toronto, Ontario, 2001.

9.9   Kulak, G.L., Fisher, J.W., and Struik, J.H.A., "Guide to Design Criteria for Bolted and Riveted Joints," Second Edition, John Wiley and Sons, New York, 1987. (free download available through the Research Council on Structural Connections at http://www.boltcouncil.org/guide1.htm)

9.10 Kulak, G.L., "High Strength Bolting for Canadian Engineers," Canadian Institute of Steel Construction, Willowdale, Ontario, 2005.

9.11 ASTM F959–06, Standard Specification for Compressible-Washer-Type Direct Tension Indicators for Use with Structural Fasteners, American Society for Testing and Materials, West Conshohocken, Pennsylvania, USA.

9.12 ASTM F1852-05, Standard Specification for "Twist Off" Type Tension Control Structural Bolt/Nut/Washer Assemblies, Steel, Heat Treated, 120/105 ksi Minimum Tensile Strength, American Society for Testing and Materials, West Conshohocken, Pennsylvania, USA.

9.13 Canadian Standards Association, CSA–W48–06, "Filler Metals and Allied Materials for Metal Arc Welding," Toronto, Ontario, 2001.

9.14 Gooderham Centre for Industrial Learning, "Welding for Design Engineers," The Canadian Welding Bureau, Mississauga, Ontario, 2005.

9.15 Patchett, B. M. and Bringas, J. E., "Metals Blue Book, Welding Filler Metals," Fourth Edition, CASTI Publishing Inc., Edmonton, Alberta, 2003.

9.16 Canadian Standards Association, CSA–W59–03, "Welded Steel Construction (Metal-Arc Welding)," Toronto, Ontario, 2003.

9.17 Butler, L.J., and Kulak, G.L., "Strength of Fillet Welds as a Function of Direction of Load," Welding Journal, Welding Research Council, Vol. 36, No. 5, May, 1971.

9.18   Fisher, J.W., and Beedle, L.S., "Criteria for Designing Bearing-Type Bolted Joints," Journal of the Structural Division, ASCE, Vol. 94, No. ST10, October, 1968.

9.19   Fisher, J.W., Galambos, T.V., Kulak, G.L., and Ravindra, M.K., "Load and Resistance Factor Design Criteria for Connectors," Journal of the Structural Division, ASCE, Vol. 104, No. ST9, September, 1978.

9.20   Birkemoe, P.C., and Gilmor, M.I., "Behavior of Bearing Critical Double-Angle Beam Connections," AISC Engineering Journal, Vol. 15, No. 4, 1978.

9.21   Crawford, S.F., and Kulak, G.L., "Eccentrically Loaded Bolted Connections," Journal of the Structural Division, ASCE, Vol. 97, No. ST3, March, 1971.

9.22   Butler, L.J., Pal, S., and Kulak, G.L., "Eccentrically Loaded Welded Connections," Journal of the Structural Division, ASCE, Vol. 98, No. ST5, May, 1972.

9.23   Canadian Institute of Steel Construction, "Handbook of Steel Construction," Ninth Edition, Toronto, Ontario, 2006.

9.24   Plastic Design in Steel, ASCE Manuals and Reports on Engineering Practice No. 41, Second Edition, 1971.

9.25   Canadian Standards Association, CSA–A23.3–04, "Design of Concrete Structures," Toronto, Ontario, 2004.

9.26   McGuire, W., "Steel Structures," Prentice-Hall, 1968.

CHAPTER 10

BUILDING DESIGN

10.1 Introduction

The previous chapters have described the design process for individual members and connections. In the selection of the individual elements in a structure, the applied forces are known and the design procedure consists of selecting trial member sizes and then checking the trial members for compliance with the appropriate requirements of a design standard, in this case, S16–01.

The overall design process is much less definite. In a very simple situation the floor area requirements and perhaps the height restrictions for the structure will be specified; the column arrangement may also be specified by the architect, whereas the general framing scheme is left to the discretion of the designer. In general, the structural designer would have to select a gravity load resisting system and a lateral load resisting system that is both economical and acceptable from an architectural point of view. The structural designer must also interpret the requirements of the National Building Code (NBC) of Canada [10.1] for the specific project, and thus determine the loads for which the structure will be designed, as well as the approximations to be made in the analysis of the structure. Only after these decisions have been taken and the various analyses performed does the process of member selection take place. If the structure is statically indeterminate, then the process of structure analysis and member sizes selection is an iterative one.

In this chapter, the design procedure is illustrated using a single storey rectangular building [10.2] located in Ottawa, Ontario. This simple building has been selected to illustrate the design process. Other building types would challenge the designer in different ways. For example, in a multi-storey building the lateral load and stability effects become more important, while in a heavy industrial structure loads due to cranes may govern the design of many structural elements. Figure 10.1 shows the framing scheme for a light industrial building, 62.5 m × 37.5 m in plan and 6 m high. The bay sizes, 12.5 m × 12.5 m, have been established by functional requirements.

The roof is assumed to consist of a steel deck supporting rigid insulation and built-up roofing. The cross-section is shown in Figure 10.2. The steel roof deck is supported by open-web steel joists spaced at 2.5 m centre-to-centre. Special open-web steel joists are used at each column line in the structure to act as lateral supports to the roof girders at these locations. The walls consist of steel cladding supported by a girt system attached to the columns.

The roof girders are arranged in a cantilever system in which the length of overhanging segments is equal to a maximum of approximately 15 to 20% of the span. The drop-in beams are then simply supported from the cantilevered segments of the girders. This commonly used roof system for single storey buildings is sometimes referred to as Gerber girder framing. The main advantage of this system is to give the design engineer the flexibility to choose the location of the inflection points so as to optimize the design of the negative and positive moment regions. The Gerber system also possesses the benefits of continuous construction without the complications of moment-resisting connections. The spandrel girders are simply supported at the ends and continuous over intermediate or wind columns. Although no specific attempt has been made to select the proportions so as to minimize the cost of the structure, the above arrangement is considered to represent good practice [10.3].

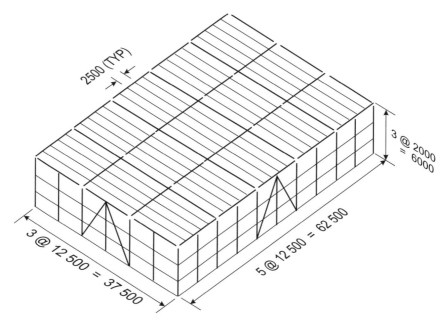

Figure 10.1 – Example Building

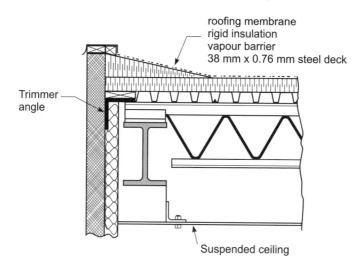

Figure 10.2 – Roof Construction

The girt system is designed to transfer the lateral wind loads from the cladding to the exterior columns. The girts would normally be designed as simply supported at the main column lines and continuous over the intermediate columns or posts, as shown in Figure

10.3(a). In this arrangement the girts are connected to the outside flange of the exterior columns. The column stability problems resulting from this arrangement are outside the scope of this textbook and, for simplicity, the girts will be designed as simply supported members spanning 6250 mm between columns and will be framed into the webs of the columns, as shown in Figure 10.3(b). Under normal conditions, this arrangement will provide complete lateral support to the columns at these points [10.2].

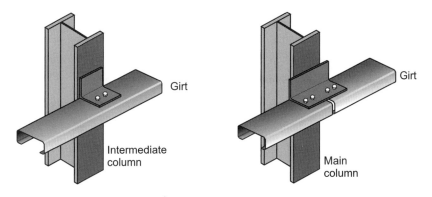

(a) Girts framed to outside flange of exterior column

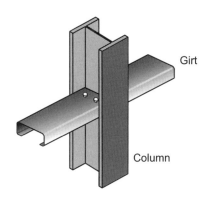

(b) Girts framed into the web of exterior column

Figure 10.3 – Common Girt Arrangements

Overall resistance to lateral load effects will be provided by bracing members in all four walls. Wind loads on the face of the building will be taken into the plane of the roof or to the foundations by the columns. The roof deck will be designed to act as a diaphragm and the loads taken out to the exterior walls and into the vertical bracing systems [10.4].

Since the purpose of this chapter is primarily to illustrate the design process, only the major elements of the structure will be designed. In many cases simplifying assumptions will be made to ensure that the design is illustrative of the basic material contained in earlier portions of this text. It is expected that the resulting design will be reasonably efficient. However, alternative methods of treating various facets of design may be more economical for particular situations or particular fabricators.

10.2 Loads

10.2.1 Dead Load

The dead load supported by a roof girder in the example building includes the weights of the materials shown in Figure 10.2, in addition to the weight of any mechanical units on the roof, ductwork carried through the joists, lighting fixtures, fans, etc., as well as the weight of the steel girder itself. Typical weights of commonly used materials are given in the Handbook of Steel Construction [10.5] as well as in various manufacturer catalogues.

For a 12.5 m× 12.5 m bay size, the specified dead load carried by a main girder in the example building can be estimated for preliminary design as:

roofing	0.35 kN/m²
insulation	0.10
steel deck	0.10
ceiling	0.05
ductwork and fixtures	0.25
open-web steel joists	0.10
Total	0.95 kN/m² = 0.95 kPa

10.2.2 Snow Load

The live load that governs the design of roof systems for most locations in Canada is that caused by snow. The specified loading due to snow accumulation on a roof, S, is determined by multiplying the specified ground snow load, S_s, by the basic roof snow load factor, C_b, the wind exposure factor, C_w, the slope factor, C_s, and the snow accumulation factor, or shape factor, C_a. An associated rain load, S_r, is added to the snow load just determined.

Clause 4.1.6 of the NBC [10.1] prescribes the values to be used for C_b, C_w, C_s, and C_a. The basic roof snow load factor, C_b, has been selected as 0.8, based on surveys of snow loads on roofs. The other factors are dependent upon the degree of shelter, roof slope and shape, and the amount and type of local projections that could cause drifting of the snow. The wind exposure factor, C_w, is usually taken as 1.0 where winter winds are not strong or frequent enough to produce significant reductions in roof loads. For flat roofs the roof slope factor, C_s, is taken as 1.0 since no reduction in load would take place as the result of sliding. Finally, the accumulation factor, C_a, reflects the shape of the roof and potential for snowdrift. In this example, the roof is flat and has no projections, which eliminates the potential for local accumulation of snow on the roof. The accumulation factor is therefore set equal to 1.0.

The specified snow load on the roof of a building is given as:

$$S = I_s [S_s (C_b C_w C_s C_a) + S_r]$$

where I_s is the importance factor for snow load, given as 1.0 for ultimate limit states of normal buildings, S_s and S_r are the 1-in-50-year ground snow load and the associated rain load, respectively. For a building located in Ottawa, Ontario, Table C-2 of the National Building Code gives S_s = 2.4 kPa and S_r = 0.4 kPa. The basic roof snow load factor, C_b, is governed by the characteristic length of the roof, l_c, defined as:

328

$$l_c = 2w - w^2/l$$

where w is the smaller plan dimension of the roof, namely, 37.5 m, and *l* is the larger plan dimension, namely, 62.5 m. The characteristic length is therefore equal to 52.5 m. For characteristic lengths less than 70 m the basic snow load factor is taken as 0.8. The wind exposure factor, C_w, is taken as 1.0, assuming that the building is not located in an exposed area. For a flat roof, the slope factor, C_s, is 1.0. The shape factor, C_a, for a flat roof where there is no snow accumulation is equal to 1.0. Therefore, the specified snow load on the roof for the conditions described is:

$$S = 1.0[2.4 \ (\ 0.8 \times 1.0 \times 1.0 \times \ 1.0) + 0.4] = 2.32 \ \text{kPa}$$

In principle, another loading case that should be considered is that due to ponding induced by a 24 hour rainfall (termed the specified rain load). This is to be considered when the position, shape, and deflection of the roof make such accumulation of water possible, even though adequate drainage has been provided. Generally, loads produced by the ponding of rainwater are not a governing design condition in regions of heavy snow loads, such as in the example considered here. Therefore, rain load will not be considered in this example. However, there are a few regions of Canada where snow loads are small and the roof design may be governed by ponding considerations.

10.2.3 Wind Load

Wind forces on low, flat roof buildings result in pressures on the windward wall, suctions on the leeward and side walls, and suctions over the roof. Using the simple procedure suggested in the NBC, the external pressures or suctions caused by wind acting normal to a building's surface are given by:

$$p = I_w \, q \, C_e \, C_g \, C_p$$

where

p	=	the specified external pressure or suction normal to a surface, kPa
I_w	=	importance factor for wind load, given as 1.0 for buildings of normal importance.
C_e	=	$(h/10)^{0.2} \geq 0.9$ for buildings on open level terrain with only scattered buildings, trees or other obstructions. The reference height above grade, h, is measured in metres. For the building considered, the exposure factor is therefore taken as 0.9 over the full height of the building.
$C_g \, C_p$	=	external pressure coefficient, including the gust effects, acting normal to a surface and used for the design of the primary structural members or cladding. The appropriate design values for small buildings are found in Figure I-7 of the Structural Commentaries of the NBC when the considering the primary structural actions arising from wind load acting on all surfaces (e.g., for the design of the lateral bracing system). Figure I-8 of the Commentaries applies to design of the structural elements in walls and cladding. Figure I-9 applies for the design of the structural elements in the roof elements.

329

q = the reference velocity pressure, kPa, from Appendix C, Climatic Data for Building Design in Canada, of the NBC.

The Structural Commentaries of the NBC provide the values for the product C_pC_g for various locations around low rise buildings, such as for the example building. When used for the design of a structural member, the value of C_pC_g is also dependent on the tributary area of that member.

For the wall members such as the girts and the wind columns, the value of C_pC_g is obtained from Figure I-8 of the Structural Commentaries. Positive pressure coefficients vary from 1.3 for tributary area greater than 50 m^2 to 1.75 for tributary areas less than 1 m^2. The negative pressure coefficients vary from -2.1 to -1.5 in the end zones of the building and from -1.75 to -1.5 in the remaining portions of the exterior walls. The value of C_pC_g for roof elements varies from 0.35 to 0.50 for positive pressure and from -1.5 to -5.4 and varies with location on the roof and whether the roof has overhang or not.

The reference velocity pressure, q, is obtained from Appendix C of the NBC. For the design of structural members for strength, i.e., for the ultimate limit states, q is the reference velocity pressure that has a probability of 1 in 50 of being exceeded in any one year. For Ottawa, this value is 0.41 kPa. When drift or deflection checks are made, serviceability limit states, a 1 in 10 probability value of q is used. For Ottawa, this value is 0.30 kPa.

In addition to the external pressures and suctions on the outside of the building, air leakage around doors and windows results in an internal pressure or suction, p_i. This depends on the amount and locations of the openings and is given by

$$p_i = I_w \ q \ C_e \ C_{gi} \ C_{pi}$$

where

p_i = the specified external pressure or suction normal to a surface, kPa

C_e = 0.90 for this building, as determined above

C_{pi} = ± 0.7 (uniformly sealed low building), internal pressure coefficient

C_{gi} = 1.0 (uniformly sealed low building), internal gust factor

For a low building with large openings that must be operational during severe windstorms, such as a fire hall or aircraft hanger, the internal gust factor should be taken as 2.0.

For this example building, the internal pressure for the ultimate limit state condition is calculated as

$$p_i = 0.41 \times 0.9 \times (\pm 0.7) \times 1.0 \ = \ \pm 0.26 \text{ kPa}$$

where the coefficient of 0.7 implies that a number of small openings exist, distributed non-uniformly around the structure.

10.2.4   Earthquake Loads

In most areas of Canada it is necessary to design a building structure to resist wind and earthquake loads, combined separately with dead and live loads, as appropriate. For special structures, and for those particularly susceptible to dynamic effects, a dynamic analysis of the structure may be required [10.1]. For most other structures, an equivalent static load approach is usually satisfactory. In either case, the requirements of the NBC specify the design procedures. In most areas of Canada, the design will be governed by either wind acting together with dead and live loads in the appropriate combinations, or by earthquake loads acting together with dead and live loads. Loads due to wind and earthquake need not be considered together. Only wind loads will be considered in this example and, while the basic approach to earthquake loads is similar, there are some differences and complexities that go beyond the scope of this text. In particular, care must be taken in the design of members and connections to ensure that the ductility assumed in the analysis of the lateral load resisting system is achieved in the finished structure. (See Clause 27 of S16–01 for details.)

10.3 Design of Roof System

A plan view and end elevation view of the roof framing scheme is shown in Figure 10.4. The steel deck is selected to span the 2500 mm distance between the open-web steel joists. Joists 600 mm in depth are selected to span the 12 500 mm distance between the main girder lines. Both these items are normally selected from manufacturer catalogues and they must satisfy both strength and deflection considerations. "Typical joists" are designed primarily to resist uniformly distributed loads delivered to the joists through the steel deck. These joists are connected to the top flange of the supporting girders by field welds, as shown in Figure 10.5(a), and are designed to resist the loading conditions specified in Clause 16.5.1 of S16–01 [10.6]. Bridging is used to stabilize the joists during construction, and sometimes permanent bracing may also be needed to stabilize the joist members in the completed structure.

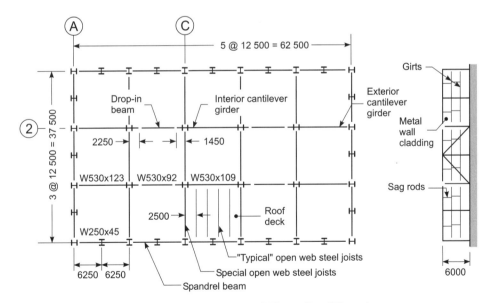

Figure 10.4 – Example Building – Roof Framing

Along the column lines, special open-web steel joists, called tie-joists, are provided. These joists are connected to the top flange of the girder and to the column, as shown in Figure 10.5(b), in order to provide stability to the upper part of the column and to the

331

compression (bottom) flange of the girder at these locations. The tie joists are designed in accordance with the requirements of Clause 16.5.12 of S16-01.

The interior segment of a typical cantilever girder system is shown schematically in Figure 10.6. Concentrated loads act on the girder member at each joist location and at the point of attachment of drop-in beams at the ends of the cantilevered portions of the girder. These loads are shown in Figure 10.6. The girder is supported vertically at each column. The top flange of the girder segment is supported laterally by the diaphragm action of the roof deck. At each column line, lateral support is also provided adjacent to the bottom flange of the girder by the attachment of the lower chord of the tie joist, as illustrated in Figure 10.5(b).

Under these conditions, and with the overhanging length less than approximately 12% of the span, it has been shown that the girder can be designed as a laterally supported member [10.2]. For other proportions, or for unusual loading conditions, the strength of the girder system may be reduced because of the propensity to buckle laterally [10.3, 10.7].

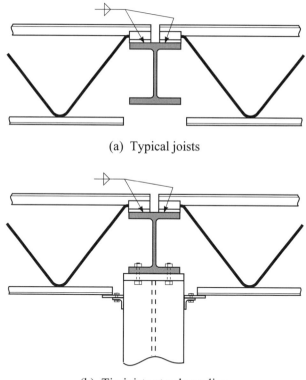

(a) Typical joists

(b) Tie-joists at column line

Figure 10.5 – Joist Construction to Interior Girder

The NBC requires that the girder system be designed to resist the following load combinations: (1) dead load plus the uniform snow load acting over the entire area, and (2) dead load plus 100% of the uniform snow load over any one portion of the area and 50% of the uniform snow load acting over the remainder of the area. Under these requirements, the maximum negative moment occurs at the column when full snow load is considered to act on the drop-in beams and the cantilever portions of the girder.

The greatest length of negative moment region will occur under the condition that only 50% of the uniform snow load is applied to the portion of the girder between the columns. This condition is significant in assessing the lateral stability of the system [10.3]. The bending moment diagram for this case is shown in Figure 10.6 (a).

The moment diagram corresponding to the maximum positive bending moment is shown in Figure 10.6(b). This condition is achieved when only one-half of the uniform snow load is applied on the drop-in beams and the corresponding cantilever portions of the girder with the full snow load applied over the portion of the girder between columns.

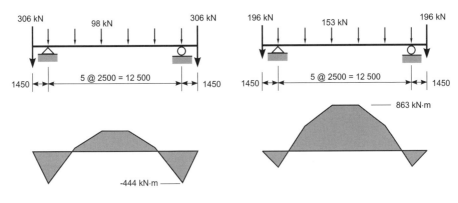

(a) Longest negative moment region (b) Largest positive moment

Figure 10.6 – Design Conditions – Interior Girder

The factored loads are calculated using the right hand side of Equation 1.1 and Table 1.3. For this example, the loads applied to the girder system are equal to the joist reactions and are based on a tributary area of $2.5 \text{ m} \times 12.5 \text{ m} = 31.3 \text{ m}^2$. The loads from the drop-in beams are equal to the reactions from two joists. At the specified load level, recalling from Section 10.2 that the specified dead load is 0.95 kPa and the specified snow load is 2.32 kPa, the loads at each joist location are:

Dead load $= 31.3 \times 0.95 = 29.7 \text{ kN}$, say, 31.0 kN in order to provide an allowance for the weight of the girder itself.

Snow load $= 31.3 \times 2.32 = 72.6 \text{ kN}$

Wind load (positive external pressure and interior suction):

$$p - p_i = I_w \left[q \ C_e \ C_g \ C_p - q \ C_e \ C_{gi} \ C_{pi} \right] \text{ (see Section 10.2)}$$

where $p_i = I_w \ q \ C_e \ C_{gi} \ C_{pi} = 1.0 \times 0.41 \times 0.9 \times 1.0 \times -0.7 = -0.26 \text{ kPa}$

and $p = I_w \ q \ C_e \left(C_p \ C_g \right) = 1.0 \times 0.41 \times 0.9 \times 0.35 = 0.13 \text{ kPa}$

Wind load $= 31.3 \times (0.13 - (-0.26)) = 12.2 \text{ kN}$

The factored loads, corresponding to dead and full snow load as principal loads and wind load as companion load, are then:

Factored load (100% S) $= 1.25$ D $+ 1.5$ S $+ 0.4$ W

$$= (1.25 \times 31.0) + (1.5 \times 72.6) + (0.4 \times 12.2) = 153 \text{ kN}$$

The factored loads, corresponding to dead load and 50% snow load as principal load and wind load as companion load, are:

Factored load (50% S) $= (1.25 \times 31.0) + (1.5 \times 72.6) \times 0.5 + (0.4 \times 12.2) = 98 \text{ kN}$

The appropriate loads and the corresponding bending moment values are shown in Figure 10.6, where the maximum moment caused by the factored loads is 863 kN · m.

Using Equation 5.7, the required plastic section modulus can be computed by assuming that the section selected will meet the requirements for a Class 2 section:

$$Z_x \text{ req'd} = \frac{M_{max}}{\phi F_y} = \frac{863 \times 10^6 \text{ N} \cdot \text{mm}}{0.90 \times 350 \text{ N/mm}^2} = 2740 \times 10^3 \text{ mm}^3$$

A W530× 109 section has a plastic section modulus of $2830 \times 10^3 \text{ mm}^3$ and meets the requirements for a Class 1 section. Additional calculations, not included here, show that shear strength requirements are satisfied.

The maximum live load deflection has been calculated at the specified load level and determined to be 36 mm. The allowable deflection for a girder supporting an asphaltic roof membrane is 1/240 times the span, or 52 mm; again, a W530× 109 section will be satisfactory.

Calculations similar to those outlined above were used to select the exterior cantilever girders, W530× 123 sections, and the drop-in beams, W530× 92 sections. The final member sizes are shown on the roof plan in Figure 10.4.

The presence of the intermediate columns means that the roof area tributary to a spandrel beam is reduced and, even with the added dead load due to exterior wall construction, a much lighter section can be used for the spandrels than was required for interior girders. For this building, it can be established that W250× 45 sections are adequate.

One possibility for connection of the drop-in beam to the cantilever girder is illustrated in Figure 10.7. The fasteners and plates in this connection must transfer a reaction of 306 kN through the eccentricity resulting from the detail of the joint. This design can proceed in accordance with the principles developed in Chapter 9. Girder-to-column connections will be discussed below in conjunction with the selection of columns.

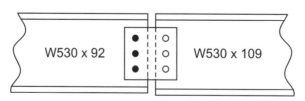

Figure 10.7 – Drop-in Beam Connection

10.4   Design of Interior Columns

The interior columns are designed as axially loaded members, restrained at the lower end by the base plate connection and at the upper end by the restraint provided by the special joist arrangement. See Figure 10.5(b). A detail of this connection is shown in Figure 10.8(a).

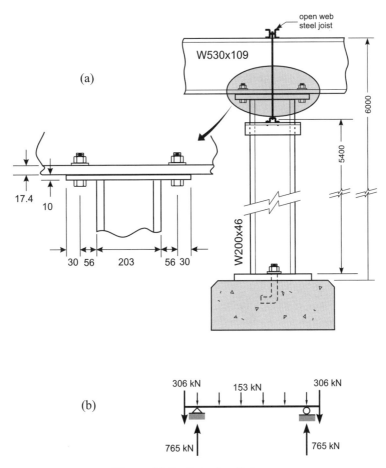

Figure 10.8 – Interior Column

Several different approaches are in use for the design of this type of column arrangement. In accordance with Clause 10.3.1 of S16–01, the length of the column will be assumed equal to the distance between the top of the base plate and the centroid of the lower chord of the joist, which in this case is 5400 mm.

The maximum axial load on an interior column will occur when the tributary area is subjected to full snow load plus full dead load as principal loads and downward wind pressure on the roof plus internal suction as companion loads. This condition is shown in Figure 10.8(b), and the factored axial load on the column is calculated as 765 kN. As an initial trial, a W200×46 section is selected. Assuming that failure is accompanied by weak axis buckling (with r_y = 51.2 mm for the W200×46 section), and further assuming that the column is pinned at the top and restrained by the action of the standard "pinned" base plate connection (G = 10.0) at the bottom, the effective length factor is 0.98 (Figure 4.21). The corresponding slenderness ratio is:

$$\frac{KL}{r} = \frac{0.98 \times 5400}{51.2} = 103$$

The slenderness factor, given by Equation 4.15, is:

$$\lambda = \frac{KL}{r}\sqrt{\frac{F_y}{\pi^2 E}} = 103\sqrt{\frac{350 \text{ MPa}}{\pi^2 \times 200\,000 \text{ MPa}}} = 1.37$$

The factored compressive resistance of the column is calculated using Equation 4.21 as:

$$C_r = \phi A F_y \left(1 + \lambda^{2n}\right)^{-1/n}$$

$$= 0.90 \times 5860 \text{ mm}^2 \times 350 \text{ MPa} \left(1 + 1.37^{\,(2 \times 1.34)}\right)^{-1/1.34}$$

$$= 753 \times 10^3 \text{ N} = 753 \text{ kN}$$

Since this section provides a column capacity that is only about 2 percent smaller than required, the W200×46 section is considered acceptable. In many cases, a square hollow structural section (HSS) would provide a more economical choice, especially for the interior columns.

One way of connecting the column base to the footing is shown in Figure 10.8(a). In this example, the column tensile force due to wind uplift less the countering dead load is small. (Note that in calculating counteracting effects, a load factor less than unity must be used.) The horizontal force to be resisted at the base (caused only by the possible out-of-plumb of the column) is also small. Thus, welds of nominal size can be used to connect the base plate to the column. These welds are present primarily to ensure the strength and stability of the column during the erection of the steel. Likewise, anchor rods of nominal size (e.g., 20 mm diameter) can be provided to aid in placing the column and to provide resistance against small, uncalculated, horizontal forces. A base plate with dimensions sufficient to transfer the column axial force of 765 kN can be selected in accordance with the procedures outlined in Section 9.12, assuming that the concrete compressive strength is known.

At the top of the column, the cap plate is provided simply as a practical convenience to assist in the connection between the girder and the column. The length of the cap plate is selected to provide sufficient space for bolting to the underside of the girder, and the plate is of nominal thickness. As at the column base, the horizontal force and the wind net uplift force are small. Thus, the welds used to attach the cap plate to the column are nominal and the bolts are selected to be compatible with the size of the girder and column.

As the 765 kN force passes from the column into the girder web, failure of the girder web can take place due either to local crippling of the web or as a result of overall buckling of the web over most of its depth. These problems were discussed in Section

5.12. In this example, the capacity of the web must be calculated in accordance with Equations 5.27(a) and 5.28(a), as follows:

$$B_r = \phi_{bi}\, w\, (N + 10\,t)\, F_y$$

$$= 0.80 \times 11.6 \text{ mm} \left[206 \text{ mm} + 10 \times (10 \text{ mm} + 18.8 \text{ mm}) \right] \times 350 \text{ MPa}$$

$$= 1600 \times 10^3 \text{ N} = 1600 \text{ kN}$$

$$B_r = 1.45\, \phi_{bi}\, w^2 \sqrt{F_y\, E}$$

$$= 1.45 \times 0.8 \times 11.6^2 \times \sqrt{350 \times 200\,000}$$

$$= 1300 \times 10^3 \text{N} = 1300 \text{ kN}$$

In these calculations, w is the web thickness for the W530×109. The length of bearing, N, is taken as the column depth, 206 mm, and the associated thickness t is the combined thickness of flange for the W530×109 and the cap plate thickness. Alternatively, the length of bearing could have been taken as the length of the capping plate, 375 mm, with a corresponding thickness t equal to the flange thickness of the W530×109. In this case, the bearing capacity obtained from Equation 5.27(a) would be 1830 kN. In order for this latter calculation to be valid, however, the thickness of the capping plate would have to be sufficient to ensure a uniform pressure distribution over the full capping plate length. The bearing capacity is found to be governed by Equation 5.28(b). Since the governing capacity, 1300 kN, is greater than the applied factored force, 765 kN, the arrangement is satisfactory.

Another important aspect of the detail at the top of the column, shown in Figure 10.8(a), is the positive lateral support provided along the top of the girder by the roof deck (and the attachment of the top chord of the joist) and the support provided adjacent to the cap plate by the attachment of the lower chord of the joist. The attachment at this point is consistent with the assumption that the design length of the column extends from the centroid of the lower chord of the joist to the top of the base plate, and the assumption that the girder is laterally supported at the compression (bottom) flange at each column line.

10.5 Design of Wall System

The general arrangement of the wall framing system is shown in Figure 10.4. Intermediate columns, mid-way between the main column lines, are used to provide reaction points for the girts and also serve as interior supports for the continuous spandrel beams. As a consequence, provision must be made to transfer the lateral force caused by wind from the top of the intermediate column into the roof deck diaphragm. In addition, the top of each intermediate exterior column is laterally supported by special bracing members framing into the bottom joist chords or to the roof deck diaphragm. Hence, lateral support is also provided to the bottom flange of the continuous spandrel beam. Using the intermediate exterior columns, the girts must now span only a distance of 6250 mm. For simplicity, the girts will be designed as simply supported over the 6250 mm span, although in most cases the continuous system shown in Figure 10.3(a) would be used.

The wall cladding must span between the girts and is usually attached to the girt system by means of self-tapping screws. The wall cladding is partially self-supporting, but its weight is also taken through the girt system. It can be assumed, however, that the weight of the wall cladding does not induce significant bending moments in the girts. The girts are supported vertically at their points of attachment to the columns and also at mid-span by sag rods. In turn, the sag rods are carried by spandrel beams, as illustrated in Figure 10.4.

Under these conditions the girts need to be designed solely to withstand the lateral loads caused by wind action. If the resultant force on the cladding is directed inward, the outside flange of the girt will be subject to compression. This situation is shown in Figure 10.9(a), where the outside flange of the girt is restrained from movement out of the plane of the applied load by its attachment to the wall cladding. If the resultant force on the girt is directed outward, as shown in Figure 10.9(b), then the inner flange of the girt is subject to compression and is restrained from out-of-plane movement only at the points of attachment to the columns and at the sag rod locations (Figure 10.9(c)).

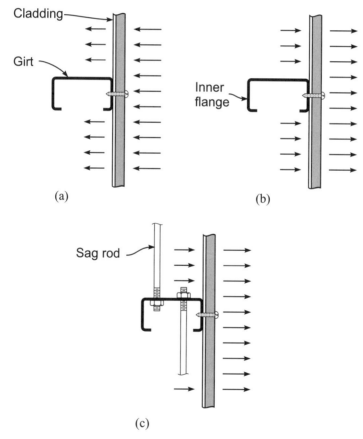

Figure 10.9 – Girt Attachment

For low buildings, the NBC prescribes pressure and gust coefficients for the various structural elements and the wall cladding as a function of their tributary areas and locations. These coefficients correspond to peak pressures due to wind from any direction

338

for the element under consideration. For the girts in this example, coefficients are given for two areas of the building, w and e (Figure 10.10). The area e identifies the portion of the structure over which higher localized suctions and pressures will occur. The extent of the area e is determined by the value of a quantity Z, shown in Figure 10.10, which for this example is given as 40% of the height of the building:

$$Z = 0.40 \times 6000 \text{ mm} = 2400 \text{ mm}$$

The tributary area of one girt is

$$A_T = 6250 \text{ mm} \times 2000 \text{ mm} = 12.5 \times 10^6 \text{ mm}^2 = 12.5 \text{ m}^2$$

From Commentary I of the Structural Commentaries to the NBC and for areas

w: $C_p C_g = +1.6$ and -1.7 (A negative value indicates suction)

e: $C_p C_g = +1.6$ and -2.0

The loading condition that can give rise to the situation shown in Figure 10.9(a) will occur when the girt is subject to a coincident maximum external pressure and maximum internal suction.

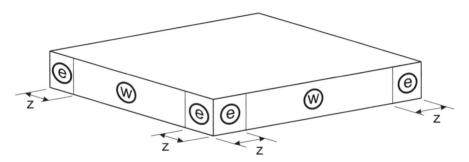

Figure 10.10 – Wind Pressure Zones

Thus, for area w:

$$p - p_i = I_w \left[q \ C_e \ C_g \ C_p - q \ C_e \ C_{gi} \ C_{pi} \right]$$

where $p_i = I_w \ q \ C_e \ C_{gi} \ C_{pi} = 1.0 \times 0.41 \times 0.9 \times (-0.7) = -0.26$ kPa (see Section 10.2)
and $p = I_w \ q \ C_e \ (C_p \ C_g) = 0.41 \times 1.0 \times (+1.6) = 0.66$ kPa .

Therefore, the net pressure $= p - p_i = 0.66 - (-0.26) = 0.92$ kPa and the load on the girt at the specified load level is 0.92 kPa $\times 2$ m $= 1.84$ kN/m .

The loading condition that can give rise to the situation shown in Figure 10.9(b) will occur when the girt is subject to the maximum external suction and maximum internal pressure. Thus, for area e:

$$p - p_i = q \ C_e \ C_p \ C_g - q \ C_{ei} \ C_{pi} \ C_{gi}$$

$$p_i = q \ C_{ei} \ C_{pi} \ C_{gi} = +0.26 \text{ kPa} \qquad\qquad \text{(see Section 10.2)}$$

$$p = q \ C_e \ (C_p \ C_g) = 0.41 \times 1.0 \times (-2.0) = -0.82 \text{ kPa}$$

Therefore the net pressure $= p - p_i = -0.82 - (+0.26) = -1.08$ kPa and the load on the girt will be -1.08 kPa $\times$ 2 m $= -2.16$ kN/m (i.e., suction)

This loading will govern the selection of the girt because the load is larger than in the first case and, in addition, the moment must be resisted in the laterally unsupported condition. Figure 10.9(c) illustrates the detail at a sag rod location, where a restraining couple can be developed by the action of the sag rods and the attachment of the girt to the cladding [10.8]. Thus, the girt is laterally unsupported along the compression flange over the 3125 mm distance between the sag rod and the column, but is considered to be laterally supported at the columns and at sag rod locations.

The sections normally used for girts are cold-formed sections of steel having a yield strength of approximately 350 MPa. The factored design moment for a typical girt, spanning a distance of 6.25 m between columns and subjected to a wind load of 2.16 kN/m is 12.7 kN·m. This maximum moment is matched against the factored moment resistance specified by a manufacturer. The moment capacity is governed by lateral buckling of the section over a 3125 mm unsupported length. The section selected for this example is a cold-formed channel 229S89-218M from the Handbook [10.5], with the selection governed by lateral torsional buckling capacity. A detail of the girt-to-column connection is shown in Figure 10.3(b). This arrangement provides displacement and torsional restraint to the column. The column will either buckle in a flexural mode about the weak axis between the brace points or it will buckle in a flexural mode about the strong axis. When the girt arrangement is as shown in Figure 10.3(a), the girts provide weak axis translational restraint but the torsional restraint may be ineffective. Torsional buckling, with the axis of twisting located at the brace point, is a possible mode of failure in this case. The reader is referred to Chapter 12 of Reference [10.10] for additional information on this topic.

10.6   Design of Exterior Columns

The arrangement of a typical exterior column is shown in Figure 10.11. The framing details are intended to be typical of column A2 in Figure 10.4. Loading on the column consists of an eccentric vertical load produced by the roof dead, snow and wind loads and transverse loads produced by the effects of wind pressure or suction. The dead load of the cladding will be small by comparison and will be neglected. The vertical load is transferred to the inner flange of the column through the girder-to-column connection and the transverse loads are delivered through the girt connections, approximately at the third-points of the column.

Although the tributary area of the column for wind is larger than that of the girt, the pressure coefficients can conservatively be taken to be the same as those for the girt.

The column is restrained at the base by the action of the base plate and at the upper end by the restraint offered by the connection to the girder. The latter effect will be assumed small in this example. The column is assumed to be braced laterally at the upper end by the spandrel girders and at the third points by the girts.

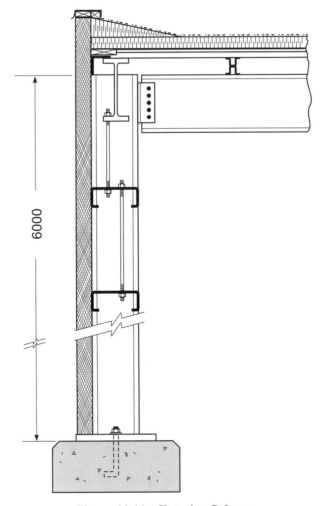

Figure 10.11 – Exterior Column

Considering first the action of vertical dead, snow and wind loads only, the calculated girder reaction produced by the factored dead and live loads is 436 kN. Assuming that the column depth is nominally 200 mm, the moment produced by the eccentricity is approximately

$$436 \text{ kN} \times (100 \text{ mm} + 60 \text{ mm}) = 69\,760 \text{ kN} \cdot \text{mm} = 70 \text{ kN} \cdot \text{m}$$

where the eccentricity includes the half-depth of the column as well as an assumed distance from the face of the column to the gauge line of the bolts in the connection.

Assuming that a W200× 36 section will be used in this location, the interaction equations developed in Chapter 8 will be used to check the adequacy of the section. The W200× 36 section meets the requirements for a Class 1 section and the pertinent cross-sectional properties are listed in the CISC Handbook:

$A = 4570 \text{ mm}^2$	$r_x = 86.7 \text{ mm}$	$r_y = 40.9 \text{ mm}$
$t = 10.2 \text{ mm}$	$d = 201 \text{ mm}$	$Z_x = 379 \times 10^3 \text{ mm}^3$

$$I_x = 34.4 \times 10^6 \text{ mm}^4$$

The factored axial load on the column is $C_f = 436$ kN and the factored end moment is $M_{fx} = 70$ kN·m. The gravity loading condition is shown in Figure 10.12(a).

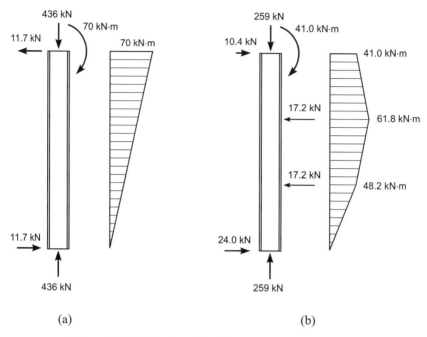

(a)   (b)

Figure 10.12 – Design Conditions – Exterior Column

For the cross-section, the factored compressive resistance of the section is:

$$C_r = \phi \, A \, F_y = 0.9 \times 4570 \text{ mm}^2 \times 350 \text{ MPa} = 1440 \times 10^3 \text{ N} = 1440 \text{ kN}$$

and the factored moment resistance is given by Equation 5.7:

$$M_{rx} = \phi \, Z_x \, F_y$$

$$= 0.9 \times 379 \times 10^3 \text{ mm}^3 \times 350 \text{ MPa} = 119 \times 10^3 \text{ N} \cdot \text{mm} = 119 \text{ kN} \cdot \text{m}$$

Since the frame is a braced frame, the second-order effects due to sway are resisted by the bracing system. The elastic buckling strength of the member is:

$$C_e = \frac{\pi^2 \, E \, I_x}{L^2} = \frac{\pi^2 \times 200\,000 \text{ MPa} \times 34.4 \times 10^6 \text{ mm}^4}{(6\,000 - 530/2)^2}$$

$$= 2060 \times 10^3 \text{ N} = 2060 \text{ kN}$$

Because the smaller end moment is zero, the equivalent moment factor is to be taken as $\omega_1 = 0.6$.

The factor U_{1x} for in-plane strength (Equation 8.11) is determined as

$$U_{1x} = \frac{\omega_1}{1 - \dfrac{C_f}{C_e}} = \frac{0.6}{1 - \dfrac{436}{2060}} = 0.76$$

The cross-sectional strength interaction equation, Equation 8.21(a), then is:

$$\frac{C_f}{C_r} + \frac{0.85\, U_{1x}\, M_{fx}}{M_{rx}} \leq 1.0$$

$$\frac{436}{1440} + \frac{0.85 \times 0.76 \times 70}{119} \leq 1.0$$

$$0.68 < 1.0 \qquad\qquad\qquad \text{Satisfactory}$$

For the in-plane strength check, K for strong axis bending is taken as 1.0 and the strong axis slenderness ratio is:

$$\left(\frac{KL}{r}\right)_x = \frac{1.00 \times (6000 - 530/2)}{86.7} = 66.1$$

where the length of the column has been taken from the base plate to the mid height of the girder. The non-dimensional slenderness factor is calculated from Equation 4.20 as:

$$\lambda = \frac{KL}{r}\sqrt{\frac{F_y}{\pi^2 E}} = 66.1\sqrt{\frac{350\ \text{MPa}}{\pi^2 \times 200\,000\ \text{MPa}}} = 0.88$$

For weak axis bending, the girts, together with the action of the cladding, effectively divide the column into three segments and prevent out-of-plane movement at these points. Thus, the weak axis slenderness ratio is:

$$\left(\frac{KL}{r}\right)_y = \frac{1.00 \times (6000/3)}{40.9} = 48.9$$

The overall in-plane strength is checked using the interaction expression Equation 8.21(a), where C_r is taken as C_{rx}. Therefore, λ will be based on $(KL/r)_x = 66.1$ and C_{rx} is given by Equation 4.21.

$$C_r = \phi\, A\, F_y \left(1 + \lambda^{2n}\right)^{-1/n}$$

$$= 0.90 \times 4570\ \text{mm}^2 \times 350\ \text{MPa}\, \left(1 + 0.88^{\,(2\times1.34)}\right)^{-1/1.34}$$

$$= 965 \times 10^3\ \text{N} = 965\ \text{kN}$$

M_{rx} is still taken as 119 kN·m.

Therefore, checking the overall (in-plane) strength interaction expression, Equation 8.21(a):

$$\frac{C_f}{C_{rx}} + \frac{0.85\, U_{1x}\, M_{fx}}{M_{rx}} \leq 1.0$$

$$\frac{436}{965} + \frac{0.85 \times 0.76 \times 70}{119} = 0.83 < 1.0$$

For lateral-torsional buckling, the interaction expression is checked again using Equation 8.21(a). In this circumstance $U_{1x} \geq 1.0$; C_r is based on $(KL/r)_y$ (1173 kN) and M_{rx} is based on Equation 5.23. However, M_{rx} based on Equation 5.23 still yields a value of 119 kN·m, a reflection that the column is braced at the third points by the girts. Therefore, Equation 8.21(a) becomes

$$\frac{C_f}{C_{ry}} + \frac{0.85\, U_{1x}\, M_{fx}}{M_{rx}} \leq 1.0$$

$$\frac{436}{1173} + \frac{0.85 \times 1.0 \times 70}{119} = 0.87 \leq 1.0$$

Thus, the W200×36 section is adequate in this situation to resist the axial force and bending moments produced by dead, snow and wind loads acting on the roof.

When lateral wind forces are taken as the principal forces, the snow load becomes the companion load. Load case 4 from Table 1.3 indicates that the wind load factor is now 1.4 and the snow load factor is 0.5. Under this condition the axial force on the column is reduced, but the lateral wind forces, transferred through the girts to the columns as lateral forces, increase. This maximizes the bending moment in the exterior columns. The reaction from each joist on the girder system will be reduced from 153 kN (dead and snow loads as principal loads plus wind as companion load) to a value of:

Factored load (dead and wind as principal) = 1.25D + 1.4W + 0.5S

$$= (1.25 \times 31.0) + (1.4 \times 12.2) + (0.5 \times 72.6) = 92.1\,\text{kN}$$

The dead and live loads, 31.0 kN and 72.6 kN, respectively, have been determined previously. As a result, the axial force on the exterior column is reduced to 259 kN and the end moment produced by the load eccentricity is 41 kN·m. In addition, the wind acting on the wall cladding delivers concentrated transverse loads to the columns at the third points, as shown in Figure 10.12(b). The factored wind loads are based on a tributary wall area 6.25 m long× 2.0 m high and on an external suction of -0.72 kPa in zone e and suction on the exterior surface, combined with an internal pressure of 0.26 kPa (both at the specified load level). The reaction delivered by the girt to the column at the factored load level is then:

Girt load = 1.4 × 6.25 m × 2.00 m × (−0.72 kPa − 0.26 kPa)

= 17.2 kN

The total bending moment diagram, resulting from the transverse loads and the eccentric vertical load, is shown in Figure 10.12(b). The maximum bending moment is 61.8 kN·m and $\omega_1 = 1.0$ (point loads present between ends of member) and $U_{1x} = 1.0/(1 - (259/2060)) = 1.14$.

The cross-sectional strength interaction expression is:

$$\frac{C_f}{C_{rx}} + \frac{0.85\, U_{1x}\, M_{fx}}{M_{rx}} \leq 1.0$$

$$\frac{259}{1440} + \frac{0.85 \times 1.14 \times 61.8}{119} = 0.68 \quad < \quad 1.0$$

The overall in-plane strength interaction expression is again checked, but this time using

$$C_r = 965 \text{ kN} \cdot \text{m} \quad \text{and} \quad M_{rx} = 119 \text{ kN} \cdot \text{m}$$

$$\frac{C_f}{C_{rx}} + \frac{0.85 \, U_{1x} \, M_{fx}}{M_{rx}} \quad \leq \quad 1.0$$

$$\frac{259}{965} + \frac{0.85 \times 1.14 \times 61.8}{119} = 0.77 \quad < \quad 1.0 \qquad \text{(Satisfactory)}$$

For the case of lateral-torsional buckling, the interaction expression is checked using Equation 8.21(a). Here again $U_{1x} = 1.14$, C_r equals 1173 kN, based on $(KL/r)_y$, and M_{rx}, based on Equation 5.23, is $119 \text{ kN} \cdot \text{m}$. Therefore, Equation 8.21a becomes

$$\frac{C_f}{C_{rx}} + \frac{0.85 \, U_{1x} \, M_{fx}}{M_{rx}} \quad \leq \quad 1.0$$

$$\frac{259}{1173} + \frac{0.85 \times 1.14 \times 61.8}{119} = 0.72 \quad < \quad 1.0$$

The W200×36 is found to be satisfactory for the two load cases checked, one that maximizes the axial force in the member, and one that maximizes the bending moment in the member. Although the shear calculations are not presented here, the shear resistance should be checked. It rarely governs the design of rolled shapes, however.

As was the case with the interior column, particular attention must be given to the design of the details and provision of bracing mechanisms to ensure the integrity of the member.

10.7 Roof Diaphragm Considerations

Although many of the individual members in the structure shown in Figure 10.1 have now been designed to resist the vertical dead, snow and wind loads and the horizontal loads caused by wind, the capacity of the structure to transfer the horizontal load to the foundations has not yet been established.

As an example, wind blowing perpendicular to the long face of the building shown in Figure 10.1 will produce pressure on the wall cladding on the windward face of the structure and suction on the leeward face (in addition to other effects). The cladding system, including the girts and exterior columns, has been designed to resist the equivalent forces on the areas tributary to the individual members. This same action, however, produces a net lateral force on the building that must be transferred to the foundations.

In some buildings, resistance to lateral load is provided within each line of columns in the structure. In these structures, wind forces are transferred from the wall cladding through the girts to the exterior columns, then resisted directly by the stiffness of each line of columns (and the appropriate girders, etc.) parallel to the wind direction. In the example building, however, and in many light industrial structures, resistance to lateral load is not provided along the interior column lines and the entire lateral force on the structure must be resisted in the exterior walls. In this situation, the wind loads are transferred through the wall cladding and girts to the exterior columns in the walls perpendicular to the wind direction. These exterior columns are, in turn, supported at the base by the foundation and at the top by the roof. The entire roof must then act as a deep horizontal girder so that the loads brought into the plane of the roof by the exterior columns can be resisted by bending and shear in the roof deck. The reactions for this horizontal roof girder are provided by vertical trusses in the end walls of the structure parallel to the direction of the wind.

The loading pattern illustrated in Figure 10.13 is for wind blowing against the long face of the building. The loads delivered to the roof diaphragm at each exterior column location are based on a tributary wall area 6.25 m long and 3.0 m high (the wind load on the lower half of the panel is taken directly into the column footing through the anchor rods). For the building as a whole, the NBC gives the peak pressure coefficients, $C_p C_g$, for the windward face as +0.75 (pressure) and for the leeward face as –0.55 (suction). Since the interior pressure is exerted equally against all interior surfaces, the net effect on the diaphragm action is zero. Just as with the design of the girts, zones of higher wind pressure or suction are present at the ends of the building face. For this building, the length of the end zone can be taken to be equal to the bay spacing, 6.25 m.

Therefore, the factored wind forces, P_f, are—

For the main portion of the windward wall:

$$P_f = \alpha_L \ A_T \ I_w \ q \ C_e \ (C_p \ C_g)$$

$$= 1.40 \times (6.25 \text{ m} \times 3.0 \text{ m}) \times 1.0 \times 0.41 \text{ kPa} \times 0.9 \times 0.75$$

$$= 7.3 \text{ kN} \quad \text{(positive pressure, as shown)}$$

For the main portion of the leeward wall:

$$P_f = \alpha_L \ A_T \ I_w \ q \ C_e \ (C_p \ C_g)$$

$$= 1.40 \times (6.25 \text{ m} \times 3.0 \text{ m}) \times 1.0 \times 0.41 \text{ kPa} \times 0.9 \times (-0.55)$$

$$= -5.3 \text{ kN} \quad \text{(suction, as shown)}$$

For the end zone, the value of $C_p C_g$ for the windward face is 1.15 and –0.80 for the leeward face. Thus, the forces for a 6.25 m width of building are—

For the windward end zone:

$$P_{fe} = 1.40 \times (6.25 \text{ m} \times 3.0 \text{ m}) \times 1.0 \times 0.41 \text{ kPa} \times 0.9 \times 1.15 = 11.1 \text{ kN}$$

For the leeward end zone:

$$P_{fe} = 1.40 \times (6.25 \text{ m} \times 3.0 \text{ m}) \times 1.0 \times 0.41 \text{ kPa} \times 0.9 \times (-0.80) = -7.8 \text{ kN}$$

The loads at the corner columns (the braced frame bent) are one-half of P_{fe}, that is, 5.6 kN and – 3.9 kN. Similarly, the loads at the first interior frame line are the average of P_f and P_{fe}, that is, 9.2 kN and –6.6 kN.

The increased wind load in the end zone is applied at one end of the building and creates torsion on the structure. This effect accounts for the non-uniform nature of the wind pressure on the structure and its torsional effect. The end zone where the increased wind load is applied is selected so as to maximize the torsion applied on the building. Torsion results when the line of action of the resultant wind force does not go through the shear centre of the building, where the shear centre corresponds to the centroid of the shear stiffness of the various lateral load resisting elements in the building. For this example building the lateral load resisting elements consist of bracing in the exterior walls as shown in Figure 10.13(a). Since the bracing is symmetrical about the geometric centre of the building, the shear centre is located at the geometrical centre of the building. Therefore, the increased wind load can be applied at either end of the building.

The forces are summarized in Figure 10.13(a). The shear force of 81.1 kN in the end wall is determined from a torsional analysis that is summarized in Figure 10.14. The shear force must be resisted by the action of the trussed bay in the side wall, as shown in the elevation view in Figure 10.13(b). Four braced frames, identified as B_1 to B_4 in Figure 10.14, have been designated to resist the lateral loads. Since there are four unknown shear forces, the selected bracing system is statically indeterminate. Basic considerations of equilibrium, force versus displacement relationship, and compatibility of deformations have to be used to determine the force in the braced frames. The equations for V_1 to V_4 presented in Figure 10.14 were obtained from such considerations.

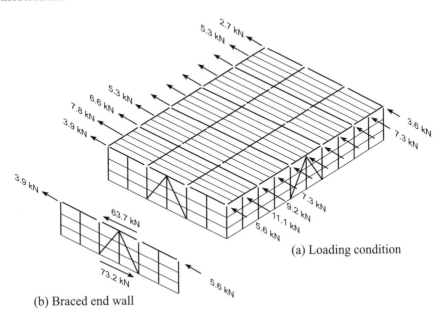

Figure 10.13 – Loading Condition – Roof Diaphragm

As shown in Figure 10.14, the force in braced frame B_1, which is parallel to the applied loads, is obtained from:

347

$$V_1 = \frac{W_R}{2} + \frac{W_R \, e \, d_1}{4 \sum_{i=1}^{} d_i^2}$$

where W_R is the sum of all the lateral forces shown on the building in Figure 10.13(a) (139 kN) and e is the distance from the shear centre and the wind force resultant (e = 2.28 m for this example).

$$V_1 = \frac{139}{2} + \frac{139 \times 2.28 \times 31.25}{2 \times (31.25^2 + 18.75^2)} = 69.5 \text{ kN} + 3.7 \text{ kN} = 73.2 \text{ kN}$$

$$V_2 = \frac{139 \times 2.28 \times 18.75}{2 \times (31.25^2 + 18.75^2)} = 2.2 \text{ kN}$$

$$V_3 = 69.5 \text{ kN} - 3.7 \text{ kN} = 65.8 \text{ kN}$$

$$V_4 = -V_2 = -2.2 \text{ kN}$$

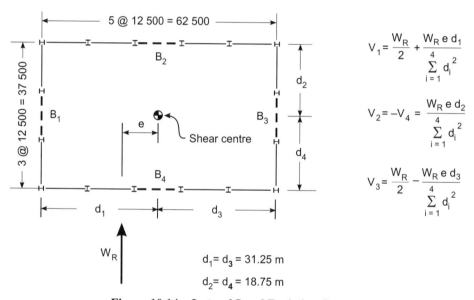

Figure 10.14 – Lateral Load Resisting System

The maximum shear force is 73.2 kN in braced frame B_1. The torsion component for this example is 3.7 kN, namely, about 5% of the shear force in the braced frame. The magnitude of the torsion contribution varies depending on the geometry of the building and the location and number of lateral load resisting elements in the building. It should be noted that if the wind forces had been assumed to act in the opposite direction, the maximum shear force would be located in braced frame B_3. Therefore, both braced frames B_1 and B_3 will be designed for the same shear force. The shear force in braced frames B_2 and B_4 is very small. This is usually the case for lateral load resisting elements in the walls perpendicular to the direction of the lateral forces. However, the design shear in these braced frames will be governed by the wind blowing against the short face of the building. A torsion analysis can be carried out to determine these forces. Such an analysis will indicate that the shear force in B_2 and B_4 is smaller than the shear force in B_1. It is common practice for small buildings like the one considered in this example to use the same bracing member sizes in both directions. Therefore, the braced end wall shown in Figure 10.13(b) will be the only one that will be designed in this example.

Figure 10.15(a) shows the loading condition for the roof diaphragm of the example building. The shear force diagram and bending moment diagram are shown in Figures 10.15(b) and (c), respectively. The concentrated moment shown in Figure 10.15(a) results from the contribution of braced frames B_2 and B_4. The web of the girder is formed by the steel roof deck. The top chords of the open-web joist system, the top flanges of the main roof girder system, and the interconnection among the various elements also participate in diaphragm action. The flanges of the girder are assumed to be formed by the perimeter framing members, such as the continuous edge angle shown in section in Figure 10.2. The edge angles also serve as connecting elements between the roof deck and the wall cladding.

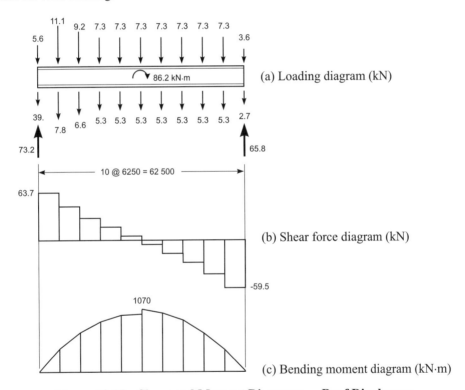

(a) Loading diagram (kN)

(b) Shear force diagram (kN)

(c) Bending moment diagram (kN·m)

Figure 10.15 – Shear and Moment Diagrams — Roof Diaphragm

The Canadian Sheet Steel Building Institute has published a design guide [10.4] that outlines the various provisions that must be met in order that the roof system will function properly as a girder or diaphragm. In this example, with the maximum bending moment value of 1070 kN·m and a "girder" depth of 37.5 m, the force that must be resisted by the flanges (the continuous edge angles) along the long sides of the structure is 1070 kN·m / 37.5 m = 28.5 kN.

The roof system must also be capable of resisting the shears appropriate to the particular location. The shear capacity of the roof will depend upon the thickness of the steel deck, the connections between the deck units and the top chord of the joists, and between the joists and the main girder system [10.4]. For example, along the short sides of the structure the connection between the roof deck and the spandrel girders must be capable of resisting a total force of 63.7 kN (see Figure 10.13).

The discussion above relates to the design of the roof diaphragm for wind blowing perpendicular to the long face of the building. Similar considerations apply for wind perpendicular to the short face. Load transfer can also be achieved by designing the primary roof system so that it forms a horizontal truss, rather than using the diaphragm action of the steel deck. Since the deck must be provided in any case, however, the additional costs of ensuring diaphragm action appear to be less than that involved in the use of a horizontal truss system [10.2].

10.8   Frame Stability Considerations

In Chapter 8, the stability effects were discussed as they affected the members of moment resisting frames. For structures of the type used in this example, stability is provided by direct acting bracing. An elevation view of one such braced bay is shown in Figure 10.13(b). Other means of obtaining stability and resisting the lateral loads are also used, such as vertical trusses and shear walls. For these structures, Clause 8.7 of S16–01 requires that the forces in the members of the lateral load resisting system also be amplified for the second order effects.

The most common approach to the bracing design is to assume that only one of the diagonal members in a bay will act (in tension) for each wind direction. Thus, each diagonal member must be proportioned to resist a tension force due to the wind loading. For the example building, a reasonable estimate of the tension force in the diagonal brace can be obtained from the base shear of the end frame (see Figure 10.13(b)) as

$$T_{ft} = 73.2 \text{ kN } \sqrt{6.25^2 + 6.00^2} \text{ m} / 6.25 \text{ m} = 101 \text{ kN}$$

This value will have to be adjusted to reflect the additional forces due to sway of the structure, as will be discussed below.

A single angle, for example, would adequately resist this load and provide room for easy connection detailing. However, the use of a single angle might result in an excessive slenderness ratio, based on an unsupported horizontal length of 6250 mm (diagonal length = 8664 mm) (see Clause 10.4.2 of S16–01). If excessive slenderness is a problem in this situation, a larger member could be used or provisions made to attach the diagonal members to the girts.

Under the action of wind, the structure will deflect laterally. Assuming that the roof deck is rigid in its own plane, this implies that each column in the structure will sway an amount equal to this deflection. The effect of this movement on the side wall columns is shown in Figure 10.16(a) by the dashed lines. If any one column in the structure is isolated, as shown in Figure 10.16(b), it is apparent that a horizontal force, $H = C \Delta/h$, must be developed at the column base as a result of the deflection of the structure. An equal and opposite force must be transferred through the roof diaphragm to the side walls of the structure, where it will be resisted by the vertical bracing in the same manner as the forces caused by wind.

Since each column in the structure will undergo a similar sway movement under the action of wind and dead load, the effective lateral shear on the structure will be increased by an amount, $\Sigma C \Delta/h$, where the summation includes all the vertical loads acting on the structure. Referring to Figure 10.13, the factored horizontal force due to factored wind that must be resisted by the vertical bracing in the undeformed position is 73.2 kN. A notional load of 0.005 times the gravity loads is also added to this base shear, in accordance with S16 Clause 8.7.2. This will be increased by the factor U_2 , as required by Clause 8.7.1.

Two load cases must be considered, namely, load case 3 from Table 1.3 (dead and snow as principal loads and wind as companion load) and load case 4 (dead plus wind as principal loads and snow as companion load).

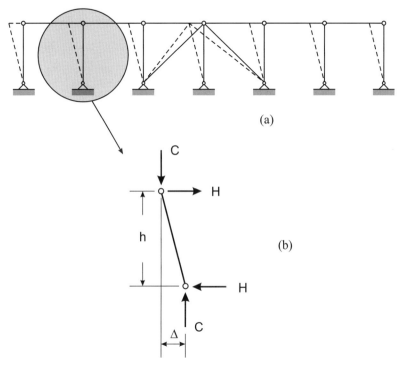

(a)

(b)

Figure 10.16 – Frame Stability Considerations

(a) Dead and snow as principal loads and wind load as companion load

In order to determine U_2, the deflection under the combined factored wind and notional load is required. Because bracing is provided in the two external walls, only one-half of the building's tributary area contributes to the gravity loads for computing the notional load and the factor U_2 .

Dead Load $= 1.25 \times 1.00$ kPa $\times 37.5$ m $\times 62.5$ m $/ 2 = 1465$ kN

Snow Load $= 1.5 \times 2.32$ kPa $\times 37.5$ m $\times 62.5$ m $/ 2 = 4078$ kN

Notional Load $= 0.005 \times (1465$ kN $+ 4078) = 27.7$ kN

Total Lateral Load $= 0.4/1.4 \times 73.2$ kN $+ 27.7$ kN $= 48.6$ kN

Note that in the above equation the lateral load of 73.2 kN is a factored wind load. It is therefore multiplied by the ratio 0.4/1.4 to obtained the factored companion load. It is also noted that the effect of wind suction on the roof, described in Figure I-7 of reference [10.1], was neglected in the above calculations. Its effect as a companion load is small and it is conservative to neglect the uplift wind pressure when assessing the stability of the structure.

The brace force is obtained by multiplying the horizontal shear by the ratio of the brace length to the horizontal projection of the brace length.

Brace Force $= (8664 \text{ mm}/6250 \text{ mm}) \times 48.6 \text{ kN} = 67.4 \text{ kN}$

Assuming that the tension brace will be connected with a bolted connection and that A'_{ne} will be $0.6 \, A_g$ to allow for shear lag and the effect of the holes (see Chapter 3), the deflection due to the factored wind load can be estimated by first calculating the area of the tension brace.

$0.85 \, \phi \, A'_{ne} \, F_u > 67.4 \text{ kN}$

$0.85 \times 0.90 \times 0.6 \, A_g \times 450 \text{ MPa} > 67.4 \text{ kN}$

$$\therefore \, A_g = \frac{67.4 \times 10^3 \text{ N}}{0.85 \times 0.9 \times 0.6 \times 450 \text{ MPa}} = 326 \text{ mm}^2$$

This required area based on strength requirement is small, as it often is. Another consideration in the design of bracing members is the slenderness, L/r, requirement outlined in Clause 10.4.2.2 of S16-01. The maximum permissible slenderness, L/r, is 300. For a member length of 8664 mm, this means that the minimum r value required is 29 mm. Using the tables of section properties in the Handbook of Steel Construction, the lightest available section that provides this minimum r value provides an area much larger than required for strength. For example, a WT205×23 ($r_y = 29.5$ mm, $A = 2950 \text{ mm}^2$) just meets the slenderness requirement but provides an area of 8.6 times the required area.

The extension of the brace under the factored load is PL/AE. The horizontal component of that extension (the sway of the structure) can be obtained by multiplying this extension by the ratio of the horizontal projection of the brace length to its actual length. Thus, the sway can be calculated as

$$\Delta_f = \frac{6\,250}{8\,664} \times \frac{67.4 \times 10^3 \text{ N} \times 8\,664 \text{ mm}}{2\,950 \text{ mm}^2 \times 200\,000 \text{ MPa}} = 0.71 \text{ mm}$$

$\sum C_f = 1465 + 4078 = 5543 \text{ kN}$

$$U_2 = \frac{1}{1 - \left[\dfrac{5543 \text{ kN} \times 0.71 \text{ mm}}{67.4 \text{ kN} \times 6000 \text{ mm}} \right]} = 1.01$$

Therefore, the base shear including the second-order effect is $1.01 \times 48.6 \text{ kN} = 49.1 \text{ kN}$. The corresponding force in the brace can now be calculated from this value as $(8664/6250) \times 49.1 = 68.1 \text{ kN}$.

(b) Dead plus wind as principal loads and snow as companion load

The factored snow load (companion load) on half of the building's tributary area is

Snow Load $= 0.5 \times 2.32$ kPa $\times 37.5$ m $\times 62.5$ m $/ 2 = 1\,359$ kN

Dead + Snow $= 1\,465$ kN $+ 1\,359$ kN $= 2\,824$ kN

Notional Load $= 0.005 \times 2\,824 = 14.1$ kN

Total Lateral Load $= 73.2$ kN $+ 14.1$ kN $= 87.3$ kN

$$\text{Brace Force} = \frac{8664 \text{ mm}}{6250 \text{ mm}} \times 87.3 \text{ kN} = 121 \text{ kN}$$

$$\Delta_f = \frac{6\,250}{8\,664} \times \frac{121 \times 10^3 \text{ N} \times 8\,664 \text{ mm}}{2\,950 \text{ mm}^2 \times 200\,000 \text{ MPa}} = 1.3 \text{ mm}$$

$$\Sigma C_f = 4123 \text{ kN}$$

and then $\quad U_2 = \dfrac{1}{1 - \left[\dfrac{2824 \text{ kN} \times 1.3 \text{ mm}}{87.3 \text{ kN} \times 6000 \text{ mm}} \right]} = 1.01$

The base shear, including second-order effects, is therefore 1.01×87.3 kN $= 88.2$ kN. The corresponding force in the brace can be calculated from this value as $(8664/6250) \times 88.2 = 122$ kN.

From the same assumptions made in case (a), the required gross area of the bracing member is determined as:

$$A_g = \frac{122 \times 10^3 \text{ N}}{0.85 \times 0.9 \times 0.6 \times 450 \text{ MPa}} = 591 \text{ mm}^2$$

This is considerably smaller than the area provided by the selected member ($A = 2950$ mm^2). The slenderness requirement for the tension brace still governs the design.

In summary, the governing case is dead load and wind load as the principal loads and snow as the companion load. Each truss in the side wall (along the short side of the building) must be designed to resist a total horizontal force of 88.2 kN and the diagonal members in that braced frame must be designed for a tensile force of 122 kN. In this particular building, the second-order effects were very small (about 1%).

Light steel trusses were used for the roof of the Shaw Conference Centre
(Photo courtesy of Collins Industries)

10.9 Summary

This chapter describes the essential elements in the design of a single storey rectangular building. The object was not to extend the material presented in previous chapters, but rather to illustrate the procedures involved in applying member selection techniques in a design situation. The example used in this chapter was necessarily simplified for this purpose.

References

10.1   "National Building Code of Canada 2005," issued by the Associate Committee on the National Building Code, National Research Council of Canada, Ottawa, 2005.

10.2   Chien, E., "Single Storey Building Design Aid," Canadian Institute of Steel Construction, Toronto, Ontario, 1987.

10.3   "Roof Framing with Cantilever (Gerber) Girders & Open Web Steel Joists," Canadian Institute of Steel Construction, Toronto, Ontario, 1989.

10.4   "Design of Steel Deck Diaphragms," Canadian Sheet Steel Building Institute, Cambridge, Ontario, B13-06, 2006.

10.5   Canadian Institute of Steel Construction, "Handbook of Steel Construction," Ninth Edition, Toronto, Ontario, 2006.

10.6   Canadian Standards Association, CAN/CSA–S16–01, "Limit States Design of Steel Structures," Toronto, Ontario, 2001.

10.7   Essa, H.S. and Kennedy, D.J.L., "Design of Steel Beams in Cantilever Suspended Construction," Journal of the Structural Division, American Society of Civil Engineers, Vol. 121, No. 11, 1995.

10.8   Birkemoe, P.C., "Behaviour and Design of Girts and Purlins for Negative Pressure (Suctions)," Proceedings, 1976 Canadian Structural Engineering Conference, Canadian Steel Industries Construction Council, Toronto, Ontario.

10.9   Canadian Standards Association, CAN/CSA–S136–01, "North American Specification for the Design of Cold Formed Steel Structural Members," Toronto, Ontario, 2001.

10.10   Structural Stability Research Council, "Guide to Stability Design Criteria for Metal Structures," Fifth Edition, T. V. Galambos Editor, John Wiley and Sons, New York, 1998.

Notes

CHAPTER 11

FATIGUE

11.1 Introduction

Fatigue is the initiation and propagation of microscopic cracks into macro cracks by the repeated application of stresses [11.1]. A discontinuity in the crystal structure of a metal or an initial crack will grow a small amount each time a load is applied to the part. Growth occurs at the crack front, which is initially sharp. Even at relatively low loads, meaning stresses less than the yield strength of the material, there will be a high concentration of stress at the sharp front, and plastic deformation (slip on atomic planes) takes place at the crack front. Continued slip results in a blunted crack tip, and the crack grows a minute amount during this process. Upon unloading, not necessarily to zero, the crack tip again becomes sharp. The process, termed fatigue crack growth, is repeated during each load cycle [11.2]. The potential for fatigue crack growth exists in every steel structure that is loaded repetitively. Fortunately, it usually requires a relatively large number of cycles of loading before significant crack growth takes place. Therefore, many civil engineering structures need not be designed against fatigue. For example, even though a high-rise building undergoes cyclic loading (wind), the number of cycles that will occur over the design life of the building is small enough that cracking due to fatigue is not a concern.

In civil engineering practice, fatigue life is an issue that must be examined for structures such as bridges, cranes, towers, and any such structure that is subjected to a large number of cycles of repeated loading. If fatigue cracking does occur, it can produce failure of the part as the crack grows to a size such that the remaining portion of the cross-section is no longer adequate to carry the imposed forces. Another possible mode of failure is that the fracture limit state is reached (*brittle fracture*) after a fatigue crack has grown to a critical size [11.2].

Although the definition of fatigue given above included the initiation of cracks as well as their propagation, fabricated steel structures inevitably contain significant metallurgical or fabrication-related discontinuities and most also include stress concentrators such as weld toes. This means that, in practical terms, the initiation phase of fatigue crack growth does not exist in fabricated steel structures. All of the fatigue crack growth comes through propagation of an existing flaw, defect, or discontinuity[1].

The task of the structural engineer is to proportion those structural members that have a potential for failure by fatigue crack growth so that they have a sufficiently long life as compared with the design life of the structure. As we will see, this will be done in the environment that some probability of failure must be accepted: in reality, there is no

---

[1] In the welding standards, defects are defined as imperfections that must be repaired, whereas flaws are imperfections that are small enough that repair is not required. The term *flaw* will generally be used in this Chapter.

structure that can be designed for zero probability of failure. The design will be carried out in the expectation that flaws will be present initially in all fabricated steel structures and that all such members will contain residual stresses of relatively high magnitude. A concomitant feature is that it is possible in the design process to identify the size of flaws that are permissible and then to use this information as the basis for both initial inspection of the structure as well as on-going inspection. This latter feature is not yet well-developed in design specifications, and the usual procedure is to accept as permissible flaw sizes consistent with the specifications that accompany the fabrication processes, e.g., the welding specifications.

As will be seen in the following sections, the evaluation of the fatigue strength of a steel member when cracking results from the imposed forces is not a complicated design process. However, the stresses that drive crack growth can also be produced as a result of relative displacement of one component to another. This behavior is more difficult to evaluate, but fatigue crack growth from this source is an important issue.

11.2   Sources of Flaws in Fabricated Steel Structures

The kinds of flaw that can occur in a fillet-welded detail are shown in Figure 11.1. These include partial penetration and lack of fusion, porosity and inclusions, undercut or micro-flaws at the weld toe, and cracking or inclusions around a weld repair or at start-stop locations or at arc strikes. Although the fabricator of the structure and those responsible for the fabrication inspection will attempt to minimize these flaws, it is neither practical nor economically possible to eliminate them in all cases.

In some cases, a "flaw" is an expected result of the type of fabrication process and has no effect on the life of the member. For instance, the partial penetration shown in Figure 11.1 is a natural consequence of the fillet-welded connection: it is not expected that the two fillet welds will merge in the central region of the connection. Since the "crack" represented by the lack of penetration is parallel to the direction of the (bending) stress field, the crack will not open up under the application of stress. Consider a detail involving mechanical fasteners—an I-shaped beam with a cover plate fastened to the beam flange with bolts. The region between bolt lines is a "flaw" or "crack," but, since the discontinuity is parallel to the stress field, the "crack" does not grow and therefore its presence does not affect the fatigue strength of the member.

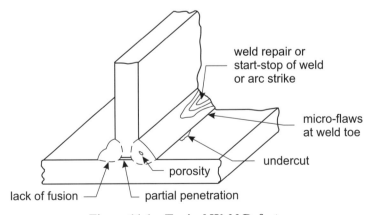

Figure 11.1 – Typical Weld Defects

The flaws that exist in all fabricated steel structures are a consequence of the manufacturing process of the steel itself and of the normal fabrication processes. Flaws in rolled shapes arise from surface and edge imperfections, irregularities in mill scale, laminations, seams, inclusions, etc., and from mechanical notches resulting from handling, straightening, cutting, shearing, and so on. In a rolled shape, crack growth can start from one of these sources. Comparatively, the "unaltered" rolled shape presents the most favorable fatigue life situation. However, there are not many practical cases in which a rolled shape does not have some kind of attachment, connection, or some other kind of alteration.

Mechanical details, in which holes are drilled or punched and forces are transferred by means of bolts (or, in older structures, by rivets), are a common way of making connections. Drilled or sub-punched and reamed holes give some reduction in fatigue life as compared with an unaltered member, but the difference usually is not very great. Punched holes give a greater reduction in fatigue life than do drilled or sub-punched and reamed holes because of imperfections at the hole edge arising from the punching process. In either case, the crack usually starts at the edge of the hole. If preloaded high-strength bolts are used, the disturbing effect of the hole is largely masked by the presence of the high local compressive stresses introduced by the bolt. In this case, fatigue cracking can start from a surface flaw rather than from the edge of the hole. This is the consequence of microscopic movement of one connected part relative to another ("fretting fatigue").

Broadly speaking, any mechanical detail has a better fatigue life than does its equivalent welded detail. The types of flaws introduced when welding is used have already been discussed. In addition to the fact that more flaws will be present when welding is used, inspection for defects is more difficult than is the case for mechanically fastened details. Likewise, repair of welded details is often difficult. Prohibiting the use of welded details in fatigue situations usually is not a practical option, however.

11.3 Basis for Design Rules

An examination of all the features that might influence the growth of fatigue cracks has shown that the fatigue life of a fabricated steel structure is associated principally with three factors [11.3, 11.4, 11.5]. These are:

the number of cycles of loading to which the member is subjected;

the type of detail under examination; and

the stress range at the location of the detail.

The stress to be calculated is simply the nominal stress at the location of the detail, and it can be determined using the usual mechanics of materials approach. This simple representation of stress is possible because selection of the detail itself implies inclusion of the stress concentration for that detail.

Stress range is the algebraic difference between the maximum nominal stress and the minimum nominal stress at a given location. The use of stress range, rather than maximum stress or some other representation of stress (e.g., ratio of maximum stress to minimum stress) is a reflection of the fact that fabricated steel structures always contain residual stresses of high magnitude [11.1]. (The fatigue strength of an annealed specimen—meaning, no residual stress—must be described in other terms.)

It is also significant that the yield strength of the steel itself does not affect fatigue crack growth.

The outcome of the research, both experimental and analytical, that was used to develop the relationships between stress range, fatigue life expressed in terms of number of loading cycles to failure, and the type of detail under investigation showed that there is a linear relationship between stress range and number of cycles when each of these is expressed in logarithmic form. This relationship is [11.1]

$$\log N = \log M - m \ \log \Delta\sigma_r \qquad (11.1a)$$

or, alternatively

$$N = M \ \Delta\sigma_r^{-m} \qquad (11.1b)$$

In these equations, N is the number of stress cycles to failure, $\Delta\sigma_r$ is the stress range, and M and m are numerical constants determined from regression analysis of the test data. The value of m, which is the slope of the straight line expressed by Equation 11.1(a), is usually taken as 3 for all cases involving normal stresses.

11.4   Design Rules Given by Standards

The rules used for the fatigue strength design of fabricated steel structures given in CSA S16–01 [11.6], in the Canadian Highway Bridge Design Code [11.7], and in the AASHTO specification [11.8] follow the representation of fatigue strength given by Equation 11.1. The rules are similar generally, but differ in the long-life region of behaviour. This will be discussed below. The S16 requirement, given in Clause 26.3.2, is that

$$F_{sr} = \left(\frac{\gamma}{n\,N} \right)^{1/3} \ \geq \ F_{srt} \qquad (11.2)$$

In the first part of this equation, F_{sr} is the stress range ($\Delta\sigma_r$ in Equation 11.1), N is the number of passages of a moving load, γ is the same as the constant M in Equation 11.1, and the exponent 1/3 is, in fact, 1/m, where m has been taken as 3. Thus, Equation 11.1(b) simply has been rearranged to obtain Equation 11.2 by solving for the stress range and giving the constant m the unique value of 3.

The remaining term in Equation 11.2, the term n, has been included to account for those cases where a single passage of a moving load gives more than one stress range at a given detail.[2] It is self-evident that each stress range created at a given detail as a moving load passes over the structure must be acknowledged in the design. It is not obvious, however, that in many cases vibrations set up by the moving load create additional stress ranges. These cannot be easily quantified by the designer. Both the AASHTO Specification and the Canadian Highway Bridge Design Code provide guidance on this

---

[2]   In the S16 Standard, the term n is defined as the number of stress range cycles at a given detail for each application of load.

point. For example, these two sources require that n = 5 be used for a cantilever girder in recognition that vibrations cause stress ranges even after the moving load has left the girder span. This aspect should not be overlooked, although in many cases n = 1 will be used.

The term F_{srt} in Equation 11.2 is the constant amplitude threshold stress range, which is the stress range (for constant amplitude loading case only) below which a crack will not grow. In other words, if the nominal stress range is always less than this value, it can be expected that fatigue crack growth will not take place. (When the stress ranges are less than the constant amplitude fatigue limit, the appropriate constant to be used is γ', and the value $m = 5$ is to be used. This is illustrated in Example 11.3)

Both AASHTO and the Canadian Highway Bridge Design Code identify an inequality that is only one-half that in Equation 11.2. Thus, the design equation in these standards is

$$F_{sr} = \left(\frac{\gamma}{n\,N}\right)^{1/3} \geq \frac{F_{srt}}{2} \tag{11.3}$$

The inequality in this equation is derived from experience with highway bridges. In this case, the great majority of fatigue stress ranges are the result of the passage of trucks ("fatigue trucks") that are small relative to the design truck. (The design truck is the vehicle used for strength evaluation of the bridge.) Even when the fatigue trucks produce stress ranges values that are always less than the constant amplitude threshold stress range, it has to be recognized that a truck larger than the fatigue truck will pass over the bridge occasionally. If this truck produces a stress range greater than the constant amplitude threshold stress range, fatigue crack growth can take place and it can take place now for all stress range cycles. Based on measured values, it is judged that this truck can be twice as large as the fatigue truck [11.1], and this is why the factor of 2 is introduced into the inequality portion of the design equations given by the highway bridge design codes (Equation 11.3).

The fatigue life representation is shown pictorially in Figure 11.2. The sloping solid line (slope of −3) is the equality portion of Equations 11.2 and 11.3. The solid horizontal line is the constant amplitude threshold stress. If it is known that only one stress range is present at the detail, then the sloping solid line and the horizontal solid line are used, as per Equation 11.2 and the S16–01 Standard. As just described, both highway bridge standards cited assume that there can be some stress ranges larger than the constant amplitude fatigue limit. For these standards, the solid sloping line, the broken sloping line, and the horizontal broken line at the value $F_{srt}/2$ are used. (The broken line at a slope of −5 is discussed following.)

The question remaining is, what representation should be used with the S16 Standard when more than one stress range is present at the detail? This is handled in Clause 26.3.3 of S16, where it is required that a summation of the separate effects be done. This summation (known as the Palmgren–Miner rule) is described in Section 11.5.1. The effect is to introduce a different fatigue life limit in the long-life region. From the intersection of solid sloping line and the solid horizontal line, a line at the slope of −5 is used in the S16 rules. This is also shown in Figure 11.2. Thus, for the usual case (not all stress ranges are the same), S16 prescribes a two-part sloping straight line.

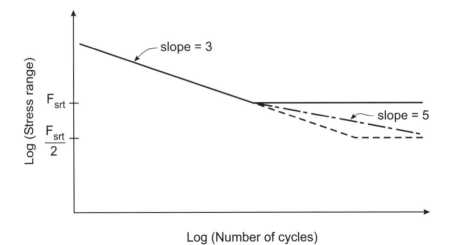

Figure 11.2 – Fatigue Life Curves

There is no general agreement as to which is the best fatigue life representation to use in the long-life region. The choice made for the highway bridge standards seems reasonable because it reflects measurements of the effect of truck traffic taken at various bridge sites. The different approach taken by S16 has some similarities to that used in European practice, but it is also a matter of engineering judgment.

The information for fatigue strength design is given in the various standards as a family of curves similar to the single case depicted in Figure 11.2. (Of course, the information necessary to carry out fatigue life calculations is also given in the standards.) For instance, eight fatigue life categories (details) are given in S16. The decision as to which category is appropriate is made with the help of pictorials, such as those given in Figure 11.3.

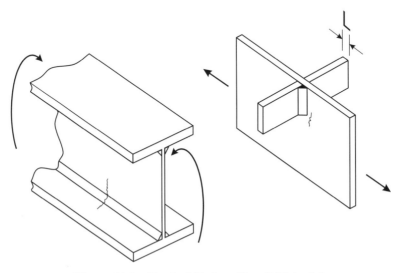

Figure 11.3 – Typical Fatigue Detail Pictorials

The two details shown in Figure 11.3 are among the many depicted in Figure 2 and Table 9 of the S16 Standard [11.6]. The beam section, in which three plates have been welded together to form an I–shape, is designated as Category B if either fillet welds or complete penetration groove welds are used or as Category B1 if partial penetration groove welds are used. The category for the longitudinally loaded plate containing the fillet-welded attachment will depend on the length of the attachment, L. It can be Category C (when L is less than 50 mm), Category D (L between 50 mm and 12 times the detail thickness, but less than 100 mm), Category E (L greater than either 12 times the thickness or 100 mm and the detail thickness is less than 25 mm), or Category E1 (limits on L as for Category E but detail thickness is greater than 25 mm). Such pictorials and the associated table in S16 enable the designer to assign a given detail to one of the eight fatigue categories.

The individual fatigue strength curves were selected on the basis of the mean of the test data less two standard deviations (of fatigue life). This means that there is a small probability of failure, about 2%. As pointed out earlier, some probability of failure has to be acknowledged, and the value selected seems to give reasonable results in practice.

Trying to obtain the number of cycles permissible for a given stress range (or, *vice versa*) directly from a figure like Figure 11.2 is difficult. However, the Standard provides the necessary information to compute the desired quantity by providing the constant M (Equation 11.1). Table 11.1 gives these values for the various fatigue categories, and also gives the constant amplitude fatigue threshold, F_{srt}. (The notation of Table 11.1 is consistent with that used in Equations 11.2 and 11.3.)

Table 11.1 – Fatigue Life Constants

Detail Category	Fatigue Life Constant γ	Fatigue Life Constant γ'	Constant Amplitude Threshold Stress Range, F_{srt} (MPa)
A	$8\ 190\times10^9$	223×10^{15}	165
B	$3\ 930\times10^9$	47.6×10^{15}	110
B1	$2\ 000\times10^9$	13.8×10^{15}	83
C	$1\ 440\times10^9$	6.86×10^{15}	69
C1	$1\ 440\times10^9$	9.92×10^{15}	83
D	721×10^9	1.66×10^{15}	48
E	361×10^9	0.347×10^{15}	31
E1	128×10^9	0.0415×10^{15}	18

Example 11.1

The overhead crane in a small manufacturing operation uses a simply-supported crane girder of 8 m span. The section used for the girder is to be made by fillet-welding three plates into an I-shape like that shown in Figure 11.3. The flange plates are 350 mm wide by 22 mm thick and the web plate is 306 mm by 14 mm. The moment of inertia of this section is 448×10^6 mm^4. The main use of the crane will be to transport a 300 kN ladle from one end of the shop to the other. The crane travels in such a position that the crane girder receives a maximum 80% of the total load as a reactive force. It can be assumed that this force comes onto the girder as a single concentrated load. Information from the owner is that the crane will make no more than two trips per hour at this load level, this will be the only significant load, the work schedule will not exceed 10 hours per day five days per week, and the design life of the building is 40 years.

Is the fatigue life of this crane girder satisfactory? Use the S16–01 Standard.

Solution:

Number of stress cycles (equals number of load cycles, in this case) —
$N = (2 \text{ cycles/hr}) (10 \text{ hr/day})(5 \text{ days/wk}) (52 \text{ wk/yr}) (40 \text{ yr}) = 208\,000$ cycles.

Detail category and permissible stress range — This beam corresponds to one of the pictorials illustrated in Figure 11.3. According to the S16 Standard, this is a Category B detail.

It is preferable to calculate the permissible stress range rather than trying to read values on a log–log plot. From Table 11.1, the constant $\gamma = 3930 \times 10^9$ for Category B. Then, using Equation 11.2 and the value $n = 1.0$, we calculate—

$$F_{sr} = \left(\frac{\gamma}{n\,N} \right)^{1/3} = \left(\frac{3930 \times 10^9}{1.0 \times 208\,000} \right)^{1/3} = 266 \text{ MPa}$$

We note that this calculated value meets the inequality requirement of Equation 11.2, given that $F_{srt} = 110$ MPa for this detail.

Calculate actual stress range –

$$\sigma_{min} = 0 \qquad\qquad \sigma_{max} = M_{max}\, y/I$$

$$M_{max} = P\,L/4 = \left(300 \times 10^3 \text{ N} \times 0.8 \right) \,(8\,000 \text{ mm}) / 4 = 480 \times 10^6 \text{ N} \cdot \text{mm}$$

$$\therefore \sigma_{max} = (480 \times 10^6)(175 \text{ mm}) / (448 \times 10^6 \text{ mm}^4) = 188 \text{ MPa}$$

and, $\Delta\sigma_r = 188 - 0 = 188$ MPa .

Since the actual range of stress (188 MPa) is less than the permissible range of stress for this detail (266 MPa), the situation is satisfactory.

Comments:

1. The number of stress cycles is not always equal to the number of load cycles. Designers should be alert for cases where a single passage of load produces more than one stress cycle, as could occur, for example, when a multiple axle vehicle traverses a member or when continuous beams are used.

2. Since stress due to dead load is always present in the member, the change in stress ($\Delta\sigma_r$) is always simply equal to the change in stress produced by the moving (i.e., live) loads.

3. Another way of looking at the problem is to compare the number of cycles that would be permitted at the actual stress range of 188 MPa with the number of

cycles that actually occur. In this example, the number of cycles permitted by the S16 standard for a stress range $\Delta\sigma_r = 188$ MPa is (using Equation 11.1b):

$$N = M \, \Delta\sigma_r^{-m} = \left(3\,930 \times 10^9\right) \, (188)^{-3} = 591\,000 \text{ cycles}$$

Since the expected number of cycles over the life of the structure is 208 000, this alternative examination shows again that the situation is satisfactory.

11.5 Fatigue Assessment for Variable Stress Ranges

In the discussion so far, it has been implicit that the stress range at the detail under investigation can be established easily and that counting or predicting the number of cycles is straightforward. As might be anticipated, things are not always simple in either of these categories: loading histories are usually quite complex. The designer has to deal with the reality that stress ranges of different magnitude take place at the detail and that these stress ranges are applied for varying numbers of cycles. A way of dealing with the problem of how to account for the occurrence of different stress ranges that take place at the location of a given detail is necessary.

11.5.1 Cumulative Fatigue Damage

In this section, a method is presented that accounts for the damage that results when different stress ranges are applied for various lengths of time. Although both linear and non-linear damage theories are available, the one that is customarily used in civil engineering practice is a linear theory that is easy to understand and apply, and which gives satisfactory results. This is the linear damage rule first proposed by Palmgren in 1924 and further developed by Miner in 1945 [11.9]. It is known as the Palmgren–Miner rule, and it simply assumes that the damage fraction that results from any particular stress range level is directly proportional to the number of cycles applied at the stress range, n_i, and inversely proportional to the fatigue life at the stress range, N_i, namely, n_i / N_i. The total damage from all stress range levels that are applied to the detail is, of course, the sum of all such occurrences. According to the Palmgren–Miner rule, fatigue failure occurs when this sum reaches unity. This can be written in equation form as a requirement that:

$$\Sigma \frac{n_i}{N_i} \leq 1 \tag{11.4}$$

where n_i = number of cycles that take place at stress range level i
$\quad N_i$ = number of cycles that would cause failure at stress range level i.

The rule is obviously very simple. It has two major shortcomings; it does not consider sequence effects and it is independent of the amplitude of the stress cycles. To at least some degree, both of these factors are not consistent with observed behaviour. However, when residual stresses are high and when plasticity is restricted (usually the case in structural engineering applications), it is known that these factors have only a small influence. Moreover, the approach gives reasonable correlation with test data and it has the considerable advantage that it is easy to use. Most specifications advise that the Palmgren-Miner rule can be used to account for cumulative damage. It should also be noted that the term "failure" in these definitions is not intended to be taken literally. It is to be interpreted as the permissible fatigue life, that is, the value represented by the mean life less two standard deviations on the log stress range vs. log number of cycles plot.

Example 11.2

The beam of Example 11.1 had been designed, fabricated, and erected when the owner decided that, in addition to the loads that had already been stipulated, it will be necessary for the crane to be able to also accommodate one trip per hour at a load level of 350 kN. (See Example 11.1 for all other details). Is the fatigue life of this crane girder still satisfactory?

Solution:

1. Number of cycles at the old load level was 208 000 ($= n_1$)
2. Number of cycles to failure at the old load level was 591 000 ($= N_1$)
3. Number of cycles at the new load level is –

   $N = (1 \text{ cycle/hr}) (10 \text{ hr/day}) (5 \text{ days/week}) (52 \text{ weeks/yr}) (40 \text{ yr})$

   $= 104\ 000 \text{ cycles} (= n_2)$

4. Number of cycles to failure at the new load level (N_2) is obtained as follows:

   By proportion, the stress range for the 350 kN load is (350/300) (188 MPa) = 219 MPa. For fatigue Category B, calculation of the number of cycles that would be permissible at the stress range of 219 MPa is $(2 \times 10^6) (125/219)^3 = 372\ 000$. Thus, $N_2 = 372\ 000$.

5. Finally checking Equation 11.4

$$\Sigma \frac{n_i}{N_i} = 1 \text{ or,}$$

$$\frac{n_1}{N_1} + \frac{n_2}{N_2} = \frac{208\ 000}{588\ 000} + \frac{104\ 000}{372\ 000} = 0.35 + 0.28 = 0.63$$

Since the total effect ("damage") of the two different stress ranges is less than 1.0, the crane girder is still satisfactory.

Example 11.3

In a final revision, the owner has identified that yet another stress range exists, 90 MPa, and its projected number of cycles is 800×10^3. Is the fatigue life of this girder still satisfactory?

Solution

The latest stress range is less than $F_{srt} = 110 \text{ MPa}$ for this Category B detail. According to Clause 26.3.3 of S16, these cycles are to be included in the Miner-Palmgren summation using the appropriate value of γ' and the value $m = 5$. Thus, we have (using the information already contained in Example 11.2)

$n_1 = 208 \times 10^3$ cycles; $\qquad N_1 = 591 \times 10^3$ cycles

$$n_2 = 104 \times 10^3 \text{ cycles;} \qquad N_2 = 372 \times 10^3 \text{ cycles}$$

and for the new loading—

$$n_3 = 800 \times 10^3 \text{ cycles}$$

and using $F'_{sr} = \left(\dfrac{\gamma'}{n\,N} \right)$

$$N_3 = \frac{47.6 \times 10^{15}}{90^5} = 8060 \times 10^3 \text{ cycles}$$

where the constant $\gamma' = 47.6 \times 10^{15}$ was obtained from Table 11.1. The summation now is written as

$$\frac{n_1}{N_1} + \frac{n_2}{N_2} + \frac{n_3}{N_3} = \frac{208\,000}{588\,000} + \frac{104\,000}{372\,000} + \frac{800\,000}{8\,060\,000} = 0.35 + 0.28 + 0.10 = 0.73$$

Since the summation is <1, the beam is still satisfactory in fatigue.

It is sometimes convenient to express the Palmgren–Miner cumulative fatigue damage rule (Equation 11.3) in terms of an equivalent stress range. We wish to calculate an equivalent stress range, $\Delta\sigma_e$, that acts for the number of cycles to which the detail is actually subjected, N, and has the same effect as the variable stress ranges [11.1]. Thus, using the Palmgren–Miner statement of damage (Equation 11.3) it is required that

$$\Sigma \frac{n_i}{N_i} = \frac{\Sigma\,n_i}{N_e} \tag{11.5}$$

In this equation, the left hand side represents the damage under the variable amplitude stress cycles, for which the terms were defined under Equation 11.4. The right hand side expresses the damage under the constant amplitude equivalent stress range, i.e., $\Delta\sigma_e$. Each of N_i and N_e correspond to the number of cycles to failure—one for the variable amplitude stress ranges and the other for the equivalent, constant amplitude, stress range.

Equation 11.1(b), which expressed the failure condition in a general way, can now be applied to Equation 11.5. Thus, $N_i = M\,\Delta\sigma_i^{-m}$ applies to the left hand side of Equation 11.4 and $N_e = M\,\Delta\sigma_e^{-m}$ applies to the right hand side. Making the substitutions—

$$\Sigma \frac{n_i}{M\,\Delta\sigma_i^{-m}} = \frac{\Sigma\,n_i}{M\,\Delta\sigma_e^{-m}}$$

The term M is a constant and can be eliminated from the equation. Then, solving for the equivalent stress range

$$\Delta\sigma_e^{\,m} = \Sigma\,\frac{n_i\,\Delta\sigma_i^{\,m}}{\Sigma\,n_i} \tag{11.6}$$

Calling $n_i/\Sigma\, n_i = \alpha_i$, that is, α_i is the fraction that any particular portion of the stress range is of the total number of cycles, then Equation 11.6 is written as

$$\Delta\sigma_e{}^m = \Sigma\, \alpha_i \,\Delta\sigma_i^m$$

Finally, solving for the equivalent stress range, we have

$$\Delta\sigma_e = \left[\, \Sigma\alpha_i \,\Delta\sigma_i^m \,\right]^{1/m} \tag{11.7}$$

Example 11.4

Use the equivalent stress method to determine the percentage of life that has been expended by the loading applied to the beam of Example 11.2.

Solution:

All of the necessary data are available in the solutions to Examples 11.1 and 11.2. In summary, these are –

n_1 = 208 000 cycles1 n_2 = 104 000 cycles

$\Delta\sigma_1$ = 188 MPa $\Delta\sigma_2$ = 219 MPa

N = 208 000 + 104 000 = 312 000 cycles

Using Equation 11.7 to calculate the equivalent stress range –

$$\Delta\sigma_e = \left[\left(\frac{208\,000}{312\,000}\right)\left(188^3\right) + \left(\frac{104\,000}{312\,000}\right)\left(219^3\right)\right]^{1/3} = 199.4 \text{ MPa, say, 200 MPa}$$

For this Category B detail and the equivalent stress range of 200 MPa, the number of cycles to failure can be calculated (Equation 11.1b) as –

$$N = M\,\Delta\sigma_r^{-m} = \left(393\text{x}10^{10}\right)\left(200^{-3}\right) = 491\,000 \text{ cycles}.$$

Since the actual number of cycles is 312 000, the percentage of life expended is (312 000/491 000) 100% = 64%.

Comments:

The same result was also seen in the solution to Example 11.2, where the Miner's summation was 0.63, which is the same, allowing for round-off errors. Whether the solution proceeds by the method shown in Example 11.2 (Miner's summation) or by that shown in Example 11.4 (equivalent stress range method) is simply a matter of choice.

The equivalent stress calculation given by Equation 11.6 is valid only when a single value of m applies to all stress ranges.

11.5.2   Analysis of Stress Histories

Situations often arise where the applied loads create stress levels and stress counts (number of cycles at a given stress level) that are much more complicated than those given in the previous examples. For example, if the crane in Example 11.1 is carried by a continuous beam over several intermediate supports, more than one stress cycles is applied per trip at a given location. This results because loading adjacent spans causes stress cycles in addition to the cycle created when the crane passes directly over the location under examination. For this more general case, one trip is termed a loading event and the stress variation at a given point in the structure during such an event is called a stress history.

Figure 11.4(a) shows an example of stress variation in an element subjected to a loading event. The information cannot be used directly in the Palmgren-Miner rule, Equation 11.4, without application of a stress counting method in order to tabulate values for the number of cycles, n_i, to be used for the different stress range levels. Several counting methods have been developed for various applications, and Reference [11.3] provides a summary. A widely-used method is the so-called *reservoir method*, and it will be the only one illustrated here. (The reservoir method is well-suited to hand-calculations and is convenient for graphical analyses of short histories. Another commonly used method, the *rainflow method*, is more suited to computer analyses of long stress histories. The rainflow and reservoir methods give identical results for most cases.)

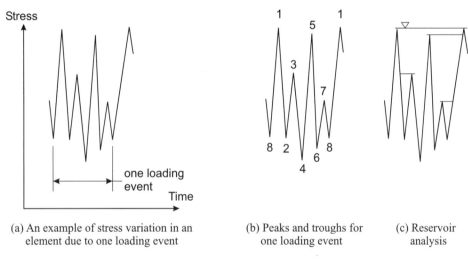

| (a) An example of stress variation in an element due to one loading event | (b) Peaks and troughs for one loading event | (c) Reservoir analysis |

Figure 11.4 – Analysis of Stress Histories

Example 11.5

The numerical values of the peaks and valleys for the stress history depicted in Figure 11.4(b) are shown in the table. Apply the reservoir counting method in order to identify the stress ranges in this stress spectrum and then evaluate the effects of 3.5 million loading events of this stress history acting on a beam that uses longitudinal fillet welds to connect the flanges to the web.

Peak/Trough No.	Stress (MPa)
1	93
2	18
3	55
4	8
5	85
6	10
7	37
8	18

Solution:

It was identified in Example 11.1 that this is a Category B detail. The reservoir counting method can conveniently be tabulated, as follows:

Drain from Trough No.	Water Level at Peak No.	Stress Range (MPa)
4	1	$93 - 8 = 85$
6	5	$85 - 10 = 75$
2	3	$55 - 18 = 37$
8	7	$37 - 18 = 19$

The damage resulting from each of these four stress ranges can now be calculated:

Stress Range, $\Delta\sigma$ (MPa)	Fatigue Resistance (cycles)	Damage due to 3.5×10^6 Loading Events, n_i / N
85	6 399 350[*]	0.55[†]
75	9 315 560	0.38
37	77 867 700	0.04
19	572 970 000	0.01

Damage summation: $\sum n_i / N = 0.98$

[*] Sample calculation: Using Eq. 11.1(b) $N = (3\,930 \times 10^9)(85^{-3}) = 6\,399\,350$ cycles

[†] Sample calculation: Using Eq. 11.4 $n_i / N = 3.5 \times 10^6 / 6.399 \times 10^6 = 0.55$

In this case, the detail meets the requirement that the damage summation must be less than unity.

11.6   Fatigue Crack Growth Under Combined Stresses

Throughout the discussion so far, it has been emphasized that the stresses to be used in the fatigue life evaluation are those corresponding to the nominal stress as obtained from a mechanics of materials level of analysis. The detail classification given in any of the design standards mentioned includes the effect of local stress concentrations due to weld shape, discontinuities, triaxial conditions, and so on. Only in exceptional cases, around large openings, for example, will a more sophisticated analysis be required. Occasionally, also, it might be necessary to investigate the combined effect of normal and shear stresses.

For a case in which both tensile and shearing stresses are present in significant quantities at a given location, the principal stresses should be calculated and the stress range corresponding to those stresses then used in the fatigue life evaluation. Of course, for this examination to be necessary, both the tensile and shear stresses must be concurrently present at that location during a given loading event.

In unusual situations, shear stress alone can be significant. The test results show that the general relationship between stress range and number of cycles still exists, and the design or evaluation proceeds as before.

When tensile and shear stresses are present at the same location but do not occur simultaneously under a given loading event, the individual components of damage can be added according to a Palmgren–Miner summation, as follows [11.1]:

$$\left[\frac{\Delta\sigma_e}{\Delta\sigma_r} \right]^3 + \left[\frac{\Delta\tau_e}{\Delta\tau_r} \right]^3 \leq 1 \qquad (11.8)$$

where σ and τ refer to normal stresses and shear stresses, respectively. The subscript e means a calculated equivalent stress range (see Equation 11.7) and the subscript r refers to the permissible stress range for the detail.

11.7   Fatigue Cracking from Out-of-Plane Effects

Most of the discussion in this chapter has centered around the influence of normal stresses on pre-existing flaws or cracks in a fabricated steel element. The assumption has been that the stresses can be calculated, usually at an elementary level. In many instances, however, fatigue crack growth results from the imposition of deformations, not stresses [11.10]. Although it is possible in some of these cases to calculate a stress range, this is usually after the fact, i.e., after a fatigue crack has already been detected. The designer is not likely to be able to identify the need for such a calculation in the course of his work. As will be seen, this type of fatigue crack growth results from the imposition of relatively small deformations, usually out-of-plane, in local regions of a member. These deformations are not usually anticipated in the design process. The main defense against this source of cracking is proper detailing, and this, in turn, must reflect engineering judgment as to what types of situations can lead to crack growth from out-of-plane effects.

Figure 11.5 illustrates the phenomenon with an example. Standard practice for many years was to cut transverse stiffeners short of the bottom (tension) flange so as to not introduce a relatively severe detail for fatigue if the stiffener is welded to the flange at that location. (There are also practical reasons for cutting the stiffener short: the stiffener will have to be made to a precise length if it is to extend exactly from flange to flange.) The height of the gap is usually quite small. If lateral movement of the top flange relative to the bottom flange should take place, large strains can be imposed in the gap region because of the significant change in stiffness between the stiffened and unstiffened (gap) regions of the web. The strains that are produced typically are so large that it may take relatively few cycles for a crack to propagate [11.11]. The flange movement could be the consequence of transverse forces in a skew bridge, for example, but often it is a consequence of shipping and handling.

The detail in Figure 11.5 shows a crack emanating from the weld toe at the bottom of the stiffener. Often, the crack will also extend across the toe of the fillet weld at the underside of the stiffener and for some distance into the web. Up to this stage, the crack is more or less parallel to the direction of the main stress field that will be experienced by the girder in service. Thus, if the source of the displacement-induced fatigue can be identified and eliminated, further growth of the crack is unlikely. However, if crack growth has gone on for some time, the crack likely will turn upwards or downwards in the web, and thus be aligned in the most unfavorable orientation with respect to service load stresses.

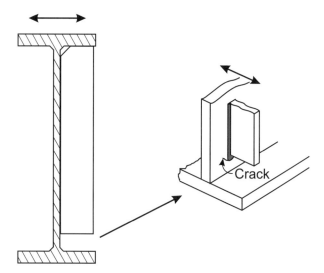

Figure 11.5 – Example of Fatigue Cracking Due to Out-of-Plane Movement

The detail just described (Figure 11.5) has been the source of fatigue cracks in many locations in the past. In a new design, the situation can be handled in different ways, reducing the possibility of fatigue crack growth due to this cause.

A way of dealing with the type of crack shown in Figure 11.5 is to drill holes at the end of the crack, thereby changing the sharp crack front to a "crack" front with an extremely large radius: see Figure 11.6. In preparation for drilling, the area should be cleaned and dye penetrant used to locate the extremity of the crack tip as accurately as possible [11.10]. The hole should then be drilled with its trailing edge at the location identified as the crack front. In this way, it can be reasonably certain that the hole has indeed intercepted the crack front. A typical hole size used for this procedure is 12 mm.

The hole should be drilled carefully and then, if necessary, lightly ground to remove scratches and burrs. If the hole is simply left open, the location can be monitored for the possibility of further crack growth. If clearances permit, a high-strength bolt can be placed in the hole and pretensioned. The introduction of high compressive stresses into this region is an effective way of increasing the fatigue life in this locality. A disadvantage is that if the original fatigue crack continues to grow, it cannot be observed until it appears from under the bolt head or washer.

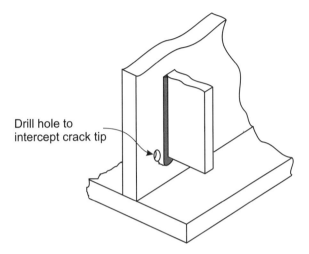

Drill hole to intercept crack tip

Figure 11.6 – Repair of a Fatigue Crack

It must be emphasized the hole-drilling technique is directed toward stopping crack growth from the in-plane stresses. If the origin of the problem was cracking from out-of-plane displacements, this has to be addressed first. When hole drilling is carried out but the out-of-plane displacements are allowed to continue, it is unlikely that the attempted repair will be effective. Recent experience has shown that under these conditions, the crack will start at the "far side" of the drilled hole and then be driven by in-plane stresses. If the crack has entered the flange, a more direct repair is required, probably addition of a flange splice.

Figure 11.7 shows one way that has been demonstrated as effective in stopping the out-of-plane displacements that drive a crack at a stiffener termination.

Another illustration of a case in which out-of-plane movement can produce fatigue cracks is shown in Figure 11.8, where a floor beam is attached to a connection plate that is welded to the web of a girder. Under the passage of traffic, the floor beam will rotate as shown. As this rotation occurs, the bottom flange of the floor beam will tend to lengthen and the top flange will tend to shorten. Lengthening of the bottom flange will not be restrained because it is pushing into the web of the girder, which is flexible in this out-of-plane direction. However, because the top flange of the girder is restrained by the deck slab, shortening of the top flange of the floor beam can only be accommodated by deformation within the gap at the top of the connection plate. This type of deformation is shown in the detail in Figure 11.8.

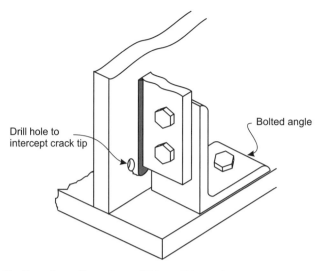

Figure 11.7 – Repair to Stop Out-of-Plane Distortion Induced Fatigue Cracks

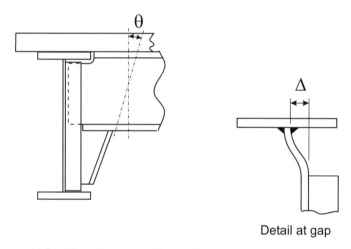

Detail at gap

Figure 11.8 – Floor Beam-to-Girder Connection

The situation hypothesized in Figure 11.8 has been confirmed by field measurements taken by Fisher [11.11]. Moreover, the field study showed that each passage of an axle caused a significant stress range at the top of the connection plate. In this situation, fatigue cracks could develop either at the weld at the top of the connection plate or at the web-to-flange fillet weld of the girder, or both. The residual tensile stress in this small gap would tend to be very high because of the proximity of the two welds. It can be expected that fatigue cracks could occur under relatively few cycles of load, although of course the fatigue life will depend largely upon the deformation, Δ, that actually takes place as a result of the rotation of the floorbeam.

Example 11.6

Given:

Figure 11.8 illustrated a floor beam to girder connection where out-of-plane cracking could occur. The detail is repeated here, as Figure 11.9. This detail corresponds to a transversely loaded fillet welded attachment with welds parallel to the direction of the primary stress. The primary stress in this case is that created by local bending of the web gap as it undergoes a distortion Δ. According to S16–01, unless the end of the welds is ground smooth the detail is Category E.

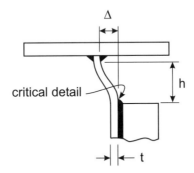

Figure 11.9 – (Example 11.5)

The web plate thickness in Figure 11.9 is t = 12 mm, the length of the gap is h = 15 mm, and a measurement of the displacement of the gap shows that Δ = 0.003 mm. What is the fatigue life of this detail?

Solution:

Application of moment-area theorems, or reference to a design handbook, will show that the moment at the end of a fixed ended beam that is displaced an amount Δ is

$$M = \frac{6 \, EI \, \Delta}{h^2}$$

Therefore, the stress is

$$\sigma = \frac{M \, y}{I} = \left(\frac{6 \, EI \, \Delta}{h^2}\right)\left(\frac{t}{2}\right)\left(\frac{1}{I}\right) = \frac{3 \, E \, \Delta \, t}{h^2}$$

Since the displacement Δ is varying as the floor beam rotation takes place, this stress is, in fact, the stress range, Δσ. Thus, for the specific quantities given:

$$\Delta\sigma = \frac{(3) \, (200\,000 \text{ MPa}) \, (0.003 \text{ mm}) \, (12 \text{ mm})}{(15 \text{ mm})^2} = 96 \text{ MPa}$$

The number of cycles for a Category E detail that can sustain a stress range of 96 MPa can be calculated using Equation 11.1(b), with the fatigue life constant M ($\equiv \gamma$) in that equation taken from Table 11.1 as 361 x 10⁹. Thus,

$$N = \left(361x10^9\right)\left(96^{-3}\right) = 408\,000 \text{ cycles}$$

Comment:

This example shows that even a very small amount of out-of-plane displacement can have a significant effect on fatigue life. In this case, the fatigue life of this Category E detail is significantly reduced by the 0.003 mm displacement.

There are many other sources of out-of-plane fatigue cracking or locations for secondary (uncalculated) stress. For example —

Restraint At Simple End Connections. Many end connections are designed as "simple," that is, it is assumed that no moment is transmitted. However, even simple connections do carry some moment, and this means that the connection elements will deform under the moment. End rotation at web framing angles causes the angles to deform and load the rivets, bolts, or welds in ways not contemplated by the designer. If the loading is cyclic, fatigue cracks may develop in the angles themselves or in the bolts, rivets, or welds. In the cases of the mechanical fasteners, prying forces develop that may cause fatigue cracking under the heads.

Floor Beam or Stringer Connections to Girders, Diaphragm and Bracing Connections. A significant source of fatigue cracking in the past has been the result of connection of floor beams or stringers to girders, including box girders. Often the connection is made to transverse girder stiffeners. When these stiffeners are not attached to the flanges, a detail used in the past, large strains can be set up in the gap at the web-to-flange junction of the girder. Fatigue cracking in the welds can result at this location, which is a zone of high residual tensile stress. Lateral bracing attached to horizontal connection plates welded to girder webs will produce out-of-plane flexing of the web, another location for fatigue cracking of the connection welds.

Coped Beams. In order to facilitate the easy connection of one flexural member to another, the flange of one of the members is often cut back, as is illustrated in Figure 11.10. (In other cases, the flanges may simply be narrowed: this is called a "blocked" beam.) In the case of coped beams, either the top or bottom flange, or both, may be coped. The cope is usually made by flame-cutting the material, and experience shows that this is often done in an unsatisfactory manner. The radius of the cope will often be small and the cutting done unevenly. In addition to the potential for fatigue cracking created by such workmanship, the flame-cutting process can leave a region of hardened and brittle material adjacent to the cut.

The coped end of the beam is at a location of theoretical zero stress since the connection must necessarily be one that does not transmit moment and the shear force is carried by the web. Nevertheless, it is known that the region of the cope can have significant stresses. There are many examples of fatigue cracking at cope locations [11.10], and the best solution in the case of a new design is to avoid copes entirely. If copes must be included, the workmanship and inspection must be of a high standard. Specific information on the fatigue life of a coped beam can be found in Reference [11.12].

Rotation of Beam or Girder Flanges by Direct Loading. The most obvious example of this is the case of railway beams or girders. Particularly in older members, it was common to place the ties directly on the top flange of the flexural members in the floor system. Thus, a stringer flange, for example, can be rotated as traffic passes over the structure. If the flange is too flexible in this direction, cracking can occur at the web-to-flange junction.

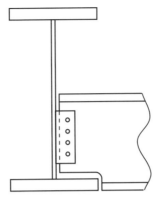

Figure 11.10 – Bottom Flange of Floor Beam Coped at Connection to Girder

References

11.1 Fisher, J.W., Kulak, G.L. and Smith, I.F.C., "A Fatigue Primer for Structural Engineers," National Steel Bridge Alliance, American Institute of Steel Construction, Chicago, Illinois, 1998.

11.2 Broek, D., "The Practical Use of Fracture Mechanics," Kluwer Academic Publishers, Dordrecht, The Netherlands, 1989.

11.3 Gurney, T.R., "Fatigue of Welded Structures, 2nd Edition," Cambridge University Press, 1979.

11.4 Fisher, J.W., Frank, K.H., Hirt, M.A., and McNamee, B.M., "Effect of Weldments on the Fatigue Strength of Steel Beams," National Cooperative Highway Research Program Report 102, Highway Research Board, Washington, D.C., 1970.

11.5 Fisher, J.W., Albrecht, P.A., Yen, B.T., Klingerman, D.J., and McNamee, B.M., "Fatigue Strength of Steel Beams With Transverse Stiffeners and Attachments," National Cooperative Highway Research Program, Report 147, Highway Research Board, Washington, D.C., 1974.

11.6 Canadian Standards Association, CAN/CSA–S16–01, "Limit States Design of Steel Structures," Toronto, Ontario, 2001.

11.7 Canadian Standards Association, CAN/CSA–S6–00 (R2005), "Canadian Highway Bridge Design Code," Toronto, Ontario, 2005.

11.8 American Association of State Highway and Transportation Officials, "AASHTO LRFD Bridge Design Specifications," SI Units, Third Edition, Washington, D.C., 2004.

11.9 Bannantine, J.A., Comer, J.J., and Handrock, J.L., "Fundamentals of Metal Fatigue Analysis," Prentice-Hall, Englewood Cliffs, (New Jersey), 1990.

11.10 Fisher, J.W., "Fatigue and Fracture in Steel Bridges: Case Studies," Wiley Interscience, 1984.

11.11 Fisher, J.W., "Fatigue Cracking in Bridges from Out-of-Plane Displacements," Canadian Journal of Civil Engineering, Vol. 5, No. 4, December 1978.

11.12 Cheng, J.J., "Design of Steel Beams with End Copes," Journal of Constructional Steel Research, Vol. 25, 1993.

Table 1
CHEMICAL COMPOSITION

CSA G40.21 Grade	Chemical Composition (Heat Analysis) Per Cent[14]								
	All_percentages_are maxima unless otherwise indicated								
	C	Mn[16]	P	S	Si[12,13]	Other[2]	Cr	Ni	Cu[9]
260W	0.20[15]	0.50/1.50	0.04	0.05	0.40	0.10	—	—	—
300W[5]	0.22[15]	0.50/1.50	0.04	0.05	0.40	0.10	—	—	—
350W	0.23	0.50/1.50	0.04	0.05	0.40	0.10	—	—	—
380W[6]	0.23	0.50/1.50	0.04	0.05	0.40	0.10	—	—	—
400W	0.23[17]	0.50/1.50	0.04	0.05	0.40	0.10	—	—	—
480W	0.26[17]	0.50/1.50	0.04	0.05	0.40	0.10[19]	—	—	—
550W	0.15	1.75[7]	0.04	0.05	0.40	0.15	—	—	—
260WT	0.20[15]	0.80/1.50	0.03	0.04	0.15/0.40	0.10	—	—	—
300WT	0.22[15]	0.80/150	0.03	0.04	0.15/0.40	0.10	—	—	—
350WT	0.22[15]	0.80/150[7]	0.03	0.04	0.15/0.40	0.10[8]	—	—	—
380WT[6]	0.22	0.80/1.50[7]	0.03	0.04	0.15/0.40	0.1 0	—	—	—
400WT	0.22[17]	0.80/150[7]	0.03	0.04[18]	0.15/0.40	0.10[8]	—	—	—
480WT	0.26[17]	0.80/1.50[7]	0.03	0.04[18]	0.15/0.40	010	—	—	—
550WT	0.15	1.75[7]	0.03	0.04[18]	0.15/0.40	0.15	—	—	—
350R	0.16	0.75	0.05/0.15	0.04	0.75	0.10	0.30/1.25[10]	0.90[10]	0.20/0.60[10]
350A	0.20	0.75/135[7]	0.03	0.04	0.1 5/0.50	0.1 0	0.70[11]	0.90[11]	0.20/0.60
400A	0.20	0.75/1.35[7]	0.03	0.04[18]	0.15/0.50	0.10	0.70[11]	0.90[11]	0.20/0.60
480A	0.20	1.00/1.60	0.025[20]	0.035[18]	0.15/0.50	0.12	0.70[11]	0.25/0.50[11]	0.20/0.60
550A	0.15	1.75[7]	0.025[20]	0.035[18]	0.15/0.50	0.15	0.70[11]	0.25/0.50[11]	0.20/0.60
350AT	0.20	0.75/1.35[7]	0.03	0.04	0.15/0.50	0.10	0.70[11]	0.90[11]	0.20/0.60
400AT	0.20	0.75/1.35[7]	0.03	0.04[18]	0.15/0.50	0.10	0.70[11]	0.90[11]	0.20/0.60
480AT	0.20	1.00/1.60	0.025[20]	0.035[18]	0.15/0.50	0.12	0.70[11]	0.25/0.50[11]	0.20/0.60
550AT	0.15	1.75[7]	0.025[20]	0.035[18]	0.15/0.50	0.15	0.70[11]	0.25/0.50[11]	0.20/0.60
700Q	0.20	1 .50	0.03	0.04	0.15/0.40	—	Boron 0.0005/0.005		—
700QT	0.20	1 .50	0.03	0.04	0.1 5/0.40	—	Boron 0.0005/0.005		—

Notes:
1. For full details, consult GSA Standard G40.20/G40.21 . Usual deoxidation for all grades is killed.
2. Other includes grain refining elements Cb, V, Al. Elements (Cb, V) may be used singly or in combination — see G40.20/G40.21 for qualifications. Al, when used, is not included in summation.
3. May have 1.50% Mn.
4. May have 0.32% C for thicknesses over 20 mm.
5. For HSS 0.26% C and 0.30/1 .20% Mn.
6. Only angles, bars, and HSS in 380W grade, and only HSS in 380WT grade.
7. Mn may be increased—see G40.20/G40.21 for qualifications.
8. 0.01/0.02% N may be used but N ≤ 1/4 V.
9. Copper content of 0.20% minimum may be specified.
10. Cr+Ni+Cu ≥ 1.00%.
11. Cr + Ni ≥ 0.40% and for HSS, 0.90% Ni max.
12. Si content of 0.15% to 0.40% is required for type W steel over 40 mm thickness, HSS of WT, A or AT steel, or bar diameter except as required by Note 13.
13. By purchaser's request or producer's option, no minimum Si content is required provided that 0.02% Al is used.
14. Additional alloying elements may be used when approved.
15. For thicknesses over 100 mm, C may be 0.22% for 260W and 260WT grades and 0.23% for 300W, 300WT, and 350WT grades.
16. For HSS Mn 1 .65% for 400 yield, I .75% for 480 yield and 1 .85% for 550 yield steels.
17. For HSS 0.20% C.
18. For HSS 0.03% S.
19. For HSS 0.12%
20. For HSS 0.03% P

Editor's Note: Tables 1 to 4 inclusive in this Appendix relate to steel materials covered by GSA Standards G40.20 and G40.21. These Tables are provided for convenience of instructors teaching courses in structural steel design and should not be used for design purposes. The GSA standards should be consulted for complete information.

Table 2
GRADES, TYPES, STRENGTH LEVELS*

Type	Yield Strength, MPa							
	260	300	350	380	400	480	550	700
W	260W	300W	350W	380W**	400W	480W	550W	—
WT	260WT	300WT	350WT	380WT‡	400WT	480WT	550WT	—
R	—	—	350R	—	—	—	—	—
A	—	—	350A	—	400A	480A	550A	—
AT	—	—	350AT	—	400AT	480AT	550AT	—
Q	—	—	—	—	—	—	—	700Q
QT	—	—	—	—	—	—	—	700QT

*   See CSA-G40.20/G40.21

**   This grade is available in hollow structural sections, angles, and bars only.

‡   This grade is available in hollow structural sections only.

Table 3
STRUCTURAL SHAPE SIZE GROUPINGS FOR TENSILE PROPERTY CLASSIFICATION

Shape Type	Group 1	Group 2	Group 3	Group 4	Group 5
W Shapes	W610x82–92 W530x66–85 W460x52–106 W410x39–85 W360x33–79 W310x21–86 W250x18–67 W200x15–71 W150x13–37 W130x24 & 28 W100x19	W1000x222–399 W920x201–313 W840x176–226 W760x134–314 W690x125–265 W610x101–241 W530x92–219 W460x113–213 W410x100–149 W360x91–196 W310x97–158 W250x73–167 W200x86 & 100	W1000x412-488 W920x342-446 W840x299-433 W760x350-389 W690x289-384 W610x262-341 W530x248-331 W460x235-286 W360x216-314 W310x179-283	W1000x539-976 W920x488-1188 W840x473-922 W760x434-865 W690x419-802 W610x372-732 W530x370-599 W460x315-464 W360x347-818 W310x313-500	
M Shapes and Super Light Beams	To 56 kg/m				
S Shapes	To 52 kg/m	Over 52 kg/m			
H Shapes		To 152 kg/m	Over 152 kg/m		
C Shapes	To 30.8 kg/m	Over 30.8 kg/m			
MC Shapes	To 42.4 kg/m	Over 42.4 kg/m			
L Shapes	To 13 mm	Over 13 to 20 mm	Over 20 mm		

Note: Tees cut from W, M, and S Shapes fall in the same group as the shape from which they are cut.

*See CSA G40.20/G40.21

380

Table 4
MECHANICAL PROPERTIES SUMMARY

CSA G40.21* Type	Grade	Tensile Strength F_u (MPa)	Nominal Maximum Thickness t (mm)	F_y(MPa) min. t ≤ 65	F_y(MPa) min. t >65	Usual Maximum Shape Size Group	F_y (MPa) min. Groups 1 to 3	F_y (MPa) min. Group 4	F_y (MPa) min. Group 5	Usual Maximum Wall Thickness (mm)	F_y (MPa) min.
W	260W	410-590	200	260	250	4	260	260			
	300W	450-620[1]	200	300	280	3	300			16	300
	350W	450-650[2]	150	350	320	2	350			16	350
	380W	480-650				2[3]	380			16	380
	400W	520-690	20	400		1	400			16	400
	480W	590-790	20	480		1	480			16	480
	550W	620-860	14	550		1	550			16	550
WT	260WT	410-590	150	260	250	5	260	260	250		
	300WT	450-620	150	300	280	5	300	290	280		
	350WT	480-650	60	350	320	4	350	330		16	350
	380WT	480-650								16	380
	400WT	520-690	20	400		2	400			16	400
	480WT	590-790	20	480		1	480			16	480
	550WT	620-860	14	550						16	550
R	350R	480-650	14	350		1	350				
A	350A	480-650	100	350	350	5	350	350	320	16	350
	400A	520-690	40	400		2	400			16	400
	480A	590-790	20	480						16	480
	550A	620-860	14	550						16	550
AT	350AT	480-650	100	350	350	5	350	350	320	16	350
	400AT	520-690	40	400		2	400			16	400
	480AT	590-790	20	480						16	480
	550AT	620-860	14	550						16	550
Q	700Q	800-950	65	700							
QT	700QT	800-950	65	700							

[1] 410-590 MPa for HSS only.
[2] Upper bound F_u = 620 MPa for HSS.
[3] For angles only.
* See CSA-G40.20/G40.21.

Table 5

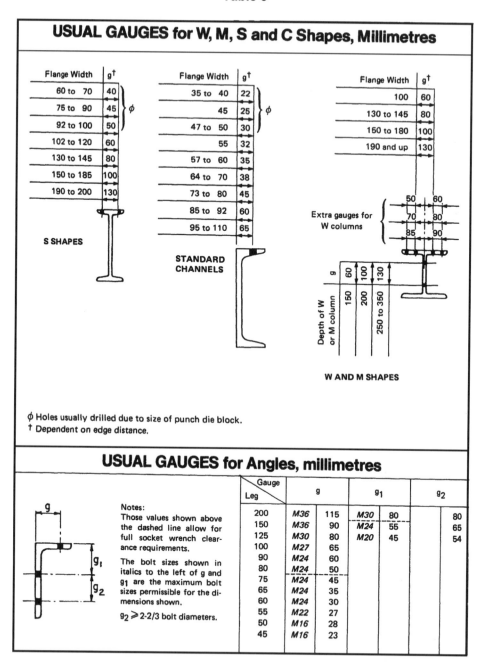

USUAL GAUGES for W, M, S and C Shapes, Millimetres

Flange Width	g†
60 to 70	40
75 to 90	45
92 to 100	50
102 to 120	60
130 to 145	80
150 to 185	100
190 to 200	130

S SHAPES

Flange Width	g†
35 to 40	22
45	25
47 to 50	30
55	32
57 to 60	35
64 to 70	38
73 to 80	45
85 to 92	60
95 to 110	65

STANDARD CHANNELS

Flange Width	g†
100	60
130 to 145	80
150 to 180	100
190 and up	130

Extra gauges for W columns

	50	60
	70	80
	85	90

W AND M SHAPES

Depth of W or M column: 150 → 60, 200 → 100, 250 to 350 → 130

ɸ Holes usually drilled due to size of punch die block.
† Dependent on edge distance.

USUAL GAUGES for Angles, millimetres

Notes:
Those values shown above the dashed line allow for full socket wrench clearance requirements.

The bolt sizes shown in italics to the left of g and g_1 are the maximum bolt sizes permissible for the dimensions shown.

$g_2 \geqslant$ 2-2/3 bolt diameters.

Gauge Leg	g		g_1		g_2
200	M36	115	M30	80	80
150	M36	90	M24	55	65
125	M30	80	M20	45	54
100	M27	65			
90	M24	60			
80	M24	50			
75	M24	45			
65	M24	35			
60	M24	30			
55	M22	27			
50	M16	28			
45	M16	23			

382